Effective Documentation

The MIT Press Series in Information Systems
Michael Lesk, editor

Nested Transactions: An Approach to Reliable Distributed Computing, J. Eliot B. Moss, 1985

Advanced Database Techniques, Daniel Martin, 1986

Text, Context, and HyperText: Writing with and for the Computer, edited by Edward Barrett, 1988

Effective Documentation: What We Have Learned from Research, edited by Stephen Doheny-Farina, 1988

Effective Documentation

What We Have Learned from Research

edited by
Stephen Doheny-Farina

The MIT Press
Cambridge, Massachusetts
London, England

This book was printed and bound by Halliday Lithograph in the United States of America.

Library of Congress Cataloging-in-Publication Data

Effective documentation: What we have learned from research
/edited by Stephen Doheny-Farina.
p. cm. -- (The MIT Press series in information systems)
Includes bibliographies and indexes.
ISBN 0-262-04098-0
1. Communication of technical information. 2. Technology -- Documentation. I. Doheny-Farina, Stephen. II. Series.
T10.5.E34 1988
601.41--dc 19 88-19921
CIP

Contents

Series Foreword

In the tradition of the shoemaker's children going barefoot, there is today a communications gap facing technical writers. Considerable research has been done on writing but it is less widely known than it should be. *Effective Documentation* contains sixteen research papers discussing many aspects of technical writing and should help close this gap.

In many studies of human-computer interaction, there are no easy answers. The fight between icons and words for commands still rages and seems as unlikely to be resolved as many theological disputes. Circumstances alter cases in this area as in many others. But familiarity with research results will help you select which circumstances matter in your case. Unfortunately, the absence of a single right answer does not mean that there are no wrong ones!

One general principle that does come forward is the difficulty of doing documentation in isolation. Just as a skilled tutor at your elbow (or Mark Hopkins at the end of the log) is perhaps the best way to learn how to use a computer system, an interactive approach to both writing and reading documentation is effective. Documentation written while a program is being developed, and done interactively with the developers, is more likely to be not only successful documentation, but also to lead to a better program. And documentation that requires active participation from the user is more likely to be effective training than a manual which is only read (if not completely ignored). Thus, the writers should use their communications skills as much as possible to involve both their colleagues and their customers in the process of learning. They should refute the old canard that "documentation stands between the user and the computer," using writing as a bridge rather than an obstacle.

Other important ideas in this book are principles of graphic design. People "like" pictures; and without suggesting that all computer manuals be issued as comic books, intelligent use of illustration and graphics can help a great deal with user problems. There is also a discussion on how to do research in this area, for those companies willing to extend their own research efforts to include not only the technical side of their products but also the documentation and interface design.

Perhaps the most important lesson from these papers, however, is the discussion of the documentation process as a process. It is important for workers in this area to realize that explaining a computer product does not begin with blank paper and end with a printed manual. New computer services and products need attention to education and documentation just as they need attention to fire safety, RF interference, and other basic points of technical design. Research of the sort explained in this book may be far from converting writing from an art into a science; but it can convert an isolated and often scorned step into one that participates in the overall design process, and by doing so improves not only the instructional material but the overall efficiency of the product and its users.

Michael Lesk

I Introduction

Methods and Results: A Range of Possibilities

Stephen Doheny-Farina
Technical Communication
Clarkson University
Potsdam, NY

At the 34th International Technical Communication Conference in May 1987, a group of technical communicators, communication researchers, and teachers of technical communication met to discuss communication issues and problems that call for further research (**1**). After much discussion, an interesting conflict arose: the communicators and teachers identified many areas that they believed needed further investigation, while the researchers pointed out that some very useful studies have been and are being conducted in many of those areas.

In a brief follow-up discussion it was noted that many of the findings of those studies are relatively inaccessible to practitioners, teachers, and students of technical communication. Either the research is being published in forums that do not reach these audiences, or the findings are being written in research report styles that blunt the usefulness of the findings for those audiences.

In recent years, however, we have seen the publication of some excellent sources of research-based guidelines for writers and designers of instructional texts and other media (e.g., Felker, 1981; Duffy and Waller, 1985; Hartley, 1985; see the chapter by Debs in this volume for a detailed discussion of these and other sources). Still, I and others felt that there may be room for a new collection of research-related material that: **a**) is directed towards a wide range of technical communication professionals, **b**) discusses issues related to both the text and the computer screen, and **c**) explores the contexts of usability -- that is, those environmental factors that influence the writing and reading of technical documentation. As you will see, some of the chapters in this book discuss research results and methods in the larger contexts of organizations and documentation cycles.

The purpose of this book, then, is to offer a range of useful information for technical writers, document designers, managers of technical writing departments, technical communication researchers, and teachers and students of technical communication.

The book's contributors have primarily taken one of three approaches to presenting this "useful information." The authors either: 1) report on specific research projects that they themselves have undertaken; 2) review the implications of a wide variety of empirical research on a given topic or topics -- research not conducted by the authors; or 3) discuss how technical communicators may incorporate research activities within the documentation cycles of their organizations.

Taken as a whole, the book provides in-depth discussions of:

- Research into User Learning and Performance,
- Research into Format and Graphic Design,
- Research into the Management of Documentation Processes, and
- Analyses of Research Methods for Technical Communication.

While I will provide a brief overview of these issues in this Introduction, I first want to discuss what I see as the book's major underlying messages -- messages intertwined in opposing views of what empirical research can do for us and how we should go about doing that research.

Differing Views of Research

As I began to read and edit the chapters, I started to see that, at the most general level, the book would provide two inextricable messages. One involves the results, the other involves the methods of research.

In order to examine these messages, it is useful to begin with a quote by Frank Smith, the editor of ***Technical Communication,,*** the journal of the Society for Technical Communication. In an editorial that prefaced a special journal issue devoted to research, Dr. Smith -- who has been a strong and vocal supporter of research in technical communication -- described an ideal conception of what research does:

> I submit that we must change our habitual approach to our jobs. Typically, we work on the basis of intuition and folklore, and when a client asks us why we want to change his expression or his table or his organization, our only answer is that we **think** it's more effective our way. The client is perfectly justified in that case to say the **he** thinks it isn't. We need to be able to say that experimental research has proven *conclusively* that our recommended approach is superior. And if we

> are to do that, we must learn what has been *proven* and who is doing the work and where it is being published. And those of us who have the proper training and bent of mind and circumstances must begin or accelerate controlled experiments designed to test the old saws and establish *new truths*. (p. 5, 4th Quarter, 1985; my italics)

The contributors to this book do indeed discuss research results that can help technical communication professionals improve the ways that they do their jobs. Yet, invariably, the overarching message that the authors convey is this: while the results of these studies provide useful insights, human communication is complex and we must *not* assume that these results are absolutely *conclusive*. Fine. Anyone who has read research reports by competent researchers will not be surprised to hear these authors caution readers not to take their results as the final word. On the other hand, we will want to know if we are *on the way* to discovering those conclusive "new truths" that Dr. Smith seeks. Some would say yes, some no.

I am going to guess that some readers may look at the research findings reported in this book and assume that, well, applied research into technical communication is in its infancy and it will take years more of study before we can make any absolute conclusions; but if researchers are rigorous, thoughtful, and careful, they will eventually uncover those truths. In contrast, others will look at these results and say that, try as we might, we will *never* be able to find absolute conclusions that prove new truths because all knowledge is situational and, therefore, no research findings can be generalized to larger populations.

You will hear both points of view in this book. Accordingly, you will hear conflicting messages about how we should conduct research in technical communication. A careful reading of the book will reveal differing approaches and differing assumptions about the nature of research. Some authors promote research that is very *localized* -- research, for example, that is geared to the specific demands of a particular task in a particular company. Other authors promote research that attempts to discover *fundamental principles* that should guide all communication of a certain type.

The relative merits of each approach have been argued for years. If such debate helps to spur research on both sides, then it is useful; if it is merely an occasion for bashing those with whom we disagree, then we can dispense with it. I hope that the information in this book -- *eclectic as it is* -- will be both useful for practitioners and stimulating for researchers. While each chapter has many dimensions, the following note a few of the highlights.

Research into User Learning and Performance

One of the primary issues that faces technical writers concerns the amount of information to provide for users. Should writers explain everything or just some things? Should writers provide information in lengthy "natural" language, or should they use concise, "truncated" language? **Charney, Reder, and Wells** first provide an overview of research into these questions by describing the debate between "the expounders vs. the minimalists." They then discuss their own studies which explore how well users learn and perform when supplied with either elaborated or minimal information. Overall, their findings indicate that elaborations can enhance learning and performance in certain circumstances.

The use of elaborated natural language is also advocated by the research of **Hunt and Vassiliadis.** But even as they make this recommendation, these authors caution us to be wary of assuming that this conclusion can be carried across differing populations of computer users. In contrast, the case for the minimalists is provided by the research reported by **Carroll, Smith-Kerker, Ford, and Mazur** (2). These studies show that users perform tasks more efficiently when using minimalist instructional texts.

In addition to the issue of elaboration vs. truncation, **Charney, Reder, and Wells** also explore the most efficient ways to construct tutorials that teach computer use. The authors investigate whether users learn best when they are faced with tutorials that **a)** contain prescribed exercises that must be worked out by the user, **b)** contain "already worked out" examples of user tasks, or **c)** allow users to decide which tasks to try, enabling the users to experiment and fail until they succeed. The studies reported provide insight into the ways that people learn how to use computers. Computer learning is also investigated in the chapter by **Carroll, Mack, Lewis, Grischkowsky, and Robertson** (3). Their research shows that people who are engaged in "active learning" -- choosing which problems to solve and experimenting until the problem is solved -- learn how to use a word processor more quickly and efficiently. In addition, the use of active-learning tutorials is also supported by **Rubens.** Her study suggests that technical writers should employ active-learning tutorials whether they are designing printed or online documentation.

How well users perform tasks may be related to how they prefer to use documentation. **Ramey** reports on user preferences from a number of previously published studies as well as her own investigations. In presenting ways that users want to use computer documentation, Ramey offers some insights into how users process information. She says, for example, that computer use is more like hearing than reading; moreover, users are resistant to reading. That is, when learning how to use the computer, they prefer to be using the machine, not reading the documentation.

Online documentation allows people to use the documentation *while* using the computer. As noted above, the relative effectiveness of online and printed documentation is investigated in a study by **Rubens**. While her study shows that one medium is not clearly better than the other, we can assume that more and more technical writers will be designing and writing a great variety of online documentation. After pointing out that hardcopy conventions do not necessarily transfer to online presentations of information, **Bradford** reviews both research and expert opinion in order to advise hardcopy writers who must plan online documentation.

Research into Format and Graphic Design

While technical writers may be expert in the presentation of verbal information, they may know considerably less about the optimal ways to design formats and present graphical information. **Rubens and Rubens** devised three different format designs and tested users abilities to perform tasks, and search and retrieve information with the three formats. This study is part of a larger attempt to isolate the numerous format design variables that make documents easier to use.

In an overview of research on the presentation of graphics, **Lewis** reviews studies that explore how we can a) represent realistic images, b) illustrate concepts, and c) understand the ways that differing types of readers use graphics. Finally, Lewis suggests how technical writers can use these findings to design graphics for computer documentation. While most of this research involves textual information, **Krull** reviews graphics as they can be employed online. In particular, Krull reviews research into a number of graphic interface devices, such as icons, windows, and pull-down menus.

Research into the Management of Documentation Processes

Most of the research reported in this book is devoted to the study of textual or online strategies and features. In recent years, some researchers have moved away from such a tight focus on the words and pictures. They have started to examine the social and organizational factors that influence writing processes. For technical writers, managers can be a major organizational force upon them, exerting a powerful influence on the process of producing usable documentation. **Chisholm**, in an exploratory survey of technical writers, discusses the common failures of management and some accepted solutions to those problems.

Many of these management problems stem from the use of an outmoded documentation cycle that relegates documentation to an add-on function that occurs at the very end of the product development cycle. **Baker**, like Chisholm, argues that the documentation process must become -- from the outset -- a part of the product development cycle. While both of these authors note the complexity of this inclusive cycle, **Mirel**, in an account of a case study of writers who produced an in-house user manual, provides a detailed analysis of the complexities of managing writers, programmers, and others who all become a part of the documentation process.

Analyses of Research Methods for Technical Communication

As stated earlier in this introduction, there is an underlying current of methodological issues running through this book. This current begins with the chapter by **Morgan**, who speaks to readers who are interested in what research may offer, but who may not know much about how research is conducted. Morgan provides an overview of research theories and methods that will help technical communicators become more critical readers of research reports.

While Morgan does not promote one type of research over another, other authors do: **Charney, Reder, and Wells** argue that we must turn to experimental research in order to discover the optimal ways to present instructions in texts. In contrast, **Hunt and Vassiliadis** conclude that no matter how rigorous, all research is context-bound and, therefore, we cannot hope to discover *the* optimal approach that will apply to all instructional material. In addition, **Mirel** argues that usability research must go beyond a focus on merely textual features to a focus on the uses of texts in users' social and organizational contexts.

Finally, both **Gould and Doheny-Farina** and **Baker** suggest ways that technical communicators can develop research programs for their companies. Baker suggests ways that technical communicators can develop an *in-house* research program by developing a human factors lab and integrating human factors research into a company's documentation cycle. Gould and Doheny-Farina discuss the techniques, constraints, and benefits of going *outside* of the technical writers' companies to study users working in their actual work environments.

This Book in Context

It is important to realize that this book is one of a small but earnest group of research-based resources for technical communicators. Accordingly, **Debs** begins the book with reviews of other publications that offer technical communication guidelines based on research. While surveying a number of the major books and journals, Debs summarizes some of the key information that can be found in the best of those sources.

A Note on the Format

You will see that there are inconsistencies in the ways that many of the following chapters are printed (e.g., a few chapters may be right justified while many others are ragged right). Please do not mistake these inconsistencies as evidence of lazy editing or careless production. So that this book could be printed as quickly as possible, The MIT Press required the authors to produce camera-ready final drafts of their chapters. The book was then printed from those final drafts. We allowed for minor differences as long as the chapters were consistent within a set of general specifications. This process, while a bit more cumbersome for the authors, has enabled The MIT Press to shorten the production time by nearly a year.

Acknowledgments

This book is the result of much hard work by its authors. I would like to thank them for putting up with my continual and often petty demands -- especially my "I-want-it-yesterday" deadlines. In addition, I would like to thank my former colleagues at the University of North Carolina, Charlotte -- Fred Smith, Mark West, Robin Hemley, and Stan Patten -- for their psychological and logistical (thanks, Stan!) support. Finally, I am indebted to Frank Satlow and Terry Ehling of The MIT Press for their guidance throughout the development of this book.

Notes

(1) This "discussion session" at the ITCC (Denver, May 1987) was organized and run by John Beard of Wayne State University and myself. The participants filled out a questionnaire, broke into discussion groups, and then reported to the entire group in an open discussion period.

(2&3) Both of these chapters are reprinted from the journal, *Human-Computer Interaction*, published by Lawrence Erlbaum Associates.

II Overview: Research Findings and Designs

1 A History of Advice: What Experts Have to Tell Us

Mary Beth Debs
Department of English Writing Program
University of Cincinnati
Cincinnati, OH 45220

How does one go about writing usable documentation? Do callouts aid the reader? Are advance organizers, summaries, and glossaries worth the extra pages? Should writers approach preparing manuals about hardware the same as they do software? What role does instruction play in reference manuals? Is there a difference between a usable text and a readable one? Is creating a usable text part of the writing process or is it more a matter of design? In the face of a new project, where does a writer go to find out what choices he or she should be making?

Few technical writers have the luxury of finding a user reading over their shoulders. In fact, many companies actually screen their writers from the product's eventual user, sometimes out of necessity or a peculiar notion of resource allocation. A company may keep the audience unknown and at a distance by not allowing writers to spend exploration and evaluation time with customers, for example, or by denying the opportunity to test the effectiveness of a manual as readily as that of any other product. In addition to a writer's learning through experience, usability research and testing provide an important route toward finding success with readers - toward discovering the extent and consistency of their likes and dislikes, expectations, patterns for accessing and retrieving information. While such testing offers improvements to the manual that may be at hand, research related to usability helps to establish guidelines which will enhance the effectiveness of every generation of documentation to follow.

Within the last five years, a handful of authors and editors have written articles and produced books that offer advice on the optimum ways to present technical information. This chapter will review the most significant and accessible of these publications, so that novice and expert writers can better choose useful sources of general information. Before reviewing what the experts have had to tell us, I will place this advice in context by providing a brief overview of the relationship that has developed between text design and technical documentation.

Early Publishing and Technical Materials

The way technical literature looks and reads today is, to a large extent, part of the heritage we have received from publishers and audiences of the seventeenth century. Although such features as alphabetization, indices, title pages, annotation, cross-referencing, section titles, and even page tabs were experimented with by occasionally adventurous scribes during the middle ages, their use became established and to some extent conventionalized during the century after the introduction of the printing press (Eisenstein, 1979). Manuals, self-help books, and textbooks, teaching topics that ranged from baking to mining and architecture, proliferated. Readers learned to expect books to be organized in certain ways and they began to anticipate the design features of particular types of books, such as the step-by-step numbering of "how-to" books. At first, printers were concerned with maintaining the aesthetic qualities of the script manuscript within the printed book, but as improvements were made in the printing press itself and in the industry, publishers, printers, and authors developed a new aesthetic for typography and design and experimented with textual and pictorial features to enhance a reader's ability to use the book. Their innovations influenced how readers store information as part of one's learning process. Their innovations also contributed to a general concern for systemizing knowledge and to new ways of doing so in a number of fields (Eisenstein, 1979).

During the same century, the style of English prose was being shaped by the Royal Society's promotion of utilitarianism. The Royal Society dealt with "natural philosophy" (which became known as science by the mid-1800's) as well as with matters falling under categories generally academic and specifically technical. In a now well-known passage from his History of the Royal Society, Thomas Sprat praises the attempt by the members

> to reject all the amplifications, digressions, and swellings of style: to return back to the primitive purity, and shortness, when men delivered so many things, almost in an equal number of words. They have exacted from all their members a close, naked, natural way of speaking; positive expressions; clear senses; a native easiness: bringing all things as near the Mathematicall plainness, as they can: and preferring the language of Artizans, Countrymen, and Merchants, before that of Wits, or Scholars.

Often viewed as a reaction to the figurative and ornamental excesses of what has been called "Ciceronian" rhetoric, this movement privileging the practice of plain language represents a concerted and deliberate effort to make language first and primarily useful (Adolph, 1968). Sprat's manifesto continues to echo in many of our business and technical writing texts today - often at cost to the "usefulness" of such stylistic devices as metaphor and analogy which, in the hands of a good writer, have a demonstrated capacity to help readers develop and learn scientific and technical concepts (Halloran and Bradford, 1984).

Modern Trends

Today, the proliferation of technical publications continues, reflecting both the demands of an increasingly literate and technically oriented society as well as the pressures created by the rapid introduction of technical innovations, such as the computer, into the marketplace. We can divide most technical information, presented to the reader in the form of textbooks, manuals, self-guidance books, and labels on products, into two major categories: informational and instructional. Publications with a primarily informational purpose include reference materials, product information labels, and specifications. These publications are designed to maintain or improve the reader's ability to efficiently access any desired information. Publications with a primarily instructional purpose include anything from popular press explanations of technical subjects to materials that accompany specific products, telling the reader how to use (or how not to use) the equipment or product. Their design is generally less dependent on discrete pieces of information, and more intent on developing for the reader a systematic approach to the subject or task at hand. Computer documentation could fall under either of these categories.

Offering a different system of categories which focuses on the reader's intent rather than the publication's general purpose, Sticht (1985) identifies two major classes of what he calls "reading tasks": reading-to-learn and reading-to-do. A reading-to-learn task requires the reader to extract and store information, essentially to remember it; the reader will rely on previewing and reviewing, outlining and underlining. In a reading-to-do task, the information can be "looked up, used, and may then be forgotten." Sticht suggests that the information offered in a publication that is task-oriented acts as a kind of "external memory." In either case, we can see that the reader approaches the information in a text with the intent of using it, either immediately or in a later application.

I have included this discussion to outline some of the areas of theory, research and practice which bear on both the writer's and reader's determination of whether or not information has been presented in a usable way, and to suggest the range of fields involved. In providing a usable text, there is a contract established between the writer and the reader. The writer must be conscious of the audience's expectations, strategies, and motivations in reading the material - even though members of the audience themselves may not be consciously aware of their own approaches. At a basic level, the reader expects a document to look like something - that is, like another manual or reference book. Conventions which begin to meet these expectations have been incorporated in the print media since the first book was published. In addition, the reader expects a document to "read well." Thus, we introduce a concern for the quality of writing along with the contemporary notion of readability. At another level, the reader expects to use the information contained in a publication, either to learn or to apply it to performing a task directly at hand. To this end, the writer must use text features to effectively and appropriately guide the reader through the text and to provide for the reader to successfully interact with the text in performing a task. These features may involve typography, layout, organization, graphics, and structural aids.

While the "reading-to-learn" task has been a long-standing concern of textbook publishers, educators, and psychologists, understanding the demands of the "reading-to-do" task took on additional importance during World War II when the military was suddenly faced with the need to teach the maintenance and operation of newly developed equipment and weaponry to a moderately literate population. Since documentation is partly responsible for carving out markets for new computer products, it has to do with both learning and doing. Since, in its many different forms, documentation may address audiences from the novice computer user to the expert, the writer will find the set of expectations to be a complex one at best, and sometimes a conflicting one.

Journals

Reflecting this complexity, current theory and research available to the technical communicator comes mostly piecemeal from a wide range of fields. Major contributions come from research in reading, typography, and instructional design. Table 1 lists selected journals which regularly publish articles focused on text features that aid usability.

Table 1
Selected Journals Containing Articles Related to Usability

Information Design and Typography
Educational Communication and Technology Journal
Ergonomics
Human Factors
Information Design Journal
Journal of Typographic Research
Simply Stated (newsletter)
Visible Language

Reading
Journal of Applied Psychology
Journal of Educational Psychology
Journal of Experimental Psychology
Journal of Verbal Learning and Verbal Behavior
Memory and Cognition
Reading Research Quarterly

Technical and General Writing
ACM Sigdoc Asterick
IEEE Transactions on Professional Communication
Iowa State Journal of Technical and Business Communication
Journal of Technical Writing and Communication
Technical Communication
Written Communication

Media
AV Communication Review

In the past, the journals in reading and psychology have tended to offer empirical studies usually focused on very narrow questions concerning word, phrase, and sentence characteristics and their effects on readers' comprehension and retention of material; jargon abounds. The technical communication journals frequently publish general articles on documentation writing. Information Design Journal and Visible Language are two readable journals of particular interest to writers concerned with the design and presentation of a wide array of technical information.

I would also consider adding the new monthly trade magazine on desktop publishing, Publish!, and the quarterly Magazine Layout and Design to the list. Publish!, for example, has carried a regular feature describing the history and aesthetic appeal of particular typefaces. (New books being published on the subject of desktop publishing also hold the promise of offering useful if limited introductions to design features, particularly typography. Two recent titles include The Illustrated Handbook of Desktop Publishing and Typesetting and Design for Desktop Publishing.)

Design Books for a Personal Reference Library

Although writers still *write* technical documents, there has been recently a steady shift toward writers gaining an understanding of how to *design* the presentation of technical information. Three books with this focus are particularly distinctive because they also serve as excellent compendiums of the theoretical discussions and research found scattered in the journals of various fields. Most importantly, they are filled with useful information, and would prove invaluable as a reference collection on the shelf of any technical communicator. And, since there is nothing finer for a student of document design than a good bibliography, each offers an excellent list of references.

The first of these books is the second edition of James Hartley's Designing Instructional Text (1985). Basing his recommendations on studies published in British and American journals, Hartley fully discusses fifteen topics, from typesizes, typefaces, and spacing, to the special demands of designing forms and generating electronic text. He generously illustrates each topic with "before and after" examples and case histories, and he concludes each chapter with a useful summary of the main points. The design of the book itself is an example of how theories can be applied to instructional materials, and how deviation from those theories can still produce an effective text. What particularly strikes me about this work, however, is Hartley's detailed and reasoned presentation of research findings, his noting of limitations of any guidelines as they are presented, and the variety of instructional materials and applications he considers. He presents a rationale, evaluates examples based on that rationale, then demonstrates the effectiveness of revising material according to a given principle. He also considers the demands of different audiences, and occasionally focuses on children's interactions with textbooks. Although I find the overall organization and layout of the text sometimes too confusing to use it solely as a reference guide, it proved to be well worth reading through - twice so far.

Guidelines for Document Designers (D. Felker et al., 1981) is the second book I would add to the bookshelf. In a carefully ordered presentation, twenty-five principles having to do with writing (at the sentence level), organization, typography and graphics are explained, again with "before and after" examples (drawn primarily from government and industry). Research studies which support each principle are summarized at the end of the sections. The guidelines themselves appear to be deceptively simple: "Make a table of contents for long documents," "Avoid using all caps," "Write short sentences." Nonetheless, the text, which includes comments on the examples, related principles, and sensible qualifications to prevent applying the principles too rigidly, serves as a valuable primer for any novice writer and offers more than one new consideration to the experienced designer.

The third book, Designing Usable Texts (1985), is a collection of fourteen articles edited by Thomas Duffy of Carnegie-Mellon University and Robert Waller from the British Institute of Educational Technology. The scope here is again generally wide, including instructional, reference, and procedural texts. Several articles examine the roles of writers and editors; and the two concluding articles offer methods for evaluating texts. According to the editors, Designing Usable Texts was compiled "in the belief that recommendations about text design from whatever source must be soundly argued, properly tested, consistent with the research evidence, but also realistic, affordable, and intuitively acceptable." To a large extent, the authors have met their stated goal, though the reader may suffer some from the density of material, a characteristic common to academic prose styles. Students of document design research may find interesting and useful particular sections of articles which summarize research from different fields: i.e., research on learning in the chapter by John Carter; on the theory of studying in the chapter by Thomas H. Anderson and Bonnie B. Armbruster; literacy by T. Sticht; and readability research by Richard P. Kern.

A fourth book I would add to the shelf of any writer who works with graphics is The Display of Quantitative Information (1983) by Edward Tufte. Devoted exclusively to "a celebration of data graphics," this often gracious text examines and criticizes various examples of graphics, their design features, aesthetics and techniques. It offers a rare combination of history, theory, and application, and makes a series of principles available to even the most novice designer.

Advice Experts Agree On

The books reviewed above offer two advantages to the technical communicator: 1) they view writing as an integral part of text design, discussing such features as organization and structure as interrelated means for enhancing a reader's use and comprehension of a document; 2) the principles of design which they offer are based on a careful consideration of recent research as well as established convention; they are likely to warn against too rigid an adherence to deceptively simple rules and formulae. Given the long history of publishing, it is surprising that only a relatively small amount of research has been conducted so far on document design. Consequently, however, the authors of the above texts are fairly consistent in identifying a limited but specific set of guidelines or rules-of-thumb for the document designer. This advice, arranged into four categories, is summarized in the following paragraphs.

Design Process. Experts agree that, whether a document is produced by a single author or a team made up of a writer, graphic artist, editor, and printer, its effectiveness and ultimate success originate in the planning stages. For technical documents, planning traditionally involves careful analyses of the task to be described, the purpose, audience, and the audience's interaction with the text and the task at hand (for example, assembling the components of a personal computer system); a writer must be especially careful in selecting material necessary for the reader and eliminating nonessential material (Felker et al., 3). Most importantly, a writer should work to develop and have at hand a repertoire of methods, strategies, and models to draw from when addressing various audiences; these options would include structuring devices such as advance organizers, summaries, and lists as well as stylistic choices and alternatives to simple text presentation (Orna, 1985; Hartley). In selecting from this repertoire, writers and designers depend upon their assessment of the readership (usually established in terms of age, education level, and familiarity with the subject or task), their understanding of the purpose the reader has (i.e., finding or verifying information, learning procedures, following instructions), and their anticipation of the conditions under which the document may be used (Orna, 30-31). Empirical evaluation, that is, controlled observations of document users particularly in the field, provides information needed both for revising the immediate document and for guiding the planning of related documents (Felker, 1985, 55-59; Hartley, 139-145).

Style and Comprehension. Readability formulas represent one response to the problem of measuring, predicting, and ultimately controlling stylistic characteristics that affect reading comprehension (Duffy, 1985). However, the experts cited here offer these formulas with caution, since undue concern with producing a good "score" by limiting sentence length and the use of multisyllabic words can just as easily result in bad prose as ignoring these guidelines can. Nonetheless, the authors do consistently recommend keeping sentences short (25 words or less), though varied, and avoiding abstract, difficult, and unnecessary words (Felker et al., Hartley). Too much information given before the subject, at the end of the sentence, or between the subject and the verb adversely affect comprehension (Felker et al., 45-48). Noun strings and nominalizations make reading more difficult; personal pronouns, concrete words, and action verbs generally insure better comprehension (Felker et al.). While most sentences should be constructed in the active voice, research does indicate that in some contexts readers have an easier time with passive voice, particularly when they anticipate emphasis being given to the object receiving the action (Felker et al., 25).

Two contributions from the Document Design Center seem particularly important to the technical communicator. First, researchers suggest that conditional statements should be handled carefully to aid the reader's comprehension. For example, if a rule or statement has several conditions or exceptions attached to it (e.g., this will happen if someone does this, or does this, and this), then the rule or statement should be stated first, followed by the conditions. If the conditions are many, they should be given as a list (Felker, 54-55; Felker et al., 50-52). Second, scenarios or short narratives can be used to illustrate concretely specific actions or situations (Felker, 53-55; Flower et al., 1983).

Organization and Structure. Experts in document design tend to talk about organization not in terms of writing but in terms of text structure. Their concern is with establishing in any document a consistent frame of reference, orienting the reader through the use of typographical cues and structural or "signpost" features. Again careful to avoid setting down absolute rules, the experts tend to draw from linguistic and reading research to suggest specific ways of controlling spatial arrangement and sequencing. For example, readers' comprehension, search strategies, and recall may be aided by making explicit how the document is organized through the use of a table of contents, overviews, and headings (Felker et al.). Chapter or section overviews highlight upcoming information or establish connections with previous information, thus providing a context for the reader (Felker et al., 15; Felker, 51). Summaries (or the related feature, advance organizers) placed at the beginning or end of sections of text seem to aid comprehension (Hartley 49-50; Carter, 1985, 150-151). Informative headings, consisting of questions or statements as opposed to simple labels, are used by readers to search for, recall, and retrieve information (Hartley 50; Anderson and Armbruster, 1985, 165; Felker et al., 17-20). Indexes that provide multiple cross-referencing and are set up in an indented format also help readers to use a document (Hartley, 128).

Sequencing is a feature that requires attention to spatial arrangement, linguistic units, and common sense logic. Most readers, for example, prefer vertically arranged lists to a series of items presented in continuous text; items in such a list are best set off by Arabic numbers or bullets (Hartley, 50-51). In arranging units of text, whether at the document, section, or sentence level, a writer does best by following the general "given-new" guidelines: that is, start with what the reader knows before including new information. Along these lines, Felker et al. suggest sequencing material so that general information is given before specific, permanent before temporary, information affecting many people before information that affects only a few (9-11). Logical time sequence is always an effective ordering device.

Finally, experts caution that too many spatial and typographic cues will prove confusing to any reader (Felker, 73-76).

Typography. Increasingly, writers are being given the authority to plan and control the "looks" of a document - the overall layout and typography. Many writers, however, have little if any training in this area of design; they may be unsure of the aesthetics and practicalities of using white space or may feel somewhat overwhelmed by the 2,350 typefaces from which one can choose (Hartley, 23). In general, the fewer typographic choices a designer makes, the better.

Text should look accessible. This can be accomplished by making paragraphs and sentences generally short (with some variation) and providing white space between paragraphs. With margins and leading between lines, as much as fifty per cent of a page may be devoted to white space. When possible, prose should be used rather than numbers or probability signs and figures, and reference numbers should be avoided (Hartley, 56-58).

In choosing a typeface, Hartley recommends selecting one that is "firm in line, open and even in spacing, and without idiosyncratic features" (24). Based on a number of research studies, experts further recommend using 8 to 10 point type, a line length between 50-70 characters, and ragged right margins (Felker et al., Hartley). Text in italics or all capitals slows reading speed.

Graphics. Learning theory suggests that not all members of an audience are text-oriented; many prefer learning through pictorial representations. Most of the authors strongly recommend incorprating visuals to supplement prose. Noting that illustrations can distract or attract, Hartley argues that drawings and pictures serve an "additive function," that is, readers do not recall more of the text itself but do better recall what has been illustrated. Illustrations of materials are less distracting and serve their function best if they are placed near their reference points in the text.

According to Carter, visual illustrations can simplify and "concretize" complex material, as can analogies, metaphors, and scenarios. (151). The well-equipped communicator will look for opportunities to add flowcharts, alogrithms, tables, charts, drawings and photgraphs. Here, the general rules-of-thumb require keeping things simple (e.g., using line drawings over photographs) and carefully following the conventions of labelling the parts of the illustrations (Twyman, 1985, 278; Hartley; Felker et al.).

Sources on Computer Documentation

None of the books cited above has specifically to do with computer documentation, although all provide information essential to those documentation specialists who anticipate their texts actually being used. Within the last six years, however, a number of texts have been published which offer advice to documentation writers. Most of these have been written by practitioners, and so they often use a kind of informed common sense approach and sometimes reflect a perspective that is limited to the experience of the practitioner gained during a stay at one company. On the positive side, many of them detail the steps involved in the process of writing and designing a useful manual, and most consider some of the stylistics and organizational characteristics that seem to make for good writing.

In a series of four articles, the latest published in 1986, John Brockmann reviews 18 of these texts. His ten criteria for evaluation are based on an author's inclusion of established technical practices, mix of theory and practice, methodology, discussions of graphics and reference aides, use of examples, and coverage of online documentation. To date, he has favored Geoffrey James's Document Databases (1985); Jonathan Price's How to Write a Computer Manual: A Handbook of Software Development (1984); and Sandra Pakin & Associates' Documentation Development Methodology (1983). Brockmann's own text, Computer User Documentation: From Paper to Online appeared in 1986. (A more complete bibliography of books on writing documentation is included at the end of this chapter.)

What do these experts say? Most of the books cover the same territory, but provide a variety of tidbits and examples of what one may encounter:

What is documentation? This question usually opens the text and includes a discussion of the varieties of tutorial and reference materials possible, and the differing demands of external and internal documentation.

How does the writer manage the process of writing documentation? Authors discuss the ins and outs of scheduling, resource allocation, or market analysis.

How does the writer plan the document? Authors may present one or several methods, including the use of standard outlines and specifications, task analysis, audience analysis, storyboarding, or taking a look at the competition. Brockmann explains a process of "blueprinting," preparing a plan which anticipates the requirements and content of the completed document. Layout concerns may also be included in this section, but none of the authors fully takes up the question of the limitations of a writer's choices in the face of company constraints.

How does one go about writing the document? In this part, most books offer guidelines having to do with the control of style so that the resulting writing will be readable and conversational. Incorporating research from the Document Design Center, Brockmann points out ways in which writing can be made "reader-based" through the use of examples, metaphors, cases, and scenarios. Price is one of the few authors who takes up the importance of teamwork in gathering information.

What illustrations should be included? As mentioned before, most writers are text-oriented, yet the majority of computer users may be more predominantly visually oriented. Engineers and programmers, for example, often work with models, drawings, and schemes, and prefer these to prose. Writers, then, must develop their visual senses. Consequently, these sections can be extremely valuable to the writer, since they outline the various types of graphics, their conventions of use, and the principles which insure their effectiveness.

How should a document be edited? Here again, most authors return to dictates of style. Some, however, suggest employing something akin to Buren and Buehler's (1980) levels of edit approach.

In what ways can a document be effectively reviewed, tested, and evaluated? Field testing is the number one recommendation. (For an overview of qualitative field testing methods, see the chapter by Gould and Doheny-Farina in this volume.)

How should the packaging and maintenance of the documentation be handled? This section is frequently missing; when it is included, the advice offered is quite general.

Although I have chosen to represent these "how to" texts collectively since they tend to follow this generic outline, there are significant differences in content and perspective. Zaneski, for example, is the only text to take up the issue of writer/printer relationships; his text also emphasizes policy-making and standards for manuals more than the other books do. Weiss offers another variation since his advice to writers centers on a structured or modular approach to document writing (see also Horn, 1985). Rather than suggesting ways to manage the process of writing documentation, Stuart focuses on the types of documents that are produced during the process of developing a computer system; these include proposals, specifications, and then the manual. Katzin takes a similar route, describing in detail the purpose and forms of such items as the system overview, glossaries, error/edit messages, terminal and data entry instructions, and forms design.

Perhaps most importantly, though, these books serve to identify and highlight important issues of debate in the study of documentation. For example, Price (whose text was produced with the staff of the User Education Group of Apple Corporation) is quite emphatic in telling the writer to "indulge in humor." Brockmann, quite rightly I think, argues that attempts at humor fail more frequently than they succeed; a conversational style would instill user-friendliness less dangerously. Other issues that have been dealt with only briefly in one or two of these textbooks include the need for a more detailed analysis of the relationship of the documentation to the product as well as an understanding of the place of documentation within the company; similarities and differences among hardcopy, on-line, and video tutorials; and the special demands of writing about hardware and software.

The Importance of Expert Advice

The task of communicating technical information, particularly that of preparing computer documentation, is an unusually complex process, even by today's standards. Each project addresses a different situation, different information needs, different constraints. Audiences vary widely in expectations, purposes, and strategies. The technical writer deals with the intersection of several interactions - writing and design, reader and text, user and product, conventions and innovations. Additionally, the use of electronic text - attempting to move more pieces of documentation to the computer screen - has created an entirely new set of considerations for the writer. Yet much of the research which would inform the choices a writer must make can be found only by reviewing the work being done in fields as diverse as information sciences, psycholinguistics, printing and graphic design, human factors, and reading education. Much of the advice offered to date by experts is often sound but in need of adaptation; too much remains relatively untested in different contexts. An increasing number of books and articles which combine the best of research and expert advice, however, are addressing the specific concerns of the technical writer. The experts suggest that the key to writing and designing effective documentation can be found in understanding what happens when the reader uses the text. How effectively a reader or learner uses a document depends on how well the writer anticipates and responds to the variables of that interaction.

References

Robert Adolph, The Rise of Modern Prose Style, Cambridge, Massachusetts, M.I.T. Press, 1968.

Thomas H. Anderson and Boonie B. Armbruster, "Studying Strategies and Their Implications for Textbook Design," Designing Usable Texts, eds. Thomas M. Duffy and Robert Waller, Orlando, Florida, Academic Press, 1985, pp. 159-177.

R. John Brockmann, "The New Generation of Books on Writing Computer Documentation," IEEE Transactions on Professional Communications, 29, 2 (June 1986), 35-39.

Robert Van Buren and Mary Fran Buehler, The Levels of Edit, Pasadena, California, California Institute of Technology, 1980.

John F. Carter, "Lessons in Text Design from an Instructional Perspective," Designing Usable Texts, eds. Thomas M. Duffy and Robert Waller, Orlando, Florida, Academic Press, 1985, pp. 145-156.

Thomas M. Duffy, "Readability Formulas: What's the Use?" Designing Usable Texts, eds. Thomas M. Duffy and Robert Waller, Orlando, Florida, Academic Press, 1985, pp. 113-143.

Thomas M. Duffy and Robert Waller, eds., Designing Usable Texts, Orlando, Florida, Academic Press, 1985.

Elizabeth L. Eisenstein, The Printing Press as an Agent of Change, Cambridge, Cambridge University Press, 1979.

Daniel B. Felker, et al., Guidelines for Document Designers, Washington, D.C., American Institutes for Research, 1981.

Daniel B. Felker, Janice Redish, and Jane Peterson, "Training Authors of Informative Documents," Designing Usable Texts, eds. Thomas M. Duffy and Robert Waller, Orlando, Florida, Academic Press, 1985, pp. 43-61.

Linda Flower, John Hayes, and Heidi Swarts, "Revising Functional Documents: The Scenario Principle," New Essays in Technical and Scienitific Communication: Research, Theory, Practice, eds. Paul V. Anderson, R. John Brockmann, and Carolyn Miller, Farmingdale, New York, Baywood Publishing Company, 1983, pp. 41-58.

Michael Halloran and Annette Bradford, "Figures of Speech in the Rhetoric of Science and Technology," Essays on Classical Rhetoric and Modern Discourse, eds. Robert J. Connors, Lisa S. Ede, and Andrea Lunsford, Carbondale, Illinois, Southern Illinois University Press, 1984, pp. 179-192.

James Hartley, Designing Instructional Text, New York, Nichols Publishing, 1985.

Robert E. Horn, "Results with Structured Writing Using the Information Mapping Writing(c) Service Standards," Designing Usable Texts, eds. Thomas M. Duffy and Robert Waller, Orlando, Florida, Academic Press, 1985, pp. 179-212.

Michael L. Kleper, The Illustrated Handbook of Desktop Publishing and Typesetting, Blue Ridge Summit, Pennsylvania, TAB Professional and Reference Books, 1987.

John Miles, Design for Desktop Publishing, San Francisco, Chronicle Books, 1987.

Elizabeth Orna, "The Author: Help or Stumbling Block on the Road to Designing Usable Texts?" Designing Usable Texts, eds. Thomas M. Duffy and Robert Waller, Orlando, Florida, Academic Press, 1985, pp. 19-41.

Edward R. Tufte, The Visual Display of Quantitative Information, Cheshire, Connecticut, Graphics Press, 1983.

T. Sticht, "Understanding Readers and Their Uses of Text," Designing Usable Texts, eds. Thomas M. Duffy and Robert Waller, Orlando, Florida, Academic Press, 1985, pp. 315-340.

Michael Twyman, "Using Pictorial Language: A Discussion of the Dimensions of the Problem," Designing Usable Texts, eds. Thomas M. Duffy and Robert Waller, Orlando, Florida, Academic Press, 1985, pp. 245-312.

Bibliography of Books on Writing Documentation

Adams, Kay, Ida Halasz, and R. Jerry Adams. Handbook for Developing Computer User Manuals. Lexington, Massachusetts: Lexington Books, 1986.

Brockmann, R. John. Writing Better Computer User Documentation: From Paper to Online. New York: John Wiley & Sons, 1986.

Browning, Christine. Guide to Effective Software Technical Writing. Englewood Cliffs, New Jersey: Prentice-Hall, Inc., 1984.

Cohan, Gerald, and Donald Cunningham. Creating Technical Manuals: A Step-by-Step Approach to Writing User-Friendly Instructions. New York: McGraw-Hill Book Co., 1984.

Houghton-Alico, Doann. Creating Computer Software User Guides. New York: McGraw-Hill Book Company, 1985.

Katzin, Emanuel. How to Write a Really Good User's Manual. New York: Van Nostrand Reinhold Company, 1985.

Kelly, Derek. Documenting Computer Application Systems: Concepts and Techniques. New York: Petrocelli Books Inc., 1983.

McGehee, Brad M. The Complete Guide to Writing Software User Manuals. Cincinnati: Writer's Digest Books, 1984.

Pakin, Sandra, et al. Documentation Development Methodology. New York: Prentice Hall, 1983.

Price, Jonathan. How to Write a Computer Manual. Menlo Park, California: Benjamin/Cummings Publishing Company, 1984.

Schoff, G., and P. Robinson. Writing and Designing Operator Manuals. Belmont, California: Lifetime Learning, 1984.

Skees, William D. Writing Handbook for Computer Professionals. Belmont, California: Wadsworth, 1982.

Stuart, Ann. Writing and Analyzing Effective Computer System Documentation. New York: Holt, Rinehart and Winston, 1984.

Weiss, Edmond. How to Write a Usable User Manual. Philadelphia, Pennsylvania: ISI Press, 1985.

Zaneski, Richard. Software Manual Production Simplified. New York: Petrocelli Books Inc., 1982.

2 Empirical Research Designs: Choices for Technical Communicators

Meg Morgan
Department of English
University of North Carolina at Charlotte
Charlotte, NC

Research in the area of technical communications, like many areas of the applied fields related to writing, such as business writing, has traditonally been concerned with reporting techniques that work in organizations and the classroom. The literature in the technical journals is replete with techniques that professionals have tried and have found to be "effective." Although professional perceptions are often accurate, there have been attempts in recent years to move away from anecdotal and "how-to" advice towards a more systematic inquiry into what does and does not "work."

Part of this systematic inquiry includes the use of empirical research methods drawn from the social sciences. For many professionals in technical communication, social science research methods are foreign territory. The purpose of this essay is to acquaint technical communicators new to social science inquiry with some fundamentals of the research methods used in the social sciences. You will not emerge from reading this chapter ready to "do" social science research, but you should be more able to understand studies published in research journals. You may also bring a more critical eye to studies, including those in this book. Those interested in additional information about a particular research method should consult the references at the end of this chapter.

What is Empirical Research?

Empirical research is a systematic examination of a contemporary phenomenon in order to answer questions or solve problems. Although empirical research shares similarities with other types of research, such as historical, theoretical, and linguistic (Lauer and Asher, 1988), it differs from

My thanks to Dianne Atkinson from Purdue University who read and responded to a draft of this chapter.

them because it asks questions about contemporary problems, problems in process, if you will. And because this chapter is concerned with empirical methods used in the social sciences, the focus is on strategies that can be used to understand how **people** behave within a communication situation.

Research in the social sciences can be broadly classified into three types: **qualitative research strategies, correlational research strategies,** and **experimental research strategies.** Qualitative research enables researchers to investigate the process of the problem situation or describe features of the problem. For example, a researcher in technical communication would use a qualitative design to examine **how** a writer and engineer work together to design a computer manual. The researcher would attend meetings with them, watch them consult together, and analyze the text they produced.

Correlational research enable researchers to uncover **relationships** among features or variables of a research problem. Using correlational methods, a researcher would investigate "a phenomenon that has already occurred," (Kerlinger, p. 379) variables over which the researcher has little control. For example, a researcher would use a correlational design to discover relationships between hiring practices of a computer software company and certain demographic characteristics of technical writers in that company.

A researcher who chooses an experimental design looks at outcomes or effects of a certain treatment or change from the way things normally occur. For example, if a computer software company wants to know how a training program affects the writing style of its engineers, the company researcher would design a research project to study outcomes of training.

In short, qualitative designs are concerned with **process** and **description,** correlational studies with **relationships,** and experimental studies with **outcomes** or **effects**.

Any research problem can be investigated using one or more of the research strategies represented by these three broad classifications; each method assumes a different kind of research question. The choice of one strategy over another means the researcher has defined the problem in a way so it can be solved using a particular research method. The choice of a particular research strategy comes down to that first and fundamental of precepts: the best research method is the one that answers the research question.

The rest of this chapter discusses each type of research and, where appropriate, designs within each type. I will include in my discussion a description of the design and three basic components of the design (theory, subjects, and data collection). At the end of each discussion, I will include an example of the design from current journals and texts.

Qualitative Designs: Ethnography, Case Study, Descriptive

The purpose of qualitative research methods is to answer questions about process or description. There are three kinds of qualitative research designs: ethnography, case study, and descriptive.

Ethnographers are interested in context and the relationship between people and their environment. They can trace a particular event over time, noting changes that occur within a single environment, culture or organization; they can record the effects of changes upon individuals within the organization or study how change affects the whole organization. Ethnographers can also examine practices among different cultures, environments, and organizations to see how the same phenomenon affects different people.

Case study researchers are interested in identifying features of a particular phenomenon by examining, in depth, few (perhaps only one) example of that phenomenon. Whereas the ethnographer focuses on context, the case study researcher focuses on the inhabitant, examining behaviors in relationship to objects, processes, and other inhabitants. In case studies, the subjects of the study are often isolated from the environment in order to focus more directly on their actions. One of the major purposes of case study research is to discover previously unknown aspects, features, or dimensions of the phenomenon. These aspects may become variables in follow-up correlational or experimental studies.

Descriptive studies are often large-scale attempts to identify features of an event. While a case study may focus on one or two subjects, descriptive studies examine many instances of that event, culling from masses of information peculiarities that distinguish that phenomenon from others.

Role of Theory in Qualitative Research

Qualitative research depends upon a "rich,. . . elaborate and well-organized explanation or theory. . . ." (Asher, p. 135) Theory signals what is important to examine and provides a window through which to view the problem. One researcher sensing conflict between engineers and technical writers in an organization can interpret the problem as one of "conflicting discourse communities," and examine the problem from that theoretical perspective. Another might use organizational communication theory to interpret the problem and approach an examination from a quite different perspective.

Theory also affects the kinds of information the researcher collects. A qualitative researcher cannot collect everything; theory provides guidelines which allow the researcher to limit the kinds of data collected. Theory also provides the slots, dimensions, or "bins" (Miles and Huberman, p. 28) that allow the researcher to interpret the data. Researchers do not know what ultimately will be found, only when, where, and how to look for it. A theory allows the qualitative researcher to make informed choices.

Choosing Subjects in Qualitative Research

The subjects for qualitative research are often chosen by the researcher in one of two ways: the researcher identifies a problem in which the subjects are already involved. The study by Mirel (below) provides an example of this type of choice. The second type is a situation in which the researcher has a research question that needs to be answered and chooses subjects that s/he thinks will provide answers to that question. The study by Ede and Lunsford (below) is an example of this choice.

Methods of Collecting Data

The researcher using one of the qualitative designs can use several methods to collect data, and Yin (1984) recommends using a variety of methods in the same study to increase the validity of research findings. He suggests (pp.79-89) six sources of data for qualitative researchers:

(1) **Documentation:** written evidence gathered at the scene of the research study or in relationship to the research questions. A literature search is documentation, as are letters, reports, and memos related to the study. According to Yin, such documents should be used to corroborate findings from other sources.

(2) **Archival records:** original records (budgets, maps, charts, personal records) not originally intended to serve a primarily communicative function.

(3) **Interviews and surveys:** data collected by the researcher not available through written records.

(4) **Direct observation:** method used to observe, usually as an outsider; researchers can attend meetings and activities related to the goal of the study as well as observe normally occurring conditions, such as the physical aspects of the environment or normal work or study routines.

(5) **Participant observation:** method used when the researcher is able to become a member of the group under study. As a participant observer, the researcher assumes a role within the organization and is able to

achieve an "insider' perspective (See below).

(6) **Physical artifacts:** physical evidence collected from the scene of the study. A user-written alternative to documentation issued by a software company is an artifact of a study on computer documentation.

("Qualitative" is actually a misnomer for this category in that the researcher can describe interpretations of data using numbers, either counts or percentages. However, much data collected is not countable.)

The most complete picture of an event can be obtained by collecting information from a variety of sources. For example, a researcher doing an ethnographic study of an organization might join the organization to assume the perspective of the participant observer and thus would also have access to documentation and be available to conduct interviews and surveys. Notes taken as a participant observer are the major source of data for the ethnographer.

The case study researcher might use direct observation of a phenomenon to collect needed information. Observing videotapes of users reading or composing, for example, enables the reseachers to classify user behaviors. This primary tool of direct observations through the videotapes could be augmented by interviews and documentation.

The most practical way for those conducting large descriptive studies to collect data is through surveys. Using surveys enables the researcher to ask many people questions over wide geographical areas. If necessary, surveys can be buttressed by interviews and observations, usually conducted on a smaller scale. (For a description of the ways technical communicators can use qualitative methods such as these, see Gould and Doheny-Farina in this volume.)

No matter what qualitative research method used, the researcher's presence will always be a factor in the collection and analysis of the data. The presence of a participant observer, especially in the beginning of a project, will affect subjects' behaviors. When the researcher is outside looking in, the action is still influenced by the researcher (Think of all those pictures you've taken in which you tell your subjects to ignore the camera and act "natural." Remember all those strained smiles, awkward waves of the hand, stiff postures, and disconcerting beads of perspiration.)

Examples of Ethnography, Case Study And Descriptive Research

The following section analyzes one research study from each of the designs discussed above. Research studies in this chapter were chosen because they are current, accessible, and address issues in technical communication.

Ethnography. Mirel (1987; see also the chapter by Mirel in this volume) studied the "contextual dynamics that influenced how a manual functions as a source of information in the workplace" (p. 349). Concerned that a "quality-oriented" user manual Mirel designed was not being used, college administrators asked her to observe how and why the manual was being ignored by personnel in the bursar's office. Over three months she collected data from three sources: (1) logs in which employees recorded how and when they used the manual; (2) weekly observation of activities in the bursar's office; (3) written surveys and interviews. From the data, Mirel constructed classification categories that answered her research questions.

She found that employees perceived they did not have the time to consult the manual; instead, asking for information from other workers seemed more "efficient." Even though consulting others was not always efficient, Mirel noted that social interaction met another need of the employees--the need for cohesion and support. Finally, because the supervisor assumed the role of "technical authority," Mirel found that asking advice from the supervisor was rewarded.

Mirel's study is an example of a well-designed ethnography. She asks clear research questions, is able unobtrusively to observe as a member of the environment, collects data from a variety of sources, and uses that data to suggest answers to her questions. In some ways her study is ideal because it avoids three problems that occur in many ethnographies: the lack of an initial focus, the lack of trust in the researcher, and the lack of control over time spent in the study.

Case Study. Lutz (1984) investigated how seven writers composed and revised their own documents using word processors and pen and paper. She also investigated how these writers edited a document written by another. She found, by counting instances within variables (such as total time writers spent working at each task, number of words revised or edited, number of sentences, mean number of words and sentences in the document) that while the computer aided composing and revising writers' own documents, it impeded editing someone else's document.

The design that Lutz used is actually experimental (see below) because she manipulates variables (pen and paper vs. word processing). However, the small number of subjects and the methods she used to collect data (direct observation and interviews) really make it more like a case study. As a case study, her findings cannot be attributed to people other than the seven subjects she used. Also, she cannot say that any of her variables (such as word processing) *caused* an effect on the writers' processes.

Lutz's case study is interesting, but not without flaws. For example, although she details the data she collected, she does not say how she collected it. Did she stand over the subjects as they worked or did she record them using a video recorder? Also, although characteristics of the subjects are important in case studies, Lutz provides no background except to say that "three were experienced and four professional writers." Lutz's major service is one performed in much case study research: she has identified variables (pen and paper vs. computer; revising vs. editing) which can lend themselves to a more controlled inquiry.

Descriptive. Ede and Lunsford (1986) designed a three-stage study in order to find out more about collaborative or group writing in the professions. They wanted to know the circumstances under which professionals wrote together and the processes they used to write. Ede and Lunsford randomly selected 1200 members of six professional organizations (200 from each) and mailed them a four-page questionnaire. Of the 1200 distributed, they received back 530, a response rate of almost 50%, about as good as you can expect with mail-out questionnaires.

At the second stage of their inquiry, Ede and Lunsford selected 12 respondents and sent each a more detailed eight-page, open-ended questionnaire. During the third stage, they visited selected sites to conduct observations and in-person interviews.

Their results (a good example of using numbers in qualitative research) are reported descriptively; for example, 87% of the 530 respondents reported they "sometimes write as part of a team or group" and that 59% of those who wrote together found the experience "productive" or "very productive" (pp. 69-70). The first stage of their project also produced information which helped them create constructs for understanding collaborative writing processes.

To date, Ede and Lunsford have not moved beyond describing survey results and on-site observations. Yet the amount of data they collected suggests they can also correlate information. For example, they might isolate demographic variables (age, sex, occupation, salary, type of company) and correlate these with variables such as satisfaction with collaborative writing or patterns of composing.

Correlational Research Design

The purpose of correlational studies is to examine already existing variables, to see what, if any, relationships exist among them. Correlational studies are used to show the strength, direction and shape of relationships between variables (Dyer, p. 194). For example, correlational studies have been done to show the relationship between smoking cigarettes and lung cancer. There is a high positive relationship between those who smoke and those to have lung cancer.

It is especially important to distinguish between correlation and causation because the relationship between variables may be so strong as to suggest causation when only correlation exists. For example, although studies have shown a high correlation between smoking and cancer, the cigarette industry rightly claims that scientists have not proved causation. In order to show causation, scientists would have to manipulate, not just correlate, variables. In cancer research, for example, scientists would have to administer cigarettes to one group and not to another. After several years, the researchers would test to see which group, smokers or non-smokers, developed cancer at a higher rate. The ethics of such an experimental situation mandate the use of correlational studies in this type of research.

Types of Correlational Studies

There are four types of correlational studies (Dyer, pp. 202-217):

1. **Studies that examine relationships between two sets of variables.** In this design, the researcher is trying to establish a relationship between two sets of dichotomous variables. For example, a study might examine the relationship between the amount of funding requested in proposals (high funding vs. low funding) and the acceptance rate of proposals (high rate of acceptance vs. low rate of acceptance.)

2. **Studies that examine relationships between a set of variables and an outcome.** In this design, a researcher might ask: to what extent do college major, sex, and grade point average (the set of variables) predict the successful completion of a course in computer document design (the outcome)?

3. **Studies that examine relationships among variables.** Often the researcher wants to distinguish among variables in order to reduce the number of variables in a study. Because the ideal is to produce variables that do not overlap, this type of correlational design helps separate variables in order to guarantee that each variable measures something different. For example, in studying the relationship among such potential predictor variables as sex,

age, race, grade point average, socio-economic status, and college entrance scores, a researcher might find that SES and GPA overlap. If this is so, one of these variables could be dropped from the study because they have the same effect on the outcome variable.

4. Studies that examine relationships between two sets of multi-dimensional variables. Variables often have several dimensions, so the researcher using Type 4 must carefully define what constitutes the variable. For example, a researcher might ask the question: what is the relationship between status in an organization and the ability to read and comprehend computer documentation? The variable, status, might be defined as as place in the organizational hierarchy, seniority, salary, number of people supervised, and budget; the ability to read and comprehend might be defined as scores on reading and comprehension or recall tests.

Role of Theory in Correlational Research

Like good qualitative studies, correlational designs depend on a sound theoretical basis. Without theory to support a research question, correlational studies can easily degenerate into a methodological game called "Let's Run Some Variables and See What We Can Corrolate." Statistical packages and computers make this game easy to play. It might be fun, for example, to run a correlation on the relationship between shoe size and computer ability. The correlation might even turn out to be strongly positive. But the findings are meaningless. A better approach is to predict or hypothsize outcomes based on previous related research or relevant theory, run the necessary tests, then report a finding that either supports or does not support the hypothesis or prediction.

Choosing Subjects in Correlational Research

Choosing subjects in correlational studies is a much more complicated process than choosing subjects in qualitative studies (except large descriptive studies). Technically speaking, the subjects do not even have to be human; they could be, for example, organizations or texts.

The term "population," used to some extent in qualitative research, is an important concept in correlational research. A population is "the unit to whom the researcher makes generalizations about the results of the research" (Asher, p. 48). Put another way, the "generalizibility" of a study means the extent to which findings of the research study can be applied to populations outside the immediate research population. It is important for the researcher to define clearly the population in the study because results can only be generalized to that population. (Obviously, other aspects of the study must remain the same to permit generalization.) In all three types of research, qualitative, correlational, and experimental, the researcher chooses subjects from among larger populations.

Correlational researchers often want to be able to generalize to large populations. In order to be able to do that effectively, efficiently, and economically, they often choose to study a smaller sample that represents the larger population. A researcher chooses a smaller sample from a larger population by using some system of selection, such as a table of random numbers. When the large population is non-homogenous in ways that may affect interpretation of the results, or when the researcher wants to use population variables in the analysis, the reseacher selects a sample based upon discrete units within the larger population.

For example, if you wish to examine how the variables, sex, educational level, and seniority influence how a technical document is used by employees in a company, you would select a sample from the population (the company) that represents these three variables: (1) males/females, (2) college/non-college graduates, and (3) employees with fewer than five years experience/those with over five years of experience. The sample chosen would represent employees with these characteristics within the larger population.

The issue of generalizibility is a most important one in correlational studies. Concern about those who may be affected by the results of correlational research has initiated debate in many scientific communities. Will women be affected by research using all males? Will blacks be affected by research using all whites? Although defining the population is the responsibility of the researcher, ascertaining the *limits* of generalizibility is the responsibility of the reader.

How big a sample do you need in order to obtain results that can be generalized? One way to determine the size of the sample is to assess the presence of the variable in the population. If the variable commonly occurs in the population (such as college students with acne) then you need a small sample for the study. If the variable rarely occurs in the population (such as college students with malaria), you need a larger sample.

A second way a researcher can determine sample size is to set up confidence limits for the study (Asher, pp. 164-169). Researchers determine the desired confidence levels before beginning the study by consulting tables which show relationships between numbers of subjects in a study and the confidence levels these numbers will produce. Confidence limits are reported in plus or minus percentages for the sample.

For example, the results of a study which uses a random sample of the population indicates that 45% of males with senior status in an organization are not able to comprehend a technical document; confidence levels may be reported at plus or minus 5%. The range for the **entire population** is between 40% and 50% of senior status males who cannot read and comprehend a technical document. *Generally, the greater the number of subjects, the more precise the confidence limits.*

The third way to determine an adequate number of subjects is to consider the number of variables in the study. Lauer and Asher (1988) suggest 10 subjects per variable. Therefore, if the researcher is correlating eight variables, the total number of subjects should be no fewer than 80. Fewer than 10 subjects per variable might lead the researcher to infer a relationship among variables where none, in fact, exists.

Methods of Collecting Data

Correlational researchers collect data based on new relationships that emerge from already existing phenomena, called variables. Variables are often the results of other studies (such as test scores) or characteristics that exist in the population (such as age, sex, geography, etc). There are two kinds of variables, "predictor" variables and "outcome" variables. Predictor variables, also called independent variables, are placed in the design. The outcome variable, also called dependent or criterion variable, is the result of the relationship with the predictor variables.

For example, a researcher in an organization wants to see if sex, education level, and seniority are related to the writing of successful proposals. The researcher draws a sample from the population that represents the three predictor variables and relates this sample to a measure for successful proposal writing--funding, for example. The predictor variables, sex, educational level, and seniority interact with a variable that measures successful proposal writing to show a relationship that might go something like this: 80% of successful proposals were written by female college graduates below the mid-level management status.

There is nothing stable about variables: in one study, successful proposals might be the outcome variable, in another they could be one of the predictor variables. For example, you might want to predict a relationship between the number of successful proposals and morale in a department or company. It is important for the reader to be able to distinguish predictor from outcome variables in a given study and to know how one affects the other.

Example of Correlational Study

Rowan (1987) wanted to examine characteristics in writers that made them good producers of explanatory discourse. From theory, she determined that three kinds of knowledge were necessary to produce good explanatory discourse: knowing the topic, knowing the audience, and knowing how to write (discourse knowledge). These became her predictor variables. Topic knowledge was measured by numbers of semesters of high school science and by number of credit hours of college physics taken by participants. Audience knowledge was measured by having students take a standard test of interpersonal cognitive complexity. Discourse knowledge was measured by number of semesters of high school English, credit hours in college writing courses, and scores on the verbal portion of the SAT.

The outcome variable was the score received on a writing sample in which students, after reading a scientific explanation about properties of light, were asked to explain these properties to naive fifth graders. Rowan developed a complex five-level grading scale to evaluate the written documents.

She predicted that all three types of knowledge (topic, audience, and discourse) are associated with explanatory writing skill and that topic knowledge "will account for a greater proportion of variance in explanatory writing skill" (p. 18) than audience or discourse measures. She found that topic knowledge and discourse knowledge did predict those who would have good explanatory skills, but that audience knowledge was only a weak predictor. She did not find that topic knowledge was a better predictor than either audience or discourse knowledge.

Rowan's study is a combination of correlational types 2 and 4. She looks at relationships between sets of multi-dimensional predictor variables and an outcome measure. Rowan is also careful to state hypotheses before conducting her study and to define her terms.

Experimental Research Designs

So far, I have discussed two major categories of empirical research: qualitative research and correlational research. Experimental research designs differ from these two categories in a number of ways. First, more than either qualitative or correlational research, experimental research is concerned with the issue of control. Qualitative research is identified for its unwillingness to exert control over the subjects or their environments. While more control is exerted in correlational research, it is manifested primarily in the efforts of the researcher to choose representative populations, to select appropriate variables, and to design and use accurate measurement instruments. In experimental research, the researcher controls all aspects of the subjects and environments except those being tested.

Experimental designs are different in another way: comparision. Unlike other types of research, the primary purpose of experimental research is to compare differences between and among groups. Comparision is implied in qualitative studies and correlational studies, but comparison is intrinsic to the design in experimental research, its *raison d'etre*. All three types compare findings to the theory that framed the study in the first place.

Control and comparison allow the experimental researcher to make a claim that cannot be made using any other research method: a well-designed experimental study can show a cause-and-effect relationship between a treatment and an outcome. It is only design that allows the reseacher to say that a treatment causes a result. For this reason, it is important to consider Lutz's project, discussed earlier in this chapter, a case study (or perhaps a pilot experimental study) rather than an experimental study: she cannot claim cause and effect .

In experimental research, a treatment is applied to one group and not to another to see the effect of the treatment on the group. In an organization, for example, in order to compare the effects of training on employee writing skills, one group of employees might receive training in writing software documentation while another group does not; a month later, writing samples are taken from each group to see if the training has had an effect.

In order for the researcher to evaluate the treatment, several conditions must exist. First, the two groups must be equal to each other, or at least, they must be equal on the variable being tested. Second, the treatments must differ from each other. If differences between treatments are not "maximized" (Kerlinger, p. 307), differences between groups may not emerge. Third, the researcher applies the treatment to only one group: the group that receives the treatment is the experimental group and the one without the treatment is the control group. Finally, there must be a way to measure the outcome or effect of the treatment on the group.

Role of Theory in Experimental Research

Like both qualitative and correlational research, theory plays a substantial part in the design of experimental research. It guides the research question, helps determine the research hypothesis and explain alternative hypotheses.

Choosing Subjects in Experimental Research

Experimental research begins with subjects in groups which the researcher has determined equivalent on all relevant variables. Because there are hundreds of variables in the human species, it is almost impossible to control for all variables except through a process called randomization. Using randomization, subjects are chosen at random from a larger (P). Subjects are then randomly assigned to groups, and groups assigned to either experimental or control conditions. If done precisely, randomization assures that experimental and control groups are equal to each other.

When randomization is used at all stages of the process, results are generalizable to all populations engaged in the same activities. Using the above training example, if complete randomization procedures were followed, the results received will apply to all software companies, assuming, of course, all other variables are equal.

Methods of Collecting Data

Data is the comparison of the outcomes of experimental and control groups in the study. In the training example, the writing sample is the outcome measure; writing samples of both trained and untrained groups are graded and grades compared to each other to determine which group performed better. The difference between outcomes is a good indicator of the effect of the treatment on the group. Outcomes will often only show up if the measurement instrument is sensitive enough to capture differences between groups. Thus, although designing measurement instruments that capture differences is not a major part of this chapter, it is a critical component of all experimental research.

Types of Experimental Research

There are several types of experimental research designs. The three designs I will discuss are true experiments, quasi-experiments. and multivariate design experiments.

True Experiments. In order for an experiment to be a true experiment it must meet all the conditions for experimental research: equal groups, at least one treatment group, and a method of measurement. *Using randomization to achieve equal groups distinguishes true experiments from other kinds of experimental designs.*

A representation of a true experiment has been formulated by Kerlinger (p. 331); it looks like this:

	X	**Y**	**(Experimental)**
R			
	-X	**Y**	**(Control)**

The symbol "R" means randomization; "X" means treatment group; "-X" means control group; "Y" means outcome measure. The representation shows that two groups, a treatment group and a control group, were set up and that randomization occurred before the treatment was applied. Although there are variations possible to this "basic" design, this design is the model from which the variations emerge.

Quasi-experiments. Randomization, the basic characteristic of true experiments, is not always possible. Yet good experimental design demands that treatment and control groups be equal at the beginning of the experiment. Aside from randomization, one way to assure that groups are equal is through a **pretest** administered to both experimental and control groups before the treatment is applied. This pretest/posttest model of experimental research may not have the same power to generalize as the true experiment using randomization, yet researchers can achieve satisfactory results using this design (Cook and Campbell, 1979).

The pretest/posttest quasi-experimental design requires that subjects be selected for commonalities, put into groups and pretested using the same test to assure they are equal on relevant variables After the treatment, groups are tested again. The pretest/posttest design (Kerlinger, p. 342) is displayed on the next page. Both groups are given the same pretest (Yb), then the experimental group is given the treatment (X), after which both groups are given the same posttest. *Comparisions are made between posttests, not from pretest to posttest.*

Yb	**X**	**Ya**	**(Experimental)**
Yb	**-X**	**Ya**	**(Control)**

Kerlinger points out a problem with the administration of the pretest (in addition to the extra work entailed in scoring it); a pretest can "sensitize" the treatment group to perform differently on the posttest. Therefore, posttest results may be higher than in fact they really are.

Multivariate Design Experiment. Multivariate design is a modification of true experiments. Instead of having one variable or treatment in the design, a multivariate design has more than one treatment and, in addition, examines the relationship between treatments was well as between treatment and outcome.

Again, going back to the training program example, the company might be interested in comparing three different training programs rather than comparing one type of training to non-training. In addition, it may want to vary the length of time required to complete the training program. This line of inquiry would lend itself to a multivariate design where the researcher is comparing outcomes of several simultaneous treatments on different groups and the effects of different treatments on each other.

How variables can be juxtaposed with each other (using the training program example) appears below. Graphically displayed, the training program multivariate design would look like this:

Training	Time# 1	Time# 2
# 1	Cell 1-1	Cell 1-2
# 2	Cell 2-1	Cell 2-2
# 3	Cell 3-1	Cell 3-2

This is called a 3 x 2 multivariate design. The addition of a fourth training program would make it a 4 x 2 design, and the addition of a third time to the original design would make it a 3 x 3 design. Theoretically, the addition of variables could go on infinitely, but this is not advisable.

Equal numbers of subjects should be assigned to each cell with a minimum of 10 subjects per cell (Lauer and Asher, 1988). Thus, in a 2 x 2 design, the minimum number would be 40 subjects; in a 3 x 3 design, 90 subjects, and so on.

Examples of True, Quasi-, and Multivariate Design Experiments

True Experiment. Halpern and Liggett (1984), guided by writing process theory, designed a true experiment to test differences between texts written by students exposed to instruction in rhetorical aspects (differentiating audiences, for example) and technical aspects (operating the equipment, for example) of dictation and those taught only the technical aspects.

They arranged to teach two pairs of business writing classes (84 students) at the same times. At the first meeting of the semester, they randomly assigned students to either experimental or control groups. While Liggett taught the experimental group, Halpern taught the control group. At the next hour, they reversed the pedagogy. In this way, they were able to control for different times and teachers. The outcome measure was the grade each memo received as a result of holistic scoring by several trained raters.

Halpern and Liggett did find some differences between memos dictated by experimental groups and those dictated by control groups although their findings are minimized because of the imprecision of the holistic scoring methods used to evaluate the outcome.

True experiments are difficult to design outside a controlled community, like college settings, because other communities often cannot be manipulated to the extent required by a true experiment. These researchers were able to do a true experiment because they could control the movement of subjects into groups and arrange teaching schedules to account for teaching style and time.

Quasi-experiment. Feinberg (1984) tested the effects of using a visual patterning pedagogy to teach arrangement. Her subjects were 97 undergraduates enrolled in the Illinois Institute of Technology. The experiment took six 50-minute class periods. She pretested her subjects during session #1 by asking them to write a brief essay on how computers affect their lives, and posttested them during session #6 with a similar essay. During the intervening sessions, Feinberg taught all students how to organize essays using a visualization strategy.

Although the pretest and posttest make this study look like a quasi-experiment, it is really a "one group, pretest-posttest" design (Dyer, p. 273). Feinberg does not create experimental and control groups, eliminating any possibility of comparing outcomes between groups. Instead, she compares the difference between pretest and posttest scores. Without the comparision between groups, Feinberg cannot legitimately make cause and effect statements, which she does when she says that "instruction in visual patterning is effective for improving the organizing skills of technologically oriented writers."

Feinberg could have divided her students into experimental and control groups, and administered the pretest, treatment and posttest and compared posttest scores between groups. This design would validate her claims of causality.

Multivariate Design. Soderston and German (1988) examined the relationships between analogy and person on recognition and recall using a segment of computer documentation. They conducted three experiments, the first of which will be discussed here.

This experiment examined the interaction among two sets of independent variables: (1) use of analogy vs. no analogy and (2) use of use of second person vs. use of third person. The outcome variable was the score subjects received on tests of recognition and recall. They found that subjects scored significantly higher on tests of recognition than on tests of recall, regardless of which cell they occupied. They also found that subjects using documentation with analogy scored significantly higher on comprehension scores. Other results proved statistically non-significant.

There are two problems with their design. The first problem is the small number of subjects in each cell, four, a problem recognized by the researchers. To fulfill minimum standards, there should have been 10 subjects per cell, a total of 80 rather than 32 subjects. A problem the researchers did not recognize or address was the problem of selection of subjects. They used two classes from the same university, one a freshman composition class, the other a continuing education class. However, it is not clear how they assigned students from these classes to cells or how they assigned cells to treatments.

In addition, students "volunteered" for the study because researchers did not test for prior computer knowledge but simply asked students with prior knowledge not to participate. Students could opt in or out of the study under their own volition; participation was not controlled by the researchers. Their second experiment increased the numbers of subjects per cell but did not correct the problem with the selection of students. A better designed study would have included all students and randomly assigned them to cells.

Conclusion

The title of this chapter, as you may have guessed by now, is a misnomer; research design is not really a choice of the researcher--it is a consequence of the research question. The relationship between question and design looks like this:

Questions About	Research Design
Process/Description	Qualitative
Relationships among Variables	Correlational
Effect of a Treatment	Experimental

Although there seems to be a growing animosity between qualitative researchers and the more quantitative types (McClelland and Donovan, 1986), the truth is no single phenomenon can be undestood in all of its complexity using only one research method. The squabble should not be about what research methods are best, but what methods best answer the question.

Research reports in this book or any book or periodical deserve critical readings. Design is not the only place a project can falter (measurement is another), but it is one of the most easily accessible areas to begin to a critical analysis of research findings.

References

Asher, J. W., *Educational Research and Evaluation Methods,* Boston: Little Brown and Company, 1976.

Cook, T. D. and D. T. Campbell, *Quasi-experimentation: Design and Analysis Issues for Field Settings,* Chicago: Rand McNally, 1979.

Dyer, J. R., *Understanding and Evaluating Educational Research,* Reading, MA: Addison Wesley, 1979.

Ede, L. and A. Lunsford, "Research into Collaborative Writing." *Technical Communication,* 32:4, pp. 69-70, 1985.

Feinberg, S., "Visual Patterns: An Experiment With Technically Oriented Writers." *Technical Communication* , 31:4, pp. 20-22, 1984.

Halpern, J. and S. Liggett, *Computers and Composing: How the New Technologies are Changing Writing,* Carbondale, IL: Southern Illinois University Press, pp. 72-79, 1984.

Kerlinger, F. N., *Foundations of Behavioral Research* , NY: Holt, Rinehart & Winston, 1973.

Lauer, J. and J. W. Asher, *Composition Research: Empirical Designs,* New York: Oxford University Press, 1988.

Lutz, J. A. "A Study of Revising and Editing at the Terminal." *IEEE Transactions on Professional Communication* , PC 27:2, pp. 73-78, 1984.

McClelland, B. W. and T. R. Donovan, eds. *Perspectives on Research and Scholarship in Composition,* New York: Modern Language Association, 1985.

Miles, M. B. and A. M. Huberman, *Qualitative Data Analysis* , Beverly Hills, CA: Sage Publications, 1984.

Mirel, B., "Designing Field Research in Technical Communication: Usability Testing for In-House User Documentation," *Journal of Technical Writing and Communication,* 17:4, pp. 347-354, 1987.

Rowan, K. "Cognitive Correlates of Explanatory Writing Skills: An Analysis of Individual Differences," International Communication Association, Montreal, May 1987.

Soderston, C. and C. German, "Toward Bridging the Gap Between Theory and Practice: Analogy and Person in Technical Communication." *Iowa State Journal of Business and Technical Communication,* 2:1, pp. 78-102, 1988.

Yin, R., *Case Study Research,* Beverly Hills, CA, Sage Publications, 1984.

III Textual, Graphic, and Online Information

3 Studies of Elaboration in Instructional Texts

Davida H. Charney
The Pennsylvania State University

Lynne M. Reder
Gail W. Wells
Carnegie-Mellon University

Technical writers who must produce a manual or some other instructional text are often caught between conflicting goals. On the one hand, as advocates of the readers who must understand and use the text, writers worry about leaving out any bit of information that might be important or useful. On the other hand, as employees who are accountable for producing a text at the least possible cost, they must use text sparingly: The longer the text, the higher the cost. In short, writers must constantly judge whether the importance of an explanation or some other piece of information is worth the cost of printing it. In some sense, all writers face the same fundamental question: what information should a text contain and to what extent should that information be elaborated?

In this chapter, we review several years of experimental research on this question of content and elaboration. Obviously, there can be no absolute answers to such questions. The answers must depend on factors such as the writer's purpose, the readers' intentions and abilities (i.e., their reasons for reading and their prior familiarity with the subject matter), and general human capacities for acquiring information or skills, in addition to conventional constraints on the form of the text. To narrow down the question to manageable proportions, we have focused our research primarily on individuals reading in order to learn a skill. Specifically, we focus on people who are learning to use a computer by reading a user manual.

The general strategy for our research has been to produce several versions of a computer manual that differ in systematic ways. We asked participants (generally college students) to work through the manuals. In some studies, we simply had participants read the manual; in others, participants also learned by working interactively with the computer. After removing the manuals, we asked the participants to demonstrate what they had learned by performing a set of tasks on the computer. We observed how many tasks the participants completed successfully and how long it took them to do so. By comparing the performance of participants who read the different versions of the manual, we can draw inferences about the characteristics of manuals that lead to better performance. We also employed a variety of readers in our studies: experienced computer users as well as computer novices, readers who opened a manual with a particular task in mind as well as readers who had no particular agenda. By comparing the performance of these groups of readers, we can draw inferences about the different needs of different readers.

Overview of the Chapter

This chapter is organized into four sections.

1. **Elaboration and Fact Learning**: We begin with a familiar instructional situation, reading in order to learn facts. We summarize a series of studies of how elaborations affect learning the main points in a standard college textbook.
2. **Elaboration and Skill Learning**: This section concerns the role of elaborations in skill learning. After contrasting two common viewpoints on elaborations in computer user manuals, we describe a series of studies in which we varied both types of elaborations and groups of readers.
3. **Learning by Reading, Watching, Discovering, and Working Exercises**: In this section, we consider the design of the tutorial section of user manuals, describing studies that call current designs of tutorials into serious question.
4. **Conclusion**: After summarizing our findings, we consider whether our findings may apply to texts other than computer manuals. We close by discussing how experimental research and user testing fit into the document design process.

ELABORATION AND FACT LEARNING

The question of how much elaboration to include in instructional texts was initially explored in a series of experiments with academic prose (Allwood, Wikstrom, & Reder, 1982; Reder, 1982; Reder & Anderson, 1980, 1982). The studies explored a seemingly simple question: Do elaborations help students master the central ideas in a standard introductory college textbook? To answer this question, Reder and her colleagues took chapters from several widely used college textbooks and prepared summaries of those chapters that were one-fifth as long. Students who participated in the studies either read the original chapter verbatim or read the summary. Then all participants were tested on their comprehension and recall of the main points.

Surprisingly, in study after study, the students who had read the summaries significantly outperformed the students who had read the full length chapters. The advantage for the summary group held up under a variety of circumstances. Some studies varied the timing of the test: whether the test occurred immediately after reading or after a long delay (up to one year). The type of test was varied: true/false, short answer, or free recall. Even the reading conditions were varied. In one study, students were allowed to take the materials home to read at their leisure; in other studies, the students' exposure to the materials was carefully timed and controlled. In some studies, the students read the text as connected prose; in other studies, the text was presented one line at a time. The pervasive finding was that students learned the main facts best when they studied them without elaboration.

The explanation of these rather counter-intuitive results seems to be a combination of two phenomena, one involving the ease with which information is registered or encoded in memory and the other involving the process of retrieving information from memory. Research on encoding has shown that the more time and attention a person spends studying a particular fact, the stronger that fact is encoded in memory (Bugelski, 1962; Cooper & Pantle, 1967). So whenever a student reads elaborations in a text, the elaborations divert her time and attention away from the main points that she must learn for the test. Conversely, when the student studies a summary, she can devote full attention to exactly those points that she must learn. This encoding phenomenon does not, however, completely account for the summary group's advantage. In one study, Reder and Anderson equated the total time that students in the summary group and students in the full chapter group spent studying the main points (Reder & Anderson, 1982). The students who read the full length chapters were given *extra* time to read the elaborations. Presumably, the encodings for the main points in both groups were equally strong, because students in both groups spent the same amount of time reading them. However, students in the summary group still performed significantly better on the tests. So, the handicap posed by elaborations seems also to involve retrieval: having the elaborations in memory seems to make it harder to retrieve the main point. In addition, the elaborations may make it harder for readers to distinguish important points from unimportant ones.

The finding that elaborations are often ineffectual and sometimes even detrimental to learning is a serious and curious charge. The implications for textbook production would be grave if one generalized this result to standard learning situations. One factor that we believe is crucial to the effectiveness of elaborations is the kind of learning that is expected to take place. Indeed, educators and laymen alike emphasize that it can be much less important to know a set of facts than to know how to use those facts. One goal of our research was to discover whether the advantage for summaries (or unelaborated text, generally) would remain when readers needed to *apply* the information to practice a skill, rather than simply *remembering* it. For example, reading full-length textbook chapters might be much more useful when the task is to write an essay, since composing requires deep understanding of the material and appropriate selection and development of various points.

In order to test the possibility that elaborations help people apply their knowledge, we turned our attention to computer user manuals since the task of learning to use a computer requires direct application of the information in the text.

ELABORATION AND SKILL LEARNING

Most people initially shared the intuition that elaboration is beneficial for learning facts; however, the value of elaboration for skill learning has been controversial for some time. For example, writers and researchers of computer documentation tend to fall into two quite distinct camps: the "expounders," who believe that instruction should be as complete and as explicit as possible, and the "minimalists," who believe that instruction should above all be brief and that it should leave much to the learner's own exploration.

The Case for the Expounders

The expounders' view is the more traditional: an instructional manual for novice learners should be as complete as possible; it should assume little if any prior knowledge and it should provide detailed exposition of all relevant points. Tausworthe (1979), for example, outlines several levels of detail for documenting computer software. The greatest degree of detail is called for in what he labels "Class A documentation," which he describes as follows:

> "Class A documentation is the most detailed; it contains specific definitions and detailed descriptions of every significant factor or item within the software specification..... This level of detail probably finds its most applicability in user manuals, and rightly so: The writer of a user manual is generally unavailable for consultation, so the user needs the extra detail." [Tausworthe (1979), pp. 158-159.]

For a more recent statement of a similar position, see Price (1984).

While the studies of fact learning described earlier suggested that elaboration does not always facilitate learning, we believed that elaborations might be much more beneficial for skill learning. Our first set of studies tested this possibility by comparing how well people learned skills from elaborated and unelaborated instructional texts.

STUDY 1. Evidence supporting the inclusion of elaboration emerged from our initial experimental study (reported in detail in Reder, Charney, & Morgan, 1986). For this study, we prepared two versions of a computer user manual that described the basic commands for IBM Personal Computer's Disk Operating System (PC-DOS). One version of the manual, the Elaborated version, contained many definitions, analogies, examples, overviews, explanations, and other elaborations. The Unelaborated version of the manual was about one-third as long (3500 words as opposed to 11,000), and omitted the elaborations. Appendices 1 and 2 present typical excerpts from the Elaborated and Unelaborated versions of the manual, respectively.

The participants in our study were 40 inexperienced computer users. We gave each participant one of the two manuals to read for forty-five minutes. Then we took away the manual and asked the participants to perform some tasks on the computer. (The subjects knew that the manual would not be available after the reading period.)

In addition to varying the amount of elaboration in the manuals, the experiment also simulated two common reading situations. Sometimes people have specific goals in mind and turn to instructional materials to find information relevant to those goals. At other times, people come to learn a new skill with only a general idea of how they will make use of what they learn. We simulated these two reading situations by dividing our participants into two equal groups. We gave one group advance information about the tasks they were going to perform before we gave them the manual to read. We assumed that participants in this "Task Orientation" group would then read the manual with the specific tasks in mind. The other participants (the "General Orientation" group) had no idea as they read the manual what kind of tasks we would ask them to perform. Within these two groups, half of the participants read the elaborated manual and half the unelaborated manual.

The tasks that the participants performed called directly on procedures described in the manuals: renaming files, creating subdirectories, copying and deleting files, and so on. As the participants worked at the computer, it recorded the commands and the time at which they were entered. We measured how well participants performed the tasks by counting how many tasks they were able to complete and how efficiently they worked (i.e., how much time they took and how many commands they had to issue to the computer).

Table 1: Mean Performance at Test as a Function of Elaboration and Participant Orientation, Study 1

	TASK ORIENTATION		GENERAL ORIENTATION	
	Elaborated Manual	Unelaborated Manual	Elaborated Manual	Unelaborated Manual
Proportion of Tasks Correctly Completed	.80	.80	.85	.76
Time to Complete All Tasks (in minutes)	33.5	36.1	29.4	40.2
Number of Commands Issued to Complete All Tasks	95.8	94.2	76.8	101.8

The results, summarized in Table 1, indicate that participants completed about the same number of tasks successfully with either manual. However, the results showed very different trends for how efficiently the Task Orientation and General Orientation groups completed those tasks. The Task Orientation group performed much more efficiently after reading the short, unelaborated version of the manual. On the other hand, the General Orientation group performed much better with the longer, elaborated manual. Table 1 shows this pattern most clearly for the average number of commands participants issued to complete the tasks. We infer from these results that both versions of the manual conveyed the basic information adequately, but that the elaborations influenced how efficiently readers could apply the information.

Even though we found that the shorter, unelaborated manual worked better for the Task Orientation group, the results in general support the expounders' case. Writers of instructional texts cannot assume that all learners will come to the manual with such clearly defined goals as the Task Orientation group. In fact, the participants who read the unelaborated manual without having specific tasks in mind consistently performed poorly. On balance, these learners were more greatly impeded by "under-elaborated" texts than the task-directed learners were by the "over-elaborated" version.

Study 1, then, provides some support for the traditional view that instruction should be complete and explicit. As commonly observed, however, there are disadvantages to complete and explicit documentation. In particular, users resist reading commercial manuals written according to the traditional guidelines, even when the relevant passages are easy to locate. People seem to prefer to figure things out on their own, or to ask someone for help (Wright, 1983; Scharer, 1984; Carroll, 1984). From this perspective, providing complete and detailed instruction seems to be of little practical use to the learner. Minimalist documentation grew out of an attempt to address this issue of reader motivation.

The Case for the Minimalists

Designers of so-called "minimalist training materials" proceed on the assumption that willingness to read a manual is inversely related to the manual's length, that people in general want to start doing things instead of reading about them and that therefore, instructional materials should actively encourage exploration by providing as little prose as possible. As Carroll (1984; 1988, reprinted in this volume) describes it: "The first principle of Minimalist design is to slash the verbiage; that's where the name comes from (i.e., less to read can mean better training)." Carroll, et al. put this principle into practice in a tutorial manual for a word processing system (the IBM Displaywriter System) and produced a revised manual that was one-fourth the length of the original.

Carroll, et al.'s (1988) procedure for shortening the manual included two major steps. First, they eliminated everything in the manual that was irrelevant to the task at hand (composing and printing a letter). Then, they took what was left, the relevant information, and deleted parts that readers should be able to learn on their own. It is worth emphasizing that Carroll, et al. were very selective about what information to omit. Their "missing information" is therefore quite different from the all too common blunder made in many commercial computer manuals of blithely or inadvertently leaving out crucial steps.

It is also important to note that Carroll, et al. (1988) made other changes to the minimal manual in addition to making it shorter: they clarified the terminology and organized the discussion around typical situations for users. This final category of changes undoubtedly improved the manual; however, it also obscures the results to some extent: we do not know how much the results are due to differences in elaboration and how much they are due to these other clarifications.

The manuals in Carroll, et al. (1988) were tutorial in the sense that readers were expected to try things out as they read about them. Carroll, et al. found that after working through the minimal version of the manual, participants (mostly secretaries) learned the same basic information more quickly than participants who used the commercially developed version of the manual. Furthermore, when participants went on to study more advanced topics, they learned new techniques more quickly if their initial training had been conducted with the minimalist materials. Carroll, et al. admit that these initial efforts at designing minimalist materials were exploratory (e.g., as a result of the testing, they put back some explanatory sections as well as some procedures that participants actually couldn't figure out on their own). However, their findings in the main support the minimalist position: having less to read led to equivalent or better learning at a faster overall rate.

Paradox Resolution: Identifying Components of Skill Learning

The preceding two sections leave us in a seemingly paradoxical position: The minimalists and the expounders both have experimental evidence to support them. The explanation for the different results may arise from differences in the prior experience of the participants. The participants in Carroll, et al.'s (1988) study were mainly secretaries who were very familiar with letter writing tasks. They may therefore have been more like the Task Orientation group in our study who also benefited from the less elaborated manual. An alternative explanation is that the tutorial aspect of Carroll, et al.'s manual made elaboration less necessary. We will reconsider the issue of tutorials later. For now, it is worth considering a third possibility: that depending on the situation, sometimes the minimalists are right and sometimes the expounders are right.

It is possible for both expounders and minimalists to be right if we shift the focus away from length per se. Length is not really the issue. The expounders' goal is not to write the longest manual possible; they in fact try to produce texts that are as concise and relevant as possible, given what topics must be covered. In an important respect, the minimalists try to do exactly the same thing. Obviously, the difference lies in defining what this relevant, essential information is to include.

To delve deeper into the issue of relevance, we began to consider what kinds of things people have to learn in order to acquire a skill (Charney & Reder, 1986; Reder, Charney, & Morgan, 1986). Perhaps some aspects of skill learning are easier when the instruction pertaining to them in the text is elaborated, while other aspects do not require elaborated instruction. If so, then the expounders may be including irrelevant information by giving detailed treatment to everything and not just the points that need it. Conversely, the minimalists may be underspecifying some points when learners would benefit greatly from more elaboration. In order to provide only relevant elaboration, then, it is necessary to isolate the aspects of skill learning and determine which ones may be facilitated by elaborated instruction. As we considered what is involved in learning a skill, we isolated three components. In order to perform a new skill well, a learner must:

1. Appreciate the meaning of novel concepts and the purpose of novel procedures. For example, proficient typists who have never used a word-processor must learn what things can and cannot be done on the computer. They must appreciate both the availability of automatic margin adjustment and the impossibility of underlining by overstriking what has already been typed.

2. Execute the procedures correctly. Learners must remember such details as where to position the cursor, in what order to type the arguments of a command, and whether a carriage return is required.

3. Use the procedures at the appropriate times. Learners must remember to use the procedures they have learned and know how to choose the most appropriate procedure for a particular situation.

Elaborations in a computer manual may touch on any of these topics: what concepts and procedures are involved, when they are relevant, and how one applies them. In Study 1, we used manuals that either elaborated on all of these points or on none of them.

Elaborating Different Types of Information

STUDY 2. In order to test the possibility that different components of skill learning require different degrees of elaboration, we classified the elaborations in the PC-DOS manual into two categories (Reder, Charney, & Morgan, 1986). Elaborations were classified as "conceptual" if they concerned basic concepts, such as the purpose of the Rename command, or conditions for application, such as when it is a good idea to rename a file. That is, conceptual elaborations dealt with both the first and third components of skill learning. Elaborations were classified as "procedural" if they concerned the second component, learning to issue commands correctly. Procedural elaborations included examples of correct commands, details about notational conventions, and so on. We then tested all possible combinations of the conceptual and procedural elaborations by producing four versions of the PC-DOS manual with the following combinations of elaborations:

- Rich Conceptual & Rich Procedural Elaborations
- Rich Conceptual & Sparse Procedural Elaborations
- Sparse Conceptual & Rich Procedural Elaborations
- Sparse Conceptual & Sparse Procedural Elaborations

The version that was rich in both types of elaboration was equivalent to the elaborated manual in our previous study (Appendix 1) and the version with neither type was equivalent to the completely unelaborated manual (Appendix 2). The other two versions are illustrated in Appendices 3 and 4, respectively. By using all four versions, we could determine whether the advantage we found for the elaborated manual in our first experiment was due to the conceptual elaborations, the procedural elaborations, or both.

This experiment was conducted very similarily to Study 1, except that no participants were given advance information about the tasks they would perform. This time, our participants included 40 novice computer users and 40 experienced computer users, none of whom had ever used an IBM-PC. We expected that the novices might need elaborations of both kinds, while the experienced computer users (who were already familiar with basic computer concepts) might only need the procedural elaborations.

Table 2 presents results showing how quickly subjects using each of the four manuals completed the tasks and how many commands they issued. The most efficient participants were those who had read the manuals containing rich procedural elaborations (see the two leftmost columns in Table 2). These participants finished the tasks in about 37 minutes and issued about 72 commands. In contrast, participants who read manuals with sparse procedural elaborations needed about 44 minutes and about 90 commands, significantly worse performance. Surprisingly, however, the conceptual elaborations seem to have had no effect at all. Adding rich conceptual elaborations to manuals with rich procedural elaborations was equivalent to having the procedural elaborations alone. Similarly, manuals with only rich conceptual elaborations produced performance no better than having no elaborations at all (see Table 2).

The results of Study 2 allow us to begin to sort out which components of skill learning require elaborated instruction and which do not. In particular, our participants needed little more than a summary of the conceptual information. They did not benefit from elaborations that described the concepts involved in using a computer (e.g., elaborate analogies that explained the concept of paths through subdirectories) or from advice about when and why particular commands were useful. What they did benefit from were well-chosen examples that illustrated what a correct computer command would look like in a specific plausible situation. For a more thorough discussion of these types of elaborations, see Charney and Reder (1987).

Table 2: Mean Performance at Test for Manuals with Four Combinations of Elaboration, Study 2

	RICH PROCEDURE		SPARSE PROCEDURE	
	Rich Concept	Sparse Concept	Rich Concept	Sparse Concept
Time to Complete All Tasks (in minutes)	37.4	37.7	43.5	45.9
Number of Commands Issued to Complete All Tasks	71.7	73.7	88.7	92.4

Other researchers have also found benefits for particular types of elaboration. For example, Kieras (1985) found that people learning to operate a mechanical device derive little benefit from detailed information about the internal workings of the device. However, he found that such "how it works" information is useful if the learner must *infer* the operating procedures (rather than memorizing them or looking them up) and if the "how it works" information is specific enough to enable such inferences.

The most surprising aspect of our results was the similarity of the patterns for novice and experienced computer users. Although the novices generally performed less well than the experienced computer users, they did not benefit any more than the experienced users from the conceptual elaborations. On the other hand, they did benefit just as much from the procedural elaborations. It is possible that the type of conceptual elaborations we included were not exactly what the novices needed. Nystrand's (1987) study is consistent with this possibility. Nystrand found that "high knowledge" and "low knowledge" computer users asked different kinds of questions when trying to use computer documentation. Low knowledge participants most often asked for "categorical definitions" while high knowledge participants most often asked for "further specifications." Nystrand characterized the differences in the questions as requests for topic elaborations (categorical definitions) or comment elaborations (further specification). He also found that adding the appropriate kinds of elaborations reduced the questions asked by both groups.

LEARNING BY READING, WATCHING, DISCOVERING, AND WORKING EXERCISES

While Study 2 does address some of the complaints of the minimalists, it does not address the central claim that people prefer *doing* things over reading manuals. Writers of commercial computer manuals have attempted to satisfy this preference by incorporating "tutorials" into user manuals. In this section, we will review evidence that, at least in their current form, such tutorials are inadequate for promoting skill learning. We will also discuss alternative forms of active learning that are more effective. In order to set this discussion in context, we will begin by briefly overviewing three active learning strategies that have received much attention in the cognitive and educational psychology literatures: learning by example, learning by discovery and learning by working exercises.

Learning by Example

Advocates of learning by example argue that texts should provide numerous worked-out examples that learners can use as models for solving problems on their own. A worked-out example consists of at least three parts: a specific problem to be solved, the correct solution to the problem, and an explicit sequence of steps that lead to the correct solution. The instructional text may also include the general rule that the problem exemplifies, as well as counterexamples. Worked-out examples can help people learn to recognize categories of problems and what solution strategies are appropriate to each category (Sweller & Cooper, 1985; Nitsch, 1977; Tennyson, Woolley, & Merrill, 1972). A worked-out example can also serve as a framework for constructing a solution to a new problem: the learner retrieves the example from memory and replaces terms specific to the old problem with terms relevant to the new one (e.g., Anderson, Farrell, & Sauers, 1984).

In some respects, Study 2 reported above supports the learning-by-example paradigm. Participants in Study 2 benefited from manuals that contained procedural elaborations, many of which consisted of commands that exemplified correct instantiations of an abstract syntactic "rule."

Features of the learning-by-examples approach may also be seen in the growing use of tutorials in computer manuals. The user of a tutorial follows step-by-step instructions to enter commands that demonstrate the computer's features. These tutorials are very similar to worked-out examples; the tutorial simply adds the physical activity of carrying out the instructions on the computer and allows the user to observe the computer's prompts and feedback messages at each stage along the way. Given the similarities between examples and the guided activity in tutorials, one might expect that people using tutorials would learn the same or more than people who simply read manuals that contain examples.

Discovery Learning

In complete contrast to the advocates of learning by example, advocates of discovery learning argue that people learn best when they set their own goals and explore a new domain with minimal guidance from a text or a teacher. Discovery learning maximizes the active involvement of the learner. Rather than studying problems set by a teacher (or the writer of the text), the learner invents his own problems, decides what techniques to use to try to solve the problem, and learns what works through trial and error.

Using a discovery learning approach, Carroll, Mack, Lewis, Grischkowsky, and Robertson (1985, reprinted in this volume) designed what they called a "guided exploration" manual for a word processing program. The manual described the basic features of the program very briefly but omitted certain procedural information in order to force learners to discover it on their own. Then they conducted a study comparing the Guided Exploration manual to a commercially produced tutorial manual. Participants using the guided exploration manual set their own "problems" (e.g., deciding to compose and print a letter) and tried out word processing procedures at their own initiative. Carroll, et al. found that this discovery learning group learned how to use the word processor in less time, finished criterion tasks more quickly and made fewer procedural errors than participants who worked through the tutorial manual.

Carroll et al.'s (1985) findings support our intuitions that active, hands-on involvement is superior to passively reading a text and examples, or even to obediently following tutorial exercises. However, we wonder to what other learning situations their findings will generalize. There are several reasons to believe that for some kinds of learners, discovery learning is not the optimal way to learn a skill, such as using a computer. In particular, discovery learning may cause certain kinds of problems for novices.

- Novice computer users may fail to create tasks for themselves that fully explore the system's capabilities. For example, a new computer user will probably not be able to invent a problem that clearly illustrates the uses of multiple windows or procedures for defining macros.

- Novices may never set themselves a task that demonstrates the advantages of one procedure over another. Unless they see examples of situations in which one procedure is more appropriate than another, novice computer users may stick with a procedure that they have already learned or that they find memorable even when it is significantly less efficient than some other procedure.

- Novices may develop and retain serious misconceptions unless their exploration leads to a highly salient error or problematic result.

Given these potential drawbacks to discovery learning, why did Carroll, et al. (1985) find advantages for the guided exploration manual over the tutorial manual? We conceive of discovery learning as involving two components. In the first component, learners decide to experiment with some procedure and invent a task involving those procedures. In the second component, learners work independently to solve the problems they have set for themselves. The advantages of discovery learning that Carroll, et al. found may have been due largely to this second component and not the first. However, the second component is closely related to another learning strategy, working exercises.

Working Exercises

The most familiar use of this learning strategy is in math and science textbooks in which exercises appear at the ends of chapters. Like worked-out examples, exercises set a specific problem. However, the answer to the problem and the steps for arriving at the answer are left for the learner to figure out (except when answers appear in the back of the book). Working exercises requires more active involvement on the part of the learner than studying worked-out examples; the learner must review the procedures described in the text, select appropriate procedures for a given problem, and determine how to apply the procedure to the specific case.

Working exercises differs from discovery learning in that the problems are set for the reader by the writer of the text. While these problems may not be intrinsically as interesting to the reader as those she might devise herself, they have some distinct advantages. First, the tasks may be designed to cover the full range of a system's capabilities. Second, tasks may be designed to illustrate situations in which one procedure is more appropriate than another. Finally, the tasks may be designed to anticipate and correct possible misconceptions.

It should be clear from the previous discussion that the three learning strategies lead to quite different prescriptions for what a computer user manual should look like. In our next study, we attempted to compare the effectiveness of manuals incorporating these strategies.

An Empirical Comparison of Learning Strategies

Study 3. In this experiment (Charney & Reder, 1986b), participants learned how to use the VisiCalc electronic spreadsheet. The study was conducted in two sessions: a training session and a test session that took place two days later.

In the training session, 30 participants (mainly undergraduates) studied 12 VisiCalc commands by reading a brief manual at their own pace. An example of an entry in the manual is provided in Appendix 5. Interspersed in the manual were training problem sets, consisting of three problems for each command. Participants were asked to solve the training problems whenever they appeared in the manual. While every participant read exactly the same text in the manual, the type of problem set for a given command varied from participant to participant. There were three types of problem sets:

- Tutorial. The instructions for the three problems in this set told participants exactly what keystrokes to type to reach the correct solutions. This problem set corresponded to tutorial activity.
- Exercise. The instructions in this set gave participants a specific goal for each of the three problems, but no guidance for how to reach it. Participants proceeded to solve the problems as best they could. After they finished or gave up, they were permitted to study our solution to the problem on the next page of the manual.
- Tutorial Plus Exercise. In this problem set, the first of the three training problems was a Tutorial problem and the remaining two were Problem Solving problems.

Appendix 6 presents a typical problem in its Tutorial and Exercise forms.

Every participant worked with all three types of problem set. That is, of the 12 VisiCalc commands that the manual discussed, four were presented with Tutorial training sets, four with Exercise sets and four with Tutorial Plus Exercise sets.

In order to compare learning with hands-on activity to learning by reading, we asked a separate group of 14 participants to read the manual without typing anything at the computer. The manual for this Read Only group presented the training problems in the same form as the Tutorial problems, except that participants were only allowed to study the steps, not enter them at the computer. In some sense, the training problems served the same function as worked-out examples in a textbook.

Two days after the training session, all participants were given a test consisting of 12 new problems to solve on the computer, one problem for each command. Their performance was evaluated in terms of their accuracy at solving the problems and the time they took to complete them.

Overall, as Table 3 indicates, training with exercises produced the most effective performance on the test. Participants were significantly more successful at solving test problems for commands that they had learned with Exercises or Tutorial Plus Exercises than for commands that they learned with Tutorial training alone. The form of the training problems did not affect how quickly participants could solve a problem. Table 3 also indicates that the computer interaction group performed better than the read-only group. These results support the notion that active learning situations in which people remember and apply procedures for themselves are more effective than situations in which people simply learn by studying the procedures.

Table 3: Mean Performance at Test as a Function of Types of Training Problems, Study 3

	COMPUTER INTERACTION GROUP			
	Tutorial	Exercise	Tutorial Plus Exercise	READ ONLY GROUP
Percent of Tasks Correctly Completed	.53	.66	.68	.48
Average Time Per Task (in secs.)	91	95	85	134

The overall picture that emerges from this study is inconsistent with the learning-by-example paradigm. Tutorials in general are similar to worked-out examples since both show the learner how to arrive at the correct solution. But neither the tutorial form of training nor the read-only training was very effective. More importantly, these two forms of training did not differ significantly: Carrying out the steps of the solution on the computer did not significantly improve learning over simply reading the examples in the manual. The results also indicate that our participants did not need to study an example before solving problems on their own. In particular, Tutorial Plus Exercises did not lead to better performance than pure Exercise training. While the results strongly support the efficacy of exercises, we would not conclude that exercises can completely replace examples, since our tasks required only simple applications of commands. However, the results do challenge the efficacy of existing tutorial manuals. Our evidence suggests that people learn no more from them than from simply reading the manual.

Study 3 did not directly compare exercises and discovery learning. However, our results suggest that the advantage which Carroll, et al. (1985) attribute to discovery learning may be due to the component whereby learners actively work out a method of completing the task they set for themselves. We conducted an additional study to see whether exercises are superior to discovery learning. Preliminary results suggest that learning was better when subjects were provided with exercises that set specific goals as compared with discovery learning (Reder, Charney, & Wells, in preparation).

The Placement of Exercises in a Manual

The exercises that we used in Study 3 were intended to help participants learn both *how* to apply procedures and *when* to apply them. The latter (the third component of skill learning described earlier) is one of the hardest things for an inexperienced computer user to learn. The knowledge that is needed for this component consists largely of knowledge of situations, or more precisely, associations of situations and procedures. This kind of situational knowledge is exactly what novices lack by definition: they have not *experienced* the range of situations that might arise and have not seen how to handle them effectively.

As mentioned previously, participants saw a set of three training problems for each VisiCalc command. In any of their forms (worked-out examples, tutorials, or exercises), the problems in a set illustrated a range of different situations in which the command might be useful. Yet simply applying a command three times in three different situations may not provide sufficient practice in learning to recognize when each command is most appropriate. We suspected that the timing of the opportunities to practice a procedure would have a great effect on how well people learn it. People learn better if their opportunities to study occurs at spaced intervals, rather than massing the study trials all at once (e.g., Glenberg, 1979; Madigan, 1969; Melton, 1967). We believed that this effect would generalize to skill learning because people need practice at recognizing the contexts of application. If training problems always follow the instructional text, our participants would not have to figure out which procedure was required, thereby missing practice on the third component of skill learning.

In Study 3, in addition to studying the effect of the form of training, we also investigated the effect of the placement or spacing of the training problems in the manual. For six of the twelve commands described in the manual, the training problems came all at once (the problems were "massed.") That is, immediately after reading about a given command, the participant saw three training problems that applied that command. For the other six commands, the training problems were "distributed." That is, participants saw only one training problem immediately after reading about the command. The other two problems appeared later, interspersed with problems that appeared after descriptions of other commands.

The results of the test revealed that participants were much faster at solving problems correctly for commands they had studied with distributed practice. The advantage for distributing the placement of the training problems appeared for all types of training problems (Tutorial, Exercise or Tutorial Plus Exercise). Overall, participants performed best when exercise form was combined with distributed placement.

SUMMARY AND CONCLUSIONS

We began this chapter with some surprising results that suggested that students learn the main ideas better from summaries of textbook chapters than from reading the chapters themselves. To explain these rather counter-intuitive results, we explored the possibility that elaborations are needed to promote application, rather than simply recall of the facts. Our findings on the most effective features of computer manuals address such factors as types of elaboration, types of readers, forms of interaction between the reader and the text, and methods of organization.

- With respect to *the degree and type of elaboration* in our manuals, we found:
    - No benefit from elaborations of general concepts (e.g., what is a disk drive);
    - No benefit from elaborations offering advice on when to apply specific procedures;
    - Significant benefits from elaborations on how to apply procedures (e.g., well-chosen situational examples).
- With respect to *computer users and their goals* for reading a manual, we found that:
    - Readers with specific tasks in mind need little or no elaboration in the text;
    - Readers without specific goals benefit from certain types of elaboration (i.e., those listed above);
    - Novice computer users and experienced computer users benefited from the same types of elaboration, although the experienced users were quicker and more accurate overall.
- With respect to the ways in which readers can *interact with the text*, we found that:
    - Readers who learned procedures simply by studying a manual containing worked-out examples performed most poorly;
    - Readers who learned procedures by carrying out the steps of a tutorial on the computer performed only slightly better;
    - Readers who learned procedures by working exercises that forced them to independently apply the information in the manual performed significantly better;
    - Readers who learned procedures by inventing their own problems to solve (discovery learning) may learn more than from a tutorial, but less than from working exercises.

With respect to the *organization of the manual*, we found that:

- Participants learned a procedure better when opportunities to practice it (either through tutorial or exercise training) were distributed throughout the manual, rather than only appearing immediately after the relevant instructional text.

THE RELATIONSHIP BETWEEN USER TESTING AND EXPERIMENTAL RESEARCH IN THE DOCUMENT DESIGN PROCESS

This chapter has concerned experimental research aimed at improving instructional texts through observations of readers attempting to learn from texts with various features. In concluding the chapter, we would like to comment on a related practice, user testing, and its relationship to the type of research we have reported.

The growing use of user testing is one of the most positive developments in technical writing in recent years. User testing is primarily a method of detecting and correcting problems in the draft of a document. To conduct a user test, writers give a draft of a document to a group of "users" (representatives of the intended audience of the document) and observe them using the document as they might on the job. For example, a group of consumers might be asked to read and carry out a set of instructions for assembling a stereo. The writers note places where the readers become confused or make mistakes. They use the results of user tests to revise the document which they then retest. They continue the cycle of testing and revision, producing successively better drafts of the document until it passes some criterion of acceptability. As a detection and correction mechanism, user testing represents the best means presently available to writers for ensuring that a specific document is complete, accurate and understandable from the standpoint of the intended audience. (For detailed discussions of methods of user testing, see Bond, 1985.) However, for all of its benefits, user testing is not sufficient for designing effective instructional texts. As we see it, user testing has three serious limitations.

(1) User testing simply cannot address the question of whether the writer has created the optimal document for conveying the desired information. Successive drafts in the user test cycle change largely in response to the results of earlier tests, rather than as a systematic exploration of alternative formulations. Further, user testing tends to focus on local rather than global features of the text. It is much more likely, for example, for user testing to reveal that a manual contains too much technical jargon than that it contains inappropriate elaboration. In essence, then, user testing is data-driven rather than theory-driven. That is, the decision to continue the cycle of testing and revision is governed by observations of problems in the draft rather than by theories or principles of document design. As a result, user testing provides few external guidelines for how good a document might ultimately become and little clue as to whether a radically different approach to presenting the text might not produce significant improvements in comprehensibility.

(2) It is difficult to extend or generalize from the results of a given user test. As discussed above, the methods chosen for altering the drafts of a document between tests are usually opportunistic rather than systematic. When the changes are unsystematic, it is impossible to determine which ones produced improvements in the test results. Another obstacle to generalization is that, for reasons of practicality, participants in any given user test are usually few in number and are selected from a highly specific population (i.e., the intended readers of the document). Because the sample of participants may be unrepresentative of readers in general, there is little assurance that revisions that are successful in one user test will also work for other groups of readers. This lack of generalization does not mean that user testing has no long term benefits. In fact, there is evidence that as writers conduct user tests, their sensitivity increases in detecting areas of text that will cause readers problems (Schriver, 1987). Our point here is that it is difficult to derive reliable principles for effective document design solely from the results of user testing.

(3) User testing enters the writing process at rather a late stage: after a draft has been produced. However, there are some things about readers that writers need to know much earlier, at the point at which they are generating ideas, selecting information and planning the overall shape of the document. At this early stage, writers are asking "What tends to work best for readers in this type of text?" as opposed to "Does our document work well enough for our readers?" Because user testing tends not to uncover general principles, it does not provide much help to writers at early points in the writing process.

Clearly, at an early stage in the document design process, writers need to draw on more general findings than user testing can provide, findings that only systematic experimentation can provide. The research we have reported here focuses primarily on the need for elaboration. Other experimental research (reviewed in Schriver, 1986; Felker, et al., 1980; and Wright, 1977) has aimed at making the information in a text easier to find (e.g., research on the use of headings, typography, and layout) and easier to comprehend and remember (e.g., research on vocabulary, sentence style, and order of presentation). While retaining a focus on documents and their readers, experimental document design research grows out of cognitive theories of how people learn from texts and what features of text facilitate reading and learning. Such research can provide valuable information to technical writers as they plan what information to include in their texts, how much to say about it, and how to present it. By seeking out such information in the early stages of the document design process and by user testing drafts at later stages, technical writers will maximize the likelihood that their readers will get the most out of their texts.

The work reported here was sponsored by the Office of Naval Research, Contract No. N00014-84-K-0063, and in part by Grant BNS-03711 from the National Science Foundation.

REFERENCES

Allwood, C. M., Wikstrom, T., & Reder, L. M. (1982). Effects of presentation format on reading retention: Superiority of summaries in free recall. *Poetics, 11*, 145-153.

Anderson, J.R., Farrell, R., & Sauers, R. (1984). Learning to program in LISP. *Cognitive Science, 8*, 87-129.

Bond, S. J. (June 1985). Protocol-aided revision: A tool for making documents usable. In F. Dwyer (Ed.), *Proceedings of the 1985 IBM Academic Information Systems University AEP Conference*. Alexandria, VA: IBM.

Bugelski, B. R. (1962). Presentation time, total time, and mediation in paired associate learning. *Journal of Experimental Psychology, 63*, 409-412.

Carroll, J., Mack, R., Lewis, C., Grischkowsky, N., & Robertson, S. (1985). Exploring exploring a word processor. *Human-Computer Interaction, 1*, 283-307.

Carroll, J., Smith-Kerker, P., Ford, J., & Mazur, S. (in press). The minimal manual. To appear in Human-Computer Interaction.

Carroll, J. (March 1984). *Designing MINIMALIST training materials* (Research Report 46643). IBM Watson Research Center, Computer Science Department. Also appeared in Datamation 30(18), 125-136, 1984.

Charney, D. H., Reder, L. M. (1986). Designing interactive tutorials for computer users: Effects of the form and spacing of practice on skill learning. *Human Computer Interaction, 2*, 297-317.

Charney, D. H., & Reder, L. M. (1987). Initial skill learning: An analysis of how elaborations facilitate the three components. In P. E. Morris (Ed.), *Modelling Cognition*. London: Wiley.

Cooper, E. H., & Pantle, A. J. (1967). The total-time hypothesis in verbal learning. *Psychological Bulletin, 68*, 221-234.

Felker, D. (April 1980). *Document design: A review of the relevant research* (Technical Report AIR-75002). Washington, D.C.: American Institute for Research.

Glenberg, A. (1979). Component-levels theory of the effects of spacing of repetitions on recall and recognition. *Memory and Cognition, 7*, 95-112.

Madigan, S. A. (1969). Intraserial repetition and coding processes in free recall. *Journal of Verbal Learning and Verbal Behavior, 8*, 828-835.

Melton, A. W. (1967). Repetition and retrieval from memory. *Science, 158*, 532.

Nitsch, K. E. (1977). Structuring decontextualized forms of knowledge. Unpublished doctoral dissertation, Vanderbilt University.

Price, J. (1984). *How to write a computer manual: A handbook of software documentation.* Menlo Park, CA: Benjamin/Cummings Publishing Co.

Reder, L. M. (1982). Elaborations: When do they help and when do they hurt? *Text, 2*, 211-224.

Reder, L. M., & Anderson, J. R. (1980). A comparison of texts and their summaries: Memorial consequences. *Journal of Verbal Learning and Verbal Behavior, 19*, 121-134.

Reder, L. M., & Anderson, J. R. (1982). Effects of spacing and embellishment on memory for the main points of a text. *Memory and Cognition, 10*, 97-102.

Reder, L. M., Charney, D. H., & Morgan, K. (1986). The role of elaborations in learning a skill from an instructional text. *Memory and Cognition, 14*, 64-78.

Reder, L. M., Charney, D. H., & Wells, G. W. (in preparation). Practicing the application of procedures in skill learning.

Scharer, L. (July 1983). User training: Less is more. *Datamation, 29*, 175-182.

Schriver, K., Hayes, J., Danley, C., Wulff, W., Davies, L., Cerroni, K., Graham, D., Flood, E., Bond, E. (April 1986). *Designing computer documentation: A review of the relevant literature* (Communication Design Center Technical Report No. 31). Carnegie-Mellon University.

Schriver, K. (1987). *Teaching writers to anticipate the readers' needs: Empirically-based instruction.* Doctoral dissertation, Carnegie-Mellon University,

Sweller, J., & Cooper, G. (1985). The use of worked examples as a substitute for problem solving in learning algebra. *Cognition and Instruction, 2*(1), 59-89.

Tausworthe, R. (1979). *Standardized development of computer software, Part II.* Englewood Cliffs, NJ: Prentice-Hall.

Tennyson, R., Woolley, F., & Merrill, M. (1972). Exemplar and nonexemplar variables which produce correct concept classification behavior and specified classification errors. *Journal of Experimental Psychology, 63*, 144-152.

Wright, P. (1977). Presenting technical information: A survey of research findings. *Instructional Science, 6*, 93-134.

Wright, P. (December 1983). Manual dexterity: A user-oriented approach to creating computer documentation. In A. Janda (Ed.), *Human factors in computing systems.* Boston, MA: Computer-Human Interaction Association.

APPENDIX 1
Excerpt of Elaborated PC-DOS Manual Used in Study 1

CHANGING THE CURRENT DIRECTORY -- CHDIR

The CHDIR command (short for "change directory") allows you to designate a directory as the "current" directory for a drive so that the computer will automatically look there for files or subdirectories mentioned in your commands. You can designate a current directory for each disk drive independently. Changing the current directory on the diskette in drive A does not affect the current directory on drive B. The root directory is automatically designated as the current directory for each drive when you first start up the computer. It is useful to designate a subdirectory as the current directory when you will be working primarily on the files in that subdirectory. Then you won't have to specify the path to the subdirectory in each command you issue.

FORMAT

The format of the command is:

CHDIR [loc and name of new current directory]

You can use the abbreviation CD in the command instead of typing CHDIR.

[Location of new current directory] refers to the path to the directory you want to designate as the new current directory. The last directory name on the list should be the name of the directory you want to designate.

For example, the command below designates a subdirectory called PASCAL as the new current directory in drive B:

A> CHDIR B:\PROGRAMS\PASCAL <ENTER>

The first symbol in the path is a backslash (\). This means that the path to the new current directory starts with the root directory of the diskette in drive B. The path indicates that the root directory contains a subdirectory called PROGRAMS, and that PROGRAMS contains PASCAL, the directory you want to designate as the "new" current directory. As usual, the amount of location information you need to provide depends on which directory was last designated as the current directory for the drive.

To change the current directory back to the root directory, give a command like the following:

A> CHDIR B:\ <ENTER>

The backslash (\) in the commands above symbolize the root directory. So the command above changes the current directory for drive B to the root directory.

If you forget which directory is the current directory, the computer can remind you. Enter a CHDIR command without specifying a location. The computer will display the path from the root directory to the current directory, or "\", if you are still in the root directory.

APPENDIX 2
Excerpt of Unelaborated PC-DOS Manual Used in Study 1

CHANGING THE CURRENT DIRECTORY -- CHDIR

The CHDIR command allows you to designate a directory as the "current" directory for a drive, so that the computer will automatically look there for files or subdirectories mentioned in your commands. You can designate a current directory for each disk drive independently.

FORMAT

CHDIR [[d:]path]

You can use the abbreviation CD in the command instead of typing CHDIR.

If you designate a subdirectory as the new current directory, the computer will carry out all the subsequent commands within that directory, unless you specify a path to another directory. To change the current directory back to the root directory, use a backslash as the path.

If you forget which directory is the current directory, the computer can remind you. Enter a CHDIR command without specifying a location. The computer will display the path from the root directory to the current directory or a backslash if you are still in the root directory.

APPENDIX 3
Excerpt of PC-DOS Manual from Study 2 with RICH CONCEPTUAL and SPARSE PROCEDURAL Elaborations

CHANGING THE CURRENT DIRECTORY -- CHDIR

The CHDIR command (short for "change directory") allows you to designate a directory as the "current" directory for a drive so that the computer will automatically look there for files or subdirectories mentioned in your commands. You can designate a current directory for each disk drive independently. Changing the current directory on the diskette in drive A does not affect the current directory on drive B.

The root directory is automatically designated as the current directory for each drive when you first start up the computer. It is useful to designate a subdirectory as the current directory when you will be working primarily on the files in that subdirectory. Then you won't have to specify the path to the subdirectory in each command you issue.

FORMAT

The format of the command is:

CHDIR [[d:]path]

You can use the abbreviation CD in the command instead of typing CHDIR.

If you designate a subdirectory as the new current directory, the computer will carry out all the subsequent commands within that directory, unless you specify a path to another directory. To change the current directory back to the root directory, use a backslash as the path.

If you forget which directory is the current directory, the computer can remind you. Enter a CHDIR command without specifying a location. The computer will display the path from the root directory to the current directory, or "\", if you are still in the root directory.

APPENDIX 4
Excerpt of PC-DOS Manual from Study 2 with SPARSE CONCEPTUAL and RICH PROCEDURAL Elaborations

CHANGING THE CURRENT DIRECTORY -- CHDIR

The CHDIR command allows you to designate a directory as the "current" directory for a drive, so that the computer will automatically look there for files or subdirectories mentioned in your commands. You can designate a current directory for each disk drive independently.

FORMAT

CHDIR [loc and name of new current directory]

You can use the abbreviation CD in the command instead of typing CHDIR.

[Location of new current directory] refers to the path to the directory you want to designate as the new current directory. The last directory name on the list should be the name of the directory you want to designate.

For example, the command below designates a subdirectory called PASCAL as the new current directory in drive B:

A> CHDIR B:\PROGRAMS\PASCAL <ENTER>

The first symbol in the path is a backslash (\). This means that the path to the new current directory starts with the root directory of the diskette in drive B. The path indicates that the root directory contains a subdirectory called PROGRAMS, and that PROGRAMS contains PASCAL, the directory you want to designate as the "new" current directory. As usual, the amount of location information you need to provide depends on which directory was last designated as the current directory for the drive.

To change the current directory back to the root directory, give a command like the following:

A> CHDIR B:\ <ENTER>

The backslash (\) in the commands above symbolize the root directory. So the command above changes the current directory for drive B to the root directory.

If you forget which directory is the current directory, the computer can remind you.

Enter a CHDIR command without specifying a location. The computer will display the path from the root directory to the current directory or a backslash if you are still in the root directory.

APPENDIX 5
Excerpt from VisiCalc Manual, Study 3
MOVE COLUMN OR ROW

The Move command moves the entire row or column that contains the current cell to another position on the worksheet.

PROCEDURES:

/M [FROM] . [TO] [RETURN]

Moves the contents of row or column in the [FROM] coordinate to the row or column specified in the [TO] coordinate.

The Move command requires the following information:

- The FROM Coordinates: The coordinates of a cell in the row or column that you wish to move. Visicalc automatically fills in the coordinates of the current cell (e.g., D5) as the FROM coordinates. If the current cell is not in the row or column you wish to move, type [BKSP] to erase these coordinates and type the coordinates of a cell in the row or column you want to move. Then type a period. Three periods appear on the edit line. Now you can type the "TO" coordinates.

- The TO Coordinates: The coordinates of a cell specifying the destination of the move. The TO coordinates must contain either the same column letter or the same row number as the FROM coordinates. The VisiCalc program determines whether to move a row or a column by comparing FROM and TO coordinates: if the column letter in the two coordinates is the same, then a row is moved; if the row number is the same, then a column is moved.

  The difference between the FROM and TO coordinates tells VisiCalc where to put the moved information. If the FROM coordinates (e.g., D5) have the same *column* letter as the TO coordinates (e.g., D3), then the contents of row 5 will move up to row 3. If the FROM coordinates (e.g., D5) have the same *row* number as the TO coordinates (e.g., B5), then the contents of column D will move left to column B.

VisiCalc makes room for the row or column you move by shifting the other rows and columns over. So moving a column or row to a new location does not "cover up" any other entries.

APPENDIX 6
A Typical Training Problem Presented in Tutorial and Exercise Forms, Study 3

A. TUTORIAL TRAINING

Alphabetize the names by putting the rows containing Steele and Stewart further down in the appropriate spots. Start with cell A1 as the current cell.

TYPE THIS: /M . A7 [RETURN]
/M . A7 [RETURN]

B. EXERCISE TRAINING

Alphabetize the names by putting the rows containing Steele and Stewart further down in the appropriate spots.

Feedback, appearing on the following page:

You could have used the following sequence of commands (starting with cell A1 as the current cell) to solve the preceding problem.

/M . A7 [RETURN]
/M . A7 [RETURN]

C. CONTENTS OF VISICALC DISPLAY

A	B
1 Steele	Clerk
2 Stewart	Clerk II
3 Sanders	Manager
4 Schiff	Manager
5 Sebert	Accountant
6 Snyder	Sec'y
7 Sweet	Clerk III

4 The Minimal Manual

John M. Carroll
IBM Thomas J. Watson Research Center

Penny L. Smith-Kerker
IBM Austin Laboratory

Jim R. Ford
IBM Federal Systems Division

Sandra A. Mazur-Rimetz
Micro Control Systems

The Minimal Manual was designed to address difficulties people have with state-of-the-art self-instruction manuals in learning to use powerful computing devices. It is briefer; it helps learners to better coordinate their attention between the system and the manual; it specifically trains error recognition and recovery; it better supports reference use after training. In two experiments, the Minimal Manual was shown to afford more efficient learning progress than an otherwise comparable, commercially developed self-instruction manual, and was superior in the specific areas predicted by its design.

1. Learning to use a word processor

Learning to do something new is always a difficult undertaking. Trying to get someone *else* to engage in such learning is even more challenging. Perhaps it is the challenge that has maintained learning as a traditional focus of interest in both theoretical and applied psychology. Recently, concern with learning has intensified in the study of human-computer interaction. The principal reason for this is the rapid extension of computer use to people who are not programmers or other computer professionals. Large numbers of people are learning to use computer equipment, and many of them are having trouble.

To some extent this is not surprising. Computer applications and their user interfaces are often very complex. However, some of the problems people have in learning to use computers are caused by the materials provided to help them learn. Education in the computer industry has traditionally concerned itself with the training needs of computer professionals, who indeed may be willing to study comprehensive but very thick reference manuals, and to attend expensive and intensive classes. Many new users have little interest in computer science, programming, or electronics *per se*. Rather, they are concerned with preparing manuscripts, letters, memos, and other sorts of documents (Davis, 1984; Eason, 1976). Currently, the industry is concerned that overly comprehensive materials may exhaust the patience and the technical backgrounds of users (Davis, 1984; Scharer, 1983).

The materials provided to new users often conflict with the learning styles and strategies they adopt spontaneously. Standard self-instruction training manuals and on-line tutorials require the user to proceed step-by-step through sequences of drill and practice exercises (Uhler, 1981, 1984). However, our studies of such stand-alone education showed that deliberate step-by-step progress was frequently interrupted by episodes of self-initiated problem solving (Carroll and Mazur, 1986; Mack, Lewis, and Carroll, 1983). In their statements and actions, users expressed a preference for getting started immediately on recognizably coherent tasks, like typing a letter, in favor of pursuing drill and practice. They just ignored steps and sections of the training that seemed irrelevant to their task-oriented concerns. They seemed quite willing to rely on their own inferences even though these were based only on hints gleaned from whatever system prompts and messages they noticed and on highly erratic references to the manual, and even though these inferences often led them to make mistakes.

This active orientation to learning is not what the designers of self-instruction training are designing for, and was in fact poorly supported by the training. Much of our prior work is a recounting of the many problems new users encountered as they tried to learn systems using these materials. In the work reported here, we empirically developed a training manual for the word processing functions of a very widely used, stand alone, commercial office information system. We very deliberately constructed a manual that differed from the commercially-developed self-instruction training manual in specific ways (ways our prior work had suggested would be important; see Carroll, Mack, Lewis, Grischkowsky, and Robertson, 1985). We then tested learning performance in a simulated office environment (Experiment 1) and then, to gather more detailed learning data, in one-on-one close observation (Experiment 2).

2. A Minimalist training model

Our strategy in training design is to accommodate, indeed to try to capitalize on, manifest learning styles and strategies. In particular, (a) we address the preference to get started immediately on real tasks by structuring training to accommodate this; (b) we address the preference to skip in reading by presenting less material to be read; and (c) we address errors, an important consequence of the active orientation to learning, by supporting error recognition and recovery.

2.1 Focus on real tasks and activities. A major theme in standard instructional models, such as the "systematic approach" (Gagne and Briggs, 1979; see also Mager, 1975), is the hierarchical decomposition of learning objectives. There is no reason in principle why an analysis of learning objectives could not be coupled with a synthesis of those objectives into a program of realistic tasks for learners, but in fact the standard presentations of systematic instructional design do not provide examples of this. Rather, they focus on curricula for building skills from the bottom up, via step-by-step drill and practice. In our prior work we were repeatedly struck by the tenacity with which learners would try to accomplish a real task despite the step-by-step guidance of their training materials, and by their unhappiness and lack of success when they tried to use the materials (Carroll and Mazur, 1986; Mack et al., 1983). As one of our learners put it, "I want to do something, not learn how to do everything." When learners abandoned their own goals and followed the drills successfully, they sometimes had difficulty extracting any meaning from their efforts, as one person put it "What did we do?"

New users of application systems are trying to use a tool, a tool that they believe will help them do their own work. They are not learning for learning's sake. They come to the learning task with an often considerable understanding of task-relevant concepts and the motivation to learn to use the tool in their work. Training should make it easy for them to use the knowledge they already have (e.g., a new word processor user might know what inserting a blank line is but not when referred to as a "carrier return control character in the data stream"). To the greatest extent possible, training should involve real tasks: Learners should do a real calculation with their electronic spreadsheet, one with their own numbers. People learning messaging systems should be sending messages (or at least using a convincing simulation); they should not be merely preparing and then canceling messages. This is not instructional libertarianism, it is practical psychology: The most important factor in learning is learner motivation, but this is also the factor least amenable to extrinsic control via design. If learners want to undertake a particular activity, then letting them attempt to do so is perhaps the best design step we can take.

2.2 Slash the verbiage. New users are not inclined to read training material. As one person we observed put it, while flipping pages in a manual, "This is just information." Users seem to be more interested in action, in working on real tasks, than in reading. We have found that learners are very susceptible to plunging into a procedure as soon as it is mentioned (e.g., in a preview) or of trying to execute purely expository descriptions (e.g., reviews). Of course, executing a preview may alter the system state and therefore make it impossible to execute the previewed exercise. Learners also often skip over crucial material if it does not address their current task-oriented concerns, or skip around among several manuals composing their own ersatz instructional procedure on the fly (Carroll and Mazur, 1986; Mack at al., 1983;

Self-instruction designs often respond to these reading problems by adding supplemental control information (e.g., injunctions to "not do anything before reading everything", an initial chapter on "how to use this book"). Such material is intended to keep the learner properly oriented to the self-instruction, but necessarily adds to the sheer bulk and complexity of the training material. This in turn can add to learners' reading problems: by providing an even more imposing manual they will be even more disinclined to read and by providing more separate information types to be differentiated and confused. We have explored the radical alternative of eliminating more control information to address the problem of skipping and misreading, and of presenting material once and as briefly as possible to make the training unimposing (see also Reder and Anderson, 1980).

2.3 Support error recognition and error recovery. A typical assumption in the design of self-instruction training manuals is that learners will not make errors. But when learners pursue their own goals, when they explore, or even when they mistype, training problems arise that the self-instruction materials do not address, for example making a diagnosis of what has happened and how to recover. Even if the system being learned includes invertible commands, or a general undo command, the user may need guidance to try these. Turning the system off to start over is a crude and typical approach new users take, but in all of the systems we have studied there are serious error tangles that arise as consequences of doing this (e.g., Carroll and Carrithers, 1984; Carroll and Mazur, 1986).

Users often fail to coordinate their attention between training material and system events. They may read an exercise step, carry it out, and then go on to the next, never checking whether the step worked properly. Or, a given step may trigger an episode of self-initiated exploration. In either case, the system state and the training state may become unsynchronized. Training should make it easy to check the coordination of the training and the system. It is probably too much to expect that all errors can be avoided; instead, errors are probably best regarded as an inevitable part of learning. Training materials must therefore explicitly support the recognition of and recovery from error *both* to make the materials robust with respect to user error *and* to train error recovery skills. Particularly, in self-initiated forays of exploration, errors may play a unique constructive role in facilitating the discovery of new knowledge (Piaget, 1985; Schank, Collins and Hunter, 1986).

2.4 Guided exploration. The Minimalist training model was first developed and tested in our prior work on Guided Exploration (Carroll et al., 1985). In that work, we designed a set of brief cards to replace a commercial self-instruction manual. The cards stressed real work by addressing user-relevant goals (e.g., typing something and quitting work) over purely system-relevant topics (e.g., practicing with the status line and menu control). They contained about an eighth as much verbiage as the manual. They stressed error recognition and recovery by graphically breaking down all procedural information into four meaningful components: goals, enabling hints, checkpoints and results, and error recoveries.

This design enhanced learning. Guided exploration learners spent less than half as much time in learning as did their self-instruction manual counterparts. During learning they spent less than a third as much time reading, committed half as many errors, and recovered more often from their errors. These differences persisted in a transfer of learning posttest, in which the Guided Exploration learners accomplished half again as much in half the time as did the learners who had been training via the self-instruction manual. Nevertheless, Guided Exploration learners sometimes voiced a desire for a more structured training tool, in particular, they asked for a manual. We decided to develop an experimental self-instruction manual to try to capitalize on the strengths of the Minimalist training model and the desire of learners to have a structured manual.

3. Designing a minimal manual

The Minimalist training model is not intended to be applied automatically in a single design pass. We cannot simultaneously have the briefest manual and the one that includes the greatest amount of error recovery information. As in other aspects of user interface design, and design in general, Minimalist training is developed iteratively: designed, empirically evaluated, and then redesigned (Dreyfuss, 1955).

The role played by empirical testing may be greater for Minimalist training than for standard self-instruction materials. It is typical instructional design practice to do some development testing (also called "formative" testing; Gagne and Briggs, 1979: 37-38), but this is done late in the design process and its typical outcome is the addition of further material, qualifications, cautions, and additional explanation. In Minimalist design, empirical testing must enter the process earlier, for the core domain tasks to be trained are identified empirically. Even later development testing is different: The remedy of choice for a problem should be to cut, not add (though this can be very difficult to do). The particular iterative process we employed in designing our Minimal Manual is that described by Carroll and Rosson (1985), which consists of three stages of qualitatively different empirical testing.

3.1 Design Analysis. In the first stage, we analyzed the training situation. We chose to focus on the domain of word processing and developed an empirical understanding of the core tasks new users were motivated to undertake, the ways in which training materials for them could be cut down, and the key user errors our design would have to address.

Focus on real tasks and activities. The goal of involving the learner was paramount. The chapters of our manual clearly labeled topics of interest to learners, for example, "Printing Something on Paper" instead of "Menus, Messages, and Helps." Learners created their first document only seven pages into the Minimal Manual. In the commercial manual, the creation of a first document was delayed until page 70. In the Minimal Manual, the first document creation was a letter; in the commercial manual, it was a description of office document processing. We tried to exploit users' prior domain knowledge in introducing word processing concepts; for example, text block moves were referred to as "cutting and pasting" to trade on the metaphor of physical operations on pieces of paper.

We tried to make the procedures of the Minimal Manual more open-ended than in standard self-instruction, to better resemble real work and to maintain learner motivation. Procedural details were deliberately specified incompletely to encourage learners to become more exploratory, and therefore, we hoped, more involved in the learning activity; for example, the function of the cursor step-keys was introduced with an invitation to "try them and see." Open ended exercises entitled "On Your Own," were placed at the end of each chapter, for example, "As you can see on page 4:3, more deletions, insertions, and replacements are suggested for the Smith Letter document. Practice your revision skills by trying some of these. When you have practiced enough, print out Smith Letter." Indeed, the amount of work suggested to learners by such exercises was equal to that presented by the manual's self-instruction procedures.

Figure 1 presents a page of the Minimal Manual illustrating some of these points. We discovered in our pilot work that learners quite often accidentally add lines to a document. They want to delete these "blank lines," but from the perspective of the system, this translates into deleting a "carrier return control character" (a goal no novice user would even imagine having). As Figure 1 shows, the Minimal Manual explicitly addresses this problem in the goal-vocabulary of the learner. Most of the topic chapters of the Minimal Manual include open-ended exercises in which the learner can use the system and the manual to plan and carry out some activity.

Slash the verbiage. We tried to be ruthless about verbiage, constructing a bare-bones manual, in the end 45 pages or less than a quarter the length of the commercial training manual. We achieved this by eliminating all repetition, all previews, reviews, and practice exercises, the index, the "welcome to word processing" introduction, and the troubleshooting appendix. By streamlining the manual, we hoped that repetition would not be necessary, that learners who forgot how to print for their second document would just look back at what they had already done. By addressing tasks learners understood on the basis of their prior familiarity with the domain, we hoped to avoid the need for previews and reviews, as well as the problems that occur when learners execute them. We viewed

DELETING BLANK LINES

The Displaywriter stores blank lines as carrier return **CHARACTERS.**

USE ↑ TO POSITION THE CURSOR AT THE BEGINNING OF THE SECOND LINE OF THE FIRST PARAGRAPH OF Smith Letter.

PRESS CARRIER RETURN ONCE.

You have inserted a blank line in the paragraph.

USE ↑ TO POSITION THE CURSOR AT THE BEGINNING OF THE BLANK LINE -- ALL THE WAY AT THE LEFT.

As you can see, a special highlighted carrier return character appears. This is the special character that was inserted when you originally pressed CARRIER RETURN.

PRESS THE DEL KEY.

WHEN THE DISPLAYWRITER PROMPTS YOU: Delete What?, PRESS ENTER.

The blank line disappears. You have deleted the special CARRIER RETURN character.

ON YOUR OWN

You can use these techniques to insert and then delete underlined and centered material. Experiment with deletion. When you are finished, END the Smith Letter document, and then print it out.

Figure 1. System functions as real and familiar tasks under user control the manual itself as guided practice, and eliminated further rote exercises in favor of the more realistic On Your Owns. Because we had never seen successful use of indexes and troubleshooting appendixes in training manuals, but had seen many errors triggered by their misuse, we decided that these too could be eliminated.

Chapters were organized to be brief (averaging less than 3 pages), so that learners could easily move from topic to topic. Task oriented chapter headings (e.g., "Centering and underlining") were employed so that the table of contents could itself serve as an effective index. All material not related to office work was eliminated or radically pared (the welcome overview, the descriptions of the system status line, the details on the system hardware components, the chapter entitled "Using the display information while viewing a document," etc.). We also tried to simplify wording: The term "the system" was replaced by the proper name of the system; function key names, like "CTR" were replaced by more transparent referring terms (e.g., "the CTR key"); the terms "display" and "display module" were changed to "screen"; the term "keyboard module" was changed to "keyboard".

Support error recognition and error recovery. We inventoried the principal errors of new users and included specific error recovery information to address these problems. For example, we had found that learners had trouble with the diskette name concept and often typed an incorrect diskette name when prompted, which had the effect of leaving the system hung up (i.e., prompting for a diskette that did not exist). The system function in fact provided a specific recovery procedure for this problem, but the commercially developed self-instruction manual failed to mention it (it was a compound keypress and may have been thought to be too complicated for new users, but it was also crucial for them). The Minimal Manual included the specific error recovery information for this error. Another error that was typical for learners was pressing the Cancel key without holding down the Code key (which is also illustrative of the general problem of misexecuting compound keypresses). Cancel is perhaps the best general error remedy the system offers, but has an entirely different meaning when used without the Code key, and one which leads to complex side effects. What complicates the error even more is that the recovery for pressing Cancel without holding the Code key, is pressing Cancel *while holding* the Code key (which allows this error to tangle up with itself). Throughout the Minimal Manual the key was explicitly referred to as "Code + Cancel", to stress the correct key combination both as an error prevention and as an error recovery -- and we referred to the combination frequently (to remind learners of its general use in error recovery).

We also tried to help users avoid making errors, in particular by helping them to keep the manual and the system properly coordinated. Instead of merely saying that the system would prompt for a document name, and that they should type the name and press ENTER, the Minimal Manual asked "Can you find this prompt on the display?: 'Type document name; press ENTER.'" We specified procedures incompletely in the manual when required information could be found on the display. Instead of specifying whether a given diskette should be loaded in the right or left disk drive, we left it to the learner to consult the system prompts. The manual intentionally included very few pictures of displayed system screens, to impel learners to coordinate the actual system display with description in the manual. Finally, indirect references were used as soon and as much as possible. Once learners had had some practice selecting document creation in the Typing Tasks menu via direct prompting ("Type a and press ENTER"), the manual switched to an indirect mode of reference ("Choose the item in the Typing Tasks menu to create a document").

Figure 2 presents another page from the Minimal Manual illustrating some of these points. The interrogative prompt "Can you find this prompt on the screen?" helps to coordinate the learner's attention between the system and training: If indeed the learner can find that particular prompt at that point in the training, then the system and the training are quite likely to be synchronized. Turning things around, if the learner cannot find the prompt, then an error condition is quite likely. The triangular symbols indicate error recovery information.

3.2 Subskill Testing. After the design analysis, particular design elements were empirically tested in qualitative detail. We observed typical users performing typical tasks. Our goal was to gather detailed information that could be directed at redesign. This work (carried out by Caroline Carrithers and the first author) involved about 20 learners for sessions of between 2 hr and 8 hr each. In many cases, we were gratified to find that our design worked: Problems we had inventoried for learners using the commercial manual had been eased. For example, we had seen many learners suffer from the complications of typing an unprintable character into a text file (the system suspends the print job until a special request is made by the user). A particularly difficult aspect of the error is that the feedback provided by the system is obscure; hence, learners usually do not even recognize that they have committed an error. Therefore, we had included specific information to help recognize this error and further information for recovery. And indeed, the learners we observed were successful with the error.

In other cases, our initial testing uncovered problems with the design. Three problematic subskills were document naming, canceling, and turning the system off as an error recovery. Learners still had trouble with the concept of document name despite our attempt to better clarify it in the manual. We ended up by having to add a substantial amount of additional information on the concept (almost a half page). However, this was not a matter of reinstating material we had originally purged. A specific problem in naming was that people found it

Topic 2. Typing Something.

In the terminology of the Displaywriter you will be "creating a document" -- that is, typing a brief letter. You will first name the document, as you might make up a name for a baby **BEFORE** it is actually born. Then you will assign the document to a work diskette -- this is where the document will be stored by the Displaywriter. And then, finally, you will type the document at the keyboard, and see the text appear on the screen -- your electronic typing paper!

Note: If you turned off the power at the work station between Topic 1 and Topic 2, turn it back on and re-insert the Vol. 1 program diskette.

TASK SELECTION

In the TASK SELECTION menu you choose the general kind of work that you want to do. To type (create) a document, choose TYPING TASKS.

Can you find this prompt on the screen?:
Type ID letter to choose ITEM; press ENTER.

TYPE AN a, THE ID LETTER FOR TYPING TASKS, AND THEN PRESS THE ENTER KEY.

▶ If you typed the wrong ID letter, just press BKSP (backspace) to remove the incorrect letter.

▶ If you typed the wrong letter **AND** pressed ENTER too, hold down the CODE key and press CANCL enough times to return to the Task Selection menu to start over. CANCL and REQST are on the same key. If you don't hold down CODE when you press CANCL, you will get REQST (Request) instead of CANCL. You can correct this by trying CANCL again, this time while holding down CODE.

Figure 2. Helping to coordinate user attention and to support error recovery unintuitive that a document they had not yet created had to have a name. We drew upon the metaphor of "naming a baby before it is actually born". We also included more task related motivation, expanding the bare statement "You must give a NAME to the document you are going to type." to "You must NAME documents (letters, memos) as you would label a file folder -- so you can get these documents back to work on later."

Similarly, we were persuaded to embellish our diagnosis/recovery information for the Code + Cancel error. Learners still had a lot of trouble coordinating the keypress and making sense of the consequences when they failed to do so. We added the following material to the first two references to the operation: "Cancel and Request are on the same key. If you don't hold down the Code key when you press Cancel, you will get Request instead of Cancel. You can correct this by trying Cancel again, this time while holding down the Code key."

We also observed a problem with turning the system off as an error recovery. We explicitly made use of this recovery method with the suggestion "Turn the system off, but be sure you first REMOVE ALL DISKETTES FROM THE DISKETTE UNIT." It seemed that learners were performing this *as they read it,* and therefore switching off before they read the capitalized condition (which had complicated side effects). We substituted this: "REMOVE ALL DISKETTES FROM THE DISKETTE UNIT TO AVOID DAMAGING THEM and then turn the system off." We also decided to make this recovery just a bit less attractive to learners by substituting "You must now start all over again, by reloading your programs from the program diskettes." for "You can now start fresh from the beginning." We found that turning the system off is best used as a last resort. Even if it is executed errorlessly, it disrupts work.

We had originally hoped to introduce document revision as an On Your Own execise, to have users "discover" revision instead of being taught about it. This did not work out; the subskill had to be further decomposed in order to be reliably executed by learners. These are only examples; there were many specific subskill problems we detailed and for which we then redesigned. (For further discussion of the design of the Minimal Manual, see Carroll, 1984, 1985. The Minimal Manual we developed is reproduced as an appendix to Carroll, Smith-Kerker, Ford, and Mazur, 1986).

3.3 Criterion Testing. Although reiterative subskill testing guarantees a sort of local optimization of the design, it is not directed at providing an objective benchmark assessment of the final success of the design. It is useful in the end to know just how good a design really is (e.g., relative to other contrasting designs or relative to particular usability goals). How good a training manual design did we end up with? We performed two laboratory studies to test and to better understand the empirical efficacy of the Minimal Manual design. The first of these focused on performance in 3 days of simulated office work experience. The second was somewhat more analytical in trying to expose the underpinnings of the performance effects, but also more limited in focusing on only a day-long learning experience. Sections 4 and 5 detail these experiments and their results.

4. Experiment 1

The first experiment was carried out by Penny Smith-Kerker and Jim Ford at the IBM development laboratory in Austin, Texas. The primary purpose of this experiment was to contrast a commercially developed standard self-instruction manual (SS) with the experimentally developed Minimal Manual (MM) in an office-like environment.

4.1 Method. *Design.* The design of this experiment was a between-subjects contrast of the independent variable of manual (MM or SS). Experimental sessions lasted up to 3 contiguous working days, 8 hr per day. A reiterating study-test procedure was employed. Subjects were asked to learn on their own and to perform periodic performance tests.

The system. The system we studied is a commercially available menu-based office information system. Our study focussed on its word processing function, which in practice is the function initially attempted by clerical users. Figure 3 schematizes the flow of control for the document creation task in this system, the most basic and one of the most typically engaged word processing tasks.

The system's function is initialized by loading a System Diskette. As indicated in Figure 3, this brings up a Home menu, which presents a variety of selection alternatives to the user. To create a document, the user selects "Document Tasks." This brings up the Document Tasks menu; the user selects "Create Document." This brings up the Typing menu, which presents options (e.g., formatting options) for the document to be created. The user then presses Enter, to go to the the Typing Area. In the Typing Area, the user can input text (using typewriting keyboard functions and keystroke commands, like Center and Underscore).

The keystroke command "Save" writes the user's document onto a Data Diskette and returns control to the Document Tasks menu, from which the user can create further documents, or edit or print an existent document. For example, printing a document is accomplished by selecting "Print Document" in the Document Tasks menu, specifying options in a Print menu (analogous to the Typing menu), and then pressing Enter to send the document to a printing device.

Subjects. Nineteen subjects participated in the experiment, 10 in the MM condition and 9 in the SS condition. A temporary agency screened participants for two qualities: (a) we wanted people who were experienced with routine office work,

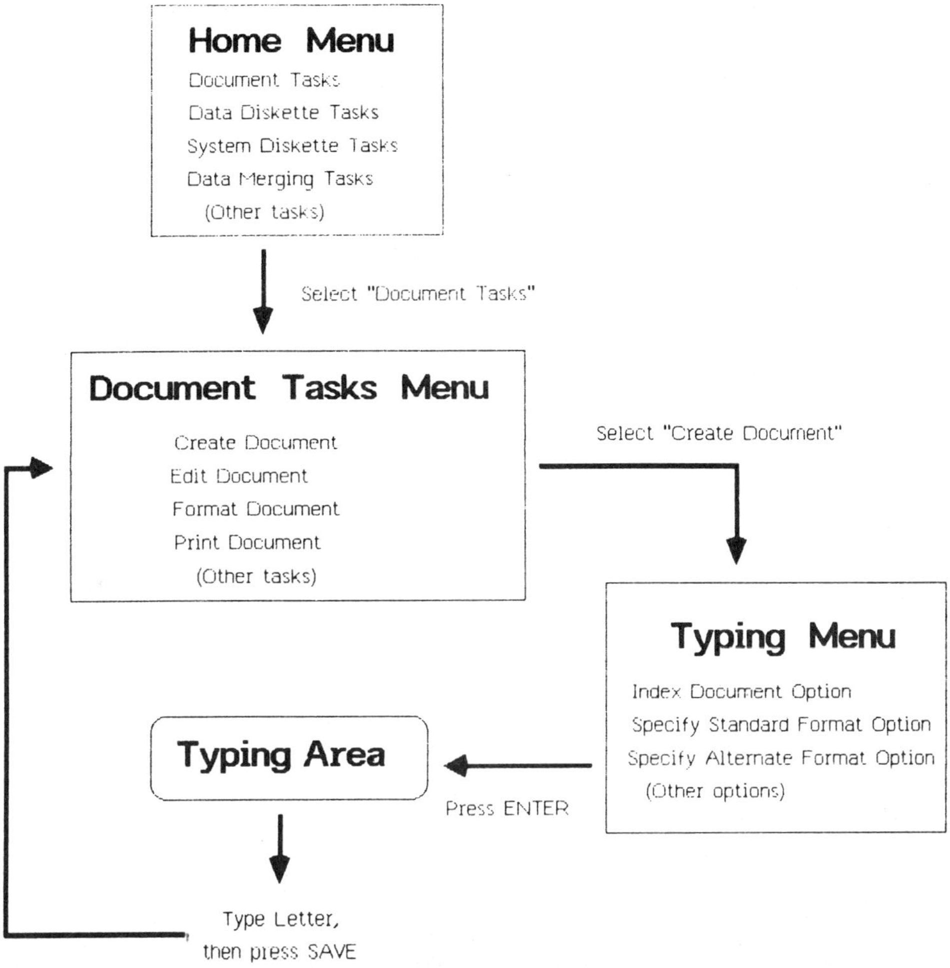

Figure 3. Flow of system control for the create a document task

Figure 3. Flow of system control for the create a document task typing in particular, and (b) we wanted people with little prior computer experience, defined in this case as less than 3 months of overall word processing experience and no experience with the particular system we studied. In fact, 10 of the subjects we obtained had less than 3 months of prior experience with word processing (4 in SS, 6 in MM), and the remaining 9 had more than 3 months experience. However, we were able to ensure that no subject had prior experience with the particular system we studied.

Subjects classified themselves into decade age ranges, the modal range of which was 25 to 34 years (8 of 19). Most subjects had had some college-level education (13 of 19). The preponderant category of prior work experience was professional secretary-typist (13 of 19); mean reported typing speed of the 19 subjects was 69 words per minute.

Procedure. Subjects were run in groups of 2 to 3 in a simulated office environment. Test rooms were outfitted with wall hangings and phones to appear office-like. The subjects knew they were participating in an experiment, but they also understood that one goal was to realistically simulate an office. Each subject was asked to imagine that a new word processor had just arrived and that they had been assigned the job of working through the training material to learn to use the equipment. We rerouted the phones of several colleagues so that they would ring in the test rooms. Subjects were asked to answer these phones and take messages. They were also given an average of two memos per day to type up on an ad hoc basis. A coffee-break room was established for the subjects, and they were encouraged to use it.

All subjects in a given group were assigned the same manual. At the beginning of the first day, and at the end of each day, an interview and administrative session was held. During the hands-on portion of the experiment, the subjects read and followed the training exercises in their manuals, and periodically (after the completion of specified groups of training topics) were given performance tasks. There was a total of 8 performance tasks, described in Figure 4. Tasks 1 through 3 addressed "basic" topics: document creation, revision, and printing. Tasks 4 through 8 addressed more "advanced" topics: multi-page documents, automatic spell checking, headers and footers, alternate formats, block text moves, and the duplication of system and data diskettes. The material for some of the advanced topics went beyond the scope of the MM and SS. For the advanced topics, subjects were provided with an additional self-instruction training manual; the same advanced manual was provided to both the MM and SS subject groups. Subjects also had access to the entire system library of reference manuals.

If subjects experienced difficulties during learning, they were permitted to telephone a simulated "hot-line" service. When using this service the subject described a problem and received help. This hot-line was staffed by a blind expert, an expert in the system who was very familiar with operational procedures in

Task 1: Create, paginate and print a one-page letter. Required business-letter formatting using line breaks and punctuation.:

Task 2: Create, paginate and print a two-page letter. Similar to Task 1, but also required underlining and simple indentation.:

Task 3: Revise, paginate, and print the letter created in Task 2. Required insertion, replacement, and deletion of text, transposition of text, and movement of a paragraph from one page to another.:

Task 4: Create, spell check, paginate and print a three-page report. Required centering, a running header and footer, both double spaced and single spaced text, and indented paragraphs.:

Task 5: Revise, paginate, and print the report created in Task 4. Required insertion, replacement, and deletion of text, revision of the header text, and movement of a paragraph within a page.:

Task 6: Revise a four-page document already created and stored on diskette. Required insertion, replacement, and deletion of text, movement of a paragraph within a page, insertion of a regular paragraph, insertion of an indented paragraph, combining two paragraphs into one, addition of a running header and footer, and underlining.

Task 7: Duplicate a diskette containing documents.:

Task 8: Duplicate a program diskette.

Figure 4. Description of Eight Performance Tasks for Experiment 1

commercial hot-lines for word processing but who was unaware of the goals of the experiment. Additionally, subjects assigned to the same room sometimes worked together on problems they experienced. We do not present an analysis of the use of these learner supports, but we included them in the procedure because both are typical of real on-the-job learning of office information systems, the sort of learning the manuals are designed to support. We had no further procedure for problem support, but if a subject had a problem so severe that nothing seemed to help and considerable time elapsed without progress, we intervened enough to get things moving again.

After finishing the prerequisite portion of the training material, each subject was allowed to undertake the corresponding performance task. During the performance task, the subject could refer to the training material (or the system reference library, or even place a call to the hot-line). Learners could work on only one performance task at a time, and could not return to a task once they had pronounced it finished.

Scoring. Two dependent measures were collected and analyzed in this experiment: (a) time to complete training and performance tasks and (b) performance on eight word processing tasks. Time was scored as the time required to read and complete the exercises in the training materials. The training materials covered the functions necessary to complete the eight performance tasks.

Each of the eight performance tasks consisted of several subtask components, specific formatting features and revisions that were scored as correct if the subject used the appropriate word processing function to achieve the desired effect. The correctness of the formatting features was determined by examining the task documents stored on diskette. The correctness of the revisions was determined by examining both the task documents stored on diskette and a record of the keystrokes produced by each subject as they completed the tasks. The performance score for each task was determined by summing the number features and revisions completed correctly.

4.2 Results. *Time.* Overall, the MM subjects required 40% less learning time than the SS subjects, $\underline{t}(17) = 3.06$, $\underline{p} < .01$. This result suggests that the Minimal Manual design accomplishes one of its design objectives -- to make learning faster. This difference was also obtained -- and of about the same magnitude -- when we looked only at the learning times for the basic topics (the material prerequisite to tasks 1 through 3), $\underline{t}(17) = 2.93$, $\underline{p} < .01$. What was perhaps more interesting, however, was that the learning time advantage for the MM group persisted also for the advanced topics (the material prerequisite for tasks 4 through 8), $\underline{t}(17) = 2.17$, $\underline{p} < .05$. As noted earlier, much of the material to be learned for the advanced topics originated in a common self-instruction manual that both the MM and the SS group studied. Thus the fact that the MM group was significantly faster at reading this material is evidence that the manual also better facilitated further learning. Figure 5 presents the summary time and performance results for Experiment 1.

Task Performance. Overall, the MM subjects accomplished 2.7 times as many performance subtasks as the SS subjects, $\underline{t}(16) = 3.63$, $\underline{p} < .01$. This analysis compares the performance score totals by subject (one subject in MM was incompletely scored and was deleted from the performance analysis). Part of the difference resides in the fact that some of the SS subjects ran out of time and hence never even attempted some of the advanced tasks. Accordingly, we also

	Minimal Manual	Standard Self-instruction
Learning time (hrs.), Tasks 1-3	5.1	8.5
Learning time (hrs.), Tasks 4-8	4.9	7.9
Performance success (subtasks), Tasks 1-8	28.9	10.2
Performance success (subtasks), Tasks 1-3	12.1	8.1
Performance time (min.), Tasks 1-3	63.0	86.4
Performance efficiency (subtasks/min.), Tasks 1-3	.23	.11

Figure 5. Overall performance measures, Experiment 1

looked at performance success for the basic tasks only. Here also the MM group outperformed their SS counterparts, however in this case by 50%, $\underline{t}(16) = 2.11$, $\underline{p} = .05$ (performance means are presented in Figure 5).

We also combined time and performance into a measure of test performance efficiency: accomplishment in the basic tasks divided by the time to perform the tasks (as noted, not enough subjects attempted the advanced material to include it too). The MM subjects were more than twice as efficient as the SS subjects, $\underline{t}(16) = 2.90$, $\underline{p} < .01$ (see Figure 5).

4.3 Discussion. Clearly, these are strong and encouraging indications that the Minimal Manual design is a better training design than the standard self-instruction manual. The key question that remains is specifically in what aspects of this design the advantage resides. Our second experiment was smaller in the scale of learning examined and less scrupulously realistic in the task-situation we presented to learners; it was designed to address the question of why the Minimal Manual design is better.

5. Experiment 2

The second experiment was carried out by Sandra Mazur and John Carroll at the IBM research center in Yorktown Heights, New York. The principal focus of the study was the contrast between a commercially developed, standard self-instruction manual (SS) and the experimentally developed Minimal Manual (MM).

5.1 Method. *Design.* The experiment had a 2x2 between-subjects design. The two independent variables were Manual, either SS or MM, and Instructions, either to "learn while doing" (LWD) or to "learn by the book" (LBB). The LWD learners were given 5 hr during which they were to perform a series of tasks using the system. The LBB learners were given 3 hr to use the manual in order to learn about the system. They were separately given 2 hr to perform a series of tasks using the system.

Subjects. A total of 32 subjects participated in the experiment, 8 in each of the four manual/instruction conditions. A temporary agency selected and screened participants for two qualities: (a) we wanted people who were experienced with routine office work, typing in particular, and (b) we wanted people with little prior computer experience. All of our participants attested to these requirements. Seven had had some exposure to computers in entering data via "canned" programs loaded by others. Both the median and the modal educational level in our participant sample was High School. Job experiences varied widely. The median and the modal amount of full-time office work experience was 5 years. The preponderant category of prior work experience was secretarial; other major job categories were counselor, switchboard operator, bank teller, accountant, and bookkeeper.

We controlled for age by attempting to balance learners across the four manual/instruction groups among six age ranges: 18 to 25, 26 to 35, 36 to 45, 46 to 55, 56 to 65, and over 66 years. We made this pseudorandom assignment on the basis of appearances only, because we did not want to call subjects' attention to age as a possible performance factor at the start of the experiment. Nevertheless, we were able to get fairly uniform distribution, X^2 (15) = 8.43, $\underline{p}$ = .9. Both the median and the modal age range in our sample was 26 to 35 years.

Procedure. The agenda for experimental sessions involved 2 hr of hands-on experience with the system in the morning, an hour lunch break, and then 3 hr of further hands-on work. The final hour of the day included a system concepts comprehension test (for which there were no significant differences). In our initial instructions we identified the main components of the word processing system and of its reference library. Subjects were encouraged to rely principally on the training manual (MM or SS), but we wanted to be realistic in making the entire system library available to those who might want to use it. (About half the subjects made some use of the reference manuals).

During the hands-on portion of the experiment, the observer sat with the subject and made detailed notes about activities and outcomes (what the subject was trying to do, what commands or selections were made, what the effects were, how errors were recovered from, etc.). All observations were time-stamped by reference to a digital timer. Subjects were encouraged to verbalize goals, plans, frustrations, and opinions throughout the session. However, the ground rules were that the observer could not answer questions or provide hints -- except in extreme situations. If a subject had failed to make progress in recovering from an error for 20 min, the observer would intervene, returning the system to the state directly preceding the error. If a subject seemed to be distressed, the observer would likewise intervene, placing the system in a familiar state (e.g., the Home menu). Three subjects became frustrated enough to ask to be excused from the experiment and were replaced.

There were a total of six performance tasks given to each learner. The tasks were typing exercises that involved use of the system's word processing function, and were presented in increasing order of difficulty (see Figure 6). For the LBB learners, Task 1 was presented after 1.5 hr of learning (and a half hour before an hour lunch break). Task 2 was given immediately after lunch. Tasks 3 through 6 were presented after a final 1.5 hr of learning. For the LWD learners, Task 1 was presented at the start of the experiment, and as each successive task was completed the next was given (with the exception that Task 2 was given during the half hour immediately after the lunch break, whether or not this was its place in the sequence).

Task 1: Create and print a letter. Required simple business-letter formatting via line skips and punctuation.:

Task 2: Create and print a letter. Similar to Task 1.:

Task 3: Create and print a bulletin. Required centering, underscoring a single word, underscoring a phrase,:

Task 4: Revise and print a bulletin. Required text block move, text block insertion, word deletion, use of text locate command, and specification of print quantity.:

Task 5: Create and print a bulletin. Required keyword indexing of the document, specification of margins, and specification of an alternate format.:

Task 6: Revise and print a bulletin. Required use of menu shortcuts via commands and the definition and use of an editing macro.

Figure 6. Description of Six Performance Tasks, Experiment 2

Learners could work on only one task at a time, and could not return to a task once they had pronounced it to be finished. Only when they had told us that a task was complete, could they go on to the next task. They were permitted to use their manual at all times.

Scoring. We scored a variety of dependent measures. Time and success for the 6 performance tasks were measured analogously to Experiment 1. Time indicated the time to complete a given performance task; success was the number of subtasks correctly completed. The LWD group contrasted with the LBB group and the subjects of Experiment 1 in that their performance times included the time it took them to learn the material as they completed the task. Scores for the systems concepts comprehension test were merely the number of questions correct.

In addition to these standard performance measures, we wanted to more analytically characterize how subjects learned and performed. We examined the allocation of attention and effort during the experiment. We measured the time it took subjects to get the system started, to load system diskettes, to get to the Typing Area, and to get printed output. During the first 1.5 hrof performance we classified subjects' activities as "reading the book", "working at the display", or "coordinating attention to both". The grain of this analysis was 30 sec (e.g., a subject had to work at the display for 30 continuous sec in order to be scored as working at the display).

We also tabulated the errors subjects made through the course of the experiment, and we measured the amount of time recovery from these errors consumed. Based on our 4 pilot subjects and the first block of eight subjects, we developed an error taxonomy for the word processing system, This included 39 of the most frequent and salient errors, organized into six categories: 3 Mechanical errors (trouble loading floppy diskettes or finding the on/off switch); 2 Manual errors (skipping text or miscoordinating the manual and the display); 16 Menu errors (selecting an exotic item or parameter from a menu, misexecuting the Code Cancel key combination); 14 Typing area errors (confusion of insert and replace mode, use of the Space Bar to advance the cursor); 3 errors which occurred in both menus and in the typing area; and the residual category of Miscellaneous. The scoring judgments were made case by case as the experimental session actually occurred. It is important to stress that the error analysis and performance success on the 6 tasks were independent measures: A subject could have perfect success on all subtasks but still make many errors, or make few errors and fail to successfully complete the performance tasks (e.g., by progressing too slowly).

The Minimal Manual stressed four general error recovery methods (the use of Cancel, Backspace, Reply, and Power off). We tabulated subjects' successful use of these methods (i.e., episodes in which the use of a recovery method actually led to error recovery) as well as unsuccessful uses. We assessed use of the MM and SS manuals for reference after training by analyzing episodes in which a subject tried to look back at material that already had been covered.

5.2 Results. Success in learning was assessed by the six performance tasks. Figure 7 summarizes the relevant results. Our analysis of the performance tasks consisted of a two-way analysis of variance (ANOVA) with Manual (MM or SS) and Instructions (LWD or LBB) as between-subject factors and Tasks (1 through 6) as a within-subject factor. For each task we scored the number of subtasks suc-

	Minimal Manual		Standard Self-instruction	
	By Book	While Doing	By Book	While Doing
Comprehension test score	20.4	23.8	14.3	20.4
Performance success (subtasks), Tasks 1-6	11.4	13.6	4.8	11.0
Performance time (min.), Tasks 1-3	71.8	121.7	104.9	130.8
Performance efficiency (subtasks/min.), Tasks 1-3	.12	.09	.05	.06

Figure 7. Overall performance measures, Experiment 2

cessfully completed. MM learners successfully completed 58% more subtasks than did SS learners, $F(1,28) = 5.31$, $p < .05$. And LWD learners completed 52% more subtasks than LBB learners, $F(1,28) = 4.48$, $p < .05$. There was no interaction of the two between-subject factors. (There was a main effect of task -- not of any interest in itself, and no interactions of task with either of the two between-subject factors).

We also applied this ANOVA design to performance efficiency: subtasks completed per unit time for each of tasks 1, 2, and 3 (too few learners attempted tasks 4, 5, and 6 to make including them meaningful). Again, we found an effect of manual: MM learners achieved 93% more per unit of time than did SS learners in tasks 1 through 3, $F(1,28) = 6.13$, $p < .05$. There was no interaction between Manual and Instructions (we again ignore the main effect of tasks; there were no interactions).

Analyzing learning. Our performance results demonstrate the learning efficacy of MM versus SS. This offers some support to the design ideas embodied in MM. We also collected data that bear more directly on the question of *how* MM affords better learning. MM was designed to allow learners to get started faster: to turn the system on, to load diskettes, to get through the menu control structure to the typing area, to print a first document. We measured elapsed time for each of these achievements. As shown in Figure 8, these measurements do indicate that the MM learners were able to get started faster than the SS learners. The MM learners were almost twice as fast to start the system up, and 20% to 40% faster to load diskettes, to reach the typing area, and to print out their first document. However, these differences were statistically significant only in the case of time to start the system up, $F(1,28) = 5.92$, $p < .05$. (For the time to start the system measure, there was also a significant interaction of Manual with In-

	Minimal Manual		Standard Self-instruction	
	By Book	While Doing	By Book	While Doing
Time to start system (min.)	4.9	8.7	16.5	8.9
Time to load diskettes (min.)	7.6	8.6	9.9	12.8
Time to reach Typing Area (min.)	40.7	35.4	60.6	33.3
Time to print out a document (min.)	42.7	56.3	72.6	53.8

Figure 8. Getting started benchmarks, Experiment 2

structions, $\underline{F}(1,28) = 5.52$, $\underline{p} < .05$, reflecting the fact that the MM/LBB group was particularly fast and the SS/LWD group particularly slow).

MM was also designed to encourage learners to coordinate their attention between the manual itself and the consequences of their actions on the system's display. We assessed this by classifying learner activities during the first 90 minutes of the experiment as "reading the book", "working at the display", or "coordinating attention to both". As Figure 9 shows, there is apparently a trade-off between the first and third of these categories. MM learners tended to spend relatively less time (29% less) reading the manual, but relatively more time coordinating their attention between the manual and the display (20% more), though this difference was nonsignificant.

	Minimal Manual		Standard Self-instruction	
	By Book	While Doing	By Book	While Doing
Reading the display (min.)	27.9	28.5	34.4	38.2
Coordinating manual and display (min.)	46.2	38.5	31.1	39.4

Figure 9. Allocation of attention in the first 1.5 hours, Experiment 2

Yet another design objective of MM was to support detection of and recovery from errors. Figure 10 summarizes our principal measures. MM learners made 20% fewer errors, $\underline{F}(1,28) = 3.11$, n.s., and spent 10% less time recovering from errors. The experimenter was forced to intervene less than half as often for MM learners as for SS learners. MM learners successfully used recommended error recovery methods 60% more often than did SS learners. Although all of the

	Minimal Manual By Book	Minimal Manual While Doing	Standard Self-instruction By Book	Standard Self-instruction While Doing
Errors and their consequence:				
Overall error frequency	187.3	188.8	224.1	261.0
Error recovery (min.)	121.7	153.3	163.7	142.3
Intervention frequency	1.0	.3	2.3	.9
Frequency of different recovery methods:				
Cancel	30.4	19.5	7.0	16.6
Backspace	12.0	12.1	9.1	10.6
Reply	1.0	1.4	1.4	3.8
Power off	3.9	5.0	2.6	1.4

Figure 10. Errors and recovery, Experiment 2

mean differences here accord with our predictions, none reached statistical significance.

MM learners did make greater use of the four specific error recovery methods that were stressed in MM, namely, Cancel, Backspace, Reply, and Power off, $F(1,28) = 7.48$, $p < .01$. There was a main effect of Recovery Method (the different recovery methods were used with varying frequencies), and an interaction of Recovery Method with Manual, $F(3,84) = 3.85$, $p < .01$ -- probably due to assorted asymmetries (Cancel was used disproportionately by the MM/LBB group, Backspace by the SS/LBB group, etc.).

Finally, MM was designed to support reference use after training. During the experiment, we noted every reference made to previously encountered information in the training manuals (i.e., reference to a section of the manual after it had been studied). We classified each reference as successful or unsuccessful according to whether the goal that prompted the reference to the manual was in fact satisfied by the reference. For each learner we then computed the ratio of successful references to the manual to the total number of references to the manual. This ratio was reliably larger for the MM learners, $F(1,28) = 4.42$, $p < .05$ (see Figure 11).

A second indication of this difference was the number of subjects who elected to make use of the system's reference library in the course of the experiment. None of the tasks we gave them required them to use any manual other than the training manual (MM or SS), but 17 of the 32 did so; 13 of these 17 were SS subjects, $p < .005$ (by the Fisher Exact Test). SS subjects spent over 20 min on

	Minimal Manual By Book	Minimal Manual While Doing	Standard Self-instruction By Book	Standard Self-instruction While Doing
Total References per subject	20.6	35.8	20.9	35
Successful References	10	13	5.6	11.6

Figure 11. References to Previously-encountered Information in Manual, Experiment 2

average referring to reference manuals in the library, whereas MM subjects spent an average of 2 min.

Targeted errors and skills. We felt that our empirically developed error taxonomy worked well for the analysis of error in this study. Only 250 (less than 4%) of the errors were classified Miscellaneous. The distribution of the 6885 observed errors among our 40 error types was very skewed (see Carroll et al., 1986, for details). Five error types seemed particularly important -- alone they accounted for over 46% of the errors; all were at least 50% more frequent than the sixth most frequent error. The five errors were Exotic choice (selecting irrelevant and advanced menu branches), Exotic parameter (altering menu defaults needlessly), Code Cancel (miscoordinating the compound keypress for Cancel), Enter to exit (trying to leave a menu without having made any selection), and Keystroke bursts (seemingly random keystrokes, usually to recover from errors).

The first three of these were errors that the MM design specifically targeted. They were important errors: Learners spent an average of 36 min recovering from the direct consequences of making these three errors, or 25% of the average total amount of error recovery time. (On average, subjects spent 145 min -- almost half their time -- recovering from errors). We performed a separate ANOVA for the sum of the frequencies of these three errors with the between-subjects variables of manual (SS or MM) and condition (LWD or LBB). There was a significant effect of manual, $\underline{F}(1,28) = 5.46$, $\underline{p} < .05$, indicating that the MM group committed these errors less often (see Figure 12).

Other specific errors targeted in the MM design were statistically more minor. Skipping text was 40% less frequent for the MM learners; Miscoordinating the manual and screen was 13% less frequent. However, together these two errors constituted less than 3% of the total errors.

As described earlier, most of the MM topic chapters had "On Your Own" open-ended exercises. Each of the MM learners spent an average of 14.2 min on these exercises (this did not differ greatly between LBB and LWD). The majority of the learners tried the On Your Own exercises for the first four topics, but very few of them tried any of the later exercises.

	Minimal Manual		Standard Self-instruction	
	By Book	While Doing	By Book	While Doing
Exotic Choice	13.5	16.6	26.5	19.6
Exotic Parameter	14.8	19.4	27.9	22.5
Code Cancel	9	16	26.3	22.4
Enter to Exit a menu	20.5	16.9	21.4	22.3
Keystroke Bursts	10.8	9.4	21	44

Figure 12. Frequencies per Subject of "Major" Errors, Experiment 2

Subjective measures. The final portion of the system concepts comprehension test consisted of attitude questions that allowed subjects to express their feelings about this learning experience. For example, we asked them if there were things they would have liked to learn but did not get to cover, and whether they would have approached the task differently if they had been learning to use the system in some other situation. A subset of the questions, however, was directed more specifically at their attitudes about overall learning difficulty in the experiment. We asked them to imagine a 10-week course in office skills, and to allot time for learning to use the word processing system. Both the median and modal response for the SS subjects was 200 hr (or 50% of the 10-week course), for MM both the median and the mode were 80 hr (or 20%), $p < .05$ (by Mann-Whitney U-test, $U = 66.5$ -- only 29 learners answered). In both Manual groups, the LBB learners estimated briefer times than did the LWD learners (LBB in SS estimated 120 hr, whereas LWD estimated 200 hr; LBB in MM estimated 80 hr, whereas LWD estimated 165 hr).

We asked the learners whether they had expected that learning to use a word processor would be difficult. Twenty-two learners answered "yes", 8 answered "no". There were no differences between the manual or instruction groups on these reported initial expectations. We asked them whether, in view of their experience in our study, they now thought that learning to use a word processor was more or less difficult than expected. The 13 SS learners who made a signed judgment were split on this question (7 more difficult, 6 less difficult), but the 13 MM learners who made a signed judgment overwhelmingly judged it to be less difficult (12 to 1), $p < .05$ (by Fisher Exact Test).

5.3 Discussion. In this experiment, MM subjects performed better and more efficiently than their SS counterparts. More importantly from an analytical perspective, they did the things the Minimal Manual was designed to facilitate: They got started faster; they coordinated attention better; they made fewer errors, in particular, errors the Minimal Manual targeted and trained against; they made better use of error recovery methods; they made better use of the training manual for later reference. The present experiment shows not only that the manual works well, it begins to show in detail why it works well.

Many of the manual differences we predicted emerged more clearly between the LBB groups than they did between the LWD groups. For example, looking only at LBB subjects, the MM group was 1.4 times faster than the SS group to start the system, 1.5 times faster to get to the Typing Area, and 1.7 times faster to print out a document (see Figure 8). During the first 1.5 hr of learning, the MM group coordinated attention between the manual and the screen 49% more than did the SS group (see Figure 9). Finally, under LBB instructions the MM group spent 35% less time in error recovery than the SS group (see Figure 10). Nevertheless, the interactions of manual and instructions were generally marginal or nonsignificant due to the great intersubject variability.

In an earlier study, Carroll and Carrithers (1984: 386) suggested a navigational analogy to understand the contrast between LWD and LBB: "Learning by the book is like navigating unfamiliar territory by following a list of very specific treasure-map instructions ('march ten paces east, then turn toward the large oak tree'). The task is well-defined until you miss a checkpoint, and then you don't know where you are. Learning by doing is like navigating unfamiliar territory by the stars. Many errors will be committed (because following a star can lead you to cliffs and rivers), but correction is always possible by simply looking up at the sky." Some results of the present study are consistent with this view: LWD had a 9% higher error rate overall than LBB, but spent a less-then-proportional amount of time in error recovery (3% more than LBB) and, perhaps more importantly, required only a third as many experimenter interventions as LBB (see Figure 10). Unfortunately, these are nonsignificant trends in the data, and hence our experiment fails to further clarify the difference between learning while doing and learning by the book.

6. General Discussion

In our introduction, we described the troubled state-of-the-art in user self-instruction, and in particular in training manuals. A variety of approaches are being explored, such as including advance organizers (Foss, Rosson and Smith, 1982) and presenting diagrammatic frameworks for training exercises (Galambos, Sebrechts, Wikler, and Black, 1984). In our own prior work, we have experimented with a Guided Exploration situation (Carroll et al., 1985) in which learners were given no manual at all but rather a set of unordered cards, each of which was directed at a particular user-pertinent goal (e.g., typing something, quitting work), but which provided only hints about how to accomplish the goal and error recognition and recovery information for when the goal was not accomplished. As mentioned earlier, our Guided Exploration learners sometimes explicitly voiced a desire to have a real manual. The Minimal Manual attempts to capitalize on the strengths of Guided Exploration and the desire of learners to have a more traditionally structured manual.

We wanted to design a training manual in the self-instruction genre, but one that allowed users to get started doing recognizably real work, one that de-emphasized reading in favor of action, and one that helped learners to avoid making errors and to recognize and recover from errors committed. Our two experiments converge on the conclusion that the Minimal Manual is substantially and reliably superior to the commercial self-instruction manual. The bases for this advantage, insofar as we can assess them now, accord with our specific design objectives. This suggests a simple and rather direct path from our current understanding of the learning problems of new users to the Minimalist training model that can address these problems. Facilitating the tasks that learners already understand and are motivated to work on, slashing the instructional verbiage they must passively read, and addressing important user errors can produce better training material than the current state of the art.

Interestingly, the Minimalist slogan that "less can be more" also may extend to the time and cost required to develop training. The analytic and subskill phases of design for the Minimal Manual together required less than a man-month of effort (Carroll, 1984a). This was a retrofitted design (MM was built out of SS), but this retrofitting created both savings and idiosyncratic obstacles: It is sometimes easier to modify an actual exemplar than to create anew, but the particular demand we placed on ourselves to have MM and SS differ only in the ways described in the introduction, definitely cost time and effort that would not have been required if we had sought only to design a good training manual. In any case, the practice of developing one training manual out of another is typical in the computing industry (the manual for Level 2.3 of a software product is developed from the manual for Level 2.2, the manual for the new word processing system is developed from that for the old one, etc.).

Many questions remain for further research and analysis, among these the questions of how far the present results can be generalized and of what specific cognitive processes underlie the learning differences between the Minimal Manual and the self-instruction manual. It may be quite important that we studied office workers learning work-related procedural skills. Our conclusions may not generalize to other areas of educational technology. It may even be significant that we studied clerical workers learning word processing. To assess the generality of the advantage of Minimalist instruction, we need to expand the investigation to other instructional domains. This is happening. On-going work by Olfman (1987) at Indiana University has, for example, developed a Minimalist manual for a spreadsheet application.

Perhaps the greatest opportunity for examining boundary conditions for the utility Minimalist instruction lies in helping development teams use this model in their work. Developers have to use *some* instructional model, and the standard self-instruction model is associated with a variety of learner problems, as described in this article. Thus the interests of research and development can converge on the strategy of regarding current development work as "appropriately scaled" research. Some of our current effort is directed at helping such development experiments take place.

Although the present studies demonstrate learning advantages of the Minimalist approach, we need to know more about the specific cognitive bases of these advantages to understand more precisely how the Minimalist approach works. Currently, we are directing some of our effort at contrasting alternate minimal manuals, each of which incorporates some but not all of the design ideas of the Minimal Manual studied here. For example, in the design of the Minimal Manual we deliberately specified some procedures incompletely, to involve the learner more in understanding and executing the procedures, and to encourage the coordination of attention between the system and the training. Black, Carroll and McGuigan (1987), using multiple alternate minimal manuals, showed a more specific effect of incomplete instructions, namely, the benefit of forcing learners to make inferences (vs. forcing covert rehearsal of procedures). We are now investigating the specific effects of different types of inferences on learning.

More broadly, we need to understand how standard self-instruction models, based on educational prescription and experience, produced training materials that were substantially inferior to our Minimalist materials. We believe that there are specific properties of the standard models that caused this difference. The "systems approach" of Gagne and Briggs (1979; see also Mager, 1975) is focused on producing a comprehensive fine-grained analysis of instructional objectives, which is a reasonable starting point for instructional design. However, it does not provide guidance in other critical areas: For example, it provides no guidance for controlling instructional verbiage; indeed, the emphasis on comprehensive decomposition of instructional objectives naturally leads to "maximalist" content. The systems approach prescribes curricula of accretional lesson sequences for the presentation of training material, *not* recognizably real task scenarios for learning. Indeed, learners are asked to periodically "demonstrate criteria", that is, to perform rote exercises in order to advance through the training curriculum (Mager, 1975: 87). Learner motivation and attitude are merely "assumed to be present" (Gagne and Briggs, 1979: 8-9), but never addressed directly by the instructional design itself. Relevant prior knowledge is similarly ignored. Carroll and Herder (in preparation) analyze in more detail how the standard model differs from Minimalist design and the consequences of these differences.

We believe that this design project has succeeded to this point because it originated both in a detailed qualitative analysis of the problems real users of word processing equipment have in realistic learning situations and in a theoretically grounded analysis of possible intervention strategies (the Minimalist training model). We suggest that when applications of cognitive science fail, it is frequently because they have addressed problems that only seem plausible in laboratory tasks. In this regard, it is important to bear in mind that the problems we identified in our design analysis of learning problems in the word processing domain are by and large *not* the problems that the designers of self-instruction training manuals set out to address.

Acknowledgment

We thank Georgia Gibson for helping to organize and run Experiment 1. We are grateful to Judy Olson, Tim O'Shea, Don Norman, Mary Beth Rosson and John Thomas for comments. This chapter is reprinted from *Human Computer-Interaction, 3,* 1987-1988, 123-153.

References

Black, J.B., Carroll, J.M. and McGuigan, S.M. 1987. What kind of minimal instruction is the best? In J.M. Carroll and P.P. Tanner (Eds.) *Proceedings of CHI+GI'87: Conference on Human Factors in Computing and Graphics Interface.* New York: ACM.

Carroll, J.M. 1984. Minimalist training. *Datamation, 30/18,* 125-136.

Carroll, J.M. 1985. Minimalist design for active users. In B. Shackle (Ed.), *Human-Computer Interaction - INTERACT '84.* Amsterdam: North-Holland, pages 39-44.

Carroll, J.M. and Carrithers, C. 1984. Blocking learning error states in a training wheels system. *Human Factors, 26,* 377-289.

Carroll, J.M. and Herder, R.E. In preparation. Why didn't Instructional Science help? Manuscript.

Carroll, J.M., Mack, R.L., Lewis, C.H., Grischkowsky, N.L., and Robertson, S.R. 1985. Exploring exploring a word processor. *Human Computer Interaction, 1,* 283-307.

Carroll, J.M. and Mazur, S.A. 1986. LisaLearning. *IEEE Computer, 91(11),* 35-49.

Carroll, J.M. and Rosson, M.B. 1985. Usability specifications as a tool in iterative development. In H.R. Hartson (Ed.) Advances in Human-Computer Interaction. Norwood, NJ: Ablex, pages 1-28.

Carroll, J.M., Smith-Kerker, P.L., Ford, J.R., and Mazur, S.A. 1986. The Minimal Manual. *IBM Research Report,* 11637, Yorktown Heights, New York.

Davis, J. 1984. What are the users doing. *Seybold Report on Office Systems, 7,* 11-18.

Dreyfuss, H. 1955. *Designing for people.* New York: Simon and Schuster.

Eason, K.D. 1976. Understanding the naive computer user. *The Computer Journal, 19,* 3-7.

Foss, D.A., Rosson, M.B., and Smith, P.L. 1982. Reducing manual labor: Experimental analysis of learning aids for a text-editor. *Proceedings of Conference on Human Factors of Computer Systems,* Gaithersberg, MD: National Bureau of Standards.

Gagne, R.M. and Briggs, L.J. 1979. *Principles of instructional design.* New York: Holt, Rinehart and Winston.

Galambos, J.A., Sebrechts, M.M., Wikler, E., and Black, J.B. 1984. A diagrammatic language for instruction of a menu-based word processing system. In S. Williams (Ed.) *Humans and machines: The interface through language.* Norwood, NJ: Ablex.

Mack, R.L., Lewis, C.H., and Carroll, J.M. 1983. Learning to use word processors: Problems and prospects. *ACM Transactions on Office Systems, 1,* 254-271.

Mager, R.F. 1975. *Preparing instructional objectives.* Belmont, CA: Pitman Learning.

Olfman, L. 1987. A comparison of construct-based and applications-based training methods for DSS generator software. Dissertation Proposal, Indiana University, Bloomington, IN.

Reder, L.M. and Anderson, J.R. 1980. A comparison of texts and their summaries: Memorial consequences. *Journal of Verbal Learning and Verbal Behavior, 19,* 121-134.

Piaget, J. 1985. *The equilibration of cognitive structures: The central problem of intellectual development.* Chicago: The University of Chicago Press.

Schank, R.C., Collins, G.C., and Hunter, L.E. 1986. Transcending inductive category formation in learning. *Behavioral and Brain Sciences, 9,* 639-686.

Scharer, L.L. 1983. User training: Less is more. *Datamation, 29/7,* 175-182.

Uhler, H.L. 1981. Training and support: Shifting the responsibility. *Seybold Report on Word Processing, 4,* 1-10.

Uhler, H.L. 1984. Training -- managers, professionals, executives. *Seybold Report on Office Systems, 7,* 1-10.

5 Exploring Exploring a Wordprocessor

John M. Carroll
IBM Thomas J. Watson Research Center

Robert L. Mack
IBM Thomas J. Watson Research Center

Clayton H. Lewis
University of Colorado

Nancy L. Grischkowsky
IBM ISG Business Application Systems

Scott R. Robertson
Rutgers University

Studies of people learning to use contemporary word processing equipment suggest that effective learning is often "active", proceeding by self-initiated problem solving. The instructional manuals that accompany current word processing equipment often penalize and impede active learning. A set of instructional materials was constructed for a commercial word processor, specifically designed to support and encourage an active learning orientation. These "guided exploration" (GE) materials are modular, task-oriented, procedurally incomplete, and address error recognition and recovery. Learners using the GE materials spent substantially less time yet still performed better on a transfer of learning post-test than learners using commercially developed self-study materials. Qualitative analysis of aspects of the learning protocols of participants suggested that active learning mechanisms may underlie this advantage.

1. Active Learning Problems

Common sense, conventional wisdom, and even psychological research all suggest that a powerful technique for effective learning is self-initiated problem solving: learning by doing, by thinking things through, by actively assimilating novel experience to prior experience (see e.g., Bransford & Johnson, 1973; Shulman & Keislar, 1966). In our own recent studies of learning to use word processing equipment, this "active" picture of human learning has been strikingly apparent (Carroll & Mack, 1984; Lewis & Mack, 1982; Mack, Lewis, & Carroll, 1983).

We have observed that learners are *overtly active* in that they seem to prefer to learn by trying things out rather than to read. While the type of self-study manual used in our studies provides hands-on experience practicing text-editing, learners take initiative to pursue their own goals. Unfortunately, these instances of active learning in the context of self-study are typically not successful because learners do not know enough about the text-editor to understand it without instruction. In particular, they have great difficulty recognizing and diagnosing errors they incur. This is in large part because learners are also *cognitively active:* that is, try to make sense of what they experience, often in ways that are misleading and worse, can sometimes rationalize away problems.

Thus, the evidence for active learning that we have observed is largely the inventory of learning *failures* in trying to use self-study instructions. State-of-the-art self-study manuals -- that accompany contemporary word-processing devices (Davis, 1984; Uhler, 1981) -- assume a more passive learner that reads explanations, then follows practice exercises, and either does not get side-tracked or is able to deal successfully with problems that come up. These manuals often do not make provisions for learners to take the initiative to learn what they want, when they want, nor do they provide support for the kinds of problems such initiative can produce.

What would happen if learners were given materials that encourage and guide active learning? To find out, we created a set of instructional materials designed to address many of the problems faced by active learners. We will describe here the nature of these new materials and the improved learning performance these materials produced.

Any study of this kind faces a serious problem in determining the effects of particular changes in training materials. We felt that a large number of substantial changes in approach would be required to deal with the active learning problems we had identified, and so an experimental program in which small, individual changes were made and evaluated sequentially seemed impractical. On the other hand, making several changes at once makes it difficult to determine the unique value of any of the individual changes.

Another challenge arises from the fact that our interest in the improved materials is really indirect: we aren't mainly interested in the effectiveness of these particular materials for the particular system we studied. Rather, we want to know whether the analysis of the learning process that led us to these changes is correct; if so, then this analysis could be applied to a range of other systems and situations. Given this objective we need to know not just whether our modified materials led to improved performance or not, but also as much as we can learn about how they led to improved performance.

In response to these problems we were led to an approach which gave us as much information as possible about what was happening during the learning process with old and new materials: the "thinking-aloud" method. Learners were asked to work with the training materials and give us a running commentary on what they were attempting to do, what problems they were encountering, and other task-related thoughts. We used these comments to characterize some aspects of the learning process that we felt would help determine how the new materials worked, and thus whether the analysis that led to the new materials was sound.

For example, the revised materials required learners to formulate their own goals while working, instead of using goals supplied by the training materials. We expected that this would lead to fewer problems understanding the goals. We relied on learners' comments and questions to assess whether this expectation was borne out. This permitted us to determine whether eliminating goals from the materials had an effect, and to determine whether our analysis of its effect was on the right track.

This choice of method brings with it some clear difficulties. Thinking-aloud is not a normal behavior, and may well affect the learning process itself. For example, learners who are thinking aloud might be more (or less) careful or methodical than learners in real situations. Making comments takes time, which must affect measures of time to complete tasks.

Despite these problems, we feel that "thinking-aloud" is a useful exploratory technique, giving some evidence about learning that is hard to get any other way. Where indications are positive, more traditional experimental techniques can be used to follow up the exploration, and can give a less problematic indication of how net performance differs for the materials being compared. We have in fact done this for some of the work described here. However, this follow-up work has used materials extensively modified again, so that they differ substantially from either set of materials discussed in the present report. This work will be reported separately. We document here what we have learned about an interesting, extreme option in the space of training designs.

Another methodological choice we made was to leave learners free to order their learning activities in any way they chose, rather than prescribing a procedure for learners to follow. This obviously complicates our comparisons, since the diversity of resulting behaviors is considerable. But our work has convinced us that controlling learner behavior is itself a major problem in the design of materials, and we did not want to beg that question by imposing artificial constraints as part of our study. We chose to handicap ourselves in the development of a model of realistic learner behavior, rather than carry out an easier development of a model of unrealistic behavior.

2. The Experiment

2.1 Guided Exploration Cards. The materials we developed consisted of a deck of large "cards", summarizing the system's functional capability. The cards were designed to meet four criteria.

Task orientation. Users of text editors are not just pressing keys. They are interested in "typing letters." That is, their goals pertain to tasks at the level of

Basic Cards
How do I use these cards?
What if I get stuck?
What are the two most important things to know before I get started?
What cards do I have?
How do I get started?
Quitting work.
Typing something.
Deletion and insertion.
Moving the cursor to a particular spot in something you have typed in.
Printing a document on paper.
Getting back something you've typed.

Advanced Cards
Making the right margins even.
Keeping lines short.
Keeping several words together.
Hyphenating.
Underlining something.
Centering something.
Short cuts: Deleting a whole line at once.
Short cuts: Other ways to delete.
Short cuts: Avoiding use of the RET key.
Short cuts: Avoiding END before printing.
Finding out when something has been printed.
Short cuts: Avoiding END before paginating.
Printing more than one document at a time.
Using help.

Figure 1. List of text-editing tasks covered by GE cards.

typing and printing documents. Each card addressed a particular functional *goal* that we believed users could better identify with. There were a total of 25 cards, divided into two sets of 11 and 14 (see Figure 1 for a list of all the cards; the cards themselves appear in the appendix to Carroll, Mack, Lewis, Grischkowsky, & Robertson, 1984). Most of our discussion focuses on the first set, which covered basic skills like document creation, text entry, moving the cursor, inserting and deleting, storing, retrieving and printing documents. The cards were packaged in an envelope, on the outside of which was pasted one further card, a general orientation to word processing titled "What is this all about?".

Four of the 11 cards in the basic set comprised a sort of "advance organizer" (Foss, Rosson, & Smith, 1982; Mayer, 1976), introducing the learners to the cards as a learning resource (an index titled "What cards do I have?", and cards labelled "How do I use these cards?", "What if I get stuck?", and "What are the two most important things to know before I get started?"). These cards were distinguished by having a different colored border than the remaining seven cards. The other cards in the basic set (as well as the second set of 14) helped the learner understand text-editing tasks (e.g., "How do I get started?", "Typing something" and "Quitting work").

These goals are task oriented in two mutually reinforcing senses. First, they name the goals users really want to undertake (as opposed to the relatively abstract and task-remote chapter topics in the self-study manual, such as "Messages and Helps"). Second, they break down the overall function of the word processing system into parts that map coherently onto what the users already know about routine office typing procedures.

A good example is the card "Typing Something" which helps the learner get to the so-called "typing area" where they can actually compose and revise their document file. This card (shown in Figure 2) refers to features and operations specific to the text-editor, but embedded in a larger and more familiar (and computer independent) context of "typing something". In contrast, the manual has separate exercises on creating documents, on the organization of the typing page, on how to end and store documents, and so on.

Incompleteness. The information on the cards was intentionally incomplete. There was no step-by-step specification for any procedure. For example, the "Moving the Cursor" card presented only hints about using the keys, not specific instructions for trying them out:

> The cursor is a brightened underscore of the screen; You can experiment with keys labelled (labels given for cursoring by forward or backward by character, word, line and paragraph). Be careful of using the Backspace key, the big Return key, and the Space bar for moving the cursor. They will actually change what you have typed in (try them and see).

The incompleteness of the cards was intended to keep the learner focussed on and involved in the learning task. We had observed in earlier work with self-study instruction that learners tended to lose track of what they were doing, because following directions is difficult and became an end in itself. For example, learners would complete exercises and exclaim "I know we did something, but I don't know what it is!". Incompleteness was intended to involve learners by inviting them to fill-in procedural details, attending more to the information on the screen, and to their own understanding of what they were trying to do and what they had learned so far. In the "Moving the cursor" example, no mention is made of the specific function of, say, the cursor key which moves the cursor to the left. Even

TYPING SOMETHING

In the terminology of the computer, you will be "creating a document". Use the Task Selection Menu to tell the computer that you want to create a document.

You can give your document any name you want, but you cannot use the same name for two different documents.

You can begin to type when you see a typing page on the screen:

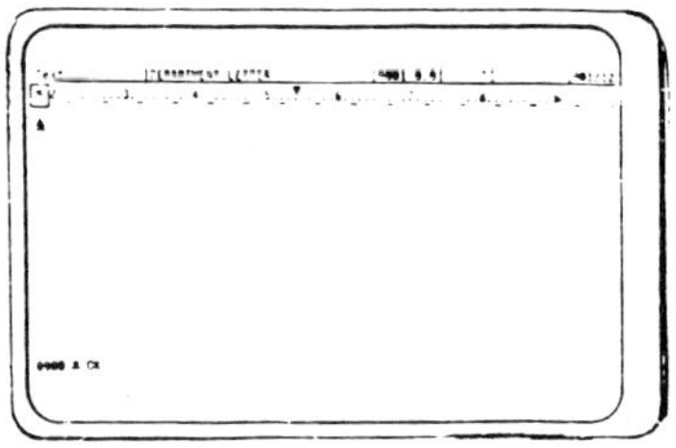

(Think of this display as a blank piece of paper but remember that you do not need to worry about margins or tabs)

Press the big RET (carriage return) key to start a new line (or to skip lines).

When you are done typing or want to leave the typing page to do something else, you want (in the terminology of the computer) to "end use" of your document: Press REQST, type the word "end", and press ENTER.

As you are typing, what you type will appear on the screen.

If you cannot get the Create menu, try 

You will see the Task Selection Menu appear and you can then try again.

Is the name of the new document unique?

Figure 2. Example of a Guided Exploration card

the warning hint about certain of the keys (which behave differently from the corresponding keys on the typewriter) ends with a challenge to try and see.

Modularity. The deck of cards was unordered. Each card attempted to address its specific procedural question without reference to material covered on other cards. Thus, (ideally) each card could be initially read, and later referred to, independently of all the other cards. In some cases this had to be compromised because of the functional organization of the system interface. For example, the system we studied queued print requests and hence forced a distinction between printing as a transaction between the user and the system interface and printing as a transaction between the system and an actual printer (and a piece of paper). Accordingly, we constructed a card for "Printing something" as well as a card for "Finding out when something has been printed". These cards referred to each other.

The cards were also modular with respect to their internal organization of information. Each consisted of a goal statement, hints, checkpoints, and remedies. The goal statement was a brief description of the subject-matter of the card, in ordinary language, as opposed to system jargon. The hints directed the learner to keys, menus, etc. that would be important in achieving this goal. The checkpoints referred to information on the screen or elsewhere that would indicate success in the goal. The remedies contained hints for recognizing errors, and suggestions about what to do in those cases.

These four procedural components were graphically blocked off on the GE cards to stress this functional decomposition to learners. An example is the card "Typing Something" in Figure 2. The modularity of the cards was intended to support self-initiated problem solving. A card could be employed by the learner at any time without untoward interaction with material covered only on *other* cards.

Safety. We wanted our learners to feel that no matter what error they had incurred, and no matter how uninterpretable their current situation, there was a way out, a way to recover. Ideally perhaps, this would have been a step-by-step "undo" key, reversing one user-command each time it was struck. Such a key would allow a learner to unravel an error situation, noting how it had occurred in the first place.

The system we were using, like many contemporary word processing systems, did not have a true undo key. Accordingly, we invented two procedures -- which we named Zot and Zap -- which provided the learner with means to return from any given system state to the Task Selection Menu (a sort of "home base" in this system). Two procedures were needed because no single recovery method would work in all situations. Zot and Zap did not undo user actions one-by-one (in general). Rather, they dumped the user back to home base. Nevertheless, we it important for users to feel they could always "get back" -- albeit ungracefully -- if they were to be confident enough to explore.

2.2 Methodology. There were two groups of six participants each. One used commercially developed self-study materials, and the other the GE materials we designed. The groups were run separately in time, the first group as a baseline. Participants were asked to use these materials to learn the basic function of a state-of-the-art commercial word processing system. Participants were asked to "think aloud" as they did so. Qualitative analysis of these think-aloud protocols, as well as quantitative assessment of performance on a transfer of learning performance test, provided bases for contrasting learning via GE with learning via the existing self-study materials.

Both groups consisted of relatively computer naive office temporaries hired from a temporary employment agency. Some had had data entry experience using VDUs but none had had word processing experience. We did not control age, and ages varied from early twenties to later fifties. All participants had substantial experience typing letters in the office environment.

The system and the training materials. The system we used is menu driven: users select tasks (e.g., print a document) by typing in command abbreviations corresponding to choices displayed in a listing (called a "menu"). The parameters of these selected tasks are then specified in subsequent menus (e.g., the name of the document to be printed, the printer to which the document should be shipped). The system's keyboard has a variety of special function keys for cursor movement, deleting, underscoring, on-line help, and so forth (that is, in addition to the conventional alphanumeric keys).

The system comes with a standard self-study training manual for user self-instruction (Davis, 1984; Uhler, 1981). This type of training material combines explanations about how to use the system with structured step-by-step practice. A learner is expected to read through each chapter, encountering a preview description, then structured practice exercises, and finally review and summary materials. In our prior work with such training approaches (Mack, Lewis, & Carroll, 1983), we found that learners often have trouble recognizing and adopting the appropriate goals in self-study training, that they often just "go through the motions" of reading and responding by rote. Recovery from error is especially problematic, since most self-study materials incorrectly presume that exercises will be successfully followed step-by-step and hence do not present error recovery procedures as such.

We have already described the general criteria for designing the GE materials. The 25 GE cards were divided into two sets. The first were described above and consisted of the basic skills needed to type, print and retrieve a document file, as well as make simple revisions (insertion and deletion). The second set of cards consisted of more advanced skills including controlling right justification of lines, preventing splitting of phrases, underlining, printing multiple copies of documents and various short-cuts for cursoring, deleting and printing.

The GE cards represented the content of 94 pages of the self-study manual (note, however that the manual contained graphical material and used a format which left a lot of empty area). The cards covered all the functions described in the manual, but obviously in a much less detailed way. For example, 23 pages of the manual (an entire topic chapter) described "system overhead" like using menus, getting prompts and messages and using help. We had no specific cards on this material. Where such material was judged necessary, it was woven into the card describing the task that required the material.

The participants' task. The twelve participants learned individually in a laboratory setting that simulated an office situation where the participant was to learn with no help from others. Participants were asked to learn basic text entry and revision skills, involving the use of menus for formatting and printing, and the interpretation of system messages. Half used the self-study materials (SS) that were part of the commercial system and half used the experimental guided exploration materials (GE).

Both groups were free to use the instruction materials as they wished. The SS materials contained extensive practice exercises and drill which participants tended to try to follow. The GE group was invited to type whatever they wanted to, but we emphasized to them that the word processor was a real tool for use in offices. If they had trouble deciding what to type, we prompted them to type something appropriate in an office, or a letter to a friend. SS participants completed training when they had worked through the manual, or as much of it as they cared to use, to their own satisfaction. GE participants completed training when they decided they had tried all the cards they were interested in, and had practiced typing. Based on pilot work, we had estimated that SS participants needed four half days to complete training, transfer task and debriefing, while the GE participants needed two half days. Participants for the two groups were hired for these respective times.

Following training, participants were given a transfer task consisting of a one-page letter which they were to transcribe into the word processor and then print out. After typing and printing the letter, participants were given a marked up copy and asked to make the indicated revisions and to print out the revised letter. Participants were permitted to refer to their training materials (GE or SS) during this transfer task.

We asked the participants to "think aloud" as they worked on both training and transfer phases: to verbalize their thoughts, plans, and concerns regarding the learning task. We remained with the participants to prompt them non-directively when they were silent and/or inactive for too long a time. The principal type of data generated by think-aloud research consists of a catalog of episodes -- critical as well as typical -- exemplifying theoretically significant points. These data were collated and taxonomized, and provide a qualitative picture of what GE learning is like.

In addition, we took time and performance measures, in particular for four menu functions (document creation, revision, formatting, and printing) and four typing display functions (line ending, word underscore, hyphenation, and deletion). Overall learning time (as defined above for each of the two groups) was recorded. The transfer task letter was scored for time and performance success with respect to the eight functions. These latter data afforded the usual quantitative contrasts, e.g., is learning via GE faster, or more efficient with respect to performance post-tests?

3. Results: Guided Exploration versus Self-Study

We present the results in two parts. First, on the basis of time and performance measurements, we establish that learning in the GE condition was more efficient (faster and more successful) than in the SS condition. Second, and on the basis of a more detailed consideration of the types of behaviors the learners engaged in, we try to explain *why* the GE learners did better. Not surprisingly, this explanation returns us to the analysis of active learning that motivated us to design the GE materials in the first place.

3.1 The Efficiency of Learning by Exploration. In both phases of the study, learning and transfer, the GE learners were faster than their SS counterparts. Learning time for GE participants was less than half what it was for SS, 3 hours and 55 minutes versus 8 hours and 5 minutes, $\underline{t}(10) = 3.14$, $\underline{p} < .01$. Learning time ranged from 1.5 hours to 6 hours in GE, and from 5 to 13 hours in SS. One apparent account of this difference rests on the sheer volume of training material with which the two groups were provided. The GE learners had only 25 page-size cards, while the SS learners had a 94 page manual (three topic chapters). As we will see below, however, there seems to be more going on than merely this.

The time advantage for GE was also evident for the transfer of learning portion of the experiment. On average, GE learners spent 40 minutes on the transfer post-test (i.e., typing, revising, formatting, and printing out a one-page letter), and SS learners spent an average of 1 hour and 12 minutes. This 49% reduction is significant, $\underline{t}(10) = 2.35$, $\underline{p} < .01$. The range of times was 30 to 50 minutes for GE learners, and 30 minutes to 2 hours and 10 minutes for SS learners.

The fact that our learners were thinking aloud may have affected the absolute magnitudes of the learning time and performance results reported above, but probably not the relative magnitudes, as all learners were subjected to the same procedure.

GE learners were also able to accomplish more on the transfer post-test. Performance on this test was analyzed into overall "initial" and "ultimate" success with each of the eight word processing functions: create, revise, format, print, line ending, word underscore, hyphenate, and delete. Initial and ultimate success were separated to preserve information regarding the self-initiated correction of errors in light of system feedback. Thus, a learner might have initially misused the word underscore or hyphenate, or filled out a menu parameter in the create document menu inappropriately, or tried to request the revise document task using the create menu -- but immediately, in light of the system's response to this, corrected the error. All such incidents were considered initial failures, but ultimate success.

The only tricky functions for scoring were line end and delete. Delete involved summing across many isolated incidents. The scoring rule used was that if the ratio of successful deletes to failures was greater than 1, the function was scored as a success overall; less than 1 was failure overall. Line end was more complex. The system we studied provides two types of line end: ordinary line end and required line end. The latter feature is used to suppress formatting, for example, to force short lines. The use of ordinary line ends throughout will produce a document that looks alright unless formatting is applied, in which case all short lines will concatenate themselves into one line. If the participant changed ordinary line ends to required line ends (in appropriate places) after formatting, this was scored as an initial failure but ultimate success. If the participant did not make these changes but did use formatting, it was scored as both initial and ultimate failure. However, if the participant never used formatting and also never used required line ends, this was scored as success (with respect to line ending --

Function	Self-Study			Guided Exploration		
	OK	Fail	Omit	OK	Fail	Omit
Create	.67	.33	--	.83	.17	--
Revise	--	.67	.33	.50	.50	--
Format	.67	--	.33	.50	--	.50
Print	.83	--	.17	1.0	--	--
Line end	.33	.67	--	.83	.17	--
Hyphenate	.50	.50	--	.83	.17	--
Underscore	--	.17	.83	.50	.17	.33
Delete	.83	.17	--	.67	.33	--
Overall	.48	.31	.21	.71	.19	.10

Figure 3. Proportion of participants initially succeeding, failing, and omitting various word processing functions in transfer post-test

and an omission with respect to formatting). Finally, if the participant always used required line ends, this was scored as failure.

The initial scoring of transfer performance is presented in Figure 3. Only four functions were used by all (GE and SS) of the learners: create, line end, hyphen, and delete. For these four functions, the GE group was more successful than the SS group (79% success versus 58%), $\underline{U} = 8.5$, $\underline{p} < .05$. (We use the Mann-Whitney U statistic in these tests since our participant sample is small, and since we cannot be certain about the underlying distribution of our data). Of course, not trying a function is failure of a sort as well. Thus a second analysis was performed taking omission of a function to be tantamount to failure. Here too the GE group performed significantly better (71% success versus 48%), $\underline{U} = 8.0$, $\underline{p} < .05$.

A similar analysis was carried out for "ultimate" success on the eight functions. For the four functions that all participants used, the GE group was more successful than the SS group (100% success versus 71%), $\underline{U} = 3$, $\underline{p} < .005$. Refer to Figure 4 for summary statistics. In the second analysis, taking omission of a function as failure, the GE group again also performed significantly better (85% success versus 63%), $\underline{U} = 6.5$, $\underline{p} < .05$.

Function	Self-Study			Guided Exploration		
	OK	Fail	Omit	OK	Fail	Omit
Create	1.0	--	--	1.0	--	--
Revise	.67	--	.33	.83	.17	--
Format	.67	--	.33	.50	--	.50
Print	.83	--	.17	1.0	--	--
Line end	.50	.50	--	1.0	--	--
Hyphenate	.50	.50	--	1.0	--	--
Underscore	--	.17	.83	.50	.17	.33
Delete	.83	.17	--	1.0	--	--
Overall	.62	.17	.21	.85	.04	.10

Figure 4. Proportion of participants ultimately succeeding, failing, and omitting various word processing functions in transfer post-test

These indications demonstrate reliable and substantial relative learning efficiency for GE relative to the SS baseline. But our main interest is not in the magnitude of the improvement itself but in determining whether the new materials changed the learning process in the way we hoped.

3.2 The Character of Learning by Exploration. Our GE materials were designed to support active learning in ways that we believed SS manuals do not. If we were successful, then there should be indications that GE learners were better task oriented, that they explored more, and that they more efficiently recognized and recovered from errors -- all relative to the SS baseline. In this section, we discuss salient learning incidents gleaned from our protocols. We have taxonomized, tabulated, and timed aspects of learner behavior for two of the document creation tasks the learners attempted in the study, the very first document creation attempted during the training portion of the experiment, and the final document creation attempted at the start of the transfer of learning test. These analyses are based to a great extent on the video record we made. Unfortunately, the tape for one participant in the SS condition was lost. Accordingly, most of the analysis is based on only 11 people.

Attention to task rather than to manual. We hoped that the GE materials would encourage, indeed require, learners to spend time using the system they were learning rather than looking at the instructional materials. Figure 5 shows how learners in the two groups spent their time. The comparison refers to the time spent on the first typed product of the two groups, from signing on through completion of the task. Apart from the transfer performance, this comparison reflects the most comparable activity on the part of participants.

	Self-Study	Guided Exploration
Initial Letter Typing Task		
Total time on task	24:59	30:00
Time reading	11:05	3:30
Time working at display	13:54	26:30
Final Letter Typing Task		
Total time on task	13:30	8:05
Time reading	1:30	:25
Time working at display	12:00	7:35

Figure 5. Average time invested in various activities during initial and final letter typing task

GE people actually spent about 22% *longer* on the initial letter typing task. However, they spent less than 12% of their time reading the training materials -- directing their attention to the display the remaining 88% of the time. In contrast, the SS people divided their time far more evenly. They spent 44% of their time reading the training manual and working at the display 56% of the time. Attending to the display -- in favor of reading -- is of course a task oriented thing to do. Nevertheless, there is some penalty attached to this strategy, at least to the extent that the GE group was somewhat slower overall.

The same activity breakdown of time was performed for the final letter the learners typed, the one in the transfer task. Both groups invested relatively more time at the display -- but the GE group more so. GE learners spent less than 5% of their time reading the training materials; SS learners a bit more than 11%. Here we see some of the payoff of the strategy of attending to the display. The GE group was 35% faster overall in the final letter typing task. (Part of discrepancy between the learning time ratio cited in section 2.1 and that cited here is due to the fact that the SS participant excluded from this analysis was also the least successful in that group).

These results complicate the simple account, suggested earlier, of the overall time advantage of GE. That account suggested that GE learners were faster (merely) in that they had less voluminous training materials to read. True enough, the GE people spent far less time reading. But they actually spent more time on the initial letter typing task -- when learners in both groups were spending relatively more time reading their training materials. But later, in the final letter typing task when both groups were spending far less time reading, the GE group was faster. This is not to say that the sheer reduction in training material volume had no effect, but only that it is in itself not the only effect.

Understanding goals during learning. We expected that GE learners would understand the goals of the exercises they carried out, since they had to devise those exercises themselves. This was borne out: no GE learner raised a question about the purpose of an activity, while this was a common occurrence for SS learners.

	Self-Study	Guided Exploration
Success	1.6	2.7
Failure	1.0	2.0

Figure 6. Frequency and Success of Exploratory Episodes Per Participant

More exploration. As described earlier, the GE materials were designed to encourage and support exploration on the part of learners. We tabulated the number of exploratory episodes learners engaged in and their outcomes -- success or failure -- for the initial letter typing task (see Figure 6). An exploratory episode was defined as an attempt by a participant to do something which (1) was not prompted by explicit instructions (e.g., most typically where relevant text has not been read at all) and/or (2) for which there may actually be a prohibition against trying or (3) is required only to recover from an error. For example, participants sometimes tried to sign on before reading how to do so or to set margins when admonished against doing so.

The success or failure of exploration can be defined in different ways. The simplest criterion, which is adopted here, is whether the participant succeeds in his or her original goal. For example, were participants able to sign on when they tried to do so on their own? Or were they able to set margins when they tried?

Of course, a looser but no less interesting criterion is whether the participant learns from his or her failure that a particular task or procedure is too difficult to learn and abandons that goal on "principled grounds". This is harder to infer, but in cases where the participant perseveres in some task despite failure we might conclude that they were not learning from exploration.

Exploratory behaviors can also be nested in that one goal can lead to subgoals than lead participants into exploring other operations. For example, trying to sign on can lead to discovery of the "locked keyboard" problem (certain errors inhibit further keyboard input until a reset key is pressed) and its resolution in the reset key. Trying to move the cursor around in a menu can lead to the discovery of related operations such as altering the content of menu fields or moving from one field to another. These are treated as separate episodes here.

It is notable that GE people engaged in over 80% more exploratory episodes than did SS people. It is also notable that exploratory episodes *do,* more often than not, eventuate in success (over 58% of the time). This provides support for our original supposition that exploratory behavior is something to be cultivated in creating a learning environment. Moreover, it indicates that we were to some degree successful in our design of the GE materials -- they did encourage and support exploration relative to our base-line.

Figure 7 gives an illustration of exploration.

Learner: OK. Now I'll try and insert the date underneath this heading.

Moves cursor down two lines, then back up one line, then back down one line.

Now I'm just playing with the keys and trying to figure out what they do.

Experimenter: Which keys are those?

Learner: The ones on the right, the Word Return, Character Advance, Word Advance, ...

Types Word Advance three times, then Line Advance once.

Experimenter: Does it seem to be in order?

Learner: Yea, it seems to do what it says it does. I'm just figuring out what it is that it exactly does.

Presses Variable Advance (for advancing through an set of menu fields), causing a reset condition (which locks the keyboard).

No. *Presses Reset, clearing the reset condition.*

That was Variable Advance. Umm.

Cursor is under a blank character in column one; there is a return character in column 2. Uses Space Bar to move cursor rightward, aligning the date she will insert with the return address already typed. (N.b. centering by hand).

Learner: OK. Now I'll add the date.

Does so.

Experimenter: What are you thinking?

Learner: Yea, I haven't really figured out, I mean I could put that date in there because I left a free line, but I'm not really sure how to insert a new line.

Maybe I can just, oh I see ... you can type it on the line that you've left or if you push Return you'll get a new line. But what if I wanted to type it in there? Oh, I guess you just, I see ...

Inserts several blank lines.

Experimenter: What are you trying to do?

Learner: I'm trying to figure out how to insert a whole new line between two lines.

Experimenter: What key are you using there?

Learner: I'm using the Line Advance. *Moves cursor down without inserting blank lines using Line Advance key..*

Oh, that's how you do it. OK, you push .. there's a distinction between Line Advance and Return. Line Advance advances what you already have and Return will put new stuff in, will put new blank lines in. So if you want to add a new line between two lines -- I don't know if its the easiest way to do it but that way that I figured out to do it -- is to push Line Advanceuntil it's under, until the cursor is under the next line, is under the line after the one where you want to insert it and then push Return and you'll get a new line and then if you push Line Advance it will go back up there and I think you can just type whatever you want. At least I'll try.

Presses Line Advance, then types "100 New Street", then presses Carrier Return, then types "Box 405", then presses Line Advance.

Well, ok, so the way you do it is after you type in a new line instead of pushing Return which will give you a new empty line, you just push Line Advance and it will go to the next line.

Figure 7. Learning by exploration: An example

In this excerpt, one of our GE participants begins by announcing a goal that she herself has determined, namely the insertion of a text line. She then experiments with operations she believes are relevant, and finally succeeds in making the insertion. More importantly though, she draws conclusions from this self-initiated undertaking. In particular, she draws a distinction between the Carrier Return operation and the operation for advancing the cursor by line. Her analysis of this distinction is in fact both superficial and incomplete, but it is quite adequate with respect to this situation. What's more, the learning "took": this person went on to deal successfully with text insertion in later portions of the experiment.

Efficient error recovery. Errors can be a troublesome fact of life for learners. In the design of our GE materials we stressed error recognition (through checkpoints) and error recovery (through remedies). An entire GE card was devoted to Zot and Zap, our two general recovery methods. These sources of information were intended to help learners keep in better touch with where they were working and what was happening. We hoped that in virtue of this fewer errors would be made, and that those that were made would be recognized as errors and recovered from more frequently and more rapidly.

	Self-Study	Guided Exploration
Unrecognized errors in initial letter	2.4	1.2
Snarled error recoveries:		
In initial letter	5.8	3.3
In final letter	4.0	1.2
Proportion of snarled recoveries that were successful:		
In initial letter	.62	.82
In final letter	.80	.86
Proportion of time spent on snarled error recovery:		
In initial letter	.36	.28
In final letter	.48	.10

Figure 8. Error recognition and recovery

To assess this, we analyzed the frequency of <u>un</u>recognized errors in our two groups (see Figure 8). For the initial letter typing task, there were an average of less than 1.2 unrecognized errors for the GE group, and 2.4 for the SS group. In other words, SS participants failed to recognize twice as many errors as GE.

We also separately examined instances of obstructing errors, that is, errors the user had to deal with in order to make any further progress with the system.

We tabulated the number of times participants committed such errors and failed to recover immediately, that is, the number of times they became snarled in recovering from the errors. In the initial letter typing task, GE people suffered an average of 3.3 of these incidents, where SS people were involved in an average of 5.8. In the final letter typing task, GE participants had an average of 1.2 snarled recoveries, where SS participants had an average of 4.0. Both groups reflect some improvement over the course of the learning task, but the GE group is consistently 40-70% better. In sum, it appears that the GE materials *did* help the learners recognize errors and avoid getting stuck in their work.

When they did get stuck in the initial letter typing task, GE learners recovered 82% of the time, where SS learners recovered 62% of the time. In the final letter typing task, the recovery rate for GE learners was 86%, and for SS learners 80%.

We analyzed this point a little further since it is possible to recover from an error by changing one's goal to suit the error condition -- that is, if you make a mistake trying some particular thing, you can simply decide to try something else. (We refer here to system-independent goals, e.g., "delete a word," not keystroke level goals, e.g., six iterations of "press CHAR DEL.") Some of the advantage in recovery for GE does seem to be attributable to goal changes, though the observed difference is not great. For the initial letter, GE learners recovered by goal changing 27% of the time, while SS learners did this 24% of the time. On the final letter the rates of goal changing were 29% for GE and 20% for SS. Excluding goal changes, the recovery rates on the initial letter were 55% for GE and 38% for SS, and on the final letter 57% for GE and 60% for SS.

While these comparisons may give an indication of improved recovery with GE, there are problems in interpreting them. Since the nature of the difficulties that learners face can be different for the two sets of materials, the recovery rates could differ, or fail to differ, for that reason. For example, since GE learners mastered more operations during learning, the problems they encountered in the final typing task might have been more subtle than those encountered by SS learners.

Another indicator of the effectiveness of the recovery instruction in the GE materials is the use of the specific operations described, Zot and Zap. We tabulated the frequency with which Zot, Zap or the equivalent was employed by learners in the initial letter typing task. In the GE group they were used an average of 3.5 times, but in the SS group they were used on average only .8 times.

Interestingly, error recoveries which involved explicit reference to the training materials were about equally frequent in both groups. In the initial letter typing task, 67% of the error recoveries involved reference to the materials, in SS this was 61%. For the final letter typing task, the figures were 33% for GE and 37% for SS.

Finally, we tabulated the time spent on error recovery in the two groups. The raw times for error recovery in the initial letter typing task were quite similar: the GE group spent somewhat less than 8.5 minutes recovering, and the SS group spent about 9 minutes. For GE this was 28% of the time on task, for SS it was 36%. For the final letter task, the raw times were different: the GE group spent less than a minute on average, where the SS group spent almost 6.5 minutes. Thus, the GE group spent 10% of their time on task recovering from error; the SS group 48%.

4. General Discussion

4.1 Why did guided exploration work? We have presented evidence that the GE materials worked better than the standard SS manual, and some evidence of how they worked. The evidence is consistent with the analysis that motivated the construction of the GE materials: learners need to think about the system they are learning, need to formulate their own goals for using the system, and need to be able to explore hypotheses about the system. Of course we cannot be sure that this analysis is correct. It may be that other aspects of the GE materials besides those we focussed on made the critical contributions. But the coincidence of improved performance with specific changes in behavior of the sort predicted by our analysis is encouraging. Active involvement with minimal material may be as effective as relatively more passive involvement with extensive material. While more complete presentation may seem objectively useful, our results suggest that such material may be simply wasted for the learner: *less can be more.*

4.2 Problems with Guided Exploration. We observed above that the most salient empirical indications of active learning are the inventories of learning failures that occur with materials designed for passive learning. Just as the analysis of these episodes helped to direct the development of our GE cards, the analysis of learning problems in the present study can direct further development of environments that support active learning.

Recalcitrant problems. Many of the problems GE learners had were quite similar to those we had seen before in studies of SS training. Learners failed to read even the briefer GE materials carefully enough. One participant failed to notice on the Typing Something card a warning *not* to try to set tabs (which involved a very complicated procedure). Throughout the learning experience, she tried over and over to set tabs -- without any success and at considerable cost in terms of getting off the track and losing time.

In another instance, a GE person was struggling with a locked keyboard (having incurred a reset condition). She tried keying several task requests to no avail and then consulted the remedies and hints on two of the cards -- not successively, but jointly. She combined the suggestions from the two cards to create a composite recovery procedure that not only failed to work, but placed the system in an unfamiliar and puzzling state.

Learners tried to generalize what they already knew, sometimes inappropriately. The participants in our study were professional typists and often tried to understand the word processing system by referring to what they already knew about typewriters (Carroll & Thomas, 1982). One person, for example, repeatedly tried to use the Carrier Return key to move the cursor down while in a menu, despite the fact that this consistently activated a warning buzzer and caused a reset (error) condition which locked the keyboard.

Expecting procedural instructions. Several of GE learners expressed a desire for more structure in the training materials. One has to be careful about interpreting learners' comments as well thought out preference judgments, but there was evidence that learners did not understand the unconventional structure of the GE materials. In particular, there was a tendency for learners to treat the intentionally incomplete "hints" in the GE materials as if they were the more familiar kind of step-by-step procedure.

If two hints appeared one above the other on a card, they were apt to be taken as temporally or logically related -- the one above either prior or prerequisite to the one below. One example is a person who successfully signed on, using the Getting Started card, but then continued to follow the card into the remedy section -- turning the power off.

Although the cards were presented unbound in a deck, learners often assumed that the ordering of the cards was crucial -- again suggesting that a procedural interpretation was being made of the card materials.

The bias toward procedurality was also evident in learners' interpretations of the system interface. For example, one person expressed the belief that the various tasks, or functions, appearing on a menu were listed in the order in which they were to be undertaken. This same person complained that the Print Card didn't tell you *how* to get the print menu -- she wanted a procedure.

Exploratory paranoia. Some learners focussed on our initial warning that some information had been intentionally omitted from the cards, and reached the conclusion that *key* information was deliberately left out. For example, one person was upset by the fact that the card dealing with formatting did not explicitly direct her to select the formatting task. This caused her to become suspicious of the GE materials.

Gaps. Learning by self-discovery produces a less predictable product than learning by a structured method such as SS. In several cases we found interesting gaps in the GE learners' knowledge. In the transfer of learning task, one participant accidentally hit the Carrier Return, inserting a blank line in her letter. This small typo exposed an interesting gap in her overall understanding of the system, for she was unable to recover at all. Her characteristic way of deleting material was to employ a key that deletes characters. Indeed, this was the only method presented in the first set of cards (many of the other GE learners discovered other deletion methods on their own). This person, however, could not come up with a method and was forced to retype the entire letter.

Another participant came to believe that it was necessary to paginate a document, that is, to lay the text out on pages, *before* creating. However, the reverse is actually true and when she attempted her premature paginations she got a message that the document did not exist. She knew something was wrong and decided to come back to the topic of pagination, but never tumbled to her actual problem. Another participant consistently tried to use the print or paginate tasks for document creation and retrieval -- despite the fact that this never worked at all. This caused a gap in her ultimate understanding of the system: she did not know how to request the document retrieval task in the transfer of learning test.

Another participant never internalized the distinction between "create document" and and "retrieve document": she persisted in trying to re-create documents (that is, to retrieve documents by way of the create task). She also never clearly made the distinction between menus and the typing page. She constantly tried to leave the typing page via a cancel key, and to leave menus via a function for storing document files

Goal problems. Our GE learners were free to pick whatever goals they wished, and they sometimes picked goals that weren't really useful, or, in some cases, were impossible. One of the participants in our study attempted to delete a special screen symbol marking the end of the typed material. This special character, however, is undeletable. Nevertheless, this person made more than ten attempts in succession to accomplish the deletion.

Our learners were experienced office personnel. Their reaction to a typewriter-like device, such as a word processor, was to set margins prior to beginning work. However, setting margins on the system was quite a complicated matter, and the cards advised learners not to try to do it. Nevertheless, several people tried, intermittently but repeatedly, to set margins. One person tried several times to move the cursor between lines in a menu with Line Return despite the fact that it never worked. Another person picked the goal of moving the cursor in a menu, which can't be done.

System restrictions. The system we studied places documents to be printed on a print queue, which has the side effect of making them inaccessible for further editing until they are actually printed out. Several participants inadvertently requested prints for documents which they then wanted to edit, that is, before actually printing the documents out. The problem for GE in this case is how to move the learner toward the correct solution -- which is to operate the printer until the queue is emptied. Giving an *ad hoc* warning or instruction is likely to be unreliable, since it may not be read or understood. Like other methods of instruction, GE has trouble in cases like this where system design imposes limitations that the learner is unlikely to reason through without help.

4.3 Where do we go from here? The results of this study are encouraging for our hypothesis that computer naive people can learn by self-discovery. But the problems outlined above are serious. Critics of discovery learning approaches (see De Cecco, 1968) have argued from such problems that exploration cannot be a general alternative to more traditional, passive approaches. How can we develop better exploratory learning environments?

Refine GE materials. We designed the GE cards by a process of iterative refinement, and that process could be continued. Some of the specific problems learners met with in the study had not appeared in earlier work, and some could no doubt be averted by simple additions to the cards.

Learner reactions suggest that more sweeping changes must also be considered. The cards provided very little explanatory material, and some learners expressed a wish for more. Such material could be made available as an optional information on the cards for learners who wanted more than simply a procedure. This might help reduce the problem of gaps in learners' understanding which we observed can result in inefficient procedures.

The tendency to treat the cards as procedures, following the information on the cards from top to bottom, might be addressed by strengthening the graphic demarcation of the parts of the cards. Some information could be moved to the back of the card to set it off better from the rest. Alternatively, *some* of the properties of the GE cards (e.g., better task orientation, greater modularity, additional error recovery information) could be incorporated into the design of a self-study manual. We are working in this direction currently, and initial results are promising (Carroll, 1984; Carroll, Ford, Smith-Kerker, & Mazur, 1984).

Make the system easier to learn. The ground-rule for our study was to improve learning only by intervening with the design of the training materials. However, designing the cards exposed design problems with the word processor we were using and suggested improvements.

Writing a card's goal statement often involved translating system jargon that appeared in menus or messages into ordinary language: the jargon should go. In describing checkpoints on the cards it was sometimes impossible to tell the learner what to look for, because there just wasn't a visible indication provided by the system. With respect to remedies, as we noted above, it became clear that no general recovery function could be defined for the assortment of common learner problems we observed. The remedies we had to describe required trying more than one thing and behaved differently in different situations.

Other problems arose during the composition and revision of documents. Learners were troubled by certain automatic features of text-editors such as automatic inserting or reflowing after deleting or format changes (see also Mack, 1984, for more investigation into these problems). This is especially true when these features are associated with seemingly familiar functions like space, backspace or return. It may be possible to design interfaces that implement these features in a more obvious way, or disguise them completely for computer naive people.

When learners explored, they ran the risk of entering unfamiliar and complex areas of the system, by intentionally or inadvertently activating advanced functions. It is possible to structure the interface so that advanced features can be disabled during learning. Carroll and Carrithers (1984) present encouraging results from this approach.

The analysis we have given is obviously incomplete. We have examined in detail only a small part of the entire learning process. We have traced the effects of only some of the features of the GE materials. For example, we have not assessed the specific effect (if any) of providing an index to the GE cards. But we feel we have provided some evidence about the value of supporting exploratory learning, and some of the problems to be dealt with in pursing this approach. We are optimistic that the guided exploration approach, especially in conjunction with system design improvements keyed to its requirements, can be developed as an effective method of user training. It has the great virtue that it lets new users get started doing meaningful work quickly, in a way that makes sense to them, and without requiring much reading.

Acknowledgement

We are grateful to Allen Spiegler for help with the data analysis. This chapter is reprinted from *Human-Computer Interaction, 1,* 1985, 283-307.

References

Bransford, J.D. & Johnson, M.K. (1973). Consideration of some problems of comprehension. In W. Chase (Ed.), *Visual Information Processing.* NY: Academic Press.

Carroll, J.M. (1984). Minimalist design. *Datamation, 30/18,* 125-136.

Carroll, J.M. & Carrithers, C. (1984). Training wheels in a user interface. *Communications of the ACM, 27,* 800-806.

Carroll, J.M., Ford, J.R., Smith-Kerker, P.S., & Mazur, S. (1984). Learning to use a word processor with the Minimal Manual. Psychonomic Society 25th Annual Meeting, San Antonio, Texas (paper available from authors).

Carroll, J.M. & Mack, R.L. (1984). Learning to use a word processor: By doing, by thinking, and by knowing. In J.C. Thomas and M. Schneider (Eds.), *Human factors in computing systems.* Norwood, NJ: Ablex.

Carroll, J.M., Mack, R.L., Lewis, C.H., Grischkowsky, N.L. & Robertson, S.R. (1984). Learning to use a word processor by Guided Exploration. *IBM Research Report,* 10428.

Carroll, J.M. & Thomas, J.C. (1984). Metaphor and the cognitive representation of computing systems. *IEEE Transactions on Systems, Man, and Cybernetics, 12,* 107-116.

Davis, J. What are the users doing. (1984). *Seybold Report on Office Systems, 7,* 11-18.

De Cecco, J.P. (1968). *The psychology of learning and instruction: Educational Psychology.* Englewood Cliffs, NJ: Prentice-Hall.

Foss, D.J., Rosson, M.B., & Smith, P. (1982). Reducing manual labor. Proceedings of National Bureau of Standards Conference on Human-Computer Interaction, Gaithersburg, Maryland.

Lewis, C.H. & Mack, R.L. (1982). The role of abduction in learning to use text-processing systems. Presented at the annual meeting of the American Educational Research Association, New York City (paper available from authors).

Mack, R.L. (1984). Understanding Text-Editing: Evidence from predictions and descriptions of text-editing procedures. *IBM Research Report,* RC 10333.

Mack, R.L., Lewis, C.H., & Carroll, J.M. (1983). Learning to use word processors: Problems and prospects. *ACM Transactions on Office Systems, 1,* 254-271.

Mayer, R. (1976). Some conditions of meaningful learning for computer programming, advance organizers and subject control of frame order. *Journal of Educational Psychology, 68,* 143-150.

Shulman, L.S. & Keislar, E.R. (1966). *Learning by discovery: A critical appraisal.* Chicago: Rand McNally.

Uhler, H.L. (1981). Training and support: Shifting the responsibility. *Seybold Report on Word Processing, 4,* 1-10.

6 No Easy Answers: Investigating Computer Error Messages

Peter Hunt
University of Wales, Cardiff, UK

Kalomira Vassiliadis
University of Thessaloniki, Greece

Why Study Error Messages?

What we read from -- or write for -- computer screens, has a critical role in the increasingly important area of person-machine interaction. Common experience is that screen messages are not always immediately informative, and that they use distorted or truncated English, or code. How long does it take, for example, for a user to decode messages like "TRANSMIT BEGINNING" which was a status message, not an instruction, or "DIM SPACE" which meant that there was not enough room on the screen for the message? (Hunt and Kirkman, 1986) This seemed to us to be an ideal area for "usability" research.

One of the main problems with any kind of language testing is the large number of variables in any text -- graphological, lexical, grammatical, tonal, semantic, and so on (Klare, 1963; Maguire, 1982). If any variable is changed, this has a "knock-on" effect on the others; the longer the text, the more complex this becomes, and the less possible it is to draw any valid conclusions.

Moreover, research on the language which appears on screens is hard to find. It is either company-confidential, or it depends on the testimony of "experienced users", rather than on empirical work, or it deals with the systems for **producing** text messages.

In our research, we concentrated on the efficiency of screen error messages. Because they are required to give precise messages in a limited space, they seemed likely to restrict linguistic variables to "testable" proportions, and therefore to yield some usable results.

With the help of a sample of more than 500 users with widely different computer skills, in three countries, we developed a series of tests, and came up with what seems ***at first sight*** to be clear and common sense guidelines for producing effective and efficient error messages. But are they as valid as they seem?

This chapter describes the tests, and we would invite you to compare your reactions with those of our sample users. We will then discuss the "user elements" which cast a good deal of doubt on the results -- and, indeed, upon a lot of "usability" research.

It is clear that the quality of system messages plays an important role in person-computer interaction, and influences the acceptabilty of software systems (Nickerson, 1969; Kennedy, 1975; Stewart, 1976; Shneiderman, 1982a, 1982b, 1984; Brown, 1979, 1983; Turner and Karasek, 1984). But "quality" in this context is an elusive thing. Not only do we have the usual linguisitic variables but there are also, as we will see, questions of tone associated with the image of the computer and the relationship (or pseudo-relationship) implied in the language (Rubenstein and Hersh, 1984). Note: we are not concerned here with matters of screen layout, as they have been dealt with quite fully (Heines, 1984), nor with the differences between reading screens and reading hard copy, as these are primarily concerned with layout of large blocks of text, or the layout of menus.

Research Procedures

How, then, can we isolate the characterisitcs of error messages? With the assistance of a major multinational computer manufacturer, we were allowed to work on a set of mainframe computer manuals. (1) Error messages which appear on the screen for this company's systems consist of a code and a message, for example:

123 ERRMESS - ERROR SOMEWHERE IN SYSTEM.

Users can look up the meaning of the code, or of the message, in the manual, where entries take this kind of format:

123 ERRMESS - ERROR SOMEWHERE IN SYSTEM
Area: Electronic mail system
Explanation: Error occurred in using address codes, and data has not been transmitted.
Rectification: Re-enter data using correct code.

How well did the messages convey the information in the manual? Indeed, if they conveyed it perfectly, there should have been no need to *have* a manual! But, of course, in many cases the full explanation and remedy would have been too long and cumbersome to fit onto a single screen, and the ideal messages would be mini-informative summaries. For our tests, we took six system messages from the manual. For each message, the **Explanation** was printed, followed by, in random order, the error message as it appeared on the screen, plus three variants. In each set, we tried to control at least one linguistic or semantic variable.

Readers of various skills and relationships with computers were then asked to state their preferences: which message expressed the explanation most clearly? There is, of course, an immediate objection to this procedure -- namely, that it is the reverse of our normal encounters with error messages. Normally, we see the message first, fail to understand it, and then turn to the explanation. However, it took very little experimentation to show that **without a context**, four error messages were impossible to evaluate.

The messages and the variants were modified in the light of experience through a series of tests, but it might be useful if we give you an example at this point. This particular message was NOT varied through the tests.

MESSAGE 1

Explanation: A keyword specified in a command is not valid for the command.

Message: 1.1 WRONG KEYWORD - CHECK VALIDITY AND SPELLING
1.2 CHECK VALIDITY AND SPELLING OF KEYWORD
1.3 UNRECOGNISED KEYWORD - CHECK VALIDITY AND SPELLING
1.4 KEYWORD CHECK VALIDITY AND SPELLING

Which of the four messages seems to express the explanation most clearly and efficiently?

The participants were selected to cover as wide a range of users as possible. For tests when we had no specific knowledge of skills, we asked users to identify themselves as one or more of these categories:

PROFESSIONAL PROGRAMMER
OCCASIONAL PROGRAMMER
HOBBYIST PROGRAMMER
NON-PROFESSIONAL USER
INEXPERIENCED USER.

Our logic was that most tests have in the past been concerned with specialist user groups -- that is, computing for dentists or lawyers, for example, rather than with skill or familiarity level within such groups.

The first pilot test covered 159 undergraduates at The University of Wales Institute of Science and Technology, Cardiff, UK. These students all classed themselves as "inexperienced users" (computing as a natural part of an undergraduate's experience is less advanced in the UK than it is in the USA). The second pilot test involved 37 professional programmers from the University Computer Centre and from the Department of Computing Mathematics of University College, Cardiff.

In these first tests, we also asked respondents to distinguish in each case between the version of the message which they thought was **CLEAREST** or **BEST**, and that which they thought **MOST APPROPRIATE**. This might seem curious at first, but it was based on experience from an earlier (unpublished) survey in which respondents were asked to judge which of a series of texts was the most readable and most suitable for a scientific audience. One respondent observed that these were not the same question.

We were, in fact, dealing with our first inkling of the flaws in any survey-based "usability" research. It is clear from work by Kirkman (1980) that certain styles may be objectively more efficient, in that they express simple meaning in plain language -- but they may well not be **acceptable**.

For example, the second-person form, found extensively in computer documentation, is intended to be "user-friendly", but because the relationship implied linguistically is artificial, it often seems to be "user-patronizing", or downright "user-insulting."

Acceptability seems to us to be a particular problem in the world of computing (where one might expect cool logic to prevail) -- perhaps because the dialect of computing is particularly seductive. To be computer-literate is now almost a social necessity, and many people seem to prefer lack of clarity for the mystique it confers. Computer-users also seem particularly prone to the inadvertent use of jargon. This is the more dangerous because much computer jargon is derived from redefining normal English words.

Significantly enough, we found that the "best/most appropriate" distinction was simply not understood by the non-experts, while the experts felt that there was no distinction to be made. This in itself is instructive; the self-image of the professional computer-user does not seem to be amenable to admitting illogical preferences, while the naive user may have attitudes to the machine, and to the concept of the machine, which do not show up directly in the results.

Some of the messages were modified, and new ones introduced, to cut out repetition, to clarify, and expand the scope of the tests. A second test battery, using five messages, was administered to 80 undergraduates, and 21 professionals.

The next group of tests (with further changes) involved technical writers, who, in the normal course of their work would either produce, work closely with, or interpret messages of this kind. In terms of the communication situation we are dealing with, these are very important subjects. They stand as both transmitters and receivers and might be expected to be highly sensitive to the problems involved. (They might also, of course, be expected to have attitudes to programmers and their messages which depend on questions of status and experience). Other tests involved groups of engineers and scientists who were participating in training courses in technical writing.

For comparative purposes, we also tested 85 Greek native speakers at the Teaching Centre of the British Council, Salonica, Greece. Their level of English was that of the first year of the Cambridge Proficiency Examination. All the subjects were inexperienced computer users.

No students seemed to have any difficulty. The only significant difference from the results with first-language speakers (in the UK and USA) was that the Greek users had a broader spread of preferences, perhaps suggesting that comprehension is the first priority, and subtleties of tone are less significant. It has certainly been observed elsewhere that second-language users of technical materials, such as computer documentation, may often prefer a jargon-ridden document to a simple one, on the assumption that it implies (and perhaps confers) a greater skill with the technology.

Finally, the tests were administered to 210 technical writers (and others involved in computing) at the Third Annual Conference on Writing for the Computer Industry, at Plymouth State College, New Hampshire USA. We will deal with the test battery used for this final experiment in some detail, noting any significant deviations in the earlier tests. Of course, there is nothing "final" about the battery as it stands; it merely indicates a careful development of our initial intuitions as to what might be tested, in view of what we found **could** be tested.

Thus, a total of 542 subjects contributed to the refining of the test battery. We would now like to present the results, to demonstrate both the linguistic and communicative points we were exploring, and the effect that the involvement of real humans had.

In the next section, we present the final versions of the tests. You might like to read each explanation, and then select the answer which is, in your opinion, best written in terms of effective, accurate, and acceptable communication. Which, in short, is most usable? We then give the figures for the New Hampshire test, and comment on them; in almost every case, the "clear" conclusions hide some very unclear implications.

Results of the Final Battery of Tests

In this section we first provide the message, followed by the survey results and a discussion of those results.

MESSAGE 1

EXPLANATION: A keyword specified in a command is not valid for the command.

1.1 WRONG KEYWORD - CHECK VALIDITY AND SPELLING
1.2 CHECK VALIDITY AND SPELLING OF KEYWORD
1.3 UNRECOGNISED KEYWORD - CHECK VALIDITY AND SPELLING
1.4 KEYWORD - CHECK VALIDITY AND SPELLING

RESULTS:	1.1:	41.4 %
	1.2:	5.9%
	1.3:	40.3%
	1.4:	12.4%

We guessed that the original message (1.3), which contained the word "unrecognised" implied that users needed to know -- or would be interested in -- how the computer worked. This is not as trivial a point as it may seem. Do users see the machine as a friend, or as a tool? Is it something which "allows" you to do things (as much documentation suggests), or something which **you** control? Is the idea of a program or a machine "failing to recognise" data, implying something quasi-human, **or** does it imply a need for specific knowledge of the inner workings of the system? Either way, it does not present a consistent "image" to the user. As Rubenstein and Hersh observe:

> To ensure ease of learning, a system must have consistent external behaviour -- behaviour independent of its internal workings. We

> call it [an **external myth**] to emphasise that what users actually see may not relate directly to the internals of the system -- bytes, files, control sections, jobs, links, and so on. (1984, p.9)

The conceptual image of the computer, therefore, did not seem to us to necessitate the quite complex (and possibly anthropomorphic) concept of a computer "not recognizing" a keyword. As far as the user is concerned, the keyword was wrong, so why not say so? The direct message also seemed to have the advantage of brevity. On that line of thought, perhaps we could cut down the information content; after all, all you need to know is that the keyword has to be checked.

All the results are, of course, tentative, but here we have an early suggestion that **more** rather than less information is required (and we should remember that most of the subjects of these tests were familiar with computing). What we did not expect was that the expression "unrecognised" would be widely popular.

This is the only example in which professional programmers deviated from, or, indeed, failed to lead, general opinion. They preferred "unrecognized" by a substantial majority. There were two reasons. First, "wrong" (1.1) is inaccurate, and the argument that it was accurate **enough** was not popular. Second, it seemed that perhaps many people objected to the tone of the message: how dare a computer address me in such a blunt manner!

Now, some of these reasons are speculative, and although we can draw broad, perhaps indicative conclusions, we must be very cautious about acting upon them. They may not be what they seem.

MESSAGE 2

EXPLANATION: An error occured in writing a record to the MV accounting file.

2.1 ERROR IN WRITING TO MV ACCOUNTING FILE
2.2 WRITING TO MV ACCOUNTING FILE IS INCORRECT
2.3 ERROR WRITING TO MV ACCOUNTING FILE
2.4 INCORRECT WRITING TO MV ACCOUNTING FILE

RESULTS: 2.1: 69.3%
2.2: 4.7%
2.3 18.3%
2.4: 7.7%

In this example, we explored the use of compressed as opposed to "natural" language. (For a discussion of truncated vs. elaborated language in documentation, see Charney, Reder, and Wells in this volume.) The original message (2.3) uses a non-standard form, which has become extremely familiar in computer use. The other three examples all include the "small" words often missed out in "computerspeak;" and even the first, which is probably closest to "normal" and unambiguous language, leaves out an article.

The popularity of 2.1 may be gratifying to anyone who is suspicious of computer language, but it should not lead us to any overconfident conclusions. Despite the fact that professional users preferred standard language even more than the writers, and the writers far more than the naive users, the pull of the dialect is still very strong elsewhere.

MESSAGE 3

EXPLANATION: A name string exceeds the maximum length required, or has a length of zero. Logical names are limited to a length of 55 characters.

3.1 NAME STRING TOO LONG OR ZERO
3.2 NAME STRING ZERO OR MORE THAN 55 CHARACTERS
3.3 INVALID LOGICAL NAME
3.4 LENGTH OF LOGICAL NAME EXCEEDED

RESULTS:	3.1:	25.7%
	3.2:	65.3%
	3.3:	4.2%
	3.4:	4.8%

Here we looked at information content of the messages, and the results show a clear preference for **more** information. The original (3.3), which was dismissed rather snappishly by one professional user as "an unacceptable message," and 3.4, which was only marginally more helpful, were much less popular than the versions which gave the reader, more precise facts. The more explicit, it seems, within reason, the better.

But again, we should not overlook those readers who told us that experts simply do not read error-messages -- and certainly do not distinguish linguistic niceties.

Some of the early versions of the test included imperatives -- in this case, "CHECK LENGTH OF LOGICAL NAME". We expected that imperatives would be popular since they are conventionally accepted as the norm for instructions. Unfortunately, simply to say "CHECK" (which, in this context, means the same in both US and UK English: "inspect") did not have any appeal.

MESSAGE 4

EXPLANATION: Either HKV could not read as input file, or a terminal read error occurred.

4.1 ERROR IN FILE READING
4.2 ERROR IN READING OF FILE
4.3 FILE READING ERROR
4.4 FILE READ ERROR

RESULTS: 4.1: 23.6%
4.2: 34.1%
4.3: 17.5%
4.4: 24.8%

The original message (4.4) is a glaring example of linguistic distortion through truncation -- and, of course, of common computer dialect. As we have seen, the dialect is very attractive, and so we should not have been surprised at the even distribution of the results. Unhappily for the common prejudice that computer professionals are all thoroughly indoctrinated into this way of writing, our professional groups voted 2-1 for version 4.2.

What we have to take into account is the growing insensitivity of the readership. "FILE READ ERROR" must be a specialist usage, as it makes no sense as an imperative, but "FILE READING ERROR" has the same structure as "MAN READING MESSAGE," and makes just as little sense in the normal linguistic community.

We would argue -- and the results so far seem to support us -- that it is undesirable to distort the language when it is not necessary for "software" reasons. It is sometimes argued that memory space is at a premium, and so messages have to be shortened, at any cost. Certainly it is rare nowadays that machine memory is so limited that the interface with the human operator has to be restricted (Hahn and Athey, 1972; Heaps and Radhakrishnan, 1977). Indeed, even if it is so, it seems curious to produce a machine which can do very many things, but which cannot be used to do them. Similarly, compression and truncation of the language would be more defensible were it consistent (Hunt and Kirkman, 1986).

MESSAGE 5

EXPLANATION: An error occurred while displaying the requested data to the output device, or while performing output operations to the summary file.

5.1 ERROR IN SUMMARY OUTPUT OR DISPLAY
5.2 CHECK DISPLAY OR SUMMARY OUTPUT
5.3 INCORRECT DISPLAY OR SUMMARY OUTPUT
5.4 ERROR DURING DISPLAY OR SUMMARY OUTPUT

RESULTS:

5.1: 18.3%
5.2: 7.7%
5.3: 5.9%
5.4: 68.1%

We had expected that the word "CHECK" would have been a good way of beginning an error message (on the grounds that it is positive and precise). The fact that "DURING", with its slower "unloading rate" but greater closeness to ordinary language was the most popular, was not only surprising, but it was rather difficult to analyse. "Ordinary" language may be inaccurate, but without testing users of this system against users of other systems, we would not be able to be more confident about the results. In short, every qualification that we can make to our results indicates the caution with which usability research results must be approached.

MESSAGE 6

EXPLANATION: A keyword in the command has not been specified with enough characters to distinguish it from another keyword acceptable in this context. [Rectification: re-enter the command].

6.1 CHECK CHARACTERS IN COMMAND KEYWORD
6.2 RE-ENTER THE COMMAND
6.3 AMBIGUOUS COMMAND - SPECIFY CHARACTERS OF KEYWORD
6.4 AMBIGUOUS COMMAND

RESULTS:

6.1: 18.1%
6.2: 13.2%
6.3: 59.6%
6.4: 9.1%

One of the more obvious objections to our procedure (indeed, to all the error messages) was that no precise action was recommended. To test the effect of a positive action being included, we added the rectification message to Message 6 above.

The imperative "CHECK" had some followers, but, as some pointed out, 6.4 (the original) is unhelpfully cryptic, and the directive 6.2 is actually rather nonsensical -- after all, if it didn't work the first time, why should it work the second time? (We can leave aside the problem that this was what it said in the manual!) Beyond the fact that the message with the maximum information was the most popular, our optimistic predictions do not seem to have been justified.

MESSAGE 7

EXPLANATION: An attempt was made to dimension a display for which there was insufficient room.

7.1 NOT ENOUGH ROOM FOR ARRAY
7.2 DIM SPACE
7.3 YOUR ARRAY IS TOO LARGE
7.4 INSUFFICIENT SPACE FOR ARRAY

RESULTS:	7.1:	31.5%
	7.2:	0.0%
	7.3:	23.2%
	7.4:	45.3%

This final example differs from the others in that it was taken from a different company and a different type of machine. This was an error message on one of Britain's most popular beginner/trainer PC's. It seemed to us that the abrupt DIM SPACE (the original, of course) was not calculated to inform or to win friends. It seems that we were not alone. Perhaps only something as extreme as this could be expected to gain unanimity -- but, again, that should not be a foregone conclusion. On some of the arguments rehearsed above, there is no reason why an expert user of the system (or of any other system) should not find that completely comprehensible, succinct, and clear.

We also tried an informal approach (7.1), a "user friendly" second-person approach (7.3), and a more formal approach (7.4). It seemed to many that the second person was perhaps too user-familiar (especially in view of this particular message) -- something that is being observed increasingly with second-person structures. More interestingly, we found (contrary to stereotypical British -- and, perhaps, American -- prejudice) that users in the USA preferred a slightly more formal approach (7.4) than their British counterparts.

What Does This Mean For Usability Research?

The conclusions from the research, **per se**, are rather obvious:

- Use short, familiar words where possible.
- Include more information rather than less.
- Use "normal" English structures; avoid truncation and compression.
- Avoid the cryptic; include action messages; and simply define the problem.
- Consider your target audience; some may require less information than others.
- Choose a consistent and appropriate external image for the machine.

So far, so good. But it should be clear by now that, more importantly, all these conclusions are tentative, and could be totally invalid for any given user or set of users. They are based on simple and preliminary investigations, and ***no matter how far the experiments were proliferated*** , in style and numbers and kinds of audience, ***the answers would remain imprecise.*** This is the nature of this particular beast; it is difficult to provide guidelines for writing system messages because of differences of opinion and the probability of incompleteness (Dwyer, 1981a, 1981b; Golden, 1980).

However, this leaves us with the more interesting aspect of this research -- that is, the attitudes displayed by the recipients of the test. It took us some time to realise that the real value of this investigation might be not where we had supposed it to be. Our comments on all these tests have indicated areas of error, misapprehension, and disagreement of many kinds. Even when we thought we had isolated one linguistic/semantic factor (as in Message 5), there were no clear conclusions. In fact, even the conclusions leave many questions unanswered.

What the investigation showed was that even in a very restricted situation, there were very many "user-centered" variables which could not easily be accounted for, and that many "obvious" and "common sense" conclusions could be called into question by them. For example, are we dealing with experts or non-experts, frequent or infrequent users? Does that make a difference?

By this, we do not mean differences to responses caused by what people **knew** -- but from **how they felt** about messages, about testing, and about us. The "human factors" of testing are paramount.

A characteristic set of responses came from our pilot test with professional programmers. Some of their responses were either neutral or encouraging:

- "More variety of messages required."
- "All versions less than ideal."
- "I don't see why the full explanation could not be given. That is the best message."

and, most usefully:

- "Some experts read only the meaning and are oblivious of the linguistic forms."

Others took exception, tacitly or openly, to researchers from a humanities department (the research was based in the Communication Studies Unit of the Department of English) finding their way into computing. There was, for example, criticism (which was perfectly valid) of the use of the jargon "readability" in the original rubric.

More subtle was the reaction of one senior professional, who took us to task because he was a specialist on a different computer system from the one used as a basis for our examples. He argued that without specific knowledge of the system, no valid judgement could be made as to the relative accuracy of the messages. This was a rather high level piece of one-upmanship, suggesting that we were too unsophisticated to realise the basic flaw in our argument. Fortunately, he was a single objector and could thus be dismissed as deviant -- a dangerous urge in itself! His preoccupation was, however, more with the validity of the **explanations**, and he felt that, if he had to choose, the shortest message would be the best.

This was perhaps the most extreme example that we encountered. The implication was that to the expert, the screen message was of very little importance in comparison with the workings of the machine. It was pointed out that the true expert user (and, of course, all but one of these messages were aimed at the expert user) really only needed, if anything, a single word: **ERROR**. "I know," the senior professional said, "when I've made an error as soon as I have hit the key. I can't be bothered to wait while a long set of messages is put onto the screen." It is, perhaps, just this sort of attitude which generates incomprehensible messages, but it cannot be so lightly dismissed.

But all of this points to the schism which any researcher on language use in the world of computers soon encounters. This is the gap of comprehension, understanding, and sympathy between various kinds of users, between developer and writer, and between machines and users. Tests which explore "fixed" items such as language, should not assume that the logic which controls computer programs extends to those who work with them.

When we are working on usability research, we have to remember that we are not simply looking at a small part of a huge system in isolation. The operation is holistic; the reading of a text on a screen (or anywhere) depends entirely upon the place of the text and the reader in a system which may have links which are not obvious. We should not, for example, isolate ourselves from what is, in effect, usability research in other fields, such as **Rezeptiontheorie** (Holub, 1984) in psychology and literary criticism, or even "deconstruction" in philosophy and literary theory (Norris, 1982).

When we let hard-copy out into the world, we can have no guarantee of how the reader will handle it. Whatever signposts we put up (after all our efforts to write a brilliant introduction, the perverse reader insists on opening our book in the middle!), we cannot guarantee the response, or even the likely response of the individual. We might assume that in scientific contexts, texts will be "closed" -- that is, a totally clear, unambiguous communicative act. "Text" is only one part of communication.

Of course, meanings are common (in common-sense terms) within "interpretive communities" (Holland, 1968) -- that is, they are understood by certain groups and types of reader. We need to ask ourselves, in usability research, whether such generalities are good enough, and how they can be applied in real terms. Even with such clearly definable groups with such common aims as those we were working with, there was remarkable scope for misunderstanding and misinterpretation.

We should then take as much notice of the findings of reception theorists, as of system designers. Anything based on response is more suspect than many of us would wish. Questions (and test batteries) always contain within themselves their implied answers. Far from there being safety in numbers, the opposite, if anything, is true. *Even "common sense" is no guide, for it is only our very* ***local*** *sense to which we can refer.*

This may seem to be a counsel of despair; but, especially with computers, we are working with tools which may eventually be able to refine our very crude judgments. Because there is a long way to go, that is no reason not to make a start.

Note

1. In the error messages, we have eradicated any indication of the company, and we must stress that the less-than-successful examples we found were a tiny minority in the documentation. Our research applies to all computer documentation, although actual forms and dialects will differ from company to company.

References

Brown, P., "Error Messages: The Neglected Area of the Man-machine Interface,"*Communications of the ACM* , 26:4, pp. 246-249, 1983.

Dwyer, B., "Programming for Uscrs," *Computers and People* , pp. 11-14, 1981a.

Dwyer, B., "A User-Friendly Algorithm," *Communications of the ACM* , 24:9, pp. 556-561, 1981b.

Golden, D., "A Plea for Friendly Software," *Software Engineering Notes* , 5, p. 4, 1980.

Hahn, K.W., and J.G. Athey, "Diagnostic Messages," *Software, Practice and Experience* , 2, pp. 347-352, 1972.

Heaps, H.S., and T. Radhakrishnan, "Comparison of Diagnostic Messages for Compilers," *Software, Practice and Experience* , 7, pp. 139-144, 1977.

Holland, N.H., *The Dynamics of Literary Response,* NY: Oxford University Press, 1968.

Holub, R.C., *Reception Theory* , London and New York: Metheun, 1984.

Hunt, P.L., and J. Kirkman, "The Problems of Distorted English in Computer Documentation," *Technical Communication* , 33:3, pp. 150-156, 1986.

Kennedy, T.C.S., "Some Behavioural Factors Affecting the Training of Naive Users of an Interactive Computer System. *International Journal of Man-machine Studies* , 7, pp. 817-834, 1975.

Kirkman, J., *Good Style for Scientific and Engineering Writing* . London: Pitman, 1980.

Klare, G.R., *The Measurement of Readability*, Ames: Iowa State University Press, 1963.

Nickerson, R.S., "Man-computer Interaction: A Challenge for Human Factors Research," *IEEE Transactions on Man-machine Systems*, 10, pp. 164-180, 1969.

Norris, C.C., *Deconstruction: Theory and Practice*, London and New York: Methuen, 1982.

Rubenstein, R., and H. Hersh, *The Human Factor: Designing Computer Systems for People*, Burlington, Mass: Digital Press, 1984.

Shneiderman, B., "How to Design with the User in Mind," *Datamation*, 9, pp. 125-126, 1982a.

Shneiderman, B., "Systems Message Design: Guidelines and Experimental Results,"*Directions in Human/Computer Interaction*, A. Badre and B. Shneiderman, eds., Norwood, NJ: Ablex, pp. 55-78, 1982b.

Shneiderman, B., "The Future of Interactive Systems and the Emergence of Direct Manipulation," *Human Factors and Interactive Computer Systems*, Y. Vassiliou, ed., Norwood, NJ: Ablex, pp. 1-27, 1984.

Stewart, T.F.M., "Displays and the Software Interface," *Applied Ergonomics*, 7:3, pp. 137-146, 1976.

Turner, J.A., and R.A. Karasek, Jr., "Software Ergonomics: Effects of Computer Application Design on Operator Task Performance and Health,"*Ergonomics*, 27:6, pp. 663-690, 1984.

7 How People *Use* Computer Documentation: Implications for Book Design

Judith Ramey

Program in Scientific and Technical Communication
College of Engineering, FH-40
University of Washington
Seattle, WA 98195

Published complaints about the inadequacies of computer documentation abound, rich with anecdotes about particularly gross misunderstandings of user needs. But when it comes to suggesting ways to improve the documentation, frequently these articles retreat into the same broad generalities that are familiar to a reader of any basic textbook on technical writing and stylistics.

What would be more helpful, of course, would be a set of detailed examinations of exactly what users look for and expect to find in the manual that accompanies the computer hardware and software that they have bought, and an equally detailed set of studies of the methods they use in working with the manual. But before anyone can offer such detailed examinations, a number of studies of documentation use must be done; and, of course, we can expect that users' habits and needs will prove to be as diverse in this area as they are in most other areas of human activity.

Pending the publication of the results of such comprehensive studies, however, we can look at currently published basic research on more general questions of document design, and at the preliminary evidence that is available from small sets of usability tests, conducted with one degree of formality or another, in order to begin to reason our way toward more functional documentation. This chapter attempts to contribute to that process, both by summarizing a small number of relevant laboratory studies and by reporting on the results of my own less formal usability tests.

Over the past three years I have conducted a number of usability tests for computer companies, among them Microsoft Corporation of Bellevue, WA, and Aldus Corporation of Seattle, WA (the makers of PageMaker desktop publishing software). Although these tests vary in topical coverage, methodology, and rigor, nevertheless the results concerning the use of documentation are surprisingly amenable to summary. Looked at as a whole, the results of these tests suggest that when people are given a task or set of tasks to carry out on a computer, in consulting the computer documentation they generally use one or another subset of a small number of habits and preferences. Although some of these habits and preferences are mutually exclusive, it appears that they all can be accommodated by a single well-thought-out book design. The following discussion specifies, in a preliminary way that can be confirmed by further research, the characteristics of such a book design. It focuses on three areas: fundamental presentational strategies in computer documentation, tools for supporting users' strategies in searching for information, and design for supporting strategies of page use.

A Prefatory Note on Test Methodologies

The usability tests that I have conducted have been focused on the documentation for and human-computer interfaces of *specific* computer products. Nevertheless, the observations conducted during the tests, the questionnaires administered during the tests, and the questions addressed in focus groups associated with the tests all attempted to take into account (to one degree or another) the subjects' basic, general expectations about and patterns of use of computer documentation.

All of these tests included the observation of subjects using a computer supported by documentation to do a set of tasks. In all cases, the subjects were encouraged to think out loud as they worked, and their comments were recorded (either manually by an observer using pencil and paper, or automatically by audiotape). However, in most of the later tests, the "thinking-aloud protocol" was not the only or even the primary means of gathering data.

In these later tests, I also gathered quantifiable data by means of a questionnaire administered at the end of each task in the task set for the test. (A test generally consisted of up to about six tasks; each task was designed to take the subject through a specific portion of the product's functionality or the documentation's coverage.) The questionnaire, which was exactly the same for all subjects and all tasks in a given test, basically asked subjects to respond to a set of questions of various types:

* yes-no questions ("Did you use the manual while doing this task?")

* ordering questions ("If you used any of the following parts of the manual during this task, number them in the order that you used them.")

* scalar ranking questions ("How easy or difficult was it to find the topics you needed to do this task?" 1 = very easy, 5 = very difficult)

* short-answer questions ("What terms did you look for that were not in the index?")

* a small number of open-ended questions ("What were your two biggest problems in using the documentation during this task?").

(Note that the questions and instructions quoted in this list are examples only, to suggest the type of material being described; they did not necessarily appear on any actual questionnaire.)

These questionnaires were very useful in providing topical continuity from subject to subject, for providing "apples and apples" comparative data between different parts of the human-computer interface or documentation, for providing a common background of information upon which to interpret the thinking-aloud-protocol results, and (in those cases where debriefings or focus groups were planned) for suggesting directions for less structured discussions and group explorations.

In many of the tests, I followed up the test procedure itself with a focus group or debriefing of all the subjects in a given category (all managers, for instance, or all secretaries), in which I attempted to probe for the thinking that lay behind their comments and responses to the questionnaires. These focus groups took place almost immediately following the test itself (following a break of from 15 minutes to one hour).

Because of the differences among the tests, the results are not directly comparable. Also, because of the nature of the particular tests that I have done, the results are directly reliable only for printed documentation, although I believe that they can be interpreted for on-line documentation as well. However, the sum of results is consistent and can be interpreted to provide rules-of-thumb about users' general expectations about and behavior with computer documentation. Based on these rules-of-thumb, we can draw conclusions about characteristics of book design that will most successfully support users in using computers.

Before looking at specific recommendations based on these usability tests, however, it is important to remind ourselves of the context in which they must be used: to design documents that somebody will use virtually in tandem with using a computer. Thus documentation design for computer systems is complicated by some of the basic characteristics of computer use itself. But at the same time it is enriched and supported by results from research in the broader area of reading habits and characteristics generally speaking. The following two sections, then, discuss 1) some of the basic problems in designing computer manuals that arise from the linkage with computer use, and 2) useful research results in the study of reading and reading comprehension.

Basic Problems in Designing Computer Manuals

The results of the tests I have done are consistent with and support the validity of three basic points that bear on the complicating characteristics of human-computer interaction -- complicating characteristics that also affect the success of documentation.

More Like Hearing than Reading

The first point is that computer use is much more like *hearing* than like reading -- users have only limited backward sweeping review of their actions so far in the course of doing a task; they cannot "skim ahead" to ascertain the relative importance or implications of what they are doing now; and they usually have only limited means available at the computer itself to determine the full scope and coverage of the functionality of the computer system. Just as hearers need cues from a speaker to help them keep track of the organization of a speech, computer users need structured documentation to provide the context for their ongoing sequences of actions. Thus, the book design of manuals (or of sets of manuals) needs to allow for providing users with a more complete view of their courses of action.

Use of Mental Models, Schemas, and Prior Knowledge

The second point is that research suggests that the ability to construct *inferences* from events or information, to be used in predicting the importance of the events or the meaning and usefulness of the information, is highly influenced by affective individual values and personal mental models, cognitive schemas, and prior knowledge. (A mental model or cognitive schema is a plan or a framework of ideas on a given topic, built in our heads out of our experience, against which we compare new experiences or information on the topic and based on which we develop further compatible expectations about the topic.) That is to say, we *reason* better about topics we care about and about topics that are already familiar.

Designers build cognitive schemas into the systems they design (either schemas they have explicitly designed to serve the user, or, inadvertently, their own schemas), and these mental models and schemas often differ from those of their users (1, 2, 3). The documentation can explain the model or schema that animates the design of the system, thus bridging the gap between the designer's understanding or point of view and the user's. Without such an explanation, users can find themselves blocked by their own preconceptions from even realizing that a different interpretation of the facts is possible, let alone required (4).

In fact, users frequently need for the documentation to provide the link between what they *want* to do and what the computer *can* do. Thus, book design also needs to provide users the ability to rely on their own pre-existing knowledge of the work they do; the documentation can exploit this pre-existing knowledge most effectively by organizing the computer's functionality into the *user's* tasks and terminology and the user's basic reasoning skills (5, 6, 7).

Designers of computer documentation must remember that users need for the documentation that accompanies a system to address these problems, which have to do with building a personally explicable, durable, and reliable informational context for using the computer to do work.

Resistance to Reading

But the situation is complicated by the fact that about one-half to three-quarters (depending on the test) of computer users (based on the sample represented by the subjects of my usability tests) want to spend very little time reading, and especially do not want to read continuous discourse -- instead, they want to spend their time on actual use of the computer itself. They skip sections that look like overviews, introductions, and so on, and scan down the page looking for specific steps that they can follow.

Therefore, book design, at the same time that it meets the above goals of providing a strong context for computer use that offsets the "hearing-like" characteristics of using a computer and that reflects the experience and goals of the users, also has to allow users to "drop into" a manual at the appropriate point, get information presented quickly in the terms they understand, and return to the task at hand, with minimum disruption of their thought processes and interruption of the work itself.

Although these sets of requirements may seem contradictory, nevertheless both can be accommodated by careful book design. What is required is a design that accommodates at least two different styles of usage equally well: a style that relies on context-setting overviews, introductions, etc., and a style that specifically wants cues to make it easy to skip over these features.

Useful Research in Reading and Reading Comprehension

Research in reading and reading comprehension offers a number of insights into the kind of text presentation that enables people to grasp information most easily (8). These studies, however, were generally carried out in the context of educational research and thus are not directly generalizable to the case of an adult reader whose reading is secondary to another activity (computer use). Nevertheless, several studies seem to support rules-of-thumb that writers have long believed and that bear directly on document design for computer systems.

One study documents the fact that readers recall information more easily when a text is organized logically, when the introductory paragraph is informative, and when the paragraphs contain topic sentences (9). Another supports the notion that people read and understand directions faster when the general organizational information for a procedure occurs *before* the directions rather than after (10).

A further study attempts to explain why conventional paragraph structure, in which a topic sentence is presented first, followed by explicitly connected coherent sentences, is preferred; it concludes that this paragraph structure improves recognition of the theme of the paragraph, lessens reading time, and improves recall. It suggests that it does this because paragraphs of this form facilitate loading the information into deeper memory and thus lessen the load on short-term memory (11).

Other studies support the idea that using signaling techniques in expository prose (for example, preview sentences, underlined headings, and logical connective phrases) increases the understandability of the prose (12). But my colleague Jan Spyridakis, in a review of the literature on signalling, warns that overall the studies are not conclusive and calls for more studies and for studies focused directly on technical communication (13).

Finally, some studies examine alternatives to prose presentations of information; one such study finds that when information was presented in three forms (prose, table, or flowchart), the prose was always slower to use and more error-prone. The other two forms yielded different results depending on the complexity of the problem; for easier problems, the table was used most rapidly, but for harder problems, the flowchart/algorithm gave fewest errors (14).

This brief survey of the research results available in the literature on reading and reading comprehension can only suggest the range of findings that can be used in documentation design for computer systems. Caution will be necessary until these results have been replicated specifically for this kind of documentation; however, the designer can work with greater confidence knowing that there is at least a provisionally sound research basis for choices in text design.

The following section recommends specific strategies in book design based on the habits and preferences expressed by the subjects in the usability tests that I have conducted.

Usability Tests: Practical Implications for Book Design

The practical implications for book design of the above points and of the results of the usability tests I have conducted can be divided into three areas: fundamental presentational strategies, tools for supporting search strategies, and page design for supporting use strategies.

Fundamental Presentational Strategies

Users consistently ask for certain strategies in documentation to make their search for information less painful and more flexible across the life of their use of the documentation. I will discuss two types of strategy: 1) user and task orientation, and 2) layering.

User and Task Orientation. Repeatedly, in the usability tests that I have conducted, the subjects have expressed frustration with their inability to figure out how to equate their understanding of the task to be done with the computer's terminology and functional organization, or to map from one to the other.

To provide users with information that is immediately usable, computer documentation must be user-oriented. This term has been used in a number of different senses; here, it means that the functionality of the computer system or application being documented must be organized into the terminology and task sequences that its users already understand or can readily grasp after brief training.

For instance, the documentation for a general business word-processing system might use the task heading "printing a form-letter" rather than "Print Merge Command" (although, of course, if the *system* is not user- and task-oriented in this way, the documentation has to go on to teach the user the equivalent terms). Also, the manual might discuss "writing a letter" and "printing an envelope" in the same general section.

Or, in a system designed to automate the business of a public library, the tasks of checking out books to a patron, seeing if a patron has an overdue book, and if so, determining the fine that is due, might all be discussed under a heading that means "transactions at the front desk." (In a system currently on the market, these activities are treated as unrelated transactions both in the menu structure and in the documentation; the librarians whom I spoke to were eloquent about this failure of logic and the unnecessary complexities it introduced into system use.)

Again, in a system that is intended to automate the preparation of overhead transparencies ("graphics" or "visuals") for people who give oral presentations, it should be easy to make "bulleted" lists (lists of items or discussion points in which each item is indented from the left margin and marked by an asterisk or other "bullet"). However, in a product for which I conducted a usability test, inserting a bullet in a master for a transparency required five to eight keystrokes (depending on the strategy), and what is worse, the word "bullet" did not occur in either the Table of Contents or in the Index -- this in spite of the fact that the subjects for the usability test identified bulleted lists as occurring on 75% or more of the transparencies they used in presentations.

But successfully user- and task-oriented documentation must go beyond plain descriptions of pieces of work you can do using the system; it ought to include two further features: *user strategies* and *anticipation of likely errors.* Again and again, across a broad spectrum of products, subjects of usability tests that I have done complain that documentation attempts to teach only two (nearly opposite) kinds of information -- the very broadest, and the most detailed: basic concepts (what a file is, for instance), on the one hand, and keystroke or menu-pick details for executing commands, on the other. Furthermore, the documentation seems to them to have been written in a vacuum -- as if no one out there in the world would actually ever have to *use* the information.

They ask for *user strategies* that help them integrate the conceptual and keystroke-level information efficiently. For instance, in documenting a word processing program that has a paragraph formatting feature, the manual could point out that if you use the formatting feature for the very first paragraph you enter, then all of your succeeding paragraphs will have the same format without your having to intervene further.

They also want *anticipation of likely errors.* For example, assume that a text editor includes a command named "substitute" that lets the user search for specified terms and replace them with others; the command uses the following syntax: "substitute *oldtext newtext.*" The fact is that no speaker of English will say "substitute for old text new text" -- the natural English syntax of this statement is "substitute new text for old text." This contradiction between the syntax of the command and the syntax called for by the identical English word means that a significant portion of the users of this text editor will get the command terms backwards most of the time. *Users want to be warned ahead of time about problems like this.* (For a discussion of natural versus truncated language, see Hunt and Vasiliades in this volume.)

Depending on the complexity of your audience, following this principle may mean that you have to prepare several manuals, one for each major segment of your audience, instead of just one.

Within a given manual, the chapter titles, headings, and subheadings must effectively organize the computer's capabilities into the terms that the user already understands; in the actual information included under each, the documentation can then present any system-specific terminology that the user needs to learn.

Again, the subjects in my tests frequently encountered instructions the intent of which they could not fathom. To paraphrase the response of many to this circumstance, "why would anybody want to *do* that?" Introductions to complicated task sequences or descriptions of tasks the use of which is not obvious should include a statement of the broader goals or uses of the actions in the user's terms.

Finally, a point that is inexplicably controversial: if the product you are documenting is intended to be directly competitive with a second product, and if that other product is already better established than yours in the market, then your index ought to include the terminology of the rival product, with cross-references to your own terminology. Some companies argue that indexing your opponents' terms both lengthens your index unnecessarily and grants unwarranted authority to your competitor; but common sense (and the results of usability tests) indicates that doing so makes the product more accessible and easier to use for people who are migrating from the old to the new product.

Admittedly, user and task orientation is much easier for vertical-market systems (all lawyers, for instance, or all engineers, or all librarians) than for truly general-purpose computers. But even when the system being documented has not been designed for a given profession or task world, it is still possible to organize the documentation around *system* tasks (for instance, "backing up the system using the tape drive" instead of a simple alphabetical list of commands), and to name those system tasks (at least in the index) according to terminology or terminologies understood by the various segments of the market.

Layering. In trying to use a system for the first time, many of the subjects in my tests rebelled against what they considered a deluge of descriptions of alternative ways to do a single action, options that could be used in more sophisticated uses of commands, etc. They wanted a section that presented only the basic, plain-vanilla approach to the task at hand -- a *skeleton* of the very basic procedure (for, say, creating a chart). On the other hand, they did not want the other information left out altogether; they wanted it to be presented in a section or sections on more advanced techniques.

Note that this preference has to do with *procedural* information; the users are not asking for a *tutorial* here, but for a task presentation that has at least two layers -- beginning and advanced. In fact, in several tests where the subjects made comments of this sort, they had previously had an opportunity to work through a tutorial. (A *tutorial* has a structure that is designed to *teach* -- it almost always uses real tasks, but they have been selected because they are convincing and efficient at conveying the rules and the power of the system; the emphasis is on building an enduring perception of the system, a mental model. A *procedure*, on the other hand, while it may incorporate explanations and may be very slow-paced, is really focused on getting the user to do the action correctly *now,* without worrying primarily about creating a lasting perception of the overall system workings.)

Tools for Supporting Search Strategies

In my tests, the following devices for supporting the search strategies of users have been studied and found to be useful; although this list certainly does not exhaust the kinds of tools that can support search strategies, it does provide some information and guidance about the needs of users in this area.

Thorough Index. The subjects in the tests I have conducted report that they rely heavily on the index of a manual to locate information; they use the index about twice as often as the table of contents to search for information.

In fact, in one test, the subjects worked through a tutorial and then returned two days afterward to attempt a set of tasks modeled carefully on the structure of the tutorial they had already done; in looking for guidance in doing steps they had forgotten, the majority turned to the index of the manual rather than to the part of the tutorial that covered a virtually identical task.

These subjects prefer a good multi-level index that includes the terms they normally use as well as the equivalent terms specific to the computer system. They also want a good system of cross-references.

Comprehensive Table of Contents. The next most frequently used tool for searching for information was the table of contents. Users want complete, informative TOCs that enable them to narrow down their search for a specific piece of information while at the same time giving them a view of the task context in which it plays a part.

Tabs. By tabs I mean the cardstock-weight dividers inserted between sections of the manual that have a stub that protrudes beyond the outside edge of the page -- the user can read the manual's section names on these stubs and can flip through the manual easily by using them. Tabs can also be implemented by printing a bar on part of the very outside edge of the page, so that the printed bars for each section are staggered down the outside edge of the closed manual ("bleed tabs"). About half of the subjects in tests where they were asked about tabs indicated that they used tabs, in conjunction with the Table of Contents, as the primary means of locating information. They wanted tabs durable (preferably laminated) and printed on both sides; some asked for additional blank tabs to be included in the package to allow them to customize the manual to their needs. Even though the other half of the subjects in these tests said that they did not use tabs, these people can more easily remove tabs than the first group can create home-made ones, so it seems wiser to include them.

Other Structural Devices. Other devices that users have asked for to help them build and use search strategies for information include internal tables of contents (at the beginning of each major subsection, for instance), cross-references (ideally with the page number, so that the user doesn't have to conduct a second search), and *alternative* tables of contents, for instance to support both the user who wants to look up a specific command name and the user who wants to search by task name instead.

Page Design for Supporting Use Strategies

The hard fact is that people simply do not want to spend their time reading computer documentation; anything that a book designer can do to lessen the textual impact of a manual will, it seems, improve its usability.

Graphic Devices. Users prefer presentations that rely on graphic cues combined with phrases, rather than full-sentence exposition.

Resemblance between the Appearance of the Product Interface and of the Documentation. With the growing popularity of products with graphic user interfaces (products for the Macintosh or for the Microsoft Windows environment or other graphics-based interfaces), users are becoming dissatisfied with the continuing dominance of text-based documentation. They want graphics-based documentation for products with graphics-based interfaces. (For a discussion of research on graphic user interfaces, see Krull in this volume.)

GUI-DOC (graphic-user-interface documentation) relies on pictures of interface parts rather than terms for them: icons, boxes, buttons, bars, and so forth. Frequently, users simply do not know and cannot recognize the terms for these graphic features; they recognize them immediately when they are *shown* them in the documentation. For instance, one subject of a usability test that I did pointed out that the document asked her to select an item from a "list box;" when she looked at the screen, there were three different boxes visible, all of which seemed to have a "selection" available. Her comment, delivered with equal parts of volume and humor, was "SHOW ME!"

Formatting and White Space. Users rely on heavy formatting for guidance of the eye and generous white space for segmenting the page. These characteristics make it easier for them to switch their attention from page to screen and back without losing their place. Without these page characteristics, they occasionally skip or repeat steps, re-read, and otherwise waste time. (For a discussion of research on format design, see Rubens and Rubens in this volume.)

Cues Marking Information Type and Function. Again and again, the subjects in my tests asked for distinctive formats and other cues to be used so that they could immediately identify the kind of information contained in a paragraph or other presentational unit. Frequently, they use these cues to organize their strategy for using the documentation rather than for using the system *per se*. That is, some users rely on examples in the documentation to inform their use of the system; others (often the minority) want the context provided by an overview before they begin to work; others want to follow a specific set of steps (as opposed to an example).

Users want overviews, introductions, etc., that are clearly visually differentiated from step-by-step procedures. Frequently, they want this information differentiated so that they can reliably skip it; for this reason, a presentation of a procedure must be sure to include all necessary preliminaries, warnings, and so forth in the form of a step (for instance, by asking the user in a separate step to determine the applicability of a warning or caution). They also want page references in the index to visually convey the distinction in the type of information; they want the page numbers for beginner information and for basic procedural information (as opposed to description) to be in a different typeface from the other entries.

They want heading levels treated typographically in such a way that they can tell where they are in a hierarchy of discussion without having to have more than one or two heading levels visible to them at a given moment. They want examples to follow a uniform format, both visually and organizationally. They want syntax diagrams to be rigorously controlled as to what they include and how they look on the page. They want in-text cross-references to be easy to see and interpret (used, for instance, to mark a procedure that also appears in the tutorial, in the advanced section, or in the command reference section, or a term that appears in the on-line help)

Conclusion

The most heartening aspect of the results of the usability tests that I have conducted is that they, generally speaking, agree with the intuitions and insights of careful and sophisticated editing and document evaluation. The collective wisdom and common sense of experienced document designers seems, pending more tests done under more rigorous laboratory controls, to be affirmed. Thus the recommendations presented here are not unusual in being radically new, but rather in being reaffirmed by recourse to users -- users whose insights have been captured not in isolation but in the process of their *using* the documents being evaluated.

References

1. Dagwell, Ron and Weber, Rob. "System Designers' User Models: A Comparative Study and Methodological Critique," *Communications of the ACM*, November 1983, Vol. 26, no. 11.

2. Carey, Tom, "User Differences in Interface Design," *IEEE Computer*, 15 (1), November 1982.

3. Mac an Airchinnigh, Michael, "Some Notes on the Representation of the User's Conceptual Model," *SIGCHI Bulletin*, a publication of ACM Special Interest Group on Computer & Human Interaction, October 1984.

4. Anderson, R.C., R.E. Reynolds, D.L. Schallert, and E.T. Goetz, "Frameworks for Comprehending Discourse," *American Educational Research Journal,* Fall 1977, vol. 14, no. 4, p. 367-81.

5. Anderson, R. C., Reynolds, R.E., Schallert, D.L., and Goetz, E.T., *op.cit.*

6. Alvermann, D.E. Smith, L.C., and Readance, J.E. "Prior Knowledge Activation and the Comprehension of Compatible and Incompatible Text," *Reading Research Quarterly,* (1985) 20, 4, 421-436.

7. Lewis, Clayton, "A Model of Mental Model Construction," *CHI '86 Proceedings,* ACM, 1986, p. 306. Describes a set of basic heuristics for interpreting common computer interaction patterns.

8. I am grateful to my colleague at UW, Jan Spyridakis, for bringing the research in reading and reading comprehension to my attention.

9. Lorch, R.F., Jr. and E.P. Lorch, "Topic Structure Representation and Text Recall," *Journal of Educational Psychology,* 1985, vol. 77, no. 2, p. 137.

10. Dixon, P., "The Processing of Organizational and Component-Step Information in Written Directions," *Journal of Memory and Language,* 26, 24-35 (1987).

11. Kieras, D., "Good and Bad Structure in Simple Paragraphs: Effects on Apparent Theme, Reading Time, and Recall," *Journal of Verbal Learning and Verbal Behavior,* 17 (1978), p. 13.

12. Loman, N.L., and R.E. Mayer, "Signal Techniques that Increase the Understandability of Expository Prose," *Journal of Educational Psychology,* 1983, vol. 75, no. 3, p. 402.

13. Spyridakis, Jan, "Authors' Plans Meet Readers' Plans," *Proceedings of the ITCC,* 1987.

14. Wright, P., and Fraser Reid, " Written Information: Some Alternatives to Prose for Expressing the Outcomes of Complex Contingencies," *Journal of Applied Psychology,* 1973, vol. 57, no. 2, p. 160.

8 Similarities and Differences in Developing Effective Online and Hardcopy Tutorial

Brenda Knowles Rubens
Myers Corners Laboratory
IBM Corporation

Introduction

There is much interest today in presenting information via a computer screen. Futurists talk of the paperless office as if it is right around the corner. However, as a friend of mine so nicely put it, the idea of the paperless office today is just about as realistic as the paperless bathroom. While most of us still shuffle paper every week at our jobs, there is a push in industry to put more and more information online. Perhaps the major impetus for this push is a financial consideration. In the long run, online information is cheaper than printed copy (Chambers and Sprecher, 1981). "As paper costs increase and electronic communication and display costs decrease, the use of computer video displays is becoming more prevalent in our society" (Merrill, 1982). Another important factor is the ease and speed of updating online documentation in comparison to hardcopy. Changes are being made so rapidly in computer systems that printed manuals are often obsolete soon after they are published. Online information can be changed and distributed in a fraction of the time it takes to make comparable changes in hardcopy.

Also, online information offers advantages to the user; this aspect is becoming more and more critical to industry as competition in the marketplace increases. (It has always been of primary importance to those of us who are the users!) An online tutorial or reference guide is easy to use at a terminal. Often trying to position a book in just the right spot at a work station is difficult. Even more often, there is no right spot available, and users awkwardly try to balance a manual on their knees or prop it between keyboard and screen.

In the case of instructional material, an online tutorial can provide different paths for a variety of users from the beginner to the more advanced user. The same features in hardcopy might call for more than one manual or at least some bothersome flipping from one section to another. An effective online tutorial can make such choices invisible to the user. In other words, the page flipping that might be required in a hardcopy text to route the user to various paths through the information must be done by the user. With an online tutorial, equivalent page flipping is done by the computer, so that users see only a smooth flow of information after they make the initial path selection. This puts an increased burden on the developers and writers of the information and less of a burden on the user.

Unfortunately, the move to put information online has not yet made the user's life that much easier. The ideal scenario is that, instead of letters, memos, messages, and other hardcopy reports we will receive all information via a computer, access it electronically, and read it on a computer screen. While electronic mail is already very much in place in many companies, the majority of workers still rely on paper copies of reports, pamphlets, books, and manuscripts. Because we tend to resist reading long passages of prose or scanning screensful of numbers and figures online, most of us resort to making hardcopy printouts of lengthy online reports (Bradford and Rubens, 1985).

Although there is a very real effort and need to reduce the amount of paper production in government and industry by using the computer as a convenient alternative medium for communicating and distributing information, the new medium itself presents unique usability problems. All too often the principles related to the design and layout of printed materials are applied indiscriminately to the design of computer video displays (Merrill, 1982). Therefore, we must consider the problems in transferring material from the printed page to the electronic screen to ensure ease-of-use for everyone who will be affected. Leaders in industry express their concern as more and more text goes online; they want empirical evidence that online text provides a productive alternative to hardcopy text.

This study looks at the differences in usability between a hardcopy, printed tutorial and an electronic, online tutorial. Developers of computer-assisted instruction (CAI) were pioneers in taking material developed for a traditional, print medium and transferring it to the new, electronic medium. Unfortunately, very few changes were made to the print-oriented programmed instruction other than putting it online and calling it CAI. Even today, "successful curriculum developers in older media treat the new medium just like the older one," but there are "great differences between the computer display and these older media" (Bork et al, 1983).

What are these differences? And does the medium contribute to or subtract from the effectiveness of a tutorial? This chapter will describe a study designed to answer these questions and find out how the medium affects the usability of the product. In this chapter I will discuss:

1. the issues involved in online versus printed texts;
2. the study itself, its design and findings;
3. suggestions for further research; and
4. the practical applications of the findings.

Online Versus Printed Text

There are important differences in online and printed text that affect usability. We do not look at a printed page and a computer screen the same way. The angle at which we view the text is different. The resolution of most video screens affects the sharpness and clarity of images online; therefore, the quality of text online suffers in comparison to the printed page (Bork, 1983). In addition, most screens can only display about 24 lines of text with from 40 to 80 characters per line depending on the hardware configuration. "Full screens of text are difficult to read and quite annoying to users. Blank space should be used in a liberal fashion with video displays" (Merrill, 1982). A standard page in a book that is completely filled with type looks much more acceptable than a full screen of text. This phenomenon is largely due to the added work reading text online poses for our eyes. While the contrast between the background and the type on a printed page is constant, the contrast between the background and type on a display screen is not because of the instability of the image. This results in a sort of flicker effect that we do not encounter when reading printed material. There is also glare from a video display, and the curved surface of the screen forces the eye to continually change focal lengths in order to read the text. Aside from these physical differences in the two media, there is the mystique that surrounds the computer.

People tend to regard the computer as "alien, mysterious and inherently difficult to use" (Mann, 1975). Such words as computerphobia and technophobia illustrate the sense of uneasiness that surrounds the medium. Indeed, the computer is a very complex medium. But until recently, too little thought and research has been given to the special difficulties in preparing information to present via a computer screen. Unfortunately, even today, the easiest method is simply to transfer text from a hardcopy medium (if it exists in this form) to the online medium with minimal effort. If any changes are made at all, more often than not, they are changes to the format of the text to make it fit on the screen better.

While there are many usability problems to address, a single study is limited in scope. The online tutorial is, perhaps, the most visible and popular type of online information for beginning computer users. Because many of these tutorials instruct new users in basic computer usage, they serve as an introduction to the computer in general and play a critical role in the diffusion process of the computer. Researchers concur that a "single well-constructed tutorial can influence (users) much more effectively than hardware considerations" (Al Awar, et al, 1981). Conversely, a poorly designed tutorial can cause even enthusiastic beginners to throw up their hands in dismay.

The Study

Three of the variables in this study are key features of CAI that earlier research in programmed instruction identified as critical to the development of effective instructional material: step size, response mode, and success rate. In addition to these variables, the presentation medium is an important independent variable.

Step size simply means the amount of text presented to the user before an action or response is required. It does not refer to the actual characters and lines of text displayed on each screen.

Response mode refers to the type of response required of the user. An *active response* occurs when a user actually has to do something such as type in a command or think of an answer to a question and key in that answer. A *passive response* occurs when a user is merely presented with information and not required to respond or is only required to select a multiple choice response from a list of several possibilities. Of course there are a variety of different types of active and passive responses. For this study, users either write or type out an answer to a question (active or constructed response); or they select an answer from a multiple choice list (passive response).

Success rate is the number of correct responses a user makes as s/he goes through the instructional material. Success rate differs from step size and response mode in that it is a dependent variable (what is measured). The step size and response mode are independent variables--variables that the researcher manipulates. For example, guided by other research, I define four levels of step size. (For a more extensive discussion of step size see "How The Study Was Conducted.") While I can manipulate response mode and step size, I cannot manipulate the number of answers a user gets correct as they go through the tutorial. Like the amount of time it takes for each user to complete the tutorial, the success rate depends on the user and not on the researcher.

The **medium** itself is an important independent variable. Does the computer influence how we process information? Several studies have concluded that we read online text significantly slower than we read hardcopy text, yet researchers have no clear idea why this is so (John Gould and Nancy Grischkowsky, 1984; Kak, 1981; Muter et al 1982; Wright and Lickorish, 1983; Shneiderman, 1983). A similar kind of study comparing editing online and hardcopy texts, found that participants edited hardcopy text much faster than online text and made fewer errors (Gould and Grischkowsky, 1984). Numerous researchers are focussing considerable attention on hardcopy and online text in an effort to understand if and how they are different (Merrill, 1982; Bork, 1983; Carroll and Mazur, 1984; Gould, 1984; Kruk and Muter, 1984).

The present study does not attempt to test all the possible differences between online and printed text. Rather, its purpose is to determine if presentation of the same instructional material both in printed form and on the computer results in differences in success rate, completion time, satisfaction, and learning over time.

Major Hypotheses

The primary research questions investigated in this study are listed below:

- Active responding (constructed response) will result in higher posttest scores than passive responding (multiple-choice).
- Posttest scores will differ between online and hardcopy users.
- Step size and medium will influence the number of errors participants make as they complete the tutorial.
- The online version of the tutorial will take longer to complete than the hardcopy version.
- Participants using the online tutorial will give it a higher rating than those using the hardcopy tutorial.

How The Study Was Conducted

To test whether step size, response mode, and medium affect participants' learning of instructional material, 80 participants completed one of 8 versions of a tutorial that differs according to step size and medium.

Step Size: A single step of information constitutes one useful chunk of instructional material. By useful, I mean that the chunk or unit of information provides information to the learner that results in a successful interaction with the computer (if executed correctly) or provides the learner with a simple but adequate definition of a specific function, operation, or term. As indicated by the following list, the four levels of the tutorial for this study comprise a 1, 6, 12, and 24 chunk step level. At the first step level, 1 unit or chunk of information is presented to the user before a response is called for. At the second step level, 6 units or chunks of information are presented to the user before a response is called for. At the third step level, 12 units or chunks of information are presented before a response is called for. And, finally, at the fourth step level, all 24 units or chunks of information are presented before responses are called for.

Medium: The tutorial was presented in either an online (CAI) version or a hardcopy version. As the following list shows, each version of the tutorial includes both constructed response (active) and multiple-choice questions (passive).

1a. 1-chunk step size: first half constructed response (active), second half multiple-choice response (passive).

1b. 1-chunk step size: first half multiple-choice, second half constructed response.

2a. 6-chunk step size: first half constructed response, second half multiple-choice.

2b. 6-chunk step size: first half multiple-choice, second half constructed response.

3a. 12-chunk step size: first half constructed response, second half multiple-choice.

3b. 12-chunk step size: first half multiple-choice, second half constructed response.

4a. 24-chunk step size: first half constructed response, second half multiple-choice.

4b. 24-chunk step size: first half multiple-choice, second half constructed response.

Procedure

All participants took a pretest to determine prior knowledge of the subject matter and filled out a demographic questionnaire. Forty users completed an online tutorial that teaches specific aspects of the programming language BASIC and some editing procedures on the IBM Personal Computer. Forty users completed a hardcopy version of the same tutorial.

Participants progressed linearly through both tutorials, responding to questions at each level of step size. They could not go back to a previous screen or page of information. In this way, size of step was strictly controlled. Participants took as long as they wanted to complete the tutorial. A pilot study conducted with 38 communications graduate students at a technological school found that students took approximately 20 to 30 minutes to complete the tutorial. The pilot study used basically the same tutorial as the present study and tested the same variables. Immediately upon completion of the tutorial, participants responded to an opinion questionnarie that asked them to rate the tutorial on several dimensions such as user preference and the tutorial's effectiveness as a teaching tool.

One week after their session with the tutorial, participants took a posttest to measure their comprehension of the instructional material. The posttest is based on the programmed text; however, the questions in the posttest do not duplicate questions from the tutorial.

Participants

The participants for this study were primarily inexperienced computer users who were unfamiliar with the BASIC programming language and the IBM Personal Computer. The 40 undergraduate communications students (24 females, 16 males) from a 4-year liberal arts school who completed the hardcopy tutorial ranged from 19 to 29 years of age with an average age of 22 and a median age of 21. The average amount of computer experience for this group was 14 months with a range in experience from 0 to 7 years. Of this group, 31 rated themselves as naive computer users, 3 had used only the word processing capabilities of the computer, and 6 said they were comfortable using a variety of software applications. Pretest scores showed that their knowledge of the subject matter taught in the tutorial was very low; 85 per cent scored 0 on the pretest.

The 40 students (23 females and 17 males) who completed the online tutorial were from a 4-year technological school; 30 were graduate students and 10 were undergraduates. The graduate students were predominantly technical communications majors with non-technological undergraduate degrees. They ranged from 17 to 55 years of age with an average age of 26 and a median age of 23. The average amount of computer experience for this group was 24 months with a range in experience from 0 to 8 years. Of this group, 19 rated themselves as naive computer users, 7 had only used computers as word processors, and 14 said they were comfortable using a variety of software applications on computers. Pretest scores indicated that their knowledge of the subject matter taught in the tutorial was very low; 90 per cent scored 0 on the pretest.

Because two of the hypotheses of this study posit differences in learning and completion times attributable to the medium, the differences between schools is a confounding source of variance in the design. In other words, differences apparently due to the media might actually be due to differences in the schools. To strengthen the study, a third group of 16 undergraduate communications students (9 females, 7 males) from the liberal arts university completed the online version of the tutorial. These data were combined with the hardcopy data collected from the same school 6 months earlier and post hoc analyses were conducted. These students ranged from 19 to 30 years of age with a mean and median age of 21. The average amount of computer experience for this group was 18 months wiht a range in experience from 0 to 8 years. Of this group, 13 rated themselves as naive computer users, 2 had only used the computer as a word processor, and 1 expressed confidence in using a variety of software applications. Everyone in this group scored 0 on the pretest.

Because the tutorial designed for this study teaches elements of the BASIC programming language and editing skills on the IBM Personal Computer, the computer experience of the respondents was a critical factor in the analyses of the data and interpretation of the results. Therefore, this potential confounding source of variance in the data was statistically controlled by using computer experience as a covariate. In this way, the varying levels of computer expertise reported by the participants did not affect the results of the study.

A pilot study revealed no problems in motivation. Students were interested in the subject matter and willing to proceed through the programmed text. Since this study assumed motivation on the part of the user and was not designed to test factors that would motivate less interested users, a student population was an appropriate audience for this study.

Instruments

The Tutorial: The tutorial developed for this study teaches fundamentals of BASIC and editing functions on an IBM PC. The online version of the tutorial is exactly the same in format and content as the hardcopy version. Common sense dictated that some wording had to be changed. For example, the hardcopy text instructs users to 'write' in their response while the online text instructs them to 'type' in their response.

The tutorial was developed from existing tutorials and manuals designed to teach BASIC on the IBM Personal Computer. The two major references were BASIC Primer I and II and IBM Personal Computer: An Introduction to Programming and Applications. I decided what material to include in the tutorial based on the intended user. Material had to be simple enough for a naive computer user to understand, and it had to include enough about how to actually use the machine to enable a naive user to feel comfortable during the session. After designing and composing the tutorial on paper, I typed the text into the computer. Because the tutorial was written to test the concept of small step size, each page or screen contains only a small amount of text--enough to represent a single unit or chunk of information. The 6, 12, and 24 step size versions were then determined by placing the questions and answers after the appropriate number of screens or pages. This format was necessary to simplify preparation of the 8 versions of the hardcopy tutorial as indicated earlier in this chapter. The pilot study gave me the average amounts of time and average success rate for each page or screen of information, and I was able to revise or delete material that took an excessive amount of time to read or proved too difficult for the majority of users. I then selected a 40 character line length which allows for ample white or empty space in both the hardcopy and online tutorial. According to prevailing research, this line length is suitable for both media (Marcus, 1982; Rehe, 1974).

The only real compromise made in designing the tutorial for this study was the deliberate elimination of textual enhancements such as graphics, illustrations, cartoons, animation, sound, color, and other highlighting techniques. I do not believe that one medium was more at a disadvantage than the other in this respect. While the print medium sacrificed graphics, illustrations, cartoons, color, and various other highlighting techniques; the computer medium sacrificed all of these plus animation and sound. While these would be interesting variables to test in future research, they would only confound the results of this study.

The Posttest: The instrument used to measure learning consisted of 38 constructed-response questions. All questions related to the instructional text; however, the posttest questions were not the same as the questions within the tutorial itself. A pilot study was conducted and each question on the posttest was subjected to an item analysis to compute item difficulties and discrimination indices. Changes were made based on the results, and questions that were too easy or too difficult were changed, replaced, or deleted.

The posttest was divided in half with each part corresponding to the constructed response or multiple-choice items in the tutorial. Each half of the posttest had a possible 19 correct answers. Ten participants completed each of the four versions of the tutorial. Within each of these versions, the tutorial questions are counterbalanced so that five participants answered the first half of the questions using constructed responses and the second half using multiple-choice responses and vice versa. Each participant received two scores on the posttest: one corresponding to the constructed response half of the tutorial and the other corresponding to the multiple-choice half of the tutorial.

Design

The design for this study is a split-plot factorial or mixed design with two between-block treatments (step size and medium) and one within-block treatment (response mode). There are four levels of step size (1, 6, 12, and 24), two levels of medium (online and hardcopy), and two levels of response mode (active and passive). Eighty students participated in the study. Participants were assigned at random to step size with ten per cell. While participants responded to both constructed response (active) and multiple-choice (passive) questions, they saw only one type of tutorial--either the online or the hardcopy version; and they experienced only one step size level of the tutorial. Response mode was systematically varied to eliminate an order effect (see discussion of conditions of the tutorial under "How the Study was Conducted"). While I will not go into details of the statistical analysis of the data, any results reported as significant means that those findings were attributable to chance less than 5 times out of 100.

Results

This study resulted in the following findings:

- Active, constructed responses have a significantly greater effect on a participant's learning of the instructional material than passive, multiple-choice responses. That is, for both the hardcopy and online tutorials, users who actively wrote out or typed in a response learned more (as measured by posttest scores) than those users who simply selected an answer from a list of multiple-choice alternatives.
- Participants who completed the online version of the tutorial scored higher on the posttest than those who completed the hardcopy version of the tutorial. In this study, online users retained more information over time than the hardcopy users.
- Both hardcopy and online users scored higher on the posttest if they maintained a high success rate and a low error rate on the questions they answered as they were going through the tutorial. In other words, errors had a negative effect on learning for the participants in this study.
- The online version of the tutorial took users longer to complete than the hardcopy version.
- Although participants rated both the online and hardcopy tutorials about the same on a satisfaction questionnaire, several of the questions revealed some interesting differences in attitudes between users of hardcopy and online information. (For a discussion of user attitudes toward online information, see Hunt and Vassiliadis in this volume).

The following sections explain these results.

Active Responding Promotes Learning

The findings concerning response mode support results from previous research in programmed instruction (Skinner, 1954; Holland, 1959; Kaess and Zeaman, 1960). As indicated by Table 1 below, learners scored significantly higher on those questions of the posttest that corresponded to the parts of the tutorial that required them to actively write or type an answer (constructed response mode). They scored lower on those questions of the posttest that corresponded to the parts of the tutorial that required them to passively select a response from a multiple-choice list.

Table 1. Posttest Mean Scores by Response			
Response Mode	Type of Tutorial		Marginals
	Hardcopy	Online	
Constructed	8.15	13.02	10.58
Multiple-Choice	6.15	11.30	8.73

Behavioral research has always emphasized the importance of active responding, and the current cognitive model of learning also emphasizes the active role of the learner in the instructional process (Wittrock, 1970). Enlisting the active participation of the user is critical to the learning process. Technical writers should seek ways to require learners to make active responses to the material regardless of the presentation medium. (For further discussion of active learning in documentation, see chapters by Charney, et al and Carroll, et al in this volume.)

Online Users Out Perform Hardcopy Users

The medium significantly affects comprehension as measured by the posttest scores. Users who completed the online tutorial scored higher than those who completed the hardcopy tutorial. Figure 1 graphs the posttest scores for both the hardcopy and online data. This graph illustrates the difference in the posttest scores for each group.

As stated earlier, the online and hardcopy groups represent two different schools.

To ensure that the difference in comprehension is due to the medium and not the schools, another group of 16 communications students from the liberal arts school completed the online version of the tutorial. Results support the finding that the medium does significantly affect the posttest scores. Once again, the online group scored higher on the posttest. Table 2 shows the means for the combined posttest scores (constructed response + multiple-choice) for both the hardcopy and online groups. Online(1) represents the online group from the technological school, and online(2) represents the online group from the liberal arts school (same subject pool as the hardcopy group). The scores of the two online groups, although from different schools, are remarkably similar.

Figure 1
Posttest Scores
Hardcopy and Online Data

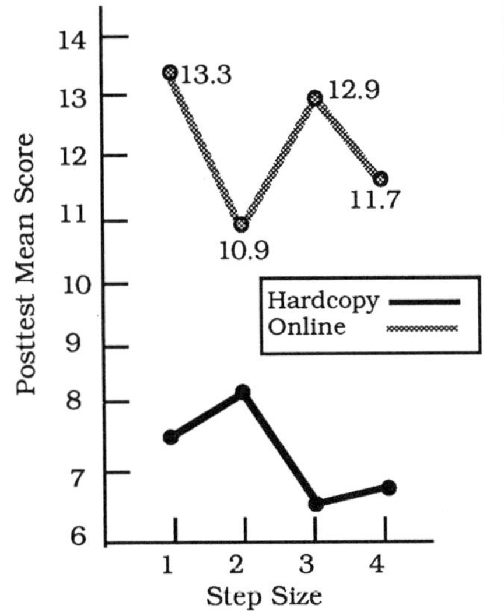

Table 2. Combined Posttest Scores				
	Mean	**Maximum**	**Minimum**	**Median**
Hardcopy	14.3	33	0	15.5
Online(1)	24.3	34	13	24.5
Online(2)	24.4	33	17	26.0

It can be argued that online users scored higher on the posttest because the subject matter being taught biased the results. I agree that other studies should be conducted using a variety of topics, and I also agree that the computer is probably not going to be the best presentation medium for every subject; however, the computer is potentially a very powerful teaching tool. The computer focusses the reader's attention on the text more effectively than a book can. It is even possible that the newness of the medium encourages users to spend more time reading material online simply because they are not used to this mode of presentation, and perhaps the increased time spent reading the material has some affect on learning. This, of course, assumes that the increased time does not result in irritation and frustration on the part of the user. But, more likely, the computer catches and keeps our attention because of its visual impact with lights and movement. More of our senses are more actively involved when we use a computer. It is a potentially more active medium that can and should demand the active participation of the user (Marvin and Winther, 1983), and these findings show the importance of active participation in learning.

Errors Affect Learning

Success rate in this study is a measure of how many answers users get correct as they go through the tutorial. The posttest score is a measure of how much information users retain one week after they complete the tutorial. There is a high correlation between success rate and the total posttest score for both the hardcopy data ($r = .57$) and the online data ($r = .49$) which indicates a strong positive relationship between success rate and the posttest score: as one increases, the other also increases. This does not mean that a tutorial can be evaluated only by the number of errors users make as they go through the material. As this study shows, the type of responses called for are very important in the learning process. Also, the questions or tasks must be relevant to the material and meaningful to the participant. They should also provide enough of a challenge to keep the users interested. Questions and tasks that are too easy fail to engage the users intellectually.

However, if the participants are required to actively respond within the tutorial and if the material is not trivial, then a high success rate might very well predict a high retention of information. It is also possible that users who score very low on a tutorial might do well on a delayed posttest especially if, because of the errors they make, they have to respond to additional questions or complete other tasks. In this way, the increase in active practice could offset the high number of errors--assuming, of course, that the participant has not already become so frustrated that nothing helps. A usability test of the material will reveal this kind of information.

Completion Times

It took the online group longer than the hardcopy group to complete the tutorial. The time it took the computer to move from screen to screen, the computer's response time, is not included in the total completion times. Table 3 shows the average time in minutes for each version of the tutorial as well as the range.

Table 3. Completion Times for Each Medium				
	Mean	**Maximum**	**Minimum**	**Median**
Hardcopy	23.48	43	14	23
Online	27.90	47	17	27

It took participants longer to complete the online tutorial by an average of 4.42 minutes. There was also a significant interaction effect between medium and step size. In other words, both the medium and the amount of material presented to users before calling for a response (step size) influenced completion time of the tutorial. Figure 2 graphs this interaction which shows that at the 1 and 6 step levels, participants completed the hardcopy tutorial considerably faster than they completed the online tutorial; but, at the 12 and 24 step levels, completion times were virtually the same for both media.

Figure 2
Interaction Between
Medium and Step Size

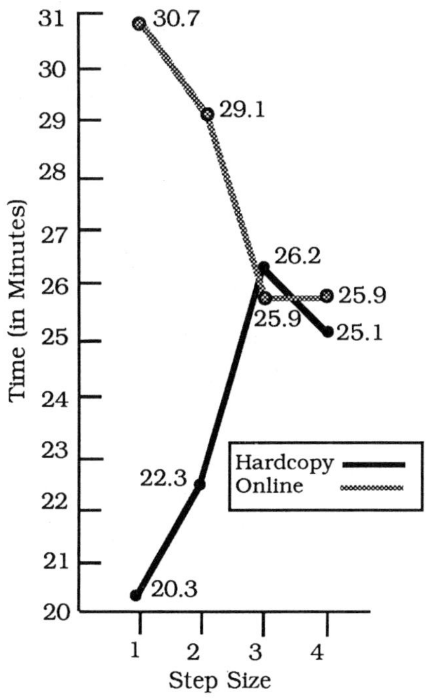

Because of the significant interaction in the data, it is unwise to attribute the difference in completion times to the medium alone. The differences in times at the 1 and 6 step levels are most likely due to the combined effects of step size and medium.

Users' Attitudes

After each group of users completed their tutorial session, they filled out a questionnaire asking about various aspects of the tutorial they had just completed. Based on research findings that indicate people's infatuation with the computer, I expected hardcopy users to express a preference for an online tutorial, rate the online tutorial higher as a teaching tool, and prefer it over the hardcopy version (Hill, 1981; Morrison and Witmer, 1983; Boettcher et al, 1983). One major problem with the opinion survey is that participants only used one medium. Had they been able to use both, their responses would have been more discriminating.

Although there is no significant difference in ratings overall between hardcopy and online groups, the responses of the users on the opinion questionnaire reveal some interesting attitudes about online information that are worth discussing. The rest of this section presents a detailed explanation of the questionnaire followed by a summary of user attitudes.

Results from this study do not clearly support earlier findings that people are either enamored or fearful of the computer. Item 1 on the questionnaire asks users whether they would prefer to use a different type of tutorial than the one they used (the hardcopy group was asked if they would prefer to use an online tutorial and vice versa). It is important to remember here that groups did not have the opportunity to try both versions of the tutorial. Table 4 shows users' responses to this question. A '1' indicates that users strongly disagreed that they wanted to use the other type of tutorial and a '7' indicates that they strongly agreed that they wanted to use the other type of tutorial.

Table 4. Preference For Other Medium

	Mean	Maximum	Minimum	Median
Hardcopy	4.25	7.0	1.0	4.0
Online(1)	4.0	7.0	1.0	4.0
Online(2)	2.5	6.0	1.0	2.0

An equal number of users in the hardcopy and online(1) groups were undecided, opposed to changing tutorials, and eager to switch to the opposite type. The online(2) users, however, were quite certain they wanted to keep the online version of the tutorial. They were, in fact, significantly more resistant to switching tutorials than hardcopy users from the same school. Nevertheless, they rated the tutorial about the same as the other two groups on how much they liked it and how effective they thought it was as a teaching tool.

Differences in users' responses on several questionnaire items between the online and hardcopy groups suggest that the larger step size versions of the tutorial are unpopular with the online users. For example, figure 3 reveals the dissatisfaction of the online(1) group with the 24 step size version of the tutorial when responses to item 1 are broken down by step size.

Figure 3
Preference for
Other Medium

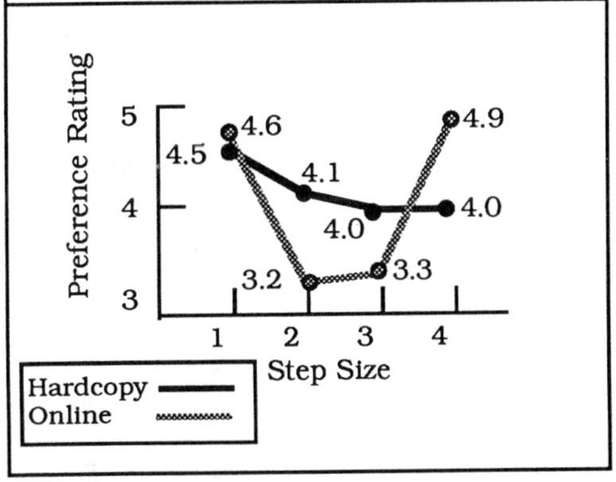

Participants who used the 24 step size version of the online tutorial were more likely to express a desire to switch to a hardcopy tutorial than any other subgroup of users. The online(2) group is not included in this graph because, at all step size levels, these users were especially resistant to changing to the hardcopy tutorial.

Figure 4 shows that the online(1) users rated the 24 step version of the tutorial lower than the other versions in effectiveness as a teaching tool, and the online(2) group rated both the 12 and 24 step versions lower than the others. Both online groups also rated the large step versions lower than the hardcopy group. Whereas the hardcopy group's rating goes up at the 24 step level, the online groups' ratings go down. Evidently, the online users are just not as comfortable with the large step size versions as is the hardcopy group. This discomfort is further evidenced in their rating of how much they liked the tutorial they were using.

The graph in figure 5 shows that the online(1) users who completed the tutorial liked all the step size levels the same except for the 24 step version that presented all of the instructional material followed by all of the questions. They rated this version lower than the others; whereas, the participants who completed the hardcopy tutorial rated the 24 step version slightly higher. Once again, the online(2) group rated the 12 and 24 step versions lower than the others.

Figure 4
Effectiveness as
Teaching Tool

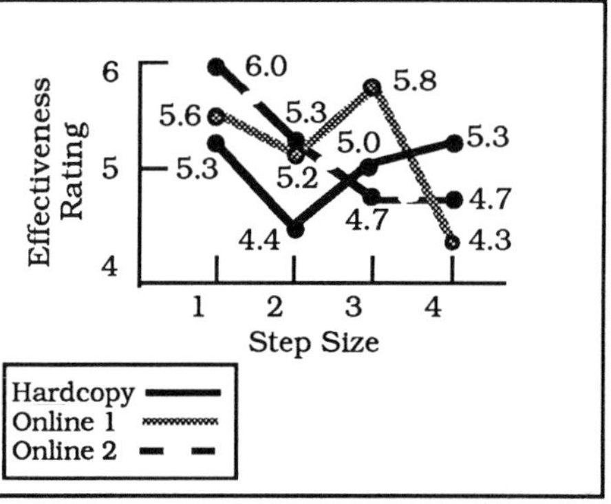

Figure 5
Like the Tutorial

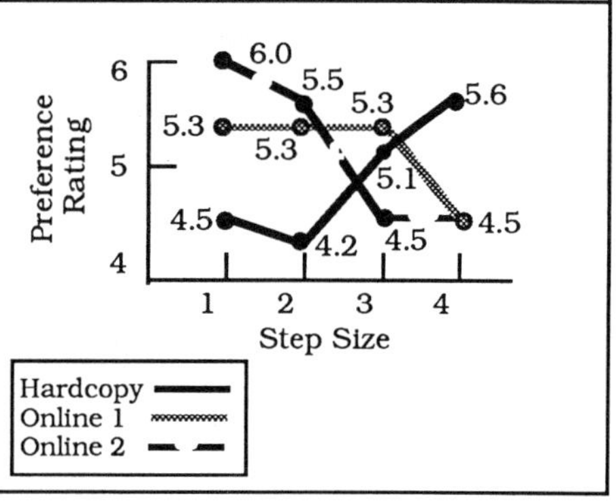

Figure 6
Easy To Read

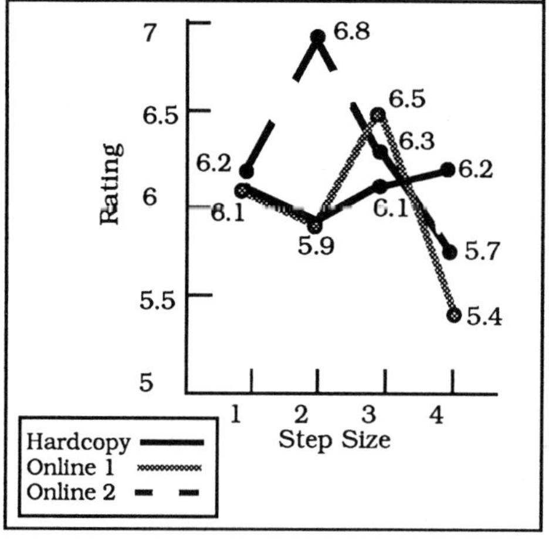

Figure 7
Easy To Understand

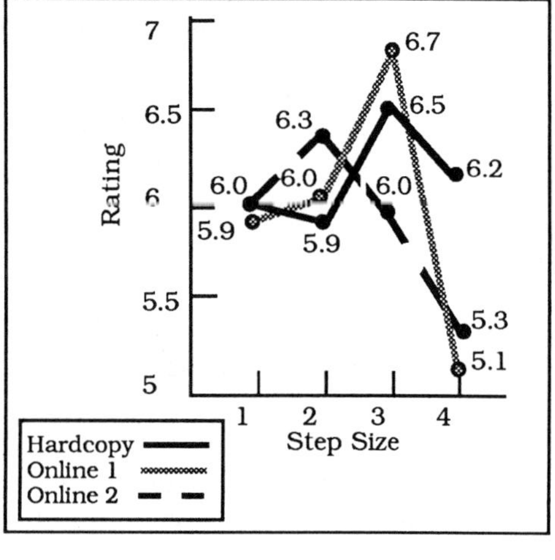

Also, participants who completed the online tutorial rated the 24 step version as harder to read and understand. Figures 6 and 7 graph hardcopy and online users responses' to each question. Overall, figures 3 through 7 suggest that online users have some difficulty with the larger step size versions of the tutorial. One explanation for this apparent difficulty is that online users do not feel comfortable with the amount of instructional material they have to read and process before they are allowed to respond to questions.

This interpretation of the data is supported by the studies referred to earlier in this chapter. Findings indicated inferior performance in users' reading and editing of online text as compared to hardcopy text. Furthermore, a survey of experienced users and writers of online information reveals that while users feel comfortable typing information into the computer, they do not feel at ease reading or editing large amounts of text on a computer screen (Bradford and Rubens, 1985).

The discrepancies between the online(1) and online(2) groups' ratings of the 12 step level point out the difficulty in establishing an optimal step size level for all online users. While the online(1) group often rated the 12 step version higher than the others, the online(2) group rated it much the same as the 24 step version of the tutorial. This is especially interesting given that on most other measures in this study, these two groups were very similar. Of course, this breakdown of the data results in only four participants for each step size level for the online(2) group; whereas, the hardcopy and online(1) groups have 10 users for each step size level. Further research is definitely indicated.

Item 5 on the opinion questionnaire refers to the four step size levels for each group. An analysis was conducted with step size and medium as the independent variables and rating as the dependent measure.

> Question 5: Consider the placement of the questions in the tutorial. Circle the appropriate number on the scale below with 1 indicating that you feel the questions occurred in the tutorial much too soon after the material being taught, 7 indicating that the questions occurred much too late after the material being taught, and 4 indicating that you were satisfied with the placement of the questions in the text.

Results showed that step size significantly affects users' responses to this question. Figure 8 illustrates hardcopy and online users' ratings for each step size. The ideal rating is 4. Ratings closer to 1 indicate that users felt questions appeared too soon after the text, and ratings closer to 7 indicate that users felt questions appeared too late after text. As the graph in Figure 8 shows, hardcopy and online users felt that questions for step size 1 appeared too soon after the text. Both online groups felt that questions for the 24 step version appeared too late after the text. All other ratings are very close to 4.

Figure 8
Users' Rating of Question Placement in Tutorial by Step Size

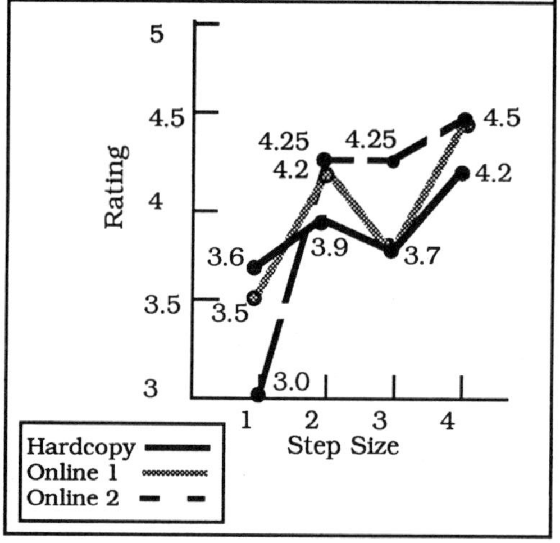

User Attitudes: Summary

These findings suggest that online users have some difficulty with the large step size versions of the tutorial tested in this study. In contrast, the hardcopy users do not seem to have similar problems. Developers of CAI should be aware of the potential danger of information overload on users especially in light of the current research which indicates that computer users have a harder time processing information online than they do when the same information is presented to them in a more traditional hardcopy format. Results of this study also indicate that an optimal step size level is not easy to determine. While online(1) users' performance peaked at the 12 step level, as reflected by lower completion time plus high posttest scores, online(2) users' performance was best at the 6 step level. Step size is a complex function of instructional content and audience as well as method of presentation and should be determined empirically through usability testing.

This study also raises some questions about users' real and perceived difficulties with online information and their learning of online instruction (as measured by posttest scores) as well as their completion times. Although results of the opinion questionnaire indicate that online users are somewhat uncomfortable with the 24 step size tutorial, their posttest scores which measure learning over time do not justify their concern. In other words, online users' posttest scores for the 24 step size version are not significantly lower than for the other versions, and, in fact, are higher than some smaller step levels. Table 5 shows the average posttest scores of hardcopy and online users for each step size.

Table 5. Average Scores for Hardcopy and Online Users

	Hardcopy	**Online(1)**	**Online(2)**
Step Size	Scores	Scores	Scores
1	7.5	13.3	11.0
6	8.2	10.9	13.8
12	6.3	12.9	11.7
24	6.6	11.7	12.7

Even though users' posttest scores do not significantly drop at the 24 step level, developers of CAI should be aware that presenting too much information before calling for active user response may discourage some computer users and does, in some situations, significantly increase reading times.

Suggestions for Future Research

While this study supports the finding that active responding results in better performance than passive responding, more research needs to be done to establish how often active responses should be solicited from users and how much interaction is necessary to promote learning. This idea also applies to instructional material of a more abstract nature. Active responses to questions within the text give learners a chance to construct their own meaningful structure using their ideas and organization strategies. This should help them in forming the mental images and associations that cognitive theorists recognize as so important to the learning process (Klaus, 1965). However, we really do not know how often a user needs this opportunity to actively respond, nor do we know the most effective types of responses to call for in various situations. Is mentally constructing an answer to a question as effective as actually writing out or typing an answer? And when is a more complicated interaction, such as actually performing a task, necessary?

We also need to find out for what subjects and in what situations do users need online information instead of a hardcopy manual or book. When do they need both? Are there instances when another presentation medium such as video or audio cassettes would be better than either? The subject matter for this study was especially appropriate for presentation on a computer. And in this study, for this subject, the computer proved more effective than a manual; however, a manual in addition to the online tutorial may have been even more effective.

We must also realize that our audience is changing. Many of the younger people entering the work force are more accustomed to reading information and doing work online. The studies referred to in this chapter may be recording a time of transition from printed text to electronic text. Future research should address this possibility.

Further research must also define the quantity and quality of active participation. It must define success rate in terms of the number and kinds of errors users should be allowed to make as well as the type of error recovery to incorporate into a program.

Practical Applications of Findings

The results of this study yield several practical guidelines for writers and developers of online tutorials, specifically, and online documentation in general.

- **Provide ample opportunities for users to actively respond to or interact with the information.** This is a must regardless of the presentation medium. Even if the documentation is intended as a reference manual rather than a tutorial, providing users with dynamic examples that illustrate function is an excellent usability aid. All documentation is, in a sense, instructional material to some degree. Whether you are trying to explain a concept or describe a specific function, you should provide examples that actively engage the user.
- **Developers of online documentation should be aware of the danger of information overload on users** especially in light of the current research which indicates that computer users have a harder time processing information online than they do when the same information is presented to them in a more traditional hardcopy format. Although this study did not find evidence to support that step size (the amount of information presented to a user before calling for a response) affects performance, it does suggest that online users in particular were somewhat uncomfortable with the version of the tutorial that presented all of the information at once before calling

for responses.

- **Provide clear and accurate instructions so that users will make as few errors as possible.** Results of this study show that there is a high positive correlation between success rate and posttest scores; the fewer errors a user makes as they go through the tutorial, the better they do on the posttest.

  In contrast to the axiom that we learn from our mistakes, we may be doomed to repeat them. In fact, users often stumble upon the truth quite by accident and count themselves lucky if they can remember what they did to achieve success. I believe that writers and developers of technical information should protect users from as many errors as possible and anticipate others by providing easy and quick error recovery.

- **Carefully consider the medium to use in communicating information.** In this study, the medium did affect performance. While I cannot offer you a prescription for when to use a particular type of presentation medium, I can offer you a checklist of things to consider:

  - Cost and resources are very real factors. If you cannot afford to develop first rate online documentation, but you can afford to develop excellent hardcopy documentation, go with what you can afford. This also applies to resources. If you have no one in your organization who is capable of designing online information and writing the program to make it a reality, and you cannot afford to hire a consultant, then you really have no choice. But consider carefully before you decide.

  - What will your audience want and what will they be able to use? If your audience is very-low tech with little or no access to computers, online information may not be a good idea. If, on the other hand, your audience uses computers routinely, online documentation may be exactly what they want and need.

  - Conduct a usability test on your documentation. Prepare prototypes of both formats and test them on your target audience. Or survey your audience to find out exactly what they need from you. If at all possible, visit your customers to keep in touch with their needs.

  - Is there any research available that you can use? Keep up-to-date on past and current research. Several hours of your time spent in the library could save your company considerable time and money. If you work for a large company, keep in contact with the people in human factors and usability. Ask for their help--often. If you work in human factors or usability, find out the kinds of information your colleagues need and design studies to help them.

We live in a multi-media environment, and each medium has unique attributes and affects us in different ways. What works in one medium might not necessarily work in another, and what proves effective in one situation might not be effective in a different situation. Developers and writers of documentation must rely on their own experience and the experience of others as reported in articles and conference presentations as they try to decide how best to communicate information to various audiences. It is important to keep up-to-date on current research because not only are the media through which we communicate information changing, the users themselves are changing. We now face a generation that has as comfortable a relationship with computers and visual media as we have with books and paper media. If we learn anything from usability research, it is that we cannot always predict how people will use products and information. In fact, research generates at least as many questions as answers; but coming up with the right questions is, really, a very important contribution.

References

1. Al-Awar, Janan; Alphonse Chapanis; and W. Randolf Ford. "Tutorials for the First-Time Computer User." *IEEE Transactions in Professional Communications* vol. PC-24, no. 1, March 1981, pp. 30-37.

2. Badre, Albert and Ben Sneiderman (Eds.). *Directions in Human/Computer Interaction.* Norwood, NJ: ABLEX Publishing Co., 1983.

3. Boettcher, Elaine G.; Sylvia F. Anderson; and Michael S. Saccucci. "A Comparison of the Effects of Computer-Assisted Instruction versus Printed Instruction on Student Learning in the Cognitive Categories of Knowledge and Application." *J. of Computer-Based Instruction*, 1981, vol. 8, no. 1, 13-17.

4. Bork, Alfred. "A Preliminary Taxonomy of Ways of Displaying Text on Screens." *Information Design J.* 3(3):206-14, 1983.

5. Bork, A.; Stephen Franklin; David Trowbridge; and Werner Feibel. "Current Projects at the Educational Technology Center." *Monitor* July/August 1982.

6. Bradford, Annette and Brenda Rubens. "Survey of Experienced Users and Writers of Online Documentation," Presented at the IBM USER-bility Symposium, Poughkeepsie, NY, June, 1985.

7. Carroll, J. M. and Sandra Mazur. "Learning to Use an Office System With an On-Line Tutorial." Research Report #RC10644 (47740), Yorktown Heights, NY: IBM Watson Research Center, 1984.

8. Chambers, Jack A. and Jerry W. Sprecher. "Computer Assisted Instruction: Current Trends." *Communicatons of the ACM*, 23:6, June 1980, pp. 332-42.

9. Gould, John D. and Nancy Grischkowsky. "Doing the Same Work with Hard Copy and with Cathod-Ray Tube (CRT) Computer Terminals," *Human Factors*, 1984, 26(3), 323-37.

10. Hill, Winfred F. *Learning: A Survey of Psychological Interpretations.* London: Methuen and Company Ltd., 1981.

11. Kak, A. V. "Relationships between Readability of Printed and CRT-Displayed Text." In *Proceedings of the Human Factors Society's 25th Annual Meeting* (pp. 137-40). Santa Monica, CA: Human Factors Society, 1981.

12. Kruk, R. S. and Paul Muter. "Reading of Continuous Text on Video Screens." *Human Factors*, 1984, 26(3), 339-45.

13. Mann, W. "Why things are so bad for the computer-naive user." *Proceedings of the National Computer Conference*, AFIPS, 44:785-87, 1975.

14. Marcus, A. "Typographic Design for Interface of Information Systems." *Proceedings Human Factors in Computer Systems* 26-30.

15. Marvin, Carolyn and Mark Winther. "Computer-Ease: A Twentieth Century Literary Emergent." *J. of Communication* 33(1), 1982, 92-108.

16. Merrill, Paul F. "Displaying Text on Microcomputers." *The Technology of Text: Principles for Structuring, Designing, and Displaying Text.* David H. Jonassen (Ed.), University of NC at Greensboro, Educational Technology Publications, Englewood Cliffs: NJ, pp. 401-13.

17. Morrison, John E. and Bob G. Witmer. "A Comparative Evaluation of Computer-Based and Print-Based Job Performance Aids." *J. of Computer-Based Instruction*, Autumn 1983, vol. 10, nos. 3 & 4, 73-75.

18. Muter, P.; Latremouille, S. A.; Treurniet, W. C.; and Beam, P. "Extended Readings of Continuous Text on Television Screens," *Human Factors*, 24, 501-08, 1982.

19. Rehe, Rolf F. *Typography: How to Make it Most Legible.* Carmel, Indiana: Design Research International, 1974.

20. Shneiderman, B. "System Message Design: Guidelines and Experimental Results." In Badre and Shneiderman, pp. 55-77.

21. Wittrock, M. C. "The Cognitive Movement in Instruction." *Education Researcher* 8, Feb. 1979, 5-11.

22. Wright, P. and A. Lickorish. "Proof-reading Texts on Screen and Paper." *Behavior and Information Technology*, 2, 227-35, 1983.

9 A Planning Process for Online Information[1]

Annette Norris Bradford
International Business Machines Corporation

For nearly 800 years, we have retrieved information from technical books, and even though presentation styles differ from discipline to discipline, most technical books support these expectations:

- The information is somewhat sequential.
- The text is divided into paragraphs and chapters.
- Pages are numbered.
- A page near the front contains the title and the names of the authors.
- Illustrations are placed near the text they explain.
- Headings indicate a shift in topic.
- Important information such as formulas is set off inside of white space.
- An index provides access to information alphabetically by topic.
- A table of contents reflects sequential organization.
- Running heads and/or feet indicate what topic is being discussed.
- Visual schemas like bulleted lists introduce sets of points.

Expectations like these constitute a kind of "technology of text," an unconscious strategy that guides us when we use printed information. We carry these expectations into every experience we have with a technical book.

But what kinds of strategies can we carry with us when we use information presented on a computer screen? Practically none that are universal. A "technology of the display screen" is still very much in its formative stages.

Even computer users of considerable experience cannot be sure that what they know about using one kind of computer system or program will help them when they learn another. There are some unwritten conventions within software packages with similar function. All spreadsheet programs, for example, use a format reinforced through years of accounting practice with paper control sheets. But specific ways of accessing screen-based information differ vastly. For the most part, every new package has its learning curve and its peculiarities of design.

---

1 An abbreviated version of this paper appeared in the *Human Factors Society Bulletin*, November 1987 (V.30, No. 11) and is reprinted with permission.

As system storage becomes a cheaper commodity, the computer industry is going to place more and more user information online, and computer users will depend upon the computer screen as a vehicle for training and information retrieval. New information delivery technologies like interactive videodisc, CD-ROM (Compact-Disk Read Only Memory)[2], and hypertext[3] both use the computer screen to interact with the user. As these technologies evolve and new technologies emerge, the lack of a "technology of the screen"—a recognized standard way of using information held in computer storage—becomes more of an issue. In time, standards will emerge, just as they did in book design. But until that time, the best that we can do as users—but more importantly in this context, as planners and designers—is to use every kind of information at our disposal to make intelligent design decisions.

The bases for such design decisions can be found in two places: empirical research and the expert (often research-informed) opinions of people who have designed online information. In this paper, I will look at both kinds of information, pointing out which sources are empirically based and which is not.

I want to concentrate on the planning process for developing online information for a computer product. To avoid any possible confusion between online information and electronic publishing[4] or electronic distribution, let me emphasize that online information is both created online and meant to be used online. Examples of this kind of information include prompts, menus, data entry panels, messages, online text perusal systems, and informational panels like those in tutorials or help facilities.

In this paper, I will begin by explaining my scheme for classifying computer users. Next I will define the genres that make up online information. With these as foundations, I will offer a series of decisions that a person or group of people planning the online information for a product should make. Under each decision, I will examine how user requirements, research findings, and expert opinion influence the decisions. Finally, I will explore a series of high-level design goals that all online information for a product should meet

---

[2] For a good overview of CD-ROM technology, read two articles in the April 1986 *IEEE Spectrum*: "The Compact Disk ROM: How it Works," by Peter Pin-Shan Chen and "The Compact Disk ROM: Applications Software," by Tim Oren and Gary A. Kildall.

[3] For a good review of hypertext, see *IEEE Computer* November 1987, "Hypertext: An Introduction and Survey," by Jeff Conklin.

[4] Electronic publishing is usually defined as "the development, storage, sale, and distribution of a product to a customer electronically via computer" (definition from "Publishers Go Electronic," in *Business Week*, June 11, 1984.

and emphasize the importance of testing online information early and frequently.

Classes of Users

Before discussing the planning needs for online information, some way of classifying the product's users is helpful. Many such classifications exist, but the one below should provide the breadth necessary to deal with users of online information. It classifies users into five groups:

- **Computer Novice**: a user completely new to computing.
- **Computer Limited**: a user who is familiar with a computer system only in so far as it fulfills a limited need. For example, some users buy computers and use them as dedicated word processors. They deal with computing only as much as is necessary to accomplish their task.
- **System Novice**: a user familiar with one operating system who is learning another.
- **System Sophisticated**: system novices who have sophisticated command of several operating systems
- **System Expert**: system administrators, people experienced with several systems well enough to provide system support.

Users cross a critical line when they move from being computer limited users to system novice users. Users above that line are have purely syntactic knowledge of the computer (the use Ben Shneiderman's terminology). Their knowledge of computing—and indeed, their use of the computer—is limited to the syntax of common commands on a given system. This kind of knowledge is system dependent and learned by rehearsal. Users below the line have acquired what Shneiderman calls "semantic knowledge." They have become familiar with at least one computer system and carry that conceptual framework with them when they learn other systems. (Shneiderman, 1982)

Bear in mind also that one user may fit into several categories based on experience with certain types of software. One might be a system sophisticated user of text processing applications and mark-up languages, for example, but a novice user of spreadsheet programs.

Classes of Online Information[5]

Just as a general agreement about types of users is necessary, so also is a consistent way of talking about classes of online information. Since a design team is typically composed of representatives from disciplines as diverse as programming, engineering, human factors, marketing, and technical writing,

---

5 Bernice Casey and Candace Soderston of the IBM Corporation in Kingston, NY contributed to the ideas in this section.

such a classification scheme allows the development team to share a common vocabulary.

This classification scheme recognizes four classes or *genre* of online information:

- Demonstrations
- Tutorials
- Online books
- Application interfaces, which include
  - Menus
  - Prompts and messages
  - Online helps
  - System metaphors and system maps

The following discussion analyzes each in terms of purpose, major design elements, and trends that are affecting the general evolution of the genre.

Demonstrations

Demonstrations are online information packages with high visual impact that serve either as marketing tools or as orientation packages for new system owners. Their purpose is to entertain, impress, or provide a very general overview for its audience. This type of package can be used effectively for marketing information and, in some instances, as an alternative to brochures or general information manuals.

Demonstration packages require very little interaction with users. Users are cast in the role of passive observers and, because of this, animation, graphics, multiple text fonts, color, and sound are particularly important. Since a demonstration is intended to provide an overview, there is little need or desire for the user to explore. Thus, the designer may want to provide only one path through the material.

The trend within this genre is toward producing true *desk-top videos* or interactive movies. Future products of this type will incorporate musical scores and sound effects, smooth animation sequences, and perhaps hooks into other output devices such as high-resolution monitors and videodisc players.

Tutorials

Tutorials are disk- or diskette-based instructional information to familiarize users with new hardware and/or software and teach them the rudiments of its use. (Bradford 1983) Tutorial have several goals:

- To bring users up to a basic level of competency
- To lead users through often-used tasks

- To demonstrate and reinforce complex skills
- To leave users feeling positive about the learning experience.

Computer tutorials run the gammet in terms of interaction style and amount of user involvement. (Bradford 1984) Here is a general summary of the kinds of computer tutorials currently available, beginning with the lowest level tutorial in term of user involvement and educational potential.

- **Automatic Page Turners**
  Some computer tutorials are automatic page turners, screen after screen of information with little chance for interaction. These tutorials are actually closer to demonstration programs.

- **Guided Tours**
  A step up from the automatic page turner is the guided tour approach, a "watch and listen" computer tutorial that demonstrates interactions on the screen while the user hears those actions described by an audiotape.

- **Simulation**
  Simulations can be used to create popular and not terribly costly (in terms of programming) tutorials. A tutorial that relies on simulation may create what looks like an actual product interface, but is actually a text file with input fields and error checking. If the user follows the tutorial's instructions carefully, the simulation is not intrusive. But if the user tries to experiment with the simulation as if it were an actual product interface, the tutorial cannot support the user.

  Simulation tutorials are particularly effective with naive users because by interacting with a simulation of the actual product interface, users can practice unfamiliar skills in an error-proof environment.

- **Tutorials Using Computer-Aided Instruction Techniques**
  Moving up the scale considerably in terms of sophistication is a computer tutorial created using Computer-Aided Instruction (CAI) tools and techniques. Tutorials that draw heavily on CAI techniques are usually able to restrict student users' progress and force remediation when students fail to score highly enough on practice exercises. These effectiveness of such techniques depends upon the environment in which the tutorial will be used. In a business office where training can be broken up with frequent interruptions, for example, it is more important that the tutorial be controlled by the student user.

- **Concurrent Tutorials**
  Tutorials may also run concurrent with the application program they teach if they can run in a hypervisor role, which means that the tutorial captures

and analyzes keystrokes before they are sent to the application to ensure that users cannot make fatal errors.

Tutorials differ from demonstrations in that users are cast in the role of active participants, not passive observers. Tutorials usually provide practice and feedback and therefore should have facilities for interpreting and responding to user input. Tutorials cannot teach unless they hold the student's attention. Color, graphics, sound, and animation may be desirable.

Tutorials are an increasingly popular way to train new users and also to influence both the marketability and usability of a product. In the March 1982 *IEEE Transactions on Professional Communications*, Al-Awar, Chapanis, and Ford noted that "the negative attitudes which many people have about computers are due partly to the way in which people are introduced to computers... A single, well-constructed tutorial can influence these [users] much more effectively than hardware considerations." (p. 30) Additionally, tutorials are self-paced and cost effective since they do not require an instructor or a classroom setting.

Some of the emerging trends in tutorial design are:

- Natural language interaction between student and online tutor. This will allow the student to ask questions and the tutorial to diagnose problems, thus enhancing the feeling of classroom dialog.

- More product or task simulation with extensive feedback, as in flight and medical training tutorials. This implies a shift away from strictly descriptive text and illustrations.

Online Books

Online books are complete product documents provided to users in an online format that can be searched, read, and often printed. The primary advantage of an online book is that users search for and retrieve information while interacting with the system, without having to search for and through hard-copy documents. Since the primary task in an online book is searching for a piece of information, the role of the user is more passive than it is with tutorial information.

The information in online books has traditionally been presented using book-like constructs (chapters or topics, indices, and tables of contents) and users are able to do such familiar hard-copy tasks as making annotations and leaving bookmarks. But without a powerful search engine, one that lets a user specify complex search arguments (such as searching for the occurrence one phrase within the same paragraph with another phrase), online books do not have much advantage over hard-copy books.

Most online books offer the user two ways to view their information: browsing and searching. Browsing an online book is not as easy as thumbing through a hard-copy document, and almost no one would read an online book "cover to cover." An online book is a reference tool, not a learning tool. Without book-like constructs like tables or contents or indices, browsing an online book would be impossible.

Since an online book is a reference tool, searching is the more popular way of accessing the book's information. Some online book systems offer only sequential string search, meaning that the users must locate and match an exact sequence of letters or words in a text. String searches are time-consuming and frustrating. Many online books are searched by means of keywords, significant phrases that serve as index terms for a data base management system. Some testing has been done to evaluate the effectiveness of information within full-text documents retrieved by means of keyword searches. Blair and Maron (1985), for example, evaluated the retrieval effectiveness of a database of 350,000 pages accessed by means of IBM's full text retrieval system STAIRS (an acronym for STorage And Information Retrieval System), which served as a representative example of a full-text document retrieval system. They found that the system retrieved less than twenty percent of the documents relevant to a particular search and was twenty times more expensive than manually indexed systems because of the cost incurred inputting and verifying each document. (Blair and Maron, 1985)

Some online books are created from data sets originally intended for printed media, but are provided to users in machine-readable form for either the display screen or local printing. In short, the information is not consciously designed for display on the screen. This practice is closer to electronic distribution than to online information and may not represent the ideal form for this genre.

Here are some examples online book systems.

- The UNIX™ operating system manuals which are available online by using the **MAN** command. (UNIX, 1980)

- The **DOCUMENT** program that serves the users of the National Magnetic Fusion Energy Computer. (Girill and Luk, 1983)

- The CONTEXT (Control of ONline TEXT) system developed by Control Data Corporation. (Hasslein, 1986)

UNIX™ is a trademark of Bell Laboratories, Inc.

- Information/Library with the Library/MVS database, a dialog-oriented online information retrieval system that runs under the MVS .

- DOMAIN/DELPHI™, the retrieval component of the Apollo™ in-house document service. (Orwick, Jaynes, Barstow, and Bohn, 1986)

Online book is the arbitrary label that I have assigned to this genre, but broadly speaking, any of the current online perusal systems available using any of the hypertext or CD-ROM retrieval systems might be called "online books." Certainly hypertext represents a significant future direction for this genre. In their review of requirements for an electronic book, Yonkelovich, Meyrowitz and van Dam explain hypertext:

Hypertext denotes nonsequential writing and reading. Both an author's tool and a reader's medium, a hypertext document system allows authors or groups of authors to link *information together, create* paths *through a corpus or related material,* annotate *existing texts, and create notes that point readers to either bibliographic data or the body of the referenced text.* (Yankelovich, Meyrowitz, and van Dam, 1985)

Hypertext breaks a longer information unit into chucks that are presented as windows on a screen. These windows associated with objects in a database so that a writer or a user of the system can create links between the objects. (Conklin, 1987) The term *hypermedia* refers to a hypertext system that links not just text but also such extensions as graphics, digitized speech, audio recordings, pictures, animation, and film clips. (Conklin, 1987)

In the future, online books should be able to integrate multifont text and high-resolution graphics. Fast-access, high-density storage devices, such as optical disks or CD-ROM, should improve their retrievability. Library workstations might be designed with dedicated keys and high-resolution monitors designed to enhance document readability.

Application Interface

The term "application interface" describes *any* information that appears on the display screen during the operation of an interactive program. Its purpose is to help users communicate with and control the underlying program, to help users perform tasks quickly and painlessly. The audience is cast in the role of active selector and performer, since applications are written to fulfill users' needs.

Apollo™ and DOMAIN/DELPHI™ are trademarks of Apollo Computer Inc.

The building blocks of an application interface include:

- Menus, lists of choices presented either as text or graphics (icons)
- Prompts, computer requests for information from the user
- Messages (both informational and warning)
- System help
- System maps and system metaphors

These building blocks have always been the same; they're present in yesterday's products as well as today's. What is different is the *way* in which they're being used today—to design screens that communicate well, promote usability, and reduce the need for documentation.

Trends in interface design include:

- Integrated, nondestructive, context-sensitive help.

- A natural language interface that lets users ask for help in everyday language.

- A movement toward the desktop or workbench metaphor and away from the traditional menu hierarchy. The user perceives that all actions are taking place on one screen, not in a vast network of separate rooms, hallways, and stairs. Some special elements of workbench designs are windows and pull-down menus.

- A movement toward more flexible graphics-based interfaces (as opposed to character-based interfaces).

- A movement toward simulation, in which the application interface reflects the look and feel of the task being done. For example, a program for finding hardware problems might let the user point to components that he or she wants to test. Simulations might call for high-resolution graphics, animation, and sound.

The section that follows will not attempt to summarize the multitude of research available on interface design. Instead, some simple guidelines and research-based principles will be offered for menus, helps, and system maps and system metaphors. (For a discussion of graphic interfaces, see Krull in this volume.)

Menus

There are various research-based and experience-based guidelines regarding the content of and arrangement of items on menus. In fact, the term "menu" is an excellent example of one of the most useful metaphors in the computer industry. Most of what we know about restaurant menus transfers when we talk about computer menus.

Here is a selective review of findings on menus.

- Researchers have repeatedly found that menu-driven interfaces are easier to use than command-driven interfaces, especially by naive and casual users. (Schneiderman, 1980; Gilfoil 1982)

- Pairing some kind of "fast path" (a command line, a layered learning system or expert function key profile) with a menu-driven interface seems to be a reasonable way to meet the needs of a range of users. A group of online experts that Brenda Rubens and I surveyed placed the need for such an alternative route through nested menus high on their list of priorities in building a menu-driven interface. (Bradford and Rubens, 1985)

  Wilbert O. Galitz in his *Handbook of Screen Format Design* suggests that when users are learning a new interface, the initiative (the "system characteristic defining who leads the dialog" between a computer and the user) "should be commensurate with the capabilities of the system user." For new and inexperienced users, he suggested that designers provide a computer-initiated dialog; for experienced users, though, permit a human-initiated dialog. (Galitz, 1982)

- Ordering items on a menu has also been tested. Where the number of choices is small and represents tasks, then the most-used-to-least-used strategy mentioned earlier works well. Where an input field is supported by a long selection list and many items may appear on the "menu," then another ordering system can be more effective. Card (1982) tested ways to organize eighteen items on a vertical menu by measuring the speed of locating designated items. He found that the most effective ordering technique was alphabetic, the second was by function, and the least effective was random. Tombough and McEwen (1982) also found a weak preference for alphabetic organization.

- Keep the number of choices low (Stahl 1985) and the number of search groups small. (Tullis 1983)

- Give each menu a descriptive title (Redish 1985). The research about headings in text can be applied here. The literature recommends descriptive headings over "cute" headings. Much of the literature on advanced organizers supported use of questions as headings.

- Group the options to reflect the topic areas covered. (Redish, 1985)

- Provide only the set of choices related to the task at hand; avoid irrelevant choices. For example, don't place a block move option on a print command menu.

- Provide a "quit without action" option to account for users who reach a menu by mistake. (Redish 1985)

System Helps
As a larger percentage of the user set moves from being computer novices or computer limited users to some degree of system sophistication, system helps grow in importance. Novices are afraid of the system and need an error-free environment like a tutorial or a training wheels system for comfortable experimentation. (Carroll and Carrithers, 1984) Sophisticated users know what constitutes a "system fatal" error and are more likely to simply experiment with a new system, using system help to avoid fatal mistakes.

Any of the five kinds of users described earlier needs to be reminded of information they have learned but seldom use. For these users, system help reminds them of information that they already know. This is the cognitive activity that Granda and Halstead-Nussloch refer to as *refreshing.* (Granda and Halstead-Nusloch, 1988)

Here are some the the concepts associated with helps:

- *Dumb versus Smart*: Traditional "dumb help" is a scrollable read-only file usually accessed by a function key; smart help has some of the characteristics listed below (like context sensitivity).

- *Destructive or Disruptive versus Window*: Destructive help replaces the part of the interface about which the user had a question with a help screen; window help does not cover the part of the screen which motivated the user to ask for help.

- *Blanket versus Context-Sensitive*: Blanket help (like dumb help) tries to answer every possible question a user could have; context sensitive help is able to sense the input field or the situation that motivated the user to ask for help.

- *System-supplied versus Customizable*: System-supplied help is a read-only piece of information that is the same for all users of a product; customizable help lets system administrators alter help text to reflect local applications or lets users add information to the help text.

A good summary of issues involved in the design of help text is found in Houghton's 1984 analysis, "Online Help Systems: A Conspectus". Aaronson and Carroll have also done some excellent analysis of intelligent help systems. (Aaronson and Carroll, 1986)

System Maps and System Metaphors

System maps and system metaphors represent two attempts at the same task: giving the user a mental image of the structure of a computer interface. In the case of a system map, the image is literal (for example, a representation of nested menus within a product interface). In the case of a system metaphor, the image is figurative (for example, "this word processing program is like a traditional office with files, waste paper cans, and desktops").

System maps are a relatively new online information device and represent a graphic form of system help. When users begin to learn new software packages, they look for cues as to the structure of the package—how the interface is arranged, how the menus are interrelated, etc. One proposal for making this process easier is to include a system map—a visual representation of the layering of information in an interface. In the February 1986 *Computerworld*, Bob Stahl suggested that system designers provide users with a "You Are Here" map similar to the diagrams we see when we enter new buildings. Such a map, Stahl contends, can provide answers to the four essential orientation questions that users ask:

- Where am I?
- What can I do from where I am?
- How do I get out?
- How can I get to other places I have either been or know about?

Stahl designed a sample system map that serves as both a system help and a cursor-selectable shortcut to parts of the product interface. (Stahl 1986)

The basic premise underlying the system map seems to be that cognitive data can benefit from a spatial orientation schema, and there is some support in the literature for this concept. For example, Herot (1984) found that people hold a conceptual image of the information contained within a physical area (such as an office or a book) by remembering something about its spatial location and orientation. Thorndyke (1981) found that good learners systematically narrowed their focus in a search to a subset of a map and learned it before moving to another subset. Good learners of spatial orientation had a variety of techniques for remembering spatial relationships, including analogies to other configurations. Poor learners were not systematic and did not chunk the learning task. (Thorndyke, 1981)

Another set of research related to the system map idea is the recent attention by the computer industry to the concept of metaphor. Ten years ago, a scan of computer industry journals would not have turned up occurrences of the word "metaphor"; the prominence of this concept today is a measure of the importance of a user's cognitive representation of a system to the process of designing an understandable user interface. Concern with finding the proper metaphor or model of a new system has become so prominent that it was the subject of parody in *Byte* magazine in December 1983. (Tom Houston's delightful exploration of "The Allegory of Software")

Here is a sampling of findings about metaphor and model that have application for system maps.

- Carey (1984) found that "developed conceptual models contribute to overall user productivity."

- Rumelhart and Norman (1981) found that analogy to create a schema for using a text editor was a very effective strategy for computer novices. Such conceptual models "should be formed by giving learners analogies based on very familiar concepts which are minimally different from the new domain."

- Lewis and Mack (1982) report that users learning a text processing system had difficulty building conceptual models of the computer system and generated incorrect models. Unguided exploration, they found, led to disorientation.

- Thomas and Carroll (1981) found that "people almost always try to learn new things by making use of past learning. New concepts are typically explained in terms of old concepts—at least initially....An existent knowledge structure is loaded into memory and used as a structural template for further learning." But they warn of inappropriate metaphors: "Misperceptions occur when interfaces and instructional materials fail to direct people to useful metaphors." Metaphors, they conclude, must be selected with sensitivity to the user set, that is, "What metaphors would this set of users adopt spontaneously? What knowledge do they have already?" (Thomas and Carroll 1981)

But metaphor's natural extension—the analogy—has historically proved to be a faulty logic tool. Just as analogies break down when carried beyond their original utility, so do conceptual models. Since the subject of the analogy and the concept being compared are not identical, the analogy eventually misleads and limits thinking. Thus analogy as an overall structuring device is discouraged by many researchers and practitioners. An example of this problem is provided by Paul Heckel in his example of a secretary who lost an important word-processing file and, after the problem of assigning duplicate names was explained to her, exclaimed, "But my filing cabinet can have two folders with the same label on them." But word processing programs do not allow this, and the metaphor "computer storage is like a filing cabinet" was misleading when carried beyond its original utility. (Heckel 1984)

Such devices as system maps and conceptual metaphors do have a utility. System maps aid in the spatial orientation of cognitive data; conceptual metaphors are useful as bridges between the familiar and the unfamiliar, especially for computer-naive users.

System maps are especially helpful in a menu-driven environment where they can explain the interrelationship between menus. But system maps require some sophisticated understanding of systems in order to interpret them correctly and are thereby more suited for non-novice users. Ironically, novices are more likely to use menu-driven systems and benefit least from system maps. System maps as product interfaces can be effective for the entire range of users. A very real limitation is the fact that system maps can become huge quickly. A product interface with 200 panels is not unusual and is difficult to represent graphically.

Planning Decisions

Here is a series of planning decisions for a product's online information. These are generalized decisions that can be adapted to the specific needs of different genre.

1. **Create or study user profiles.** Online information needs are affected by the kinds of users who will need the information. Five types of users were discussed earlier. More specific user profiles should be constructed detailing such user characteristics as education, reading level, and probable job experience.

2. **Understand the environment in which the information will be used.** User environment can place constraints on the kinds of online information that you should provide. For example, in planning the interface for a problem reporting system for remote users, packed screens might be desirable, rather than less busy screens that are considered more useable. The time required to transmit eight screens rather than two poses an environmental constraint on the design of the information. Or in a manufacturing environment, there may be a greater requirement for information to be online since manuals are easily lost in such an environment.

   To further enhance these general user profiles, consult available customer documents. Sometimes marketing documents are available the profile potential customers. Visiting representative members of the customer set is useful, as well as reading the journals and literature used by that customer set. (For a discussion of on-site research techniques, see Gould and Doheny-Farina in this volume.)

3. **Understand the market requirements for the product.** Sometimes the online information that you are planning must fit into an existing framework created not by a company but by the market. For example, the planners on a product that I worked on several years ago wanted to use the term "viewport" to describe the interface element commonly known today as a window. The term *viewport* existed in the mainframe product architecture description and was heavily favored. But a survey of the market told us that the term users would expect to see would be *window*. Without this market consistency, users might not recognize the same function across several products.

   One of the best sources of this kind of product information is the trade press who commonly review product interfaces and online information. Reading this information is recommended because you should be aware of what is already available in the market. But be careful not to be unduly influenced by what you have seen. There are a number of "look and feel" suits in the courts now challenging similarities between product interfaces regarding such elements as icons, windows, and use of the mouse. Peter Wallman writing for the *Wall Street Journal* recently made this observation:

   In some cases, judges have refused to grant copyright protection to how programs look and act on the computer screen, holding that the software's utilitarian nature falls outside the category of artistic expression covered in copyright laws. In other disputes, jurists have extended copyright protection to the "total concept and feel" of programs. (Wallman 1988)

4. **Define what tasks be performed and what kinds of expertise the users performing these tasks will have.** Task analysis is a procedure for analyzing a piece of work or **task**, breaking it into subtasks and steps, and identifying the relationship among the parts. The resulting analysis can serve as the basis for both product design and information design.

   Information design and development is an amorphous task. An engineer can hold a capacitor in her hands. A programmer can write and test code to perform tasks. But how does a writer understand what a user needs to know in order to use a particular machine or software package? Task analysis gives the writer something concrete to deal with because it provides a framework for conceptualizing a new product. This way of viewing the product makes it easier for writers to determine what to include and what to omit. (Ward 1983; Bradford 1988)

Task analysis is a popular paradigm for designing information in the computer industry. There is widespread support for organization by user task as opposed to the practice a decade ago of organizing by product function (a menu, for example, might say "Printing a File" rather than "Printer Access").

Task-oriented information is a personalized, active-voice form of information that "describes step-by-step how the user is to perform certain tasks"; product-oriented information is a more impersonal, passive-voice form of information that "describes how a product works." (Odescalchi, 1985)

Not a great deal of empirical verification of task-analysis has been done. When Savage, Habinek, and Barnhart (1982) studied menus, they found that ordering items by job title produced more errors than ordering them by function or task. Odescalchi tested task-oriented information versus product-oriented in an IBM Human Factors Lab last year and found that even though writers needed 42% more time to develop task-oriented information, 79% of the users tested preferred task-orientation and 41% showed a productivity gain due to task orientation. (Odescalchi, 1985)

Performing a task analysis on a computer industry product begins with paradigm for analyzing the new product in terms of the nine universal computing tasks.

- **Evaluation**—deciding whether or not to buy a product
- **Planning**—including the new product in the established network
- **Installation**—making the new product operational
- **Administration**—managing data processing resources
- **Operation**—checking and controlling programs
- **Customization**—tailoring the product to a specific environment
- **Application Programming**—designing, coding, compiling, debugging, and testing applications of a general purpose program to a user's specific purpose
- **Diagnosis**—identifying problems
- **End Use**—using a product for the purpose for which it was designed. (Mitchell, 1982)

These universal tasks are further broken into subtasks and analyzed in terms of the task, the user performing the task, the action, and the desired outcome. With this information, the planner can determine the information needs of the new product. (Ward 1983)

Task-orientation, then, requires some time early in the development cycle devoted not just to product function but also to potential user. It is the job of the information planner to decide what kinds of information are suited to which tasks. Online information is but one piece of the product support puzzle. Deciding which tasks requirements are best met by online information requires some attention to genre and to online capabilities.

5. **When tasks are to be supported with online information, study user profiles to decide which genre of online information is most appropriate.** By pairing information gained in the user analysis with the types of online information described earlier, it is possible to make intelligent decisions about what tasks and users benefit most from various types of online information.

   Granda and Halstead-Nussloch tested various forms of help available to users and found that online help is most likely to be accessed by users in a *refreshing* cognitive state, users who have learned information and need to merely be reminded of what they have learned. (Granda and Hallstead-Nussloch 1988)

   Although unsupported by empirical data, these generalizations can be made about online information and types of computer users:

   - Computer novices and computer limited users are most likely to use tutorials.
   - System novices are less likely to use tutorials, but, as noted above, depend more heavily on system help.
   - System experts would be most likely to use online books.
   - All users are affected by the quality of the user interface elements, such as the menus, messages, helps, and prompts. Interface flexibility in terms of allowing fast paths (Gilfoil 1982) or training wheels systems (Carroll and Carrithers, 1984), as noted earlier, is recommended.

6. **Determine how much and what kinds of information to present online.** With this determination goes the conscious decision to have some information available in both in hard-copy and online, and to present some information exclusively in hard-copy. The ever-increasing cost of quality printing paired with the ever-decreasing cost of system storage could well provoke a mad rush to place all system documentation online. (Weiss 1985) This is not necessarily appropriate, however glorious the visions of "the paperless office of the future."

   Even though I've never seen any research to support this notion, there is a folk wisdom that says certain kinds of information are not suitable for online presentation. These include:

- *System Set-Up Information.* Obviously a small system cannot provide you with help about setting itself up.

- *Small-System Hardware Problem Determination.* In a large system, not all parts of the system "die" at once. But if a small system like a personal computer has hardware problems, you can't diagnose them with a sick machine.

- *Information Requiring High-Resolution Graphics.* Integration of graphics and text on high-resolution display devices is not impossible today—but it is expensive. Often, system documentation has to address the lowest common denominator of hardware in a system.

Command and syntax summaries can be placed online effectively but are usually reinforced with a hard-copy reference tool like a summary card. Online books that contain reference information may work better online than "step-by-step" procedural books. (Hasslin, 1986)

7. **Assess whether the online information is cost justified.** The decision to include some kinds of online information (notably tutorials or intelligent help) can be costly, and the cost is usually not offset by the reduction in printing hard-copy books. Creating online information requires different skills and tools and can be costly to staff. Some of the additional demands that online information can pose include:

   - Staffing
   - Selecting appropriate tools (hardware and software)
   - Training writers on the new tools
   - Devising service and update strategies

   The point is not to discourage the use of online information, but to make planners aware of the potential problems.

8. **Decide what tools are needed to create, compile, store, and display the planned information online.** Tool search is a topic in itself, but here is a brief overview of online information tools. Typically, tools for developing online information include:

   - A development facility that usually consists of a way to edit text, determine colors and other attributes (like blinking and sound), and specify routing to other panels and to help facilities (for example, where does menu selection "1" lead to?).

   - A compile facility for processing the raw input and compressing out unnecessary space for efficient storage. Often times, in the case of system helps and interface information, this information is compiled along with the software program that the information supports.

- A run facility for displaying information and/or the program.

When product information is part of the software program, then it is useful to have a facility for displaying the information without the product itself to aid in testing and debugging. It is also useful to have a way to simulate the product interface so that the supporting information can be tested. When online books are part of the product information, then some kind of search engine is key to the successful use of the book.

In choosing a tool, be sure to select one that supports all the product needs. These include:

- *Translation* Will the online product information be translated? Expansion factors in translation are typically thirty percent over the space required for the English version.
- *Enhancements* Over the life of a product, a number of enhancements may be added. A tool should have enough flexibility to support new functions.

9. **Allow abundant time for development and testing.** Some aspects of product development view testing purely as a verification tool. For example, when a programmer writes a piece of code, testing is the means used to verify that it performs its function. But in creating online information, testing is the best design tool. Testing of online information is both formative and iterative—formative because it is the way to verify or disprove design concepts and iterative because it is not a single test but a series of tests that end with a completed design.

   Waiting to test some kinds of online information—especially interface panels, prompts, system helps, and system maps—until a running system is available is usually too late. Testing early in the development cycle, even with pen-and-paper versions of the information, allows for early detection and correction of errors.

   As you test, guard against defending your design. If only one user has a problem with your design, you don't have grounds for changing the design. But as patterns of problems emerge, redesign and retest.

   If possible, involve all members of the design team in the testing. No where does bad design become more apparent than when you watch a frustrated user. Many design arguments can be circumvented if everyone on the team has observed testing. (For discussions of the relationship of product design and documentation design, see the chapters by Baker and Chisholm in this volume).

10. **As you create the online information, keep these ideals in mind:**

- *Consistency.* More than any other aspect of design, consistency is the key to usable online information—and this consistency pervades several levels.

  - Consistency with existing software likely to exist on users' systems
  - Consistency between menus in terms of structure and assignment of function keys
  - Consistency in panel design and function keys between instructional materials like tutorials and the product interface
  - Consistency in such design elements as color and icons.

- *Transparency.* The organization of online information should be as transparent as possible to minimize learning. Any time and memory capacity devoted to learning the structure of information takes away from the other kinds of learning that need to take place for users to master the task that the software package is teaching—word processing, financial planning, etc. If information cannot be fully transparent, Stahl emphasizes, then intuitiveness is a worthy substitute. (Stahl, 1986)

- *Conciseness.* There is always more to say about a computer system than there is room to say it. Even before 1984, the computer industry was learning the difficult lesson, "Less is More." Too often, computer industry writers considered that it was the job to provide users with every piece of information that they could ever want about a computer system. The implementation of task analysis helped to get subsets of full product information into the hands of the correct users. Now the industry is emphasizing conciseness as a new goal. In fact, too much information is now equated with a poorly designed interface. (For a discussion of "the expounders versus the minimalists" see Charney, Reder, and Wells in this volume).

  Even though we allowed ourselves to become long-winded in books, we cannot afford that same luxury on the computer screen. The experts that Brenda Rubens and I surveyed were adamant about the need for conciseness, specifying minimal text, well-written and to the point. (Bradford and Rubens, 1985)

- *Order.* After task analysis has isolated the tasks performed by a machine or process, then presenting those tasks in a "most used to least used" order finds some support. When organizing information in a tutorial, I have also seen some evidence for a whole-to-parts organization (Gilfoil, 1982). Think, for example, how difficult it would be to construct a bicycle the night before a child's birthday without knowledge of what the completed toy looked like. With a vision of the whole, I often order parts using the "most used to least used" strategy.

- *Plain English.* Nowhere is straightforward language more in demand than in technical documentation—and nowhere more imperative than in writing online information. Roemer and Chapanis studied users learning a computer system with tutorials by having groups with three levels of reading ability use progressively more complex (in terms of sentence structure) instructions. They found that users of all educational levels preferred the simplest language when learning new technical information. (Roemer, 1981; Roemer and Chapanis, 1982; See Hunt and Vassiliadis in this volume)

  Tools for determining readability are historically incapable of ensuring "plain English." Even the best readability formulas are still based on word and sentence length, and there is no absolute correlation between these characteristics and the difficulty of a passage. Psycholinguistics research reveals other issues such as embedding and density of ideas to be more important in determining the reading difficulty of a piece of prose. Especially in technical documentation, reading swiftly is not always desirable. In some passages, readers need to be told linguistically and visually to "slow down and pay closer attention." That is why technical writing is characterized by more white space and more visual schemas than ordinary prose. (Halloran and Bradford, 1984)

- *Appropriate Persona.* The term "persona" (meaning the personality that a piece of writing projects) has only recently found its way into discussion of technical documentation. The ideal persona for technical documentation has traditionally been that of the detached, impersonal scientist. But as the role of the technical communicator has shifted from translator to educator, David Bradford notes, personas have become more pronounced, manifesting themselves in such elements as humor, irony, cartooning, reinforcement, personification, pronoun choice, and eloquence. (D. Bradford, 1984)

  Here are some ways that persona manifests itself in online information.

  - Reinforcing users when they do things correctly, either overtly with a message or implicitly by having the system perform as it should.

- Forgiving errors in user input that do not have catastrophic affects on the interface, such as predictable misspellings.

- Personalizing the interface, giving your information a persona. Carey in *IEEE Computer* noted that, "The personal touch also needs to be preserved. Interface designers and software implementers can be identified, both by name and by graphic, so that help comes not from the system but from an individual." (Carey 1982)

- Providing not just concepts but examples. Examples to make abstract concepts concrete. One good syntax example is worth ten screens full of parameter explanations. Pepper (1981) found that when students reviewed programming text, they looked first for clear, well-written examples.

Persona is a part of the issue of matching the information to the user.

- *Navigation.* Online information requires special attention to orientation, a constant sense of where users are in the interface and where they are going. System maps were discussed earlier as one way to help users navigate. A colleague of mine once compared online information to a deck of cards: the user sees only the card on top without understanding that card's position in the full deck or knowing how large the deck really is. (Van Oss, 1984) Compared to the book, the familiar analog tool of our experience, online information is a navigational unknown.

  Navigation aids are roadsigns, familiar landmarks in an unfamiliar environment that help compensate in part for the missing elements that compose the "technology of text" that I discussed in the beginning of this paper. Here are some sample navigation aids (Bradford 1984)

  - Monitoring markers like "1 of 6"

  - Displayed active keys for backing up, going forward, returning to the main menu, and leaving a "bookmark," a software placeholder

  - Conceptual maps and metaphors

  - Overviews and summaries (the whole set of devices know as "advance organizers" (Ausabel 1982), though their utility is often a function of the user's "prior learning, cognitive strategies, and textual content." (Jonassen, 1985)

Conclusion

Computer users are constantly changing, moving from being computer novices toward becoming system-sophisticates. In staying abreast of current research and testing the online information that we produce, we are contributing to the evolving "technology of the display screen." Providing an informed method for choosing among all the possibilities offered through research findings and technological capabilities is the goal of this paper. Good judgment and testing are our final arbiters.

References

Aaronson, Amy and John M. Carroll, "The Answer Is in the Question: A Protocol Study of Intelligent Help," *Computer Science*, 1987.

Al-Awar, J., A. Chapanis and W. R. Ford, "Tutorials for the First-Time Computer User," *IEEE Transactions on Professional Communications* 24 (March 1982), pp. 30-37.

Ausubel, D.P., "The Use of Advanced Organizers in the Learning and Retention of Meaningful Verbal Material," *Journal of Educational Psychology* 51 (1960), pp. 267-272.

Blair, David C. and M. E. Maron, "An Evaluation of Retrieval Effectiveness for a Full-Text Document-Retrieval System," *Communications of the ACM* 28:3 (March 1985), pp. 289-299.

Bradford, Annette, "Enhanced User Interface through Computer Tutorials," *Proceedings of the IEEE Professional Communications Society* (Atlanta, GA) October 1983, pp. 131-134.

Bradford, Annette, "Conceptual Differences between Online Information and the Printed Page," *Technical Communication*, 3th Quarter, 1984, pp. 13-16.

Bradford, Annette, "Levels of Sophistication in Computer-Based Tutorials: Writer and User Variables," *Proceedings of the IEEE Professional Communications Conference* (Atlantic City, NJ) October 1984, pp. 166-169.

Bradford, Annette, "What Is A Task Analysis Matrix?", *Proceedings of the 35th International Technical Communication Conference* (Philadelphia, PA) May 1988.

Bradford, Annette and Brenda Rubens, "A Survey of Experienced Users and Writers of Online Information," *Proceedings of the IEEE Professional Communications Conference,* (Williamsburg, VA) October 1985, pp. 269-274.

Bradford, David, "The Use of Persona in Microcomputer Documentation," *IEEE Transactions on Professional Communications*, PC27:2 (1984), pp. 65-68.

Card, Stuart K., "User Perceptual Mechanisms in Search of Computer Command Menus," *Human Factors in Computer Systems*, Proceedings of the Meeting of the Association for Computing Machinery, Gaithersburg, MD (March 1982), pp. 190-196.

Carey, T., "User Differences in Interface Design," *IEEE Computer* (June 1984), pp. 65-68.

Carroll, J. M. and C. Carrithers, "Training Wheels in a User Interface," *Communications of the ACM*, 27 (1984), pp. 800-806.

Conklin, Jeff, "Hypertext: An Introduction and Survey," *IEEE Computer*, November 1988, pp. 17-41.

Galitz, Wilbert O., *Handbook of Screen Design Format*, (Wellesley, MA: Q.E.D. Information Sciences, Inc., 1982).

Gilfoil, D.M., "Warming Up to Computers: A Study of Cognitive and Affective Interaction over Time," *Human Factors in Computer Systems*, Proceedings of the Meeting of the Association for Computing Machinery, Gaithersburg, MD (March 1982), 245-249.

Girill, T. R. and Clement H. Luk, "DOCUMENT: An Interactive Solution to Four Documentation Problems,' *Communications of the ACM*, 26:5 (May 1983), pp. 328-337.

Granda, Richard E. and Richard Halstead-Nussloch, "The Perceived Usefulness of Computer Information Sources: A Field Study," IBM Technical Report No. 00.3495, IBM Poughkeepsie, February 25, 1988.

Halloran, S. M. and A. Bradford, "Figures of Speech in the Rhetoric of Science and Technology," in *Essays on Classical Rhetoric and Modern Discourse*, ed. Robert J. Conners, Lisa S. Ede, and Andrea A. Lunsford. Carbondale, IL: Southern Illinois University Press, 1983, pp. 179-192.

Hasslein, Vaughn, "Marketing Survey of User Requests for Online Documentation," *Proceedings of the 33rd International Technical Communication Conference* (Detroit, MI) May 1986, pp. 434-439.

Heckel, Paul, *The Elements of Friendly Software Design*, (New York: Warner Books, 1982).

Herot, C. F., "Graphical User Interfaces," *Human Factors and Interactive Computer Systems: Proceedings of the NYU Symposium on User Interfaces*, New York, May 1982 (Norwood, NJ: Ablex Publishing Corporation, 1984).

Houghton, R. "Online Help Systems: A Conspectus," *Communications of the ACM*, 27:2 (February 1984), pp. 126-133.

Houston, T., "The Allegory of Software," *Byte*, December 1983, pp. 210-214.

Jonassen, David H., "Generative Learning vs. Mathemagenic Control of Text Processing," Introduction to Chapter 1 of *The Technology of Text: Principles for Structuring, Designing, and Displaying Text*, ed. David H. Johassen (Englewood Cliffs, NJ: Educational Technology Publications, 1985), pp. 9-45.

Lewis, C. and R. Mack, "Learning to Use a Text Processing System: Evidence from 'Thinking Aloud' Protocols," *Human Factors in Computer Systems*, Proceedings of the Meeting of the Association for Computing Machinery, Gaithersburg, MD (March 1982), pp. 387-393.

Mitchell, G.E., "Solving Problems of Information Gathering with Task-Oriented Information Design," *Proceedings of the 29th International Technical Communication Conference* (Boston, MA) May 1982, pp. C76-C78.

Odescalchi, Esther Kando, "Productivity Gain Attained by Task Oriented Information," *Proceedings of the 33rd International Technical Communication Conference* (Detroit, MI) May 1986, pp. 359-362.

Orwick, Penny, Joseph T. Jaynes, Thomas R. Barstow, and Lawrence S. Bohn, "DOMAIN/DELPHI™: Retrieving Documents Online," *CHI'86 Proceedings*, April 1986, pp. 114-121.

Pepper, J., "Following Student' Suggestions for Rewriting a Computer Programming Textbook," *Educational Research Journal* 18: 3 (1981), pp. 259-269.

Redish, Janice, "Creating Computer Menus That People Can Understand," *Simply Stated*, No. 61 (November-December 1985), pp. 1-4.

Roemer, J.M., "Learning Performance and Attitudes as a Function of the Reading Grade Level of a Computer-Presented Tutorial," Dissertation, Johns Hopkins University, 1981.

Roemer, J.M. and A. Chapanis, "Learning Performance and Attitudes as a Function of the Reading Grade Level of a Computer-Presented Tutorial," *Human Factors in Computer Systems*, Proceedings of the Meeting of the Association for Computing Machinery, Gaithersburg, MD (March 1982), pp. 239-244.

Rumelhart, D. E. and D. E. Norman, "Analogical Processes in Learning," in *Cognitives Skills and Their Acquisition*, ed. John A. Anderson (Hillsdale, NJ: Lawrence Erlbaum Associates, 1981), pp. 335-359.

Savage, R.E., J. Habinek, and T. Barnhart, "The Design, Simulation, and Evaluation of a Menu Driven User Interface," *Human Factors in Computer*

Systems, Proceedings of the Meeting of the Association for Computing Machinery, Gaithersburg, MD (March 1982), pp. 36-40.

Shneiderman, B., *Software Psychology: Human Factors in Computers and Information Systems.* (Winthrop Publishers, Inc.: Cambridge, MA, 1980).

Shneiderman, B. IBM Workshop in Interactive Systems, Kingston, NY, October 14, 1982.

Stahl, Bob, "Friendly Mainframe Software Guides Users Toward Productivity," *Computerworld*, February 3, 1986, pp. 53-56, 59, 60, 64-66.

Thomas, J.C. and J. M. Carroll, "Human Factors in Communication," *IBM Systems Journal*, 20:2 (1981), pp. 237-263.

Thorndyke, P., "Spatial Cognition and Reasoning," in *Cognition, Social Behavior, and the Environment* (Hillsdale, NJ: Lawrence Erlbaum Associations, 1981).

Tombaugh, J. W. and Scott A. McEwan, "Comparison of Two Information Retrieval Systems on Videotext: Tree-Structure versus Alphabetical Directory," *Human Factors in Computer Systems*, Proceedings of the Meeting of the Association for Computing Machinery, Gaithersburg, MD (March 1982).

Tullis, Thomas S., "The Formatting of Alphanumeric Displays: A Review and Analysis," *Human Factors*, 25:1983, pp. 657-682.

UNIX™ User's Manual, Bell Telephone Laboratories, 1980.

Van Oss, Joseph E., "Documentation Systems: Changing Products, Tools, and Theory," In *Proceedings of the 31st International Technical Communication Conference* (Seattle, WA) May 1983, pp. WE 150-153.

Waldman, Peter, "Software-Copyright Laws Are in State of Confusion," *Wall Street Journal*, Monday, March 21, 1988, p. 21, col. 7.

Ward, Robert, "A Task Analysis Primer for Technical Communicators," *Proceedings of the 31st International Technical Communication Conference*, (Seattle, WA) May 1983, pp. WE 86-88.

Weiss, Edmond, "The Next Wave of User Documentation," *Computerworld*, (September 9, 1985), pp. ID/15-ID19.

Yankelovich, Nicole, Norman Meyrowitz, and Andries van Dam, "Reading and Writing the Electronic Book," *IEEE Computer*, March 1985, pp. 15-30.

10 Usability and Format Design

Philip Rubens
Communication Research Laboratory
Rensselaer Polytechnic Institute

Brenda Knowles Rubens
Myers Corners Laboratory
IBM Corporation

USABILITY TESTING

What is usability testing and why is it important? In general, usability testing evaluates your product and/or documentation to establish that the intended audience will be able to use it effectively and efficiently. (Throughout this chapter, we use the term "product" to refer to the documentation). You may think you understand your audience, but you may know your product too well to serve as an objective evaluator. Usability testing helps determine whether or not the product you develop will be easy to use for a specific audience or audiences.

Experimental design can be, and often is, a part of usability testing, but they also exist separately. This study, for instance, was not done to test the usability of a manual for a particular audience. Instead, this study was designed as part of a larger effort to isolate differences in format and design that can make a technical document easier to use in terms of retrieval time and accuracy in performing specific tasks. In your particular situation, you may not have the luxury of numerous test participants or the expertise to conduct studies that require statistical analyses. This does not mean that you cannot test your product's usability.

You can discover a great deal about your product by developing several typical tasks that your users will actually perform. These tasks should be as detailed as possible and will probably contain several sub-tasks. For example, the ten questions in our studies simulate ten separate tasks that cover the range of work required of that product's users. The questions also force users to access information throughout the manual.

Prior to our study, we asked two people to use all three manuals in answering each of the ten questions and comment in detail regarding problems they had in using each manual. In this way, we had some idea of the strengths and weaknesses of the manuals before we began Study 1. An objective editor or writer or an external consultant could perform this type of analysis for your company. You should include this type of usability walkthrough before you begin more formal testing.

Your usability test may resemble the type of study described in this chapter, or it may be a 'find and fix' test. In this type of iterative testing, you provide test participants with tasks and focus on the problems they have completing the tasks. Problems are fixed as quickly as possible, and the product is re-tested. This process continues until no more problems can be identified, or until the kinds of problems detected are considered trivial.

Both studies reported in this chapter offer substantial support for usability testing. This type of testing is important because, as these studies show, you cannot always be sure that what you have developed will be easy to use. You may think you understand your audience, but end-users, like all humans, exhibit a full range of novel responses to tasks. To examine the different ways in which typical users react to documentation we offer two studies in this chapter. The first study focuses on three formats — a user action/system response design, a generic and clumsy manual, and a more user supportive manual. In this study, we assess search and retrieval time, and performance. Based on this study we determined the relative vitality of the manuals to support tasks and were able to reduce the test documents to two for a second study. In this study, we examined reference aids using search and retrieval time, and performance as dependent variables. Following the report for this study we offer a set of principles for employing usability as an assessment tool for documentation.

THE MANUALS

The three manuals tested in Study 1 have exactly the same content and reading level; only the format differs. Because of the formatting techniques, the manuals do have different lengths. Manual A has 49 double-sided pages, Manual B has 37 single-sided pages, and Manual C has 59 single-sided pages. Manual B, the original, is a typewritten manual. It is set solid with 8 point type on a 40 pica line on a page 48 picas deep.

Manual A is set with 8 point type and two points of leading on a 36 pica line on a page 50 picas deep. The distinguishing features of Manual A include: discourse punctuation (selective boldfacing and other textual emphasis techniques), liberal use of isolated examples, and considerable whitespace around oversize headings extended into the left margin. This text also has a reference card that can be used like an index or table of contents.

Manual C is the only text set landscape, 11 x 8 1/2 instead of 8 1/2 x 11 inches. It has 8 point type with two points of leading on a 50 pica line. The page is 43 picas deep. While this manual uses the left hand margin like Manual A, the intent of this use is to establish a "User Action/System Response" format. Considerable whitespace appears around the user actions in the left margin, and underlining is employed for emphasis within the text .

The heading system differs among all manuals. In the original manual only boldface is used for both heads and emphasis within text. This text lacks any indent practices for heading placement. The other two manuals have a heading system based on three cueing principles: type size, type style, and type position. In typographic design many researchers have found that readers, who are generally not as typographically literate as the people producing the texts, can neither appreciate nor decode subtle typographic variations. Thus, they are unlikely to see a change of two points in type size as a sufficient clue that something significant has happened within the text.

In addition, there seems to be a saturation level for typographic variation beyond which the variation loses its value for attracting attention. For instance, in one study of color, the researchers added colors to texts until every word was a different color. In the early stages of the experiment, readers attended to the colors and tried to discern their purpose. However, at some threshold the readers became confused by the colors, and, finally, when the page was saturated with color, ignored it altogether. Similar experiments have been performed with ink highlighting and underlining in texts (4, 10).

Text position is also used to exploit its substantial cueing value. In some studies, simply isolating type with additional leading around it created the perception among readers that it was a larger size than the same type set with less leading. Thus, additional leading alone can make type appear larger (6, 7, 8). Furthermore, isolating text in some manner can provide readers with important clues about the importance of that text. Examples, usually set off with additional leading and indented from the major text margins, gain emphasis from such practices. Other conventions, such as the use of a cueing area separated from the major text area, provide important retrieval information for users. In this instance, the isolation of the headers in a cueing area uses those principles discussed above.

Basic layout and typographic decisions about the general shape of the manuals were also made. These decisions became important because the original manual did nothing to support the reader seeking to resolve an error condition or complete a task. The basic features of the manuals are summarized in Tables 1 and 2, and Figure 1.

Table 1
Manual Features

Manual	Type Style	Type Size	Line Width	Page Depth
A	Sans Serif	8/10	36	50
B	Typewriter	8/8	40	48
C	Serif	8/10	50	43

Table 2
Header Characteristics

Head Level	Type Style	Type Size	Location
1	Boldface All Caps	14	Flush Left Cue Area
2	Boldface Initial Caps	11	Flush Left Cue Area
3	Boldface Initial Caps	8	Flush Left Text Area

Figure 1
Formats for Study Manuals

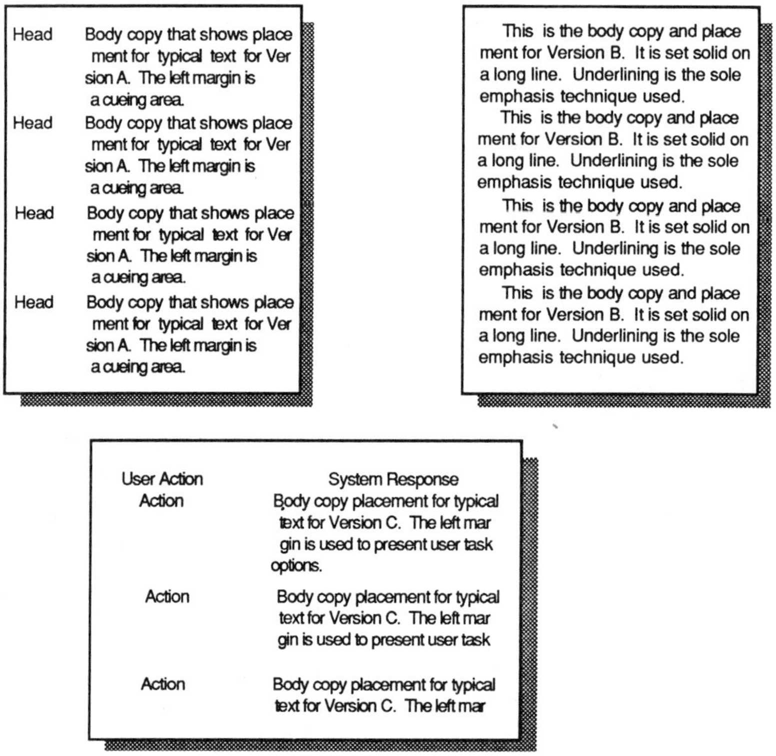

Admittedly, all of the decisions made in designing these manuals are not optimal. However, the decisions were limited to the obvious concern of the original authoring agency for production savings. That is, we recognized that they produced the original manual — Manual B — with a typewriter (or "Daisy" wheel printer) and were constrained to the basic typographic conventions offered by that device. Thus, we attempted to duplicate the page features found in the original. This decision created unusually long line lengths for the size type employed. However, all of the manuals in the study were equally disadvantaged by our decisions. Future studies of the same text will manipulate type size and style.

Specific decisions about cueing and other page formatting features were also made. As we alluded to earlier, Manuals A and C had standardized heading systems based on perception and visual acuity research (2, 3, 5, 7, 9, 12, 14). Thus, headers were emphasized by size, style, and location based on our best judgement of the relevant research for discrimination. Table 2 offers a summary of the header characteristics.

In general, we provided adequate levels of discrimination among head levels. Erdmann, for instance, reports that typical readers have difficulty discerning a difference of less than two points in type size (6). We offered three points of difference in our heading system. Furthermore, we relied on text style, in this instance boldface, and position to further distinguish among the three heading levels. We understand, once again, the inherent limitations of our decisions. Given more latitude in design, we would have employed some other features; however, in this study we wanted to maintain some similarities between the re-formatted manuals and the original (Manual B).

FOCUS ON FORMAT

One further point needs discussion: our focus on formatting variables. We did so because our interest is in time-to-productivity and task support. However, there are some compelling reasons for addressing solely formatting features.

First, a major concern of documentation groups is the page count they produce to support products. In brief, this concern refers to the raw number of impressions ejected from a printing press. Obviously, the page count will be influenced by any decision concerning the size of pages, local area features within that page — text area, the use of illustrations, the size and placement of illustrations, the use of headers, the allocation of cueing area, handling specialized notices, and the like — and the characteristics of the type and ink(s) to be imposed on a page. One example from that list should suffice to emphasize our point.

If one decides to use 10 point Palatino as body type in a publication, or publication library, each document in that library might have different size areas — based on margins, trim sizes, etc. — available for imposing type. Moreover, various sites across a corporation might not have access to the same typesetting equipment. Since type vendors and manufacturers have their own algorithms for generating fonts, the same corporation might experience different page counts although they all use the same typeface. In Figure 2 we demonstrate something of the variability of typeface based on various manufacturers of the same size typeface. The calculations for this figure are based on the same type size for a library of publications for a single corporation. Each document within this library has its own page features and the figure reflects these differences.

Figure 2
Typographic Variations

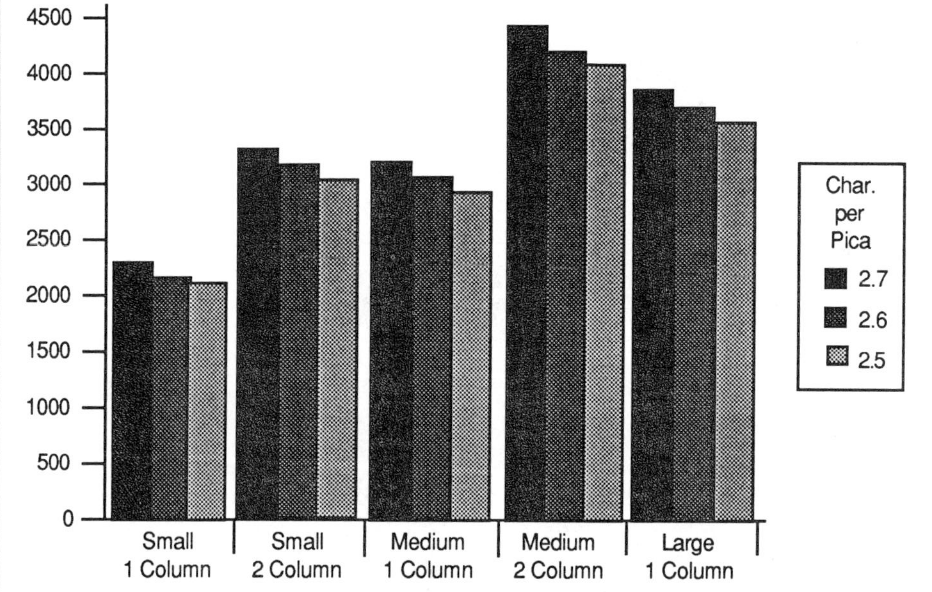

In this scenario, the medium two column size publications accommodate the most characters and the small one column size the least. This observation, in itself, is valuable information. However, the key issue is to understand the variability of the same type specifications across sites, document libraries, and individual documents. Despite these differences, all of the documents produced with the same typeface will appear, at least to the typical reader, to be identical, only the personnel concerned with page counts will be able to discern these differences.

The important issue, for our purposes, is that format as a variable is amenable to some degree of control. It provides a "look and feel" for a document that can create some very useful expectations and behaviors on the part of the reader/user. For instance, in making our decisions about the tables of contents, we consciously modeled the heading in these sections after the target headings readers were likely to be searching for in the text proper.

To further this point, most corporations do have highly developed graphic guidelines that have been imposed across the corporation. Format is much easier to control than content. Even though a company can mandate basic writing conventions, the innumerable ways of writing the same information make content more difficult to control. It is also obvious that content is the one aspect of the text that the reader must confront directly and try to ferret intention out of that content. It is unlikely that similar arguments between reader and text will occur with the format. In short, content contains the message but is fraught with ambiguity; format conveys the message and is opaque to the reader.

STUDY 1: MANUAL DESIGN AND PERFORMANCE

The initial study was broad in scope. There were a number of differences in the three manuals and to develop a design to isolate and test each feature would have required a very large number of test participants. In addition, we were not absolutely certain which features to isolate.

Therefore, we decided to begin with a test of all three manuals to determine if one of them was easier to use than the others. If we found that one manual was clearly more usable, then we would examine that manual closely, decide what features made it different than the other two, and design other studies to test specific features. In this way, we could keep the various studies fairly simple; yet, over time, gather a body of information on format features that had the potential for making the manual easy to use.

Procedure

For the first study, we provided 87 test participants with the three versions of the manual. Classes were selected based on their willingness to participate in the study. In each class, an equal number of the three versions of the manuals were distributed at random to students. First, participants completed a brief demographic questionnaire. Next, they examined the manuals for 15 minutes with the understanding that they would answer questions using the manuals when they completed their examination of them. They could not mark in the manual or make any notes as they looked through them. At the end of the fifteen minutes, participants completed a pencil and paper test to find the solutions to ten problems. (See Appendix A for a complete set of questions.) In each case, the solution had an ideal answer and location where the answer could be found.

Responses to the search task have two parts: the answer and its location in the text. In scoring the responses, both of these are counted. For instance, the answer to a question that deals with an editing function will most likely be located in the manual section on editing. If a participant gives the correct response but finds it in the wrong location, the response is counted as correct but the location is scored as an error. Participants recorded the time they began to look for an answer (start time) and the time they located the answer (stop time). This information accounts for actual search and retrieval time and does not include time spent mentally constructing responses or recording them on paper.

Eighty-seven college students (38 males and 49 females) participated in this study. They ranged in age from under 20 to over 40. The majority (68) ranged in age from under 20 to 25. Only 11 were over 30. Forty-four of the participants were graduate students and 43 were undergraduates. The level of computer ability for this group was low with 23 participants reporting no experience, 25 reporting limited skills, 14 reporting better-than-average new user skills, 19 reporting above average programming skills, and only 6 reporting the ability to program in several languages.

Design

There are two dependent variables: search and retrieval time, and performance scores. In other words, we measured the time it took to locate answers to the questions (in seconds) and the number of correct responses to the questions. Each question is worth two points — one point for the right answer and one point for the right location. There are two independent variables in the study — manual type and question type. The independent variables are under the control of the researcher. The manual type has three levels: Manual A (with reference card); Manual B (original format); and Manual C (landscape format).

Question type has two levels: simple and complex. The simple questions can be easily answered by locating the key term in the manual and copying the surrounding information. The user does not have to think very hard about the question to locate the correct answer and copy it onto the answer sheet. The complex questions, in contrast, require the user to locate the key term or terms in the text, read the surrounding information, and make some decisions about what material to include in the answer. This latter type of question requires some analysis and synthesis of information to arrive at an appropriate, and novel, answer. Simply copying information verbatim from the text is not sufficient. Each participant used only one version of the manual and answered all ten questions. In answering the ten questions, participants had to reference information throughout the manual.

Results

The statistical analyses performed on the data indicate that in this study manual format does not significantly affect retrieval time or overall performance; however, the type of question does significantly affect retrieval time ($p < .0001$) and performance score ($p < .0001$). Users score higher on the simple questions (8.6) than they do on the complex questions (6.7). While manual format does not significantly affect users' overall performance on the questions, the format does affect Manual C users' performance on simple questions ($p<.01$).

Table 3
Performance Mean Scores: Study 1

Manual	All Questions	Simple Questions	Complex Questions
A	7.9	8.9	6.8
B	7.9	9.2	6.6
C	7.2	7.7	6.8
Marginals	7.7	8.6	6.7

Discussion

This initial study, while it did not identify one manual that was clearly easier to use than the other two, suggests that the addition of formatting techniques alone does not always create usable manuals. For example, Manual C, which makes some sophisticated attempts at formatting, lacks sufficient discrimination between degree levels and task information. This lack of discrimination occurs in both typography and content.

In terms of typography, degree heads cannot be distinguished based on type size, location, or style. While some attempt has been made in Manual C to extend information into the left margin, both degree heads and task information have exactly the same position, type size, and type style. Spencer and Coe find that discriminable extension techniques do produce better retrieval rates (13). Several other researchers find that boldface type aids retrieval and learning (4, 7, 8). Since the latter techniques do not appear in Manual C, it is little wonder that subjects perform poorly.

This lack of discrimination also extends to content. For instance, the differences between MAIN COMMAND MENU 'options' and the 'variables' available within an option cannot be determined. The text uses the two terms interchangeably. Question 3 offers the most telling example of this problem: "If you exit the program from the MAIN COMMAND MENU, what command can you enter to get back into the program?" The question requires an understanding of three key terms: exit, end, and program. It also requires a knowledge of the difference between leaving a program, usually back to an operating system or a computing language, and leaving one part of a program for another.

In defining the problem, users have to discover (1) how to exit the 'program' and (2) how to get back into the program from wherever the exit action takes them. The presence of two options on the MAIN COMMAND MENU that imply 'leaving' further confuse problem definition. First, the users encounter an End command, which allows them to exit the program (the correct response). Second, they encounter an eXit command, which sends them from the MAIN COMMAND MENU to the EDITOR MENU. The term 'exit' in the question confuses them; and they select the second option, even though it does not allow them to exit the 'program.'

Question 2 offers another good example of this problem: "X performs what function in the MAIN COMMAND MENU?" Manual C users go to the correct chapter and locate a lower case 'x' on page 8, the second page of that chapter. They make their responses based on that information. Other typographic cues within the text at that point make this choice even more likely: there is a sentence that begins with a lower case 'x'. Users probably assume that the lowercase x is an option rather than a variable. The correct answer, however, appears on page 15 at the end of that chapter. Here the capital X is embedded in the word 'eXit.' Even with the X underlined, as in Manual C, it is easy to overlook. This illustrates the average reader's inability to comprehend the subtle typographic distinctions commonly encountered in computer documentation.

A more general, and typical, example of formatting problems can be found in users' responses to question 10: "If you are PUTting a file to disk and want to stop, what do you do?" Manual A users find five PUT commands on their reference card; Manual B users encounter an END command before reaching PUT; and Manual C offers heads that explain user actions rather than tasks. Users' responses indicate that they depend on the alphabetical menu listings in both the text and on the reference card. In all cases, users either encounter a method for ending the program before reaching the PUT command or they find numerous examples of the PUT command. The confusion created by these alphabetic menus mediates against their usefulness. Studies of menu organization by Barnard, et al and Loeb suggest that content or conceptually organized menus are best for long listings (2, 13).

One can conclude from this study that manual format does have some influence on performance. Users score significantly lower on the simple questions when using Manual C (Table 3). While there are no significant differences in search and retrieval times due to manuals, Table 4 indicates that Manual A users completed the questions in the least amount of time, followed by Manual B users. Manual C users took the longest to complete the ten questions.

Table 4
Question Completion Times

Manual	Total Times (Min:Sec)
A	04:35
B	05:40
C	05:55

The differences in these manuals are based entirely on format (content is the same in all three manuals). Manual A has short line lengths and uses the left hand cueing area for major heads that define tasks. Manual B has long line lengths and very little leading. Manual C has line lengths comparable to Manual A but uses the left cueing area to offer information on how users perform tasks rather than offering task categories. Based on this study, the most surprising shortcomings involved (1) Manual C and (2) the general concept of alphabetic ordering. Users seemed to search in vain for specific tasks in Manual C, and the alphabetic ordering in all manuals confused users in a variety of ways.

STUDY 2: REFERENCE STRATEGIES AND PERFORMANCE[2]

In the second study, we focussed on the original manual (Manual B) and on Manual A which fared best in the first study. We eliminated Manual C, the landscape version. Even though it utilized formatting techniques and looked as if it would be more usable than the original version; when test participants tried to answer the simple questions using Manual C, their performance scores significantly declined. For Manuals A and B, there were no significant differences in users' performance scores (Table 5) or retrieval times (Table 4); however, as Table 4 shows, the average retrieval time for Manual A was faster than for Manual B.

Reference Strategies

We examined retrieval aids because the underlying purpose of these manuals is to provide rapid error condition resolution. We included three levels of retrieval aids: index, quick-reference card, and a standardized heading and emphasis system. Each of these had two variations in the test condition. The indices were produced based on topics in one version and tasks in a second version. The quick-reference cards followed the logic of the indices but had the added feature of text page numbers on the cards, a feature not generally found on reference cards.

We hypothesized that the addition of the reference card was responsible for the quicker retrieval time, and decided to add reference aids to Manual A and B in an attempt to discover what type of reference aids contributed to ease of use. We revised and expanded the reference card from Study 1. It remained task-oriented; in other words, users located the task they wanted to do on the card; but, rather than the very terse commands listed on the card in Study 1, the revised card (Figure 3) used complete imperative sentences.

Figure 3
Task Oriented Reference Card

Using the MAIN COMMAND

To Do This:	Use This Command:	See Page
Dial a System	D	14
Go To NUMBERS FILE for Phone Numbers	N	16
Answer the Phone	A	14
Find Available Disk Space	F	15
Begin SUBCOMMAND MENU	B	14
Receive a File From the System (Download)	R	16
Send a File To the System (Upload)	S	18
Get a File From the Disk	G	15
Go to Line Editor	X	19
Create New MACRO Commands	M	16
Examine Contents of Buffer	V	19
Send Contents of Buffer to Printer	O	16
Save the File to a Disk	P	16
End the Program	E	15

Using the EDITOR COMMAND

To Do This:	Use This Command:	See Page
Get a File From a Disk	.G	22
Find Amount of Available Memory	.F	22
Set the Margins	.S	25
See the HELP Menu	.H	23
Insert Lines in the Program	.I	23
Retype an Existing Line	.R	24
Center a Line	CTRL + C	26
List a Line or Lines	.L	23
Delete a Line or Lines	.D	22
Wipe the Screen	.W	26
Send Lines to the Printer	.O	24
Clear the Current Buffer	.C	22
Save a File to the Disk	.P	24
Go to a Transfer Package	.X	26

Using the SUB COMMAND

To Do This:	Use This Command:	See Page
Alter Baud Rate	A	28
Begin Terminal Mode	B	28
Copy Incoming Data to the Buffer	C	28
Print Incoming Data	O	29
Save File to Disk	P	29
Return to MAIN COMMAND MENU	M	29
Hang Up the Phone	H	29

Also, the columns were labeled in natural language. Users located the task they wanted to do under column 1 which was labeled "To do this" and next to it under column 2, labeled "Use this Command," users found the command to accomplish the task.

A second reference card (Figure 4) attempts to deal with a serious problem in usability with the product itself; a single command has more than one function depending on what part of the product you are in. For example, if you are in the Sub Command Menu, typing and entering the command 'C' copies incoming data to the buffer. However, in the same product, if you are in the Macro Command Menu, the command 'C' clears the buffer. And you cannot always be certain where you are in the product; you have to rely on your memory. This, of course, is a serious flaw in the product; and, unfortunately, the burden falls to the documentation to make a sloppy product easy to use.

Figure 4
Matrix Reference Card

Quick Reference Card
for Standard Menu Commands

Menu Commands — Response In

	MAIN COMMAND MENU	EDITOR COMMAND MENU	SUB COMMAND MENU	MACRO COMMAND MENU	NUMBERS FILE COMMAND MENU
A	Answers Phone	—	Alters Baud Rate	—	—
	Accesses SUB COMMAND MENU	—	Begins Terminal Mode	—	—
	—		Copies Buffer on File	Clears Current Buffer	Allows Change in System Name, Phone Number, and/or MACRO
.C	—	Clears Current Buffer	—	—	—
	Dials a System	—	—	—	—
.D	—	Deletes Text From File	—	—	—
	Ends Program	—	Ends Program	Ends Program	Ends Program
.E	—	Ends Program	—	—	—
	Displays Available Disk Space	—	—	—	—
.F	—	Displays Available Disk Space	—	—	—
	Gets File From Disk	—	—	—	—
.G	—	Gets File From Disk	—	Gets MACRO File From Disk	—
	—	—	Hangs Up Phone	—	Displays HELP MENU
.H	—	Displays HELP Menu	—	—	—
	—	Allows Insertion of Text Into File	—	—	—

This second reference card tries to prevent any potential disasters by providing a matrix. It gives an alphabetical list of the commands in the first column and the five command menus that comprise the product in the next five columns. To use this matrix reference card, the user must know the commands in advance. The user then locates the command, identifies the active command menu, and discovers what that command does in that particular part of the program. With this card, the user quickly sees that the command 'C' does three different operations depending on the command menu active at the time.

In contrast, the task-oriented reference card (Figure 3) provides the task and then gives the command to accomplish the task. It is not immediately apparent from this card that one command has several functions depending on the sub command menu. However, as long as you know which menu you are in at any given time, you will be able to locate the appropriate command to accomplish a specific task by finding the task under the correct menu in the "Use This Command" column.

In addition to the reference card, we added an index to each manual. The index has one of two different types: one is command-oriented in that it lists the various command menus and the commands themselves. The other index simply compiles the headings found in the manual. In this case, the index for each of the manuals differs because it has to reflect the headings for that particular manual.

Design

Using the two kinds of reference cards and indices, we developed four reference strategies for each manual. For both Manual A and Manual B, there were four conditions:

Version 1 — Command driven index and matrix reference card

Version 2 — Command driven index and task-oriented reference card

Version 3 — Headings index and matrix reference card

Version 4 — Headings index and task-oriented reference card

Reference strategy, then, is an additional independent variable for Study 2. Question type and manual type are the other independent variables. The primary difference between the two studies is that in Study 1 there were three manual types (A, B, and C); in Study 2 there are only two manual types (A and B). The dependent variables are the same as in Study 1: performance score and retrieval time.

Procedure

Once again, participants were members of classes at a four-year technological school. All participants answered the five simple and five complex questions that comprised question type. Each participant used either Manual A or Manual B (Manual type) and only one of the four different versions (Reference Strategy). Test participants used the same procedure for examining manuals and recording times as described in Study 1.

In all, 104 test participants completed Study 2. Of this number, there were 20 females and 84 males who ranged in age from under 19 to 35. However, the majority of the participants (103) ranged in age from under 19 to 25; only 1 person was over 30. Most of these students were undergraduates (85) and 19 were graduate students. The level of computer ability was high with 37 reporting the ability to program in several languages, 33 reporting above average programming skills, 14 reporting better-than-average new user skills, 14 reporting limited new user skills, and only 6 reporting no computer abilities at all. While computing ability is higher for the subjects in Study 2, this need not cause concern because we are not comparing the two studies. If we were to do so, computing ability would be treated as a co-variate.

Results

As in Study 1, there was a significant difference in performance scores and retrieval times due to question type ($p<.00001$). Users scored significantly lower on the complex questions (7.8) than they did on the simple questions (9.2) (Table 5); and they took significantly more time (Table 6) to answer the complex questions (07:30 minutes) than the simple questions (04:32 minutes).

Table 5
Performance Mean Scores: Study 2

Manual	All Questions	Simple Questions	Complex Questions
A	8.7	9.4	8.0
B	8.3	9.0	7.5
Marginals	8.5	9.2	7.8

While there is no significant difference in performance scores due to the type of manual used or the reference strategies provided, there is a significant difference in retrieval times due to the type of reference strategy. Version 4, which uses a headings index and a task-oriented reference card, of both Manual A and Manual B resulted in the fastest retrieval times (05:06 minutes). Table 6 gives the average times for all four reference strategies.

Table 6
Reference Strategies
Mean Completion Times
(minutes:seconds)

Version	All Questions	Simple Questions	Complex Questions
1	07:15	05:31	08:58
2	05:41	04:02	07:20
3	05:53	04:12	07:24
4	05:06	03:45	06:28
Marginals	05:15	04:32	07:30

Version 4 of the reference strategies is quicker to use for all questions for both manual types (Figure 5). Reference versions 1 and 3 cause more problems for Manual B users answering the simple questions (Figure 6). Versions 1 and 3 have the matrix reference card in common; therefore, the matrix card apparently slowed down Manual B users in answering the simple questions.

Figure 5
Reference Strategy
All Questions

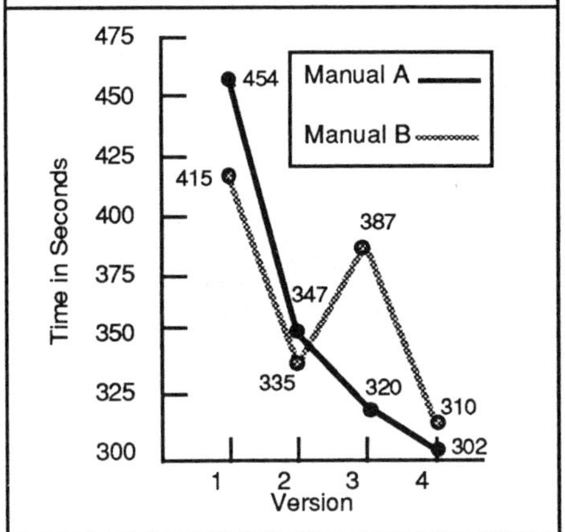

Figure 6
Reference Strategy
Simple Questions

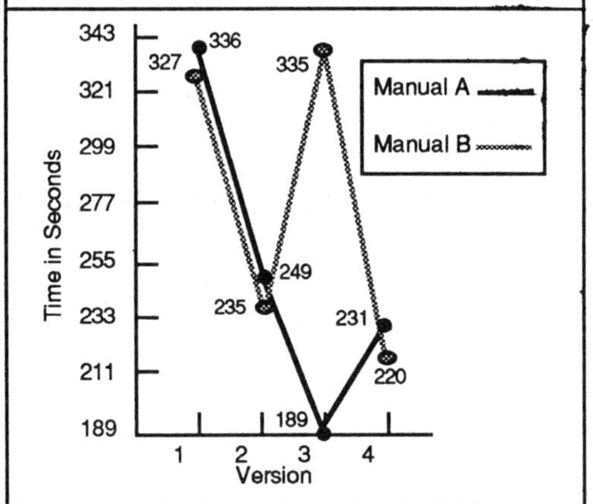

We think two factors account for these results. First, Manual B, the original manual, did not offer users distinctive headings within the text or try to set off text in any special way. Because of this, Manual B users would not be as likely to locate information just by flipping through the text and would be more likely to turn to a reference aid for help. This is where the second factor comes in — although the matrix reference card is designed to prevent users from making wrong choices, it requires some effort on their part to learn how to use it. Since we provided no instruction in how to use the reference aids, we believe that the high retrieval times for Versions 1 and 3 for Manual B users result from their attempts to understand how to use the matrix reference card.

Because performance scores do not differ significantly due to manual type or reference strategy, we know that Manual B users successfully located the answers to the questions. Did they figure out how to use the matrix reference card, or did they resort to some other means to locate the correct answers to the questions? Fortunately, we asked users to report which reference aid they used for each question: the index, the reference card, or random search. This data indicates that when Manual B users were answering the simple questions, they used the reference card 47% of the time. This information indicates that, although it took them extra time to understand how to use the matrix reference card, they did figure it out and were able to locate the correct answers.

Version 4 (headings index and task-oriented reference card) took users on average only 05:06 minutes to answer the ten questions. They spent an average of 03:45 minutes on the simple questions and 06:28 minutes on the complex questions (Table 6). This reference combination was especially effective in helping users find answers to the complex questions. Manual A and B users of Version 4 completed the complex questions sooner than users of Versions 1, 2, or 3 (Table 6). Evidently the combination of a general headings index and task-oriented reference card was more effective than a command driven index and task-oriented reference card (Version 2) for users unfamiliar with the product.

CONCLUSION

In summary, Studies 1 and 2 revealed information that surprised us. In Study 1, we found that Manual C, although it looked like an improvement over the original Manual B, was, in fact, harder to use. We would not have guessed this simply by looking at the three manuals because Manual C incorporated sophisticated formatting techniques purported by the research to increase a manual's usability. The test, however, revealed problems with Manual C that would have to be revised.

In Study 2, we felt that the reference strategy in Version 1, the command driven index and matrix reference card, would be the most effective combination. A great deal of time and effort went into the design of the matrix card by an expert user of the product. As the study shows, however, that combination resulted in the longest retrieval times. Instead, Version 4 with the task-oriented reference card and headings index produced the shortest retrieval times. It is likely that the designer of the matrix reference card was simply too familiar with the product to be able to realistically understand the problems a new user would encounter. Such design difficulties are exactly those captured by usability testing.

RECOMMENDATIONS

Based on the results of these two studies, we can offer several recommendations for designers and developers of manuals.

1. Task-oriented retrieval aids assist users in locating information. One of the most noticeable shortcomings of technical information is its propensity to offer information of varying kinds in a single document. That is, a manual will shift among marketing, operating, and descriptive information. While such shifts occur in any writing, in technical manuals such schizophrenic behavior obscures the important ways in which the manual can support tasks. Even in the basic studies reported here, an obvious case can be made for more precision in internal document information as well as the need to provide information, <u>and keys into that information</u>, that support tasks.

2. Design retrieval aids so that they do not require learning time. The matrix reference card, although a sophisticated tool for the experienced user who already knew product commands, slowed down inexperienced users. Based on the utility of this feature for experienced users, it would be tempting to develop similar supporting reference aids for even very large systems. The matrix does allow this kind of support. However, the most useful aids were those that related directly to tasks <u>and</u> provided directions, in the form of page numbers, to additional information in the supporting text. This novel approach, although admittedly costly to maintain, has significant potential for supporting user tasks.

3. If possible, provide a variety of retrieval aids and make their usefulness apparent. The reference cards in these studies, for instance, worked somewhat like an abbreviated index. In fact, when users looked at the indices, they soon discovered that they bore a striking resemblance to the reference cards. Further investigation demonstrated that the features of all reference aids were redundant with the ways in which information was presented in the manuals. The key point here is to establish an expectation within any document or document set and use that expectation as a "security blanket" the user can rely on across the possible product interactions.

4. Depend on headings and highlighting as retrieval aids. According to search methods reported by test participants in Study 2, a favorite way to find information is still random search — flipping through the manual. Therefore, headings and subheadings as well as highlighting and other visual cues within the manual itself are still very important retrieval aids. Despite the best laid publication plans, user search patterns and behaviors are still highly idiosyncratic. Thus, providing many access points and offering discriminable retrieval aids will make your documents more usable. This perception also implies that, whatever methods you use to accomplish discriminability, you must not overburden the users' ability to understand a sophisticated emphasis system. Rely, instead, on a few highly discriminable textual features and use them consistently and wisely.

5. Test your product. These studies show that you cannot always accurately predict what users will do with your product. One of the most frequent interactions users perform on new products is to test the product's limits as well as its similarity to earlier products. Such behaviors depend on guessing and intuitive rummaging. There is a certain playfulness to this approach, but it is also these early interactions that produce many novel and unpredictable interaction patterns. Since these interactions are so idiosyncratic it is unlikely that the product developers will have considered them in preparing the product. The only method for discovering such interactions and addressing the problems they create for usability is through a carefully defined and applied testing program.

FUTURE RESEARCH

We plan to continue with our research in this area by testing a variety of type sizes, fonts, image areas, local area features, and content-related issues. We also want to duplicate our study online. Eventually, we will use the formatting techniques and reference strategies to revise a different manual and test whether or not our findings transfer to other environments. We also wonder whether experienced users (someone very familiar with the product) require a different kind of documentation than inexperienced users. Finally, we will establish a model to explain the variety of ways users try to interact with information.

As we said earlier in this chapter, our goals as researchers are long-term. If you are developing products for the market place, your goals are more immediate and urgent. However, as these studies show, testing your product is essential in determining ease of use. Do not take shortcuts in usability. If you do, your users may become unwilling and unhappy test participants instead of satisfied customers.

REFERENCES

1. Barnard, P. J., et al. "Planning Menus for Displays: Some Effects of Their Structure on User Performance," *Proceedings of the IEEE Conference on Displays for Man-Machine Systems.* Bailrigg, Lancaster, England: M. W. Bailey & Company, Ltd., 1977. 130-133.

2. Bruner, J. S. "Value and need as organizing factors in reception," *Journal of Applied Psychology* 42 (1947): 33-38.

3. Burnhill, P. "Typographic Education: Headings in Text," *Journal of Typographic Research* 4 (1976): 353-365.

4. Crouse, J. H., and P. Idstein. "Effects of Encoding Cues on Prose Learning," *Journal of Educational Psychology* 63, 4 (1972): 309-313.

5. Engel, F. L. "Visual Conspicuity as an External Determinant of Eye Movement and Selective Attention," Diss. Eindhoven, Netherlands, 1976.

6. Erdmann, R. L., and A. S. Neal. "Word legibility as a function of letter legibility, with word size, word familiarity, and resolution parameters," *Journal of Applied Psychology* 52 (Oct. 1968): 403-409.

7. Foster, J., and P. Coles. "An experimental study of typographic cueing in printed text," *Ergonomics* 20.1 (1977): 353-365.

8. Hershberger, W. A., and D. F. Terry. "Typographic Cueing in Conventional and Programmed Texts," *Journal of Applied Psychology* 49 (1965): 55-60.

9. Kahneman, D., and A. Henik. "Effects of visual groupings on immediate recall and selective attention," *Attention and Performance IV.* Ed. S. Dornic. Hillsdale, NJ: Lawrence Erlebaum Associates, 1977. 307-332.

10. Klare, George R., et al. "The Relationship of Style Difficulty to Immediate Retention and to Acceptability of Technical Material," *Journal of Educational Psychology* 46 (1955): 287-295.

11. Loeb, J. W. "Differences Between Cues in Effectiveness as Retrieval Aids," Dissertation University of Southern California, 1969.

12. Poulton, E. C. *Effects of Printing Types and Format on the Comprehension of Scientific Journals.* Cambridge, England: Cambridge University Press, 1959.

13. Spencer, H. L., and B. Coe. "Typographic Coding in Lists and Bibliographies," *Applied Ergonomics* 5.4 (1974): 136-141.

14. Teicher, W. H., and M. J. Krebs. "Visual search for simple targets," *Psychological Bulletin* 81 (1974): 15-28.

NOTES

[1]This study began as a project in a Publications Practicum master's degree course in 1984. The project focussed on a common communication's package with an internal editor that could be purchased in any computer store. The manufacturer had granted permission to used the product as part of the course work. (This product is no longer available in the marketplace; it has been replaced by more current technology.)

The students were asked to take the original manual that accompanied the product and reformat it so that it would be easier to use. Students had studied the manual for months, and they had a demonstration of the product which they could review. Students also had the benefit of reading relevant research in the area of documentation design from 1980-1984 as well as what they had learned in their other courses and their combined knowledge and experience. How to approach the project was left up to the students. The result was two reformatted versions of the manual produced by two teams of students.

[2]The reference cards for Study 2 were designed by Claudia Myrland and Richard Coyle; the indexes were designed by Mary Beth Raven.

APPENDIX A: QUESTIONS FOR PERFORMANCE EVALUATION

1. What can **Parity** be referred to as?
2. **X** performs what function in the MAIN COMMAND MENU?
3. If you exit the program from the MAIN COMMAND MENU, what command can you enter to get back into the program?
4. In the SUPPORT PROGRAMS what three (3) kinds of files can be converted into textfiles?
5. In the editor what function does .F perform?
6. During initial set-up what line must be changed to configure your program?
7. If you enter **Fx** after typing **D** at the MAIN COMMAND MENU, what would happen?
8. In the NUMBERS FILE COMMAND MENU what does **S** do?
9. What does the command **.L10,20** do in the editor?
10. If you are **PUT**ting a file to disk and want to stop, what command can you use?

11 Design Principles for Pictorial Information

Elaine Lewis
College of Communication
Boston University

Pictorial information -- photographs, line drawings, diagrams, and symbol systems -- is often crucial for effective documentation. Yet many technical communicators fail to use pictures to support their prose. Because they often lack knowledge about methods of visual communication, writers may not realize when a picture is appropriate or what type of picture works best for a particular illustration need. Even designers, who are professionally trained in the use of pictorial information, often base their graphic choices on convention or aesthetics, rather than effectiveness. This chapter offers empirically supported guidelines for deciding when and how to use pictures effectively.

Computer documentation design demands a range of illustration styles to suit different information needs. Representing a piece of hardware requires some degree of realism, whereas the portrayal of an entire system could involve a more diagrammatic approach. Abstract concepts like procedures and functional relationships for systems and software require graphic analogies, such as flow diagrams or a standard set of symbols. Other uses for symbols, or icons, include providing directional cues for proper use of a manual or on-line documentation in operating systems like that found on the Apple MacIntosh.

Technical communicators must not only be sensitive to the type and function of information which needs illustration; they must also consider their audience and their medium. Not only do people process pictures differently, their comprehension ability and level of computer experience help shape their documentation requirements. While a printed manual would naturally require different illustration techniques than those appropriate for interactive, electronic documentation, some basic principles apply across media.

Scholars have addressed many of these concerns through research about the human factors of pictorial displays. Published work in psychology, communication and ergonomics offers important clues for establishing pictorial design standards.

Overview of this Chapter

I offer this chapter as a resource for those writers and designers of computer documentation who need to make decisions about illustrations. First, I will review the pertinent research literature according to the type and function of information to be portrayed, followed by a discussion of findings concerned with audience characteristics. Although the documentation requirements of printed manuals will be the major focus of this review, I will also include some research on electronic formats. The studies I cite fall into the following categories:

Representing Realistic Images
- Mental Processes in Perception
- Using Illustrations to Enhance Text
- Choosing a Style of Illustration
- Showing Spatial Relationships

Illustrating Conceptual Information
- Providing User Orientation
- Clarifying Processes and Procedures

Considering Audience Characteristics
- General Abilities and Preferences
- The Effect of Practice

In the second section of this chapter, I will interpret these research findings in order to develop principles for effective illustration of computer documentation. This section includes:

Representing Equipment, Systems and Components
- Photographs Versus Line Drawings
- Spatial Tasks for Hardware

Improving User Orientation Within a Manual

Illustrating Processes and Procedures

Review of Research

Several books and articles provide a theoretical basis and overview for picture perception and visual information processing (Biederman, 1987; Chase, 1973; Kennedy, 1974). However, this review will concentrate on primary empirical research that is relevant to decision-making about documentation design. Most of this research employs either experimental methods in the laboratory or quasi-experimental techniques in field settings.

Representing Realistic Images

Realistic images -- those which have a physical, observable counterpart -- can satisfy several information requirements for documentation. Showing hardware components and configurations is a necessity for installation guides and trouble-shooting manuals. Here pictures can enhance identification of specific parts within a system or aid solution of hardware problems. In these cases, deciding what to illustrate, and choosing between using a photograph or a line drawing, are frequent questions for designers. The search for answers should begin with an analysis of how people see and understand graphics.

Mental Processes in Perception. A quick overview of mental processes in the perception of pictorial information suggests that graphic features -- the type of lines, shapes, and tones, along with their organization on the page -- influence how people recognize and understand pictures. Our perception of these features interact with our memories of real objects and with other mental images. Pictures are encoded in memory differently than words, and we can more easily remember the information from pictures.

Most studies in perceptual psychology have focused on the perception of real, three-dimensional objects and environments rather than on picture perception. Some work has considered how people see particular illustrations, but few investigators have explored how graphic features affect visual information processing.

One exception is a series of experiments by a group of psychologists at Johns Hopkins University (Egeth, Atkinson, Gilmore, and Marcus, 1973). They tested various display configurations, compositions and sizes by measuring viewers' speed and accuracy at identifying embedded letters and linear figures. The arrangement of these shapes affected how long subjects searched for a particular letter or figure; circular arrays took longer to process than linear arrangements. Combinations of graphic features influenced subjects' error rates and reaction times in ways not predicted by then-current theories of visual information processing. Consequently, the researchers cited a need for more adequate theories of perception which could account for peoples' cognitive flexibility. Since perceiving simple letters and figures requires some processing on the cognitive level, certainly more complex pictures like those typically found in computer manuals must interact with users' cognitive processes.

Features within a picture are not seen in isolation. They are considered within the larger "context" of the picture as a whole. Moreover the entire picture is considered within an individual's experiential and cultural context. Perceived context of a picture and how we assign meaning to that picture from memory are important considerations for documentation designers.

Some psychologists and media researchers have investigated the relationships among context, meaning and memory. In a series of five related experiments, Kosslyn (1975) found evidence to support the notion that people's internal mental representations of real objects are quite similar to our perceptions of line drawings. Kosslyn's early work also suggests that when a certain object is illustrated, its relative size and context should match that of its mental representation or we may not be able to recognize and remember it. Later he and colleagues (Jolicoeur, Gluck and Kosslyn, 1984) expanded this theory of "cognitive mapping" to explore the nature of differences between how people recognize pictures and verbal descriptions. They concluded that people may have a single "memory" of an object which can be accessed by pictures or words, but that pictures retrieve this memory more quickly. We understand pictures faster than words.

People process visual and verbal information in two different "modes," with visual processing more effective in many situations. In their study about viewer processing of verbal versus visual components of print advertisements, Childers, Heckler, and Houston (1986) investigated these two different levels of processing. They suggest that pictorial encoding is more elaborate, and that people retain pictures better. In their empirical investigations, subjects remembered more detail about the pictorial components of advertisements than they remembered about the verbal passages. Subjects also recalled more of the central messages of the pictures.

Research about cognitive processes in picture perception thus suggests that people retain pictorial information better, and that they understand it more quickly than verbal descriptions of the same object. Used resourcefully, illustrations can achieve certain communication objectives better than prose.

Using Illustrations to Enhance Text. Empirical evidence overwhelmingly supports the use of illustrations to enhance text. Pictures aid comprehension and retention of complex information, and they help people solve problems more quickly.

Because pictures and words stimulate different mental processes, pictures are most often used to reinforce words. A recent compilation of 46 experiments which tested teaching materials with and without illustrations, showed that the vast majority (85 percent) support the use of pictures to enhance comprehension and retention (Levie and Lentz, 1982). This overall finding also applied to those studies which focused on specific instructional functions similar to some in computer documentation.

Illustrations can be used very effectively to reinforce descriptions of assembly tasks in hardware-oriented documentation. Stone and Glock (1981) found that subjects could assemble a toy model with significantly fewer errors if the text was enhanced by adding line drawings.

More complex procedural tasks also benefit from the addition of pictures. Booher (1975) examined six picture-word formats for their effectiveness in aiding problem-solving tasks. The formats included: text-only, pictorial-only, pictorial-related text, text-related pictorial, pictorial-redundant text, and text-redundant pictorial. In a "related" version the minor format merely reinforced the major; in a "redundant" version it duplicated the content of the major format. These different formats allowed investigation of the relative benefits of each picture-word combination. Pictorial information seemed most crucial to speed in problem solving, while textual information aided accuracy. The combinations of words and pictures were more effective than either mode alone. In fact, pictorial-related text and pictorial-redundant text were the easiest formats to comprehend, perhaps because pictures most directly enhanced the text in these versions.

While including graphics will help readers comprehend the material, the proper placement of that graphic can add to its usefulness. Whalley and Flemming (1975) found that readers spent more time studying a diagram if it was positioned in the text immediately following the sentence that first referred to it.

Incorporating illustrations will help readers understand instructions more easily and will enable them to complete the related tasks with fewer errors. However, this raises a further problem for documentaion designers: the choice between photographs or drawings to represent an object.

Choosing a Style of Illustration. Each type of picture has its strength. Simple drawings are easier to remember, but a photograph is sometimes necessary to provide the degree of realism necessary for interpretation. The choice of an illustration style should depend upon the characteristics of the object which is illustrated, along with how the information will be used.

Simple, realistic line drawings can be identified as easily as photographs, and their information is better retained. In a recent investigation, Biederman and Ju (1988) compared viewers' abilities to perceive and recognize objects when they were represented by color photographs or by line drawings. They found that simple line drawings could be identified as quickly and accurately as fully detailed, textured, color photographs. These researchers also suggest that instructional materials for assembling equipment are more easily followed when the parts are drawn instead of photographed. They argue that the advantage of drawings is not due to any intrinsic perceptual superiority, but rather to the poor quality of photographic reproduction. Reproduced photographs often lack sufficient contrast for determining the contours of the components.

Studies of the importance of verisimilitude in line drawings have generated conflicting results. Some early perceptual research implied that line drawings with exaggerated features, "cartoons," are more easily recognized, but later work contradicts this notion. Tversky and Baratz (1985) tested the relative identification speed for photographic images and political cartoons of famous people. The photographic images were more rapidly identified.

In a series of experiments, Dwyer (1968; 1969) tested eight versions of 37 illustrations which accompanied a 2000-word text teaching the anatomy and physiology of the human heart. The illustrations included simple line drawings; detailed, shaded line drawings; photographs of models of the heart; and photographs of real heart specimens. Each type of visual was represented both in black-and-white and in color. The researchers evaluated subjects on their comprehension of important concepts illustrated in the text, and on their ability to identify parts of the heart through terminology quizzes and drawing tests. Different illustration types proved better for different purposes. Photographs seemed superior for understanding concepts during an evaluation immediately after reading the material, whereas line drawings had a relative advantage for remembering these concepts during delayed tests.

Greater retention for material illustrated with line drawings is corroborated by other work as well (Peeck, 1974; Snodgrass and Volovitz, 1972). While comparing the two drawn formats for the heart material -- detailed, shaded drawings versus simple line drawings -- Arnold and Dwyer (1975) discovered that the different types seemed to develop different mental skills. The more detailed drawings enhanced overall knowledge about the subject, but they did not seem to help with more specific comprehension tasks like answering basic, factual questions. In this case, detailed drawings and simple drawings worked equally well.

In general, information shown by line drawings is more easily remembered, and in many cases drawings are as good as photographs for immediate comprehension. Photographs are better for showing an overall view of a particular piece of equipment. They also can provide depth cues. In this way photographs can be quite useful for providing background or "contextual" information. If photographs are used they should be high contrast and well reproduced.

Showing Spatial Relationships. While many of the preceding studies recommend representational photographs and line drawings for illustrating objects, some functions may be more effectively presented through abstract styles. Spatial tasks related to computer configuration and maintenance, such as the location of circuit cards in a system chassis, may be better represented by schematic drawings because they more closely parallel the way people remember information about physical places. Here the relative placement of picture elements is more important than the degree of realism.

Some empirical evidence indicates that an abstract approach is most effective for the depiction of location. Bartram (1980) tested the use of four different coding schemes for indicating a London bus route: a conventional road map, a schematic map, a list of the stops in sequential order, and a list in alphabetical order.

Although there were no significant differences in accuracy among those using the different coding schemes, the schematic map proved the overwhelmingly fastest and easiest to use when finding locations and planning routes.

This suggests that a schematic style is most effective for conveying relational information. In other words, a more simplified, abstract rendition of computer components is better than a photograph or a realistic drawing for showing spatial relationships.

Illustrating Conceptual Information

Several types of conceptual information challenge the creators of computer documentation. Most common may be the indication of directional cues for using a manual, like "continue to next page," and the illustration of software procedures, such as a "start of day procedure."[1].

Providing User Orientation. One purpose for graphic illustration concerns user orientation within a manual. Users often have difficulty finding the proper section of a computer manual, and graphic cues can help them "orient" themselves. Both "macro-orientation," like indication of overall structure and of particular sections or chapters, and "micro-orientation" within an operation or procedure can be illustrated visually. Graphically-based text organizers can determine how quickly and easily a user navigates through a manual or interactive program, and they may even help retention of the material. Bernard and Peterson (1981) found that two weeks after reading a text with graphic organizers, subjects performed much better on a comprehension test than their counterparts who used text without organizers.

Symbol systems are often used to illustrate directional concepts like "continue to the next page" or "end of procedure." Although the current general wisdom is that iconic symbols -- those which relate to a realistic image -- work best, this may not always be true.

Samet, Geiselman, and Landee (1982) tested three types of conventional, abstract symbols against their iconic counterparts. The conventional symbols were those traditionally used by the military for identifying three different army divisions. The iconic versions illustrated the divisions through more representational sym-

---

[1]Showing temporal or mathematical relationships is another area where visual information can play an important role, and many researchers have addressed appropriate techniques for this purpose. Their findings will not be discussed in this chapter, but those interested in this area should refer to one of the extensive analyses available (Beeby and Taylor, 1973; Burnhill, Hartley and Young, 1976; Cleveland, 1985; Cleveland and McGill, 1984; Macdonald-Ross, 1977; Tufte, 1983).

bols, showing pictograms of tanks and missiles. Each set of symbols was enhanced in two ways: by selectively adding thickness to the symbols' contours, and by adding a three-dimensional effect. Although subject accuracy in finding and reacting to the two types of symbols was relatively similar, people processed the conventional symbols much more quickly than the icons. Enhancements to the icons made them even less effective.

These findings are also supported by another study which evaluated a set of symbols for a helicopter screen display (Remington and Williams, 1986). Here newly created graphic symbols were slower to find and harder to identify than standard numeric symbols. Again, enhancements made the graphic symbols even less effective.

A frequent use of conventional symbol systems is for directional cues in places where people may not share a common language, such as international airports and train stations. In one study, Jones (1978) found that shape was much more important than color to convey meaning in English road signs. This finding was consistent for three different types of messages: warnings, instructions, and general information. Some of the signs included figurative elements, such as vehicles and pedestrians, and others were totally abstract, diagonal slashes and circles. More concrete versions of the signs were easier to interpret than the abstract versions.

In a different study, Jones (1983) asked subjects to create and evaluate their own pictograms for 32 abstract words. She told subjects that their aim was to develop an international symbol language. Participants tended to produce symbols with concrete, figurative illustrations. Of the ten percent of pictograms which were abstract, most incorporated symbols in conventional usage like "!" and "?". When asked to evaluate the pictograms, respondents liked the more concrete versions, with a tendency to like unique ones best.

Graphically-based text organizers can help users locate and remember the information they need from a manual. Although people find more concrete, figurative symbols preferable to abstract ones, symbols in conventional usage are superior to any new type. All symbols and icons should incorporate bold shapes with a minimum of detail and embellishments.[2]

Clarifying Processes and Procedures. Describing conceptual processes and procedures is an important function of software documentation. Empirical evidence from technical communication in other scientific fields supports the use of graphic representations of abstract procedures to enhance understanding and retention of information. Rigney and Lutz (1976) found that chemistry students

[2]For a further analysis of the use of icons, see the chapter by Krull in this volume.

who were trained using graphic analogies of electrochemical reactions comprehended the information much better than their counterparts who used textual information only. The study tested students' knowledge, comprehension, and ability to apply concepts taught by one of two versions of an interactive learning module. Both interactive lessons began with presenting the basic concepts; one described them in greater detail through a text description and the other followed the introduction with an animated computer graphic. Subjects took the same amount of time to complete either lesson. The graphic version was shown to be superior for all three of the learning variables. Students also found the graphic version more enjoyable to use, which implies the worth of pictures to strengthen motivation.

The findings of Royer and Cable (1976) support using illustrations to teach concepts about heat and electricity in physics. They tested students' relative comprehension of abstract passages which were enhanced with illustrations and verbal analogies. Both enhanced formats were understood better than unenhanced text. The format with graphic illustrations seemed to provide the best context for understanding, especially when used to clarify abstract content.

Wright and Reid (1973) evaluated the relative speed and accuracy of adults solving problems using four different information formats. Two of the formats were text-based, bureaucratic style prose and a list of short sentences, while the others were more graphic, a flowchart style algorithm and a table with two-dimensions. The problems concerned a topic new to all of the 68 subjects: the appropriateness of six space vehicles for different types of travel. Those using the prose formats were always slower and more error prone when solving the problems. The effectiveness of the two non-prose formats varied according to the difficulty of the problem-solving tasks. For easy problems the table was fastest; for more difficult ones the algorithm worked best. When the subjects worked from memory the effectiveness of the prose formats improved, with the short sentences having an edge over the bureaucratic prose. The researchers concluded that the optimum format depends upon the conditions of use and the desired learning outcome.

Indeed, technical communicators must choose information formats according to the objectives and purpose of the documentation. An often-used procedure such as "start of day" or routine maintenance should be portrayed in a style different than that used for those procedures which are performed less often, like initial system configuration. If a procedure is performed often, or needs to be remembered, it really should be illustrated. Of course, another consideration for selecting a particular style is who will be using the documentation. The next section discusses audience differences.

Considering Audience Characteristics

The characteristics of a technical communicator's audience, in our case the users of computer manuals, can determine how effective a particular format will be. Writers and designers should consider the general abilities and experience of their intended audience.

General Abilities and Preferences. Several researchers have sought to quantify individual differences in visual versus verbal information processing. Childers and colleagues evaluated four measures of differences in subjects' ability and preference for processing words versus pictures (Childers, Houston, and Heckler, 1985). They found that a strong ability in visual information processing, that is how easily a person can understand pictures, improved memory for pictures.

In fact, users' general cognitive ability affects their comprehension of documentation, perhaps even more strongly than does format. When comparing comprehension levels for picture and word formats, Levin and associates found that ability affected students' proficiency more than information format (Levin, Divine-Hawkins, Kerst, and Guttmann, 1974). Some students process both types of information easily and accurately, while others perform poorly with both.

Manipulation of illustration style improves the performance of slow learners more than that of higher achievers. One study found that high achievers learn equally well despite the illustration format (Dwyer 1975). The use of some types of visuals, black-and-white line drawings in particular, increased the performance of slow learners for comprehending objects and components. More realistic pictures seem to be most effective for improving the performance of slow learners when they are expected to learn abstract concepts. In another study, adding realistic pictures to an abstract diagram about ecological cycles helped students of low verbal ability to understand facts and relationships (Winn and Holliday, 1982).

One way graphics improve performance is through increasing users' motivation. Holliday, Brunner and Donais (1977) tested the relative worth of block figures versus color line drawings for reinforcing scientific concepts. Students with the pictures learned better and were more motivated to perform well.

In general, people like pictures, so they are useful as an aid to motivation even when they may not improve performance. Some evidence supports a preference for photographs and more realistic, detailed drawings as compared to the less realistic formats such as simple line drawings (Myatt and Carter, 1979).

The Effect of Practice. Many visual formats, especially those illustrating abstract content, seem to become more effective with user practice. Egeth and colleagues (1973) found that in repetitive identification tasks for simple line drawings, practice significantly enhanced speed and accuracy. Individual subjects' overall ability also affected their rate of improvement, with the higher ability subjects improving at a greater, and more consistent, rate.

In fact, practice may even counteract some of the initial superiority of graphic formats for some applications. Tullis (1981) tested four different formats for electronic displays of telephone testing procedures: narrative with complete words and phrases; structured narrative which used a tabular format; black-and-white graphics which showed a diagram; and color graphics which showed the same diagram in color. Accuracy did not vary across formats. Initially, response times for the two graphic formats were significantly shorter, but with practice the structured verbal format was equally effective.

Implications for Pictorial Standards

Although the findings of any individual study should not dictate when and how technical communicators use pictures, considered as a whole these research findings can recommend some useful principles. Pictures can greatly improve computer documentation as enhancements to verbal descriptions or as substitutions for text. Graphics also have utility for user orientation within a manual or interactive program. Illustrations should be used liberally within economic constraints. Here are a few empirically supported guidelines and examples of when and how to use pictures most effectively.

Representing Equipment, Systems and Components

Use pictures whenever possible to reinforce verbal descriptions of hardware. Pictures enhance comprehension of assembly and maintenance tasks typically found in installation manuals, and users remember pictorial descriptions better than those which are text-based.

Photographs versus Line Drawings. In many cases these formats can work equally well for identifying equipment and components, provided that the pictures are properly duplicated and have relatively high contrast. Instances where users must see a particular detail, or when they need an overall view of the equipment, can be exceptions. Here the choice between photographs and drawings is more clear-cut.

Line drawings are more effective when the contour of an object is important, such as when the user must differentiate among similar parts or understand a particular feature. Figure 1 shows an example of the type of detail which is less intelligible when illustrated through a photograph. The written documentation to accompany this illustration explains how to set the "forms thickness adjuster" on a printer. Users must notice both the component and the scale for successful adjustment. These details can be more difficult to see in a photograph as shown by Figure 2.

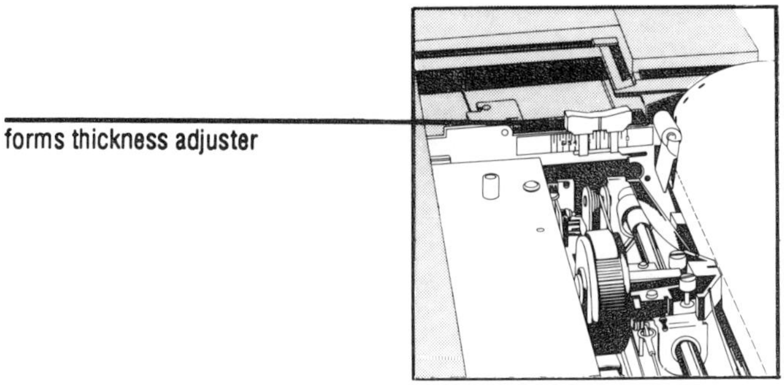

Figure 1: Line Drawing of a Detailed Component on a Printer. Copyright, 1987, by NCR Corporation. All rights reserved. Reprinted with permission.

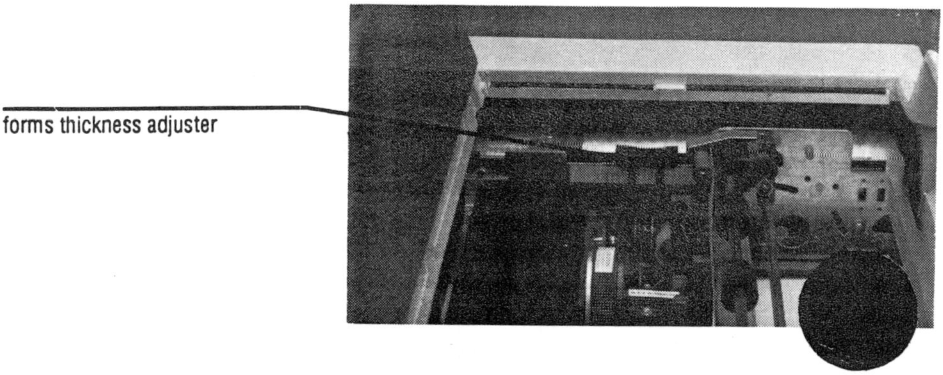

Figure 2: Photograph Where the Component Is Difficult to Find Copyright, 1987, by NCR Corporation. All rights reserved. Reprinted with permission.

In contrast, when users are asked to perform a task which involves several components on the printer, such as installing a ribbon, an overall view is most appropriate. A photograph can better provide the contextual information necessary for orientation to the printer as a whole. The photograph in Figure 3 is more effective than the line drawing in Figure 4 because it supplies the depth cues and overall orientation necessary for this task. Here the drawing may even confuse users because of its more "diagrammatic" style. In general, a realistic photograph is most effective to reinforce global understanding and to provide an adequate context for components and equipment parts.[3]

Figure 3: Photograph which Provides Depth and Context
Copyright, 1987, by NCR Corporation. All rights reserved.
Reprinted with permission.

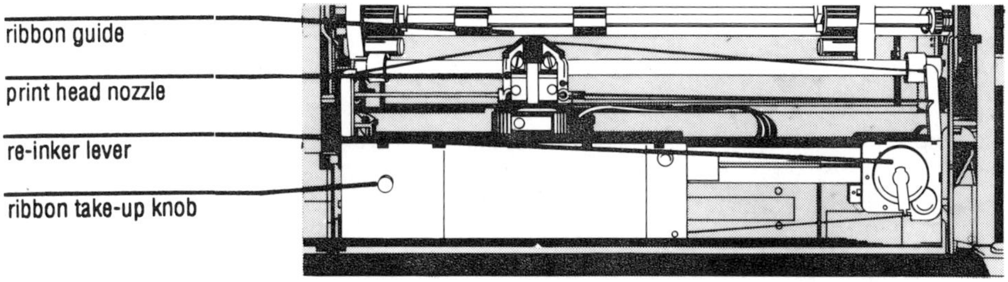

Figure 4: Line Drawing which Fails to Provide Overall Orientation
Copyright, 1987, by NCR Corporation. All rights reserved.
Reprinted with permission.

Sometimes combination of the two formats is more effective than either alone. Using photographs to show context and line drawings to highlight details employs the strengths of each illustration style.

---

[3]These pictures were evaluated during documentation prototype testing at Watzman+Keyes Information Design. Through evaluating the speed and comprehension of 100 users, we found evidence to further support the principles outlined here.

Spatial Tasks for Hardware. More abstract techniques work best for conveying spatial information related to computer configuration and maintenance, such as the relative location of components. Simplified, schematic diagrams are much more quickly understood than realistic line drawings or photographs for spatial tasks like installing a board in a system chassis. The schematic drawing shown in Figure 5 can help a technician understand the relative location and spatial arrangement of the circuit boards.

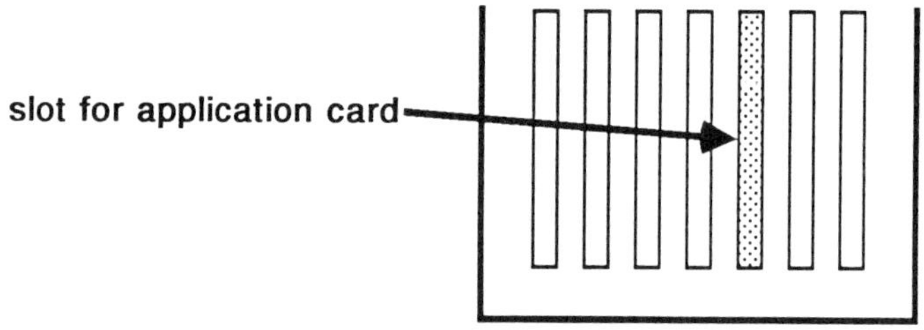

Figure 5: Boards in a Computer Chassis Illustrated Schematically

Details which would be shown by a realistic line drawing are unnecessary and could be confusing. Although a photograph would offer spatial cues through showing an overall view, it may also confuse the viewer through including irrelevant information. The schematic drawing is most effective because it selectively presents only the important features.

Improving User Orientation within a Manual

Graphic organizers can help people locate and remember information within a manual, and symbol systems can be useful as directional cues. The example in Figure 6 uses arrows and a box to guide readers through a decision point in an installation manual.

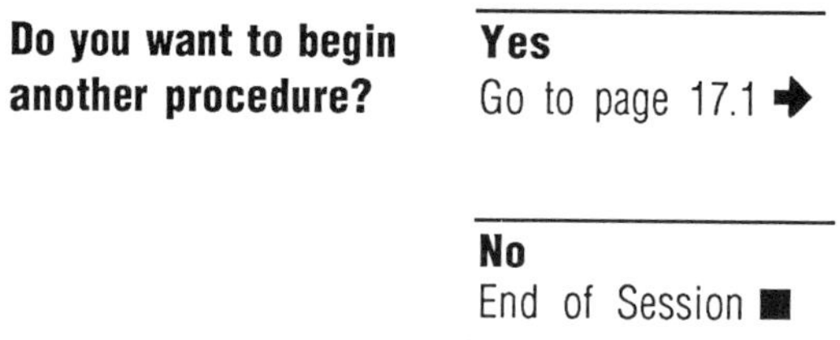

Figure 6: Example of Simple Icons for User Orientation

The choice of icons can be an interesting challenge for designers, with trade-offs between styles which are most easily understood and those which most strongly enhance user motivation. Users understand conventional symbols, like arrows and stop signs, more quickly than novel symbols. This suggests that more obvious, conventional icons are superior for material which is used one-time or only occasionally. With practice, however, users tend to prefer more unique symbols. Designing more interesting symbols for manuals or documentation sets can enhance user satisfaction.

In general, concrete symbols or icons are easier to interpret than those which are purely abstract. Bold, simple shapes are most effective for both iconic and abstract formats. A distinctive shape is more important for identification than detail or color. Other graphic embellishments, such as three-dimensional effects only degrade effectiveness.

Illustrating Processes and Procedures

Graphic analogies, like flow diagrams and hierarchical arrangement of concepts, help users complete abstract processes more quickly and with fewer errors. For easy procedures a simple table or list format works best, but complex processes require a more dimensional diagram. Figure 7 shows a diagrammatic description for the sequence of steps in a typical spreadsheet session.

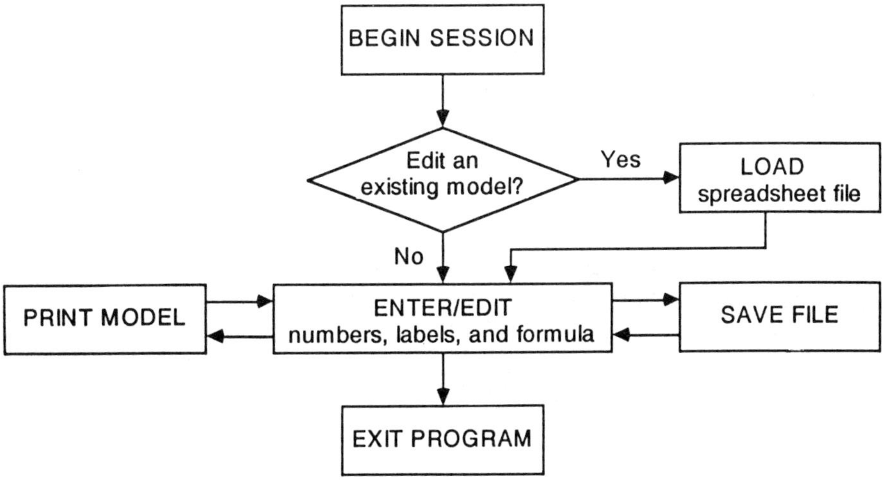

Figure 7: Flow Diagram Showing Steps in a Typical Spreadsheet Session

Although this procedure is not very complex, it includes a decision point and two iterative process options, printing and saving. The diagram concisely illustrates the relationships among all of the sub-tasks in a format more quickly understood than a purely verbal description.

The Need for More Research

Pictorial information is a vital part of effective computer documentation, and research offers some clues for the intelligent use of pictures. Unfortunately, many gaps in our knowledge remain. In my search through dozens of journals and several databases, I found few studies with direct relevance to documentation design. This dearth poses a challenge for those of us engaged in empirical work.

Research questions abound. How does the degree of realism in an illustration interact with users' performance? Which graphic features are most important for user orientation within a manual? What type of diagrams are most easily understood? How do factors like users' level of computer experience and type of task affect the usefulness of pictures? Can design principles for print media translate to electronic formats?

More generally, we need to focus on such pragmatic research issues with subjects who represent typical users. We should investigate not only how users acquire knowledge, but also how they apply it in realistic problem-solving situations.

References

Arnold, T.L. and Dwyer, F.M., "Realism in Visualized Instruction," *Perceptual and Motor Skills,* vol. 40, 1975, pp. 369-370.

Bartram, D.J., "Comprehending Spatial Information: The Relative Efficiency of Different Methods of Presenting Information About Bus Routes," *Journal of Applied Psychology,* vol. 65, 1980, pp. 103-110.

Beeby, A.W. and Taylor, H., "How Well Can We use Graphs?" *Communicator of Scientific and Technical Information,* vol. 17, 1973, pp. 7-11.

Bernard, R.M., Petersen, C.H., and Ally, M., "Can Images Provide Contextual Support for Prose?" *Journal of Educational Communication and Technology,* vol. 29, no. 2, 1981, pp. 101-108.

Biederman, I., "Recognition by Components: A Theory of Human Image Understanding," *Psychological Review,* vol. 94, 1987, pp. 115-145.

Biederman, I. and Ju, G., "Surface versus Edge-based Determinants of Visual Recognition," *Cognitive Psychology,* vol. 20, no. 1, 1988, pp. 38-63.

Booher, H., "Relative Comprehensibility of Pictorial Information and Printed Words in Proceduralized Instructions," *Human Factors,* vol. 17, 1975, pp. 266-277.

Burnhill, P., Hartley, J. and Young, M., "Tables in Text" *Applied Ergonomics,* vol. 7, 1976, pp. 13-18.

Chase, W.G., ed., *Visual Information Processing,* New York, Academic Press, 1973.

Childers, T.L., S.E. Heckler and M.J. Houston, "Memory for the Visual and Verbal Components of Print Advertisements," *Psychology & Marketing,* vol. 3, 1986, pp. 137-150.

Childers, T.L., M.J. Houston and S.E. Heckler, "Measurement of Individual Differences in Visual Versus Verbal Information Processing," *Journal of Consumer Research,* vol. 12, 1985, pp. 125-134.

Cleveland, W.S., *The Elements of Graphing Data,* Monterey, CA, Wadsworth Advanced Book Program, 1985.

Cleveland, W.S. and McGill, R., "Graphical Perception: Theory, Experimentation and Application to the Development of Graphical Methods," *Journal of the American Statistical Association,* vol. 79, no. 387, 1984, pp. 531-554.

Dwyer, F.M. "On Visualized Instruction: Effects of Students' Entering Behavior," *Journal of Experimental Education,* vol. 43, 1975, pp. 78-83.

Dwyer, F.M, "The Effect of Varying the Amount of Realistic Detail in Visual Illustration Designed to Complement Programmed Instruction," *Programmed Learning and Educational Technology,* vol. 6, 1969, pp. 147-153.

Dwyer, F.M., "The Effectiveness of Visual Illustrations Used to Complement Programmed Instruction," *Journal of Psychology,* vol. 70, 1968, pp. 157-162.

Dwyer, F.M. "Exploratory Studies in the Effectiveness of Visual Illustrations," *AV Communication Review,* vol. 18, 1970, pp. 235-249.

Egeth, H., Atkinson, J., Gilmore, G., and Marcus, N., "Factors Affecting Processing Mode in Visual Search," *Perception and Psychophysics,* vol. 13, no. 3, 1973, pp. 394-402.

Holliday, W.G., Brunner, L.L. and Donais, E.L., "Differential Cognitive and Effective Responses to Flow Diagrams," *Journal of Research in Science Teaching,* vol. 14, 1977, pp. 129-138.

Jolicoeur, P., Gluck, M.A. and Kosslyn, S.M., "Pictures and Names: Making the Connection," *Cognitive Psychology,* vol. 16, no. 2, 1984, pp. 243-275.

Jones, S., "Symbolic Representation of Abstract Concepts," *Ergonomics,* vol. 21, no. 4, 1978, pp. 573-577.

Jones, S., "Stereotypy in Pictograms of Abstract Concepts," *Ergonomics,* vol. 26, no. 6, 1983, pp. 605-611.

Kennedy, J.M., *A Psychology of Picture Perception,* San Francisco, Jossey-Bass, 1974.

Kosslyn, S.M., "Information Representation in Visual Images," *Cognitive Psychology,* vol. 7, 1975, pp. 341-370.

Levie, W.H. and Lentz, R., "Effects of Text Illustrations: A Review of Research," *Journal of Educational Communication and Technology,* vol. 30, no. 4, 1982, pp. 195-232.

Levin, J.R. Divine-Hawkins, P., Kerst, S.M. and Guttmann, J., "Individual Differences in Learning from Pictures and Words: The Development and Application of an Instrument," *Journal of Educational Psychology,* vol. 66, 1974, pp. 296-303.

Macdonald-Ross, M., "How Numbers are Shown: A Review of Research on the Presentation of Quantitative Data in Texts," *AV Communication Review,* vol. 25, 1977, pp. 359-409.

Myatt, B. and J.M. Carter, "Picture Preferences of Children and Young Adults," *Journal of Educational Communication and Technology,* vol. 27, 1979, pp. 45-53.

Peeck, J. "Retention of Pictorial and Verbal Content of a Text with Illustrations," *Journal of Educational Psychology,* vol. 66, 1974, pp. 880-888.

Remington, R. and Williams, D., "On the Selection and Evaluation of Visual Display Symbology: Factors Influencing Search and Identification Times," *Human Factors,* vol. 28, no. 4, 1986, pp. 407-420.

Rigney, J.W. and Lutz, K.A., "Effects of Graphic Analogies of Concepts in Chemistry on Learning and Attitude," *Journal of Educational Psychology,* vol. 68, 1976, pp. 305-311.

Royer, J.M. and Cable, G.W., "Illustration Analogies, and Facilitative Transfer in Prose Learning," *Journal of Educational Psychology,* vol. 68, 1976, pp. 205-209.

Samet, M.G., Geiselman, R.E. and Landee, B.M., "A Human Performance Evaluation of Graphic Symbol Design Features," *Perceptual and Motor Skills,* vol. 54, 1982, pp. 1303-1310.

Snodgrass, J.G., Volovitz, R., and Walfish, E.R., "Recognition Memory for Words, Pictures and Words and Pictures," *Psychonomic Science,* vol. 27, 1972, pp. 345-347.

Stone, D.E. and Glock, M.D., "How do Young Adults read Directions with and without Pictures?" *Journal of Educational Psychology,* vol. 73, 1981, pp. 419-426.

Tversky, B. and Baratz, D., "Memory for Faces: Are Caricatures better than Photographs?" *Memory and Cognition,* vol. 13, 1985, pp. 45-49.

Tufte, E.R., *The Visual Display of Quantitative Information,* Cheshire, CT, Graphics Press, 1983.

Tullis, T.S., "An Evaluation of Alphanumeric, Graphic, and Color Information Displays," *Human Factors,* vol. 23, no. 5, 1981, pp. 541-550.

Whalley, P.C. and Flemming, R.W. "An Experiment with a Simple Recorder of Reading Behavior," *Programmed Learning and Educational Technology,* vol 12, 1975, pp. 120-123.

Winn, W. and Holliday, W., "Design Principles for Diagrams and Charts," in D.H. Jonassen, editor, *The Technology of Text: Principles for Structuring, Designing, and Displaying Text,* Educational Technology Publications, Englewood Cliffs, NJ, 1982, pp. 277-299.

Wright, P. and Reid, F., "Written Information: Some Alternatives to Prose for Expressing the Outcomes of Complex Contingencies, *Journal of Applied Psychology*, vol. 57, 1973, pp. 160-166.

12 If Icon, Why Can't You?

Robert Krull

Communication Research Laboratory
Rensselaer Polytechnic Institute
Troy, NY 12180-3590
USERBTFO@RPITSMTS

Graphic computer interfaces like those found on the Apple Macintosh, the Xerox Star, and to be included with the IBM OS/2 Presentation Manager have developed reputations for their learnability and usability. Some analysts even have argued that computing systems will have limited acceptance in offices unless they adopt such systems (eg. Sniger, 1984). Icons, small pictures representing computer parts or functions, are a part of several graphics interfaces and have drawn a great deal of attention.

To be sure, the icons play a role in interfaces; but the icons by themselves are not the only reason these interfaces are effective. The interfaces' other features collectively play a great role. Not all icon-based interfaces are equally well designed or better than command-driven interfaces (Whiteside, Jones, Levy, & Wixon, 1985). Adding icons to a poorly designed interface will not improve it and, in fact, may detract from an interface.

Graphic interfaces have also been called ***direct manipulation*** interfaces (Shneiderman, 1987). This term probably more effectively captures how these interfaces are used. Rather than having to type file names, command names, and so on, users can point at items on the screen using a mouse or cursor keys. In effect, users can directly manipulate the items on a screen. Graphics depicting icons, window boundaries, and file names, while pleasing to look at, help users because of how users act on them. The direct manipulation interaction style reduces typing errors and eases user memory and learning loads.

Features common to many modern interfaces are summarized in Figure 1.

Figure 1

Features of Direct Manipulation Interfaces

Feature	Advantage for Users
Icons	Allow users to guess what objects do. Allows rapid scanning of the screen.
Point-and-do	Reduces memory load and typing errors.
Windows	Show two or more views of material necessary to do a task. Allow comparisons and integration of subtasks.
Pull-down menus and fast keys.	Provide memory cues to command options. Allow sampling of options without requiring extensive navigation or error recovery. Teaches command operation while showing menus.

In this chapter I discuss two major issues -- the role of icons as a computer language system; and the remaining features of graphic interfaces. In discussing the first issue, icons as a language, I will review research on the following: pictographic language systems, cuneiform and hieroglyphs, computer pictograms and analogs, pictograph grammars, and icon extensibility. I will discuss these issues, but in doing so will attempt to build an understanding of how other graphic features work. In discussing this second issue I will review research on the following topics: point-and-do execute functionality, windows, pull-down menus and fast keys. In this section I will show what these features have in common with icons. I will conclude the chapter with suggestions about when and how these features are most effectively used.

Icons and How They Work

Written forms of computer languages have evolved from arcane numeric notations such as binary arithmetic, through lower level and higher computer languages to direct manipulation interfaces. This evolution has been made possible by the computer's increasing power and has been driven by users' demands for more accommodating systems.

Written forms of natural language have also evolved, but not along the same path. Early pictographic systems gave way to cuneiform, and then to phonetic spelling systems, such as the English alphabet. Again the demand has been for increases in ease of using written language, but the features of usability are somewhat different from those of computer languages. This difference may be important in drawing parallels between the two kinds of language systems.

Pictographs of Natural Languages

Pictographs of natural languages represent their meaning independently of the sound of a spoken language -- pictures are used to stand for the visual image of objects rather than for the sound of the objects' name (Fromkin & Rodman, 1983). Highway pictorgraphs, for example, indicate an upcoming bend in a road by placing a curved arrow on a sign. The arrow is meant to depict the shape of the road rather than the sound of the word "bend". Pictograms, therefore, are very useful when people who speak different languages attempt to communicate.

Over time, natural languages extend their symbols' meanings from a single object to attributes of that object or to concepts related to it. These symbols, called ideograms, have the advantage of denoting a wider range of concepts. A disadvantage is that their meanings are less obvious. For example, highway signs, although often pictures of real objects, really stand for ideas about how drivers are to behave (Eliot, 1960). These signs require some learning by their users.

Cuneiform and Hieroglyphs

Cuneiform, written with a system of triangular marks, evolved from pictures of objects to words representing the sounds of syllables or whole words (Fromkin & Rodman, 1983). In other words, cuneiform encodes spoken names of concepts rather than how concepts look to the eye. The advantage of this and other phonetic encoding systems are that words can refer to abstract concepts with no visual form.

Being able to represent abstract concepts probably is the driving force behind the movement of most languages from pictographic to alphabetic writing. Chinese characters, for example, grew greatly in number over time and changed from pictographic representations of concrete meanings to representations of the sounds of the language for abstract meanings (Wood & Wood, 1987).

Hieroglyphs were not pictures of objects but rather symbols for the syllables of a spoken language. So hieroglyphs, although they look like icons, really work more like the alphabet of English. One might design computer writing in forms similar to cuneiform, hieroglyphs or Chinese characters, but little would be gained from such an effort. They would demand at least as much learning as commands written with an alphabet.

Pictograms of Computer Languages

Written computer languages could take several forms, differing in the symbols used and the meanings denoted. The options are shown in Figure 2. The first column in the figure contains symbol options; the second contains categories of computer terms to be denoted. The third column, containing categories from language grammars, will be discussed later in the paper.

The key here is the dimension of *iconicity* -- the degree of visual similarity between a symbol and its referent. When the referent (the concept to be represented) is concrete, it should be possible to find a pictorial symbol for it. The relationship between the symbol and the referent then could be called iconic. As the figure suggests, icons can be designed most easily for physical objects such as video display terminals, printers, keyboards and other peripherals.

When the meaning to be denoted is abstract, it may not be possible to find an unambiguous visual symbol and the sound of its name in a language may be more appropriate. The relationship between the printed alphabetic symbols for the sound of a word and their meaning is non-iconic. Since the level of encoding here involves an alphabet or numbers, both digits, one can also call it digital encoding. Palmer (1986) makes essentially the same distinction, calling the two

Figure 2

Levels of Computer Writing

Form of Encoding	Computer Level	Language Level
Iconic | Analogic | Digital	Hardware | Software | Functions	Nouns | Verbs

extremes realistic and abstract.

Computer icons have difficulty with abstract concepts (Krull, 1985). Recently developed computer icons, like modern Chinese characters, have themselves become more abstract and less obvious in meaning to users (Wood & Wood, 1987). Such icons probably don't work very well. Figure 2 pairs digital writing with abstract computer concepts -- functions such as cutting, pasting, and so on. Alphabetic writing systems seem more appropriate to these concepts, a point to which I shall return in discussing the third column in the figure.

Analogic Writing in Computing

Many concepts may be only partially captured by visual symbols; they are between the extremes on my iconicity dimension. This is probably the level at which most computer "icons" operate. They encode a part rather than the whole of a concept's meaning; they are really ***analogs***. For example, the Apple Macintosh's trash can "icon" is unlike trash cans found in most offices and functions differently from a real trash can. It only tries to capture some features common to throwing away computer and office files. Graphic symbols that are clearly intended to be analogs, such as thermometers representing the level of completion of tasks (eg. Myers, 1985), can nevertheless be helpful to users.

Unfortunately, much of computing and, indeed much of office work, deals with abstract concepts. For example, word processors might be construed as ***things*** rather than collections of functions. But specific operations of word processors -- block moves and so on -- are abstract concepts and would be more difficult to represent pictographically.

These limitations of pictographic analogs mislead users about which of several functions an analog denotes (Fahnrich & Ziegler, 1985). The problem is made more acute by users' style of learning, which tends to be spotty rather than comprehensive (Hammond & Barnard, 1985). If users had comprehensive knowledge of computer products, they could compare a particular analog to others they know about and guess its meaning by a process of elimination. Since their learning is spotty, users have to work out each analog's meaning from its visual features. Since only some of an analog's features are relevant, the end result can be that users misjudge a substantial proportion of supposedly obvious "icon" meanings (Carroll & Mazur, 1986).

A solution used by Apple and other graphic interface designers has been to apply a consistent metaphoric framework to drive icon generation. Since designers wanted to increase the use of small computers by office workers, they chose physical objects from offices to make up their metaphoric frame. Icons for graphic interfaces were given some of the attributes of their real-world counterparts so that users could guess how they worked by thinking about how real offices worked (Hemenway, 1982; Bewley, Roberts, Schroit, & Verplank, 1983).

As direct manipulation have gained in popularity, so has the term icon. It seems that currently any picture or symbol in a computer interface is called an icon, no matter what it represents. While Wood and Wood (1987) are very clear about the differences among symbols that represent concepts visually or phonetically, concretely or abstractly, they still refer to all pictorial signs as icons, a point of view that obscures how pictographs function.

Pictograph Grammars

If one looks at icon generation from the standpoint of the grammar of natural languages (Krull, 1985), icons may be easier to find for the nouns in a language than for verbs and other parts of speech. In the third column of Figure 2 I have shown why this may be the case for computer systems as well. The nouns in computer systems can be abstract concepts, but most frequently will be concrete physical objects such as hardware. I have already argued that physical objects can be represented by pictographs. The verbs in computer systems most frequently are functions or actions. These are less easily represented pictographically.

Wood and Wood (1987) agree that icons for verbs are difficult to generate and thus require users' learning their meanings. Hemenway (1982) argues that computer icons may represent either command operations (verbs) or the objects of operations (nouns). She suggests that the verbs may be represented by what they do rather than how they look. Only when these analogies are obvious to users, as when drawn from a strong and familiar metaphoric framework like a desktop, will they work well (Bewley, Roberts, Schroit, & Verplank, 1983). Even then, one should expect more successful icons for nouns than for verbs. An indication of the truth of this proposition is that most of the verbs appearing on the Apple Macintosh desktop take the form of written words.

One solution to icon ambiguity is to combine encoding systems. That is, to join icons with written labels. This form of redundant encoding can help reduce interpretation errors for icons representing objects and actions. Bewley, Roberts, Schroit, and Verplank (1983) found that users made 25 percent fewer errors when icons they were seeing for the first time were accompanied by labels. Palmer (1986) found that labels combined with icons produced more rapid, accurate visual search of computer menus than did the labels alone. In both cases, the labels seemed to make a difference in users' understanding what an icon represented. For a related discussion of research into the combination of verbal and pictorial information see Lewis in this volume.

Extensibility of Icon Systems

Another issue in generating complete icon systems is the poor extensibility of pictographic encoding. Designers may need to extend iconic systems when they add functions to a single computer product or when they attempt to link two computer products, such as a word processor and a paint program. Individual products can be extended by adding new icons or by modifying the appearance of existing ones. As products become complex, however, icons and their properties can become inconsistent with one another (Wood & Wood, 1987). The metaphor driving the icon system loses its focus, again leading to confusion (Halasz & Moran, 1982; Carroll & Mazur, 1986). For example, many computer paint programs mix pictographs of the object to be produced (such as a rectangle) with analogs of a tool for producing effects (such as a spray can). Users may become confused about whether pictographs represent effects or tools.

Links among computer software products probably work best when a common metaphor is used to generate their interfaces. Then users can employ what they know about one program to learning about another (Bewley, Roberts, Schroit, & Verplank, 1983). However, even when the icons for two programs are the same and the tasks seem similar in many ways, users may have difficulty transferring their knowledge (Ziegler, Hoppe, and Fahnrich, 1986).

Together these studies of natural language writing systems and of computer interfaces demonstrate that icons have value and limitations. They have value in reducing users' learning period. Their limitations are in handling abstract concepts and complex, extended systems. Designers should look beyond icons to other aspects of direct manipulation interfaces to find additional routes to product usability.

Beyond Icons: Other Features Of Direct Manipulation Interfaces

Point-and-Do

Traditional computer interaction requires users' typing commands from memory, which invites typing and memory errors. Some users are poor typists; all of them will make errors at some time or another. When programs have complex and rigid command syntax, users make what appear to be small errors, but which stop computers from carrying out commands (Krull & Rubens, 1986). Point-and-do, or as they are sometimes militaristically called, point-and-shoot interfaces markedly reduce the amount of typing required. They enable to users to point at command names and objects of action (such as file names and computer devices). When the pointer falls over an object on the screen and a button is pressed, the object changes in some way to tell the user that it has been selected. This feedback helps users make fewer pointing errors, and smooths their interaction with the machine.

The other helpful aspect of point-and-do interaction is its reducing user memory load. Instead of having to recall command and file names from memory, users can rapidly scan through a list of items on the computer screen. The visible list gives new users an idea of the range of things they can do (Garner, 1974) and reminds casual users of things they have done before (Holcomb & Tharp, 1985). In this way graphic interaction lets users capitalize on their spatial skills rather than requiring them to work through more difficult abstract verbal reasoning processes (Heckel, 1984; Hemenway, 1982; Shamonsky, 1985; Muter & Mayson, 1986). It can mean that users are able to do many tasks without having to search through a printed manual.

Point-and-do is most effective when the meaning of objects on the screen and their properties are unmistakable. Then users can explore interfaces, acting on screen items as if they were real (Shamonsky, 1985), guessing about appropriate actions as they go (Fahnrich & Ziegler, 1985), For example, the terms ***cut*** and ***paste*** used in many word processors having pull-down menus is fairly unambiguous. They refer to cutting a section out of a document or pasting one into a document. Less clear is that they require a user to mark a block of text to be cut or pasted prior to having the cut or paste take effect. Once users have figured that out, though, they can perform these actions without too many errors.

Less transparent are screen objects that lead users into extended dialogs. For example, ***format*** menu choices for some word processors lead to dialogs about margins, headers and footers and so on. In other word processors, ***format*** may lead to dialog about type variations such as typefaces, type sizes, and font variations such as boldface. In either case, users have to do more than just point at an item on the screen. In some cases, users will not know this in advance and may spend considerable effort returning to where they blundered into a dialog. Ideally, point-and-do interfaces should make clear what properties a screen object has.

An additional aspect of point-and-do that needs to be unambiguous is action grammar. For example, users may be faced with the following question: To delete a text file from a diskette, should they point at the text file and then point at the command ***cut*** or should they first point at ***cut*** and then at the name of the text file? Command-based computer systems normally expect the user to follow an English-like syntax of typing the command name (the verb) first and then the file name (the object). Point-and-do interfaces typically follow a physical action order of selecting an object by pointing at it (the object of the command) and then selecting the command (the verb) (Krull, 1985; Bewley, Roberts, Schroit, & Verplank, 1983). This deviation from natural language syntax and from command-driven systems (Hammond & Barnard, 1985) may be confusing to some users.

Some point-and-do interfaces are not consistent in syntax, sometimes starting with the verb and sometimes with the noun (Carroll & Mazur, 1986). The Apple program MacWrite follows English syntax for saving documents. The user points at the command ***Save as ...*** and then types the file name. This is a standard verb-object imperative sentence. MacWrite uses a different syntax for deleting text. The user must first define a section of text by pointing at it and then chooses the command *Cut*. This sequence is in a non-English object-verb order. These sequences are used very frequently with MacWrite and are sufficiently simple to be learned well. However, such inconsistency are likely to be problematic with commands users need to access infrequently.

Most point-and-do interfaces include one other feature -- reversibility. They allow users to undo what they have done. By letting users point at several objects without acting on them further, point-and-do lets users hunt for precisely the object they want. Allowing for easy reversal of actions, either through an *Undo* option or through complementary opposing actions, can save users considerable aggravation (Shneiderman, 1987; Shamonsky, 1985).

Windows

A ***window*** is an artificially bounded area, that may contain text or graphics, falling inside the physical limits of a computer screen. The area may cover the entire screen or some part of the screen. Windows may appear on a screen one after another; or several windows may coexist on a screen at one time (Card, Pavel & Farrell, 1985).

Since users often need to work with several pieces of information to complete a single task, presenting information on a computer screen in windows is advantageous. Depending on how windowing is handled, users can compare information in two windows, copy information between windows, and even work on different aspects of a task by running different software in different windows. All of these techniques save user effort and reduce user memory load. Rather than having to remember information, users can look at several pieces of information at once. Windows then serve the role of external memory banks (Card, Pavel & Farrell, 1985).

An indication of windows' value is shown by how they are used. Gaylin (1986), for example, found that users worked with about four windows at a time and that the bulk of user actions involved moving from one window to the other, searching for information. It seems that users do indeed like using windows and want access to several windows' worth of information in completing tasks (eg. Murrell, 1983).

Window Properties and Usability

Although all windows are depicted on screens using information coding, not all windows work the same way. The arrangement of windows on screens is of two basic types -- tiled windows and overlapping windows (Bly & Rosenberg, 1986; Holcomb & Tharp, 1985). Of course windows may also be arranged to appear on a screen one after the other. These ***time-multiplexed*** windows (Card, Pavel & Farrell, 1985) may also be combined with tiled or overlapped windows for a staggering range of window options.

In ***tiled*** systems windows are placed beside one another on the screen. If an additional window is placed on a screen, other windows must be adjusted to make room for it. The simplest case in this system is of one window covering the whole screen; a complex case is many windows on a screen, each of a different size and shape. A tiled, multi-window view can be quite confusing to look at because so many small windows are visible at once. The main advantages of tiled windows is that they require little manipulation on the part of users and that users can see at once all of the windows containing information (Bly & Rosenberg, 1986).

Overlapping window systems allow parts of one window to cover another window. Any one of several overlapped windows can be made to fill an entire screen. The advantages of this system are that users can apply all of their screen space to work with one window at a time without having to close other windows and that window shape can be adjusted to fit the tasks they contain. There are two main disadvantages with overlapping windows -- managing them can become an additional task users have to take care of (Bly & Rosenberg, 1986), and they produce the princess-and-the-pea problem. That is, overlapping windows can be layered like mattresses in the fairy tale about the princess and the pea. Users may know that an item of importance, the pea of the story, lies among the layers but not at which layer. Finding the item may require fiddling with several windows -- closing, resizing or moving them.

As I mentioned earlier, window depictions involve information coding. They involve coding because a designer needs to indicate to a user where a window is (its boundaries) and how to act on it. In this way windows share many properties with icons. Often window boundaries and action systems are combined. When windows are part of direct manipulation interfaces, users expect to act on windows by directly acting on them. Screen windows, like physical windows, have frames that users can manipulate and "panes" through which users can see things.

Computer window frames are depicted (or coded) through graphic characters or color or both. Different parts of window frames may operate differently and this too is shown by graphic coding. These are forms of analog language coding -- the graphic characters on the screen share a few of the properties of a physical object, but not all of the properties of the object. On most window systems, for example, you couldn't paint or alter the physical characteristics of the window frame itself and window frames disappear when one changes to another software program or turns the computer off.

Figure 3 shows a typical window. By pointing at the top of the frame, users may move the window around the computer screen. The sides of the frame may be used to resize a window by ***dragging*** them across the screen using a mouse pointer. Many windows, like this one, employ a graphic character to allow users to close the window. Here the graphic character is a small square. One might think that

Figure 3

A Computer Window

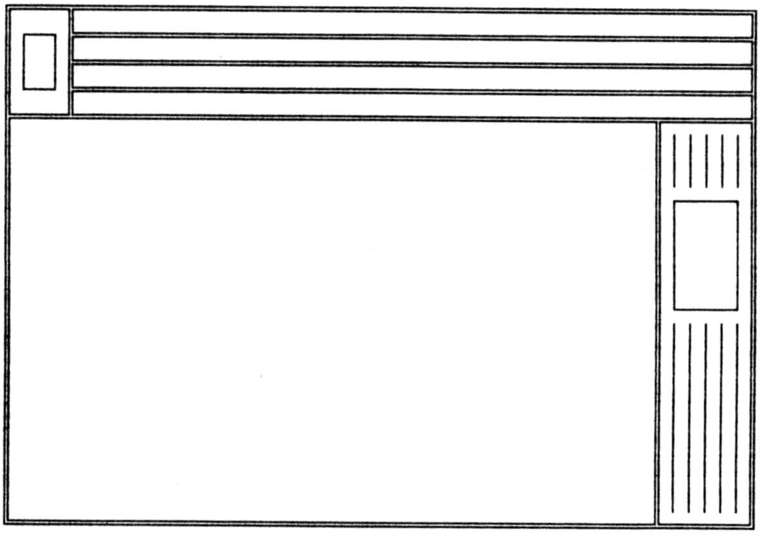

this square is an icon, but it really is not. It isn't because the picture is not of an object or any other physical item. It represents a function and therefore is encoded arbitrarily in the same way as letters on a page encode the meaning of words.

The window also includes a ***slider*** or ***elevator***. This is the rectangular box in the long channel on the right side of the window. Again this is often referred to as an icon, but is really an analog. Real windows don't have elevators; and real elevators have little in common with this graphic device other than moving up and down. For example, when one moves the box in the computer elevator, text or graphics in the adjacent window move up and down. In real elevators, the items adjacent to the elevator (people and offices, for example) stay in one location and the contents of the elevator move up and down.

These encoded aspects of windows support user learning and performance by providing flexible views of tasks if the analogic encoding is understandable to users. If, for example, users can grasp the common and different properties of real and computer windows, they may be able to guess the functions of the latter from their experience with the former. However, when the analogy is obscure, as with the close box, users cannot find a relevant real world experience to apply and will not be able to use the encoded information successfully.

Pull-downs and Fast Keys

Pull-down menus are dynamic menus that appear on a computer screen, allow some user action to be performed on the menu, and then disappear. The labels at the top level of the menu tree are always visible on the screen in an area called the ***menu bar***.

The pull-down gets its name from the physical actions users perform with a mouse to select items from the menu. Users point at a label at the top level of the menu. This causes the menu associated with the label to pull or drop downward on the computer screen. Users then slide the mouse pointer further down the menu to the item they seek. On many computer products equivalent actions can also be performed with key stroke combinations, but the name for the menu style derives from the mouse interaction pattern. Figure 4 shows the major features of a pull-down menu.

Figure 4

A Pull-down Menu with Fast Keys

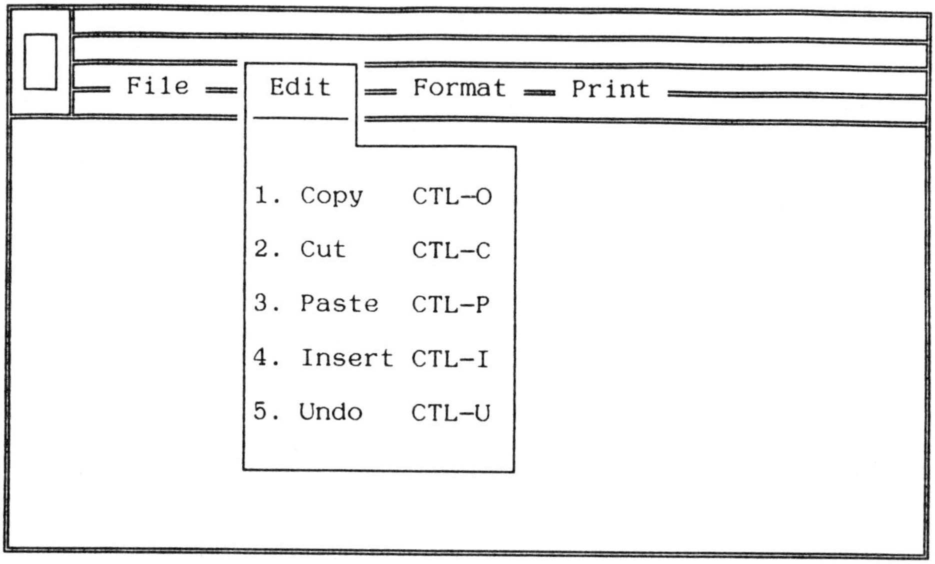

Pull-down menus share at least one usability property with windows -- they can be made to appear when they are needed and disappear when they are not. They also share some graphics features. They have boundaries marked by graphics and contain items at which users can point.

Because the pull-down menu appears at the users' request, it is easier for users to pay attention to important information. Users can concentrate on just one set of menus at a time when a menu is pulled down. Conversely they do not have to look at any menus when no menus are pulled down. Pull-downs reduce demands on user memory because they cue users about the options available and do not ask users to remember command names (Bewley, Roberts, Schroit, & Verplank, 1983).

Many pull-down menu systems also include ***fast keys*** or ***speed keys***, an indication in the menu of the keyboard command that performs the same function as a menu item. Figure 4 shows that pressing the control key and letter O together has the same effect as choosing the copy option from the menu. Every time a user looks at a menu item she also sees the corresponding key combination. Users may more quickly learn command sequences this way than by going through tutorials.

Additional advantages of pull-downs relate to users' making errors and to their navigating among menus. Pull-downs reduce the consequences of errors by allowing users easily to check a second and third menu if they don't find the item they want in the first menu. Rather than backing out of incorrect command sequences or navigating up and down the hierarchy of a conventional menu tree, users simply push their pointer to the next menu. Since research has shown that users make many navigation errors in working with menu systems (Savage & Habinek, 1984; Savage, Habinek, and Barnhart, 1982), a system allowing them easy error recovery could save considerable time.

Pull-downs also help navigation by always showing what the top level of menu choices are. This helps users guess the path likely to contain the item they are seeking. Research has demonstrated that users' guesses about complex problems are better when they know the full range of items available (Garner, 1974) and the top levels of menus probably provide such an indicator.

Finally, pull-downs probably give users a sense of security about where they are. Pull-downs don't overwrite what users have been working on. The window frame and its contents are still on the screen, showing users where they are in tasks.

Designing Optimal Interfaces

Designing effective interfaces can involve using icons. The Xerox Star and the Apple Macintosh are products whose well-known interfaces do include many icons. However, effective, modern interfaces can be produced without icons. In fact, given the rapid development of computer systems and the poor extensibility of pictographic encoding schemes, designers could be cautioned to concentrate their energies on other aspects of interface design. My guess is that pictographic coding is a transitional phase in computer interface design. Icons probably will not disappear, but they will become one among many useful parts of future interaction systems.

The areas I think most promising contain the other characteristics of direct manipulation interfaces -- point-and-do, windows, dynamics menus, and so on. Powerful operating system shells have been developed for small computers by concentrating on these features. They work well with few or no icons.

I have summarized my suggestions in Figure 5. Many existing, successful interfaces already incorporate them.

Figure 5

Applying Direct Manipulation Interface Features

Icons	* Use icons for objects but not for actions; * Add labels to icons to reduce ambiguity; * Don't use icons with abstract topics; * Don't expect icons to sustain an interface by themselves.
Point-and-Do	* To reduce typing errors, allow users to point at items on the screen; * Cue user memory by letting users see options on the screen; * Let users sample from screen options without making their actions permanent; * Follow a consistent sequence for all actions; * Provide feedback to users about their actions.
Windows	* Make available several windows to let users have more than one view of parts of tasks; * If users need flexibility, let windows be moveable and resizable; * Make window boundaries unmistakable; * Make window features obvious in meaning and consistent in functioning.
Pull-downs and Fast Keys	* Use pull-down menus to reduce window clutter; * Use pull-downs as cues to user memory; * Let users easily sample menu choices; * Show fast-key equivalents for menu choices to teach users the faster interaction mode.

BIBLIOGRAPHY

Bewley, William L., Roberts, Teresa L., Schroit, David, Verplank, William L. Human factors testing in the design of Xerox's 8010 "Star" Office Workstation. In Proc. CHI'83 Human Factors in Computing Systems (Boston, December 12-15, 1983), ACM, New York, 72-77.

Bly, Sara A. & Rosenberg, Jarrett K. A comparison of tiled and overlapping windows. In Proc. CHI'86 Human Factors in Computing Systems (Boston, April 13-17, 1986), ACM, New York, 101-106.

Card S.K., Pavel, M. & Farrell, J.E. Window-based computer dialogues. In B. Shackel (Ed). Human-Computer Interaction --Interact '84. Elsevier Science Publishers: North-Holland 1985, 239-243.

Carroll, J.M. Presentation and form in user-interface architecture. Byte, 8(12), 113-122.

Carroll, John M. & Mazur, Sandra A. LisaLearning. IEEE Computer 19(11), 1986, 35-49.

Carroll, J.M. & Kay, D.S. Prompting, feedback and error correction in the design of a scenario machine. In Proc. CHI'85 Human Factors in Computing Systems (San Francisco, April 14-18, 1985), ACM, New York, 149-154.

DeFrancis, John. The Chinese Language: Fact and Fantasy. Honolulu: University of Hawaii Press, 1984. Cited in Wood, William T. & Wood, Susan K. Icons in everyday life. In Salvendy, Gavriel, Sauter, Steven L., & Hurrel, Joseph J. Jr. (Editors) Social, Ergonomic and Stress Aspects of Work with Computers. Amsterdam: Elsevier, 1987.

Eliot, W.G. Symbology on the highways. In Whitney, E. (Ed.) Symbology: The user of Symbols in Visual Communications. New York: Hastings House, 1960.

Fahnrich, K.P. & Ziegler, J. Workstations using direct manipulation as interaction mode -- Aspects of design, application and evaluation. In B. Shackel (Ed). Human-Computer Interaction -- Interact '84. Elsevier Science Publishers: North-Holland, 1985, 693-698.

Fromkin, Victoria & Rodman, Robert. An Introduction to Language. New York: Holt, Rinehart and Winston, 1983.

Garner, Wendell, R. The Processing of Information and Structure New York: Halstead, 1974.

Gaylin, Kenneth B. How are windows used? Some notes on creating an empirically-based windowing benchmark task. In Proc. CHI'86 Human Factors in Computing Systems (Boston, April 13-17, 1986), ACM, New York, 96-100.

Halasz, F. & Moran, T.P. Analogy considered harmful. In Proc. CHI'82 Human Factors in Computer Systems (Gaithersburg, Md., May, 1982), ACM, New York, 383-386.

Hammond, N. & Barnard, P. Dialogue design: Characteristics of user knowledge. In Monk, A. (Ed.) Fundamentals of human computer interaction. London: Academic Press, 1985. 127-164.

Heckel, Paul. The Elements of Friendly Software Design. New York: Warner Books, 1984.

Hemenway, Kathleen. Psychological issues in the use of icons in command menus. In Proc. CHI'82 Human Factors in Computer Systems (Gaithersburg, Md., May, 1982), ACM, New York, 20-23.

Holcomb, R. & Tharp, A.L. The effects of windows on man-machine interfaces. Proceedings of the 1985 ACM Computer Science Conference. Washington, DC: ACM, 280-291.

Krull, R. Communicative functions of icons as computer commands. Bridging the Present and the Future: Proceedings of the IEEE Professional Communication Society, Williamsburg, VA, October 1985, 207-210..

Krull, R. & Rubens, P. Feedback and highlighting as aids to computer users. Paper presented to the International Communication Association conference, Chicago, May, 1986.

Myers, B.A. The importance of percent-done progress indicators for computer-human interfaces. In Proc. CHI'85 Human Factors in Computing Systems (San Francisco, April 14-18, 1985), ACM, New York, 11-18.

Palmer, P.A. A study comparing the effectiveness of a contextual menu versus a textual menu. Paper presented at the International Communication Association conference, Chicago, May, 1986.

Poltrock, Steven E., Steiner, Donald D., & Tarlton, P. Nong. Graphic interfaces for knowledge-based system development. In Proc. CHI'86 Human Factors in Computing Systems (Boston, April 13-17, 1986), ACM, New York, 9-15.

Savage, R.E. & Habinek, J.H. A multilevel menu-driven user interface: Design and evaluation through simulation. Norwood, NJ: Ablex, 1984, 165-186.

Savage, R.E., Habinek, J.K. & Barnhart, T.W. The design, simulation and evaluation of a menu driven user interface. In Proc. CHI'82 Human Factors in Computer Systems (Gaithersburg, Md., May, 1982), ACM, New York, 36-40.

Shamonsky, Dorothy. Scripting with graphics: Icons as a visual tool. Visible Language, XIX-2 (Spring 1985), 226-242.

Shneiderman, B. Designing the User Interface: Strategies for Effective Human-Computer Interaction. Reading, Mass.: Addison-Wesley, 1987.

Sniger, P. Office systems struggle for user acceptance. Mini-Micro Systems, 17(15), Dec., 1984, 89-92.

Whiteside, J., Jones, S., Levy, P.S., & Wixon, D. user performance with command, menu and iconic interfaces. In Proc. CHI'85 Human Factors in Computing Systems (San Francisco, April 14-18, 1985), ACM, New York, 185-192.

Wood, William T. & Wood, Susan K. Icons in everyday life. In Salvendy, Gavriel, Sauter, Steven L., & Hurrel, Joseph J. Jr. (Editors) Social, Ergonomic and Stress Aspects of Work with Computers. Amsterdam: Elsevier, 1987.

Ziegler, J.E., Hoppe, H.U., and Fahnrich, K.P. Learning and transfer for text and graphics editing with a direct manipulation interface. In Proc. CHI'86 Human Factors in Computing Systems (Boston, April 13-17, 1986), ACM, New York, 72-77.

IV The Communication Context: Management and Research

13 The Politics of Usability: The Organizational Functions of an In-House Manual

Barbara Mirel
Illinois Institute of Technology

Introduction

The current state of research into software documentation evokes images of an infinitely receding frontier. Every time researchers lay claim to new territory such as scenario-based instructions or contextualized examples, new possibilities appear on the horizon, such as complementary large-scale organizational patterns or designs for multiple audiences. Although the range of current research is expansive, it remains within the confines of a single theoretical framework, one that models comprehension as a transaction between a reader, writer, and text. Within this framework, researchers explore how the linguistic and rhetorical features that writers choose affect the meanings that readers create when they engage a text. To inquire into how readers construct meaning from manuals, studies on documentation focus on such issues as readers' schema for problem-solving; conventions associated with manuals as a genre; mental models that readers use to represent a system and its operations; psycholinguistic principles for presenting logical relationships and cohesive devices; form and content that accord with the results of audience analyses; and sociolinguistic choices for evoking particular relationships between readers and writers [1-10].

While explorations within this perspective have advanced the field of user documentation, in recent years an altogether new frontier has been opened. This frontier reaches beyond reader-writer-text interactions toward what Lester Faigley terms a "social theory of writing." This new perspective challenges researchers to refine and possibly reconceive the principles for developing effective manuals as they discover the implications of contextual dynamics. As Faigley argues, a social theory of writing "moves beyond the traditional concern for audience, forcing researchers to consider issues such as social roles, group purposes, communal organization, ideology, and finally theories of culture." [11, p. 235-36].

Two propositions emerge when, as will be the case in this essay, one analyzes the development and usability of an in-house manual in relation to the political and social dynamics of its surrounding environment. First of all, it becomes apparent that in-house documentation should be treated as a separate and distinct area of study. Unlike commercial manuals which are mass marketed, in-house manuals are written for and used in a single workplace, one in which workers need training on a new system. To develop manuals in this workplace, writers must constantly interact with all the people accountable for the system -- the users, programmers, and managers. An in-house writer's interactions with these key personnel become one part of an organization-wide effort to adjust to a technological innovation. Therefore, an in-house writer's choices consistently influence, and are influenced by, the organizational behavior that accompanies computerization. The dynamics of computerization that writers encounter range from uncertainty about how a new system will affect job tasks, status, and interpersonal communications to conflicts between programmers and users. As disseminators of information within this context, in-house writers cannot escape the social and political ramifications of their organizational roles.

A second proposition is that in-house documentation requires new definitions for usability (effectiveness). Conventionally, the usability of a manual refers to such textual qualities as comprehensibility and accuracy. Such measures of usability are necessary but not sufficient for an in-house manual. As an organizational communication, an in-house manual represents a commitment by the corporation to integrate a new technology into its day-to-day internal operations. Therefore, usability for in-house documentation also must entail satisfying the tacit purpose of helping an organization adapt to its new computer system. In the midst of uncertainty and change, the manual can function as a stabilizing force. Its standardized procedures and selective presentation of information can help negotiate between competing departmental priorities while, at the same time, assimilating readers into the knowledge and values necessary for the acceptance of computerization. In order for manuals to achieve these goals, however, users must actually use them. In this context, usability for an in-house manual ought to be measured by the degree to which the manual is actually used and by the effects of that use.

Overview of the Chapter

I will explore this concept of usability by examining the dynamic relationship between organizational responses to computerization and the development of in-house documentation. First, I will describe common organizational responses in three areas: the relationship that develops between in-house users and programmers; the communication channels that users rely on for information about the system; and the techniques that managers use to adapt to a new system. In each of these areas, I will highlight the special role that in-house manual writers must assume in order to develop and implement manuals that will satisfy the evolving social and political needs of their organizations.

After establishing the ways in which the dynamics of computerization affect the work of an in-house writer, I will propose an expanded definition of the purposes of an in-house manual. Specifically, I will identify the tacit organizational purposes that an in-house manual must satisfy in addition to its explicit aim of instructing users in operating a new system.

Finally, I will argue that current usability tests are insufficient for evaluating if a manual successfully achieves its organizational purposes. High marks on such tests for clarity, comprehensibility, and task-orientation are no guarantee that a manual will actually be valued by users as a source of information or function to dissipate organizational conflict and uncertainty. I will present a design for a usability test that can assess the actual use of a manual and its role in helping an organization successfully adapt to a new computer system.

Research Procedure

My claims about the organizational purposes of an in-house manual derive from a case study I conducted on the development of an in-house accounting system manual for cashiers in the Bursar's office in a large state university [12-13]. In this study, the in-house writer spent one and a half years developing and implementing this user's manual, working with programmers in the Administrative Computing Department (who modified and further developed the system purchased from a vendor), the cashiers in the Bursar's office, and managers from both divisions. Once a prototype manual was completed, the writer conducted a conventional usability test and found that the cashiers could easily perform the instructions and that they judged the manual to be clear and well-suited for their on-line tasks.

However, once the manual was distributed, the users rarely, if ever, referred to it, despite the fact that they continuously made mistakes in operating the system. Because many of these errors caused large-scale organizational problems in regard to billing, tuition assessments, and interest charges, the writer conducted the kind of "actual use" study that is presented in this chapter.

The purpose of the study was to determine why the manual was not used and how increased use might improve not just the efficient use of the system but also the relations between departments and users' satisfaction with their jobs. Ultimately, findings from this "actual use" testing showed that the functionality of the manual was not an independent issue but instead depended on management techniques and social interactions within and between the user and programming departments. This case study, then, provides the basis of the evidence I will use to support my arguments in the rest of this chapter.

In-House Writers in Relation to Technological Change

Usually, the need for an in-house manual arises after an organization implements a new system. When users have problems running the system and when those problems impede the productivity and efficiency of the workplace, administrators commission the production of a manual to help users master their on-line tasks. The immediate and apparent purpose of an in-house manual -- indeed, of any manual -- is the instruction of users. Writing an in-house manual would appear to be a fairly straightforward endeavor. With the system already in place and running, the writer's job appears to be simply to document in clear and accurate prose how to use particular functions and commands for certain tasks. According to many documentation specialists, conventional rhetorical strategies and linguistic principles for writing "user-friendly" documentation should be sufficient [1;14-16]. Unfortunately, such a view assumes that an in-house manual is produced in a static environment. In fact, the opposite is true.

The Politics of Documentation

Computerization sets in motion an ever-evolving set of organizational responses [17]. These responses touch on all aspects of organizational life: the restructuring of task responsibilities; the re-allocation of authority; shifts in the channels of communication; and reconceptions of the interpersonal relations both within and between various departments. Overall, these responses create an atmosphere of uncertainty and conflict [18].

The development of an in-house manual is one part of this process of adapting to a new system. Contextual dynamics associated with computerization shape writers' choices about form, content and purpose just as much as do rhetorical or linguistic considerations. Within a context of uncertainty and competing preferences, in-house writers grapple with the problem of how to write manuals for two purposes: to teach users how to operate a system and to help stabilize organizational life. These two purposes merge in every aspect of documentation development and implementation. For example, writers need to ask several questions: what do users actually need to know when programmers, managers, and users all define those needs differently? What are the boundaries of user and programmer responsibilities that both groups can agree upon? How should these boundaries be delineated within the manual? What supplemental explanations will help users become more receptive to the system, without, at the same time, provoking programmers to reject oversimplifications? What motivational incentives should accompany the distribution and use of a manual?

Far from being a straightforward process of documenting operations in a one-to-one correspondence with computer functions, in-house manual writing entails making political choices about what information to include; how to present the information to the satisfaction of users, programmers, managers and writers alike; and how to ensure the manual's use. Each of these choices forces an in-house writer to carefully "read" and interact with the strategies that individuals and departments adopt in response to a new computer system. Three particular responses to technological change present writers with the greatest challenges for developing manuals that will become valued sources of information and standardization in the workplace: (1) new interdependencies between users and programmers that are marked by conflict over how to divide responsibilities and over what knowledge should be shared or privileged; (2) patterns for accessing information in the users' office that preclude the in-flow of new knowledge; and (3) managerial techniques in the users' office that do not accommodate to the demands and potential of the new technology.

(1) Interdependencies Between Users and Programmers

New computer systems can change workers' autonomy. When the introduction of a new system changes workers' modes of operation from non-automated to computerized methods , the autonomy that some workers previously enjoyed may come to be replaced by excessive reliance on technical experts. Although users remain experts in their particular tasks, they suddenly find themselves in need of outside assistance in order to continue to perform those tasks effectively. These outside experts train them in on-line procedures, help them resolve errors, and modify and build programs to meet the needs of evolving on-line tasks.

Writers Vs. Programmers. In my case study of the accounting system manual for cashiers in the Bursar's office, I found that the cashiers turned for this technical support to programmers in the Administrative Computing Department. But the programmers also depended on the users. Programmers needed users' input as to how the system was running and how users conducted their business. Only by having this input could programmers effectively carry out their responsibility to construct new software and debug and modify existing programs.

On the surface, this interdependency between programmers and users would seem to suggest cooperative relations as the two groups are required to join together to run the system smoothly. Yet, beneath the surface, tensions often brew, occasionally escalating into overt conflict. Each group expects more than the other is either able or willing to give. In my case study, users demanded that programmers be immediately available for instruction and problem-solving. Programmers, however, resented this beck-and-call expectation for it drastically curtailed their ability to attend to what they saw as their primary work, namely program modification and development. Programmers, in turn, expected users to take initiatives and learn the system on their own so that they could become independent operators. However, users balked at this expectation, claiming to be experts in accounting, not computers. Moreover, users blamed programmers for purposely keeping technical information obscure and for wrapping their programming activities in a cloak of secrecy.

Andrew Pettigrew describes this kind of situation as "defensive-cyclical" behavior [18]. Each group, he argues, simultaneously blames the other for its intransigence and entrenches its own demands even further. As my case study shows, two possible sources for such an impasse are: (1) a lack of consensus about what constitutes the limits of each department's responsibilities and (2) the absence of agreement as to what computer-related information should be shared and how to make it accessible to all.

In-house documentation writers may find themselves confronting these types of situations. To deal with them effectively, in-house writers need to be aware of the specific sources of these kinds of problems and should be willing to take on new roles in dealing with them. The job of the in-house manual writer becomes broader than the mere translation of commands. The writer needs to make the manual a source for transmitting information about operational responsibilities and for providing explanations on how a system works.

An in-house manual plays an important role in establishing a consensus between users and programmers. Amidst factionalism, the manual acts as an impersonal, formal communication. It conveys the bounds of user and programmer responsibilities and de-mystifies system-related information without championing the interests of any one group. To do so, however, in-house writers need to actively negotiate between the contending demands and goals of users and programmers and document in the manual the outcome of their efforts.

Writers as Liaisons and Gatekeepers. These responsibilities place in-house writers in the roles of liaison and gatekeeper. As in-house writers gather information for the manual, they mediate as liaisons between users and programmers, working with both groups separately and together to reach mutually satisfying conceptions of what constitutes independent operation of the system and what body of knowledge is required for computer proficiency. As liaisons, writers need to create support teams for developing the manual and include on the team the individuals whose very participation in the manual project will help ensure the success of negotiations and a positive response to the manual once it is distributed. Specifically, writers should elicit commitments for regular participation from the users' direct supervisor, one or two users who are recognized as "resident experts," the programmer who acts as the key contact with users, and the programming manager.

Besides these development teams, in-house writers also have to organize a second support team, one that makes plans for implementing the manual. This implementation team should be composed of managers who have the authority to develop policies that will give users incentives to use their manuals. Managers from the user and programming offices should take part in the implementation team (wearing different hats here than in the support teams) as should administrators for technical support services in the organization at-large.

As writers document the results of their team meetings and incorporate the outcomes of other informal discussions in the manual, they shift to gatekeeper roles. As gatekeepers, writers are less concerned with carrying on arbitrations and more concerned with passing information along the established organizational channels. They filter and transmit information, relying on their unbiased positions in the organization to gain universal consent to the material they present. Writers must select for their manuals the content that best serves the task-oriented and political needs of the organization and must constantly guard against information overdose, on the one hand, and distortion, on the other. Ideally, gatekeeper-writers should compose standardized instructions and give enough justification for chosen procedures to make users realize the reasons behind the operation. But writers must refrain from giving too elaborate a justification so as to avoid the potential chaos of users thinking they should make their own choices about optimal procedures [19].

As successful as writers might be as liaisons and gatekeepers, their manuals will still not be effective unless users actually use them. If the stabilizing potential of an in-house manual is to take effect, the manual has to be made part of users' routines for accessing information about the system. The ways in which users exchange information must become an important area of concern for in-house manual writers.

(2) Patterns for Accessing Information in the User's Office

Probably nothing more strikingly dramatizes the difference between commercial and in-house manuals than the fact that, in the case of in-house manuals, writers are developing their manuals while in-house users are simultaneously gaining experience with the system. By the time the manual reaches users, the users have already developed routines for exchanging information about the system. Users establish intra-office cliques for sharing advice; they tacitly assign roles to resident experts; and, as noted earlier, they often turn to programmers for help. The manual enters an already established communication system, one that has been functioning for some time without the aid of formally written instructions and explanations.

User Cliques. While a manual can increase users' understanding of the system, the mere presence of a manual does not guarantee that users will alter their informal, conversational patterns for accessing information so as to include reference to the manual. Users are frequently reluctant to change these informal channels of communications because these channels provide a sense of social unity within the office. The norms that users evolve for discussing problems with the system rest on unspoken groundrules about how the office culture will integrate the new system into its activities [20]. As part of the office culture, a strong reliance on interpersonal communications can reflect two interrelated social norms -- first, that workers will respond as a group to computerization and, second, that they will sanction cooperative efforts in preference to individual, self-directed learning [21]. Combined, a group response and a sanctioning of cooperative efforts mean that workers see the building of technical competencies as a joint enterprise in learning, not one that an individual should pursue for personal advancement. Collaborative learning through ongoing conversations might level recognition for success into a group-wide accomplishment, but it also uses group accountablity to diffuse the stigma of failure.

In my case study, I observed the users at work for three months after the manual had been distributed and found that cashiers never referred to their manuals. Instead, they predominantly sought help from co-workers and continuously turned to the same two or three individuals for that help. This breakdown into two- to three-person cliques was based on geographic proximity; clique members also tended to go to lunch and on break together. Discussions of how to work the system were only one aspect of the conversations that went on among clique members. These users also frequently commiserated about their general problems with the system or the complexity of a particular student's account. This shared frustration evoked a sense of solidarity. Adding to that sense of cohesion was the fact that, during slow work periods, clique members chatted freely about extra-office events.

Resident Experts. Often the cashiers retrieved information outside their cliques by going to two or three key individuals who seemed to know the most about the system. One of these resident experts was the floor supervisor, the only employee who had regular contact with programmers. Another was the office manager who made a habit of circulating among employees and making sure that they checked all their work with him. The third resident expert was a quiet woman who rarely went to others for help but, instead, spent inordinate amounts of time in front of the screen, working through the system by trial and error. Others in the office relied on her skills as a patient problem-solver and regularly asked her for advice. By soliciting her help, the members of the office incorporated the fruits of her solitary efforts and individual learning into their communications network. The social unity achieved through shared interchanges went undisturbed.

Effects of Limited Knowledge. One consequence of these patterns of accessing and sharing information about the system was that it became a relatively closed communication system. This system, while successful in some ways, unfortunately thwarted the entry of new knowledge. Users' understanding of and proficiency with the programs could extend no further than the knowledge of the most expert worker in the office. Even the resident experts, however, lacked the conceptual understanding about the workings of the system that was essential for inferring solutions and projecting effective uses of the system. Consequently, even after working on the system for a year, users repeatedly made errors that called for programmers' intervention, a situation that increasingly frustrated and antagonized programmers and upper level management.

In such a situation, an in-house manual can be the source of the new technical knowledge that users need in order to maximize their efficiency and productivity on the system. However, given the importance of social unity for job satisfaction and innovative learning, writers must recognize that their manuals should supplement interpersonal exchanges, not supplant them.

What Writers Need to Understand. In-house manual writers need to fully understand how users acquire information, and they must create manuals that can become part of these efforts. Collaboration with users in developing a manual must, therefore, entail more than merely getting users' input about task-related procedures. Writers also must discover users' preferred sources of information. To do so, writers should closely observe when users seek help, who they turn to for help, how effective that help is, and, when the help is not effective, what gaps in information thwart success. From such observations writers can determine ways to highlight the most crucial information that their manuals need to cover and can find a language that can be readily assimilated into users' conversations.

Even after a manual is distributed, writers need to actively promote its use as a source of necessary technical explanation and instruction. For example, they can hold training sessions on how to combine the manual with other sources of help. They can involve users in updating the documentation to meet their evolving needs. But, writers cannot single-handedly institute the active use of their in-house manuals. Writers require the support of an office manager. As I will discuss in the next section, such support is not always readily forthcoming. Moreover, lack of managerial support is not just a manual-related issue but is often one part of an overall negative response by the manager to the technology.

(3) Managerial Techniques in the Workplace

Supervisory patterns play a critical role in the success of an organization's efforts to integrate a new technology into the routines of the workplace. As is suggested by the "consonance theory" in organization research, organizations are most successful when the established structures for making decisions and managing the office complement the demands and potential of a new system [22-23]. For example, when users have complex tasks in which more than one procedure is possible, the best managerial structure gives autonomous groups responsibility for those tasks, coupled with the power to determine their own choices. Conversely, for routine, single-approach procedures, a centralized decision-making authority is most effective [24-25].

Current research in organization theory takes consonance one step further by claiming that, although management structures are important, supervisory style, as an independent variable, has the greatest impact on the effective use of a new technology [17]. Supervisory style includes the methods managers use to run their offices -- methods for performing administrative duties, supervising employees, and bringing their authority to bear. To a large extent, managers are motivated by a drive for status to assume whatever style they practice . As Lawrence Mohr argues, managers make choices based on "the desire not to lose and even to gain social standing in [an] organization." [25, p. 112].

Organizations that have been newly computerized often present managers with major problems in management style. Managers seek to maintain their status while struggling to answer the new demands that a system imposes on their time as well as on their intellectual skills. They must now deal with a computer system and with their employees' interactions with the system. Because managerial responsibilities are suddenly compounded with technical ones, managers confront questions about what decision-making authority they should keep for themselves and what responsibilities for the system they should relinquish to users.

Managerial Control Vs. Technical Competence. Perhaps the worst path that managers can follow in this situation is to increase their involvement in the operation of the system without increasing their technical knowledge and capabilities. In that case, managers use increased intervention in all aspects of workers' tasks to reassert their status; they may for a time succeed in maintaining their leadership standing because all actions depend on their approval. But, in the long run, their technical ignorance impedes the dissemination of technical information in the office and leads to inefficient and unproductive operations -- perhaps even to a loss of managerial authority.

Such behavior by managers may pose the most difficult problem that in-house manual writers have to face. If technically unskilled managers set themselves up as the final source of information, their authority can be threatened by users' reference to a manual, which is a more technically reliable source than the manager. Ironically, while this managerial style is rooted in managers' attempts to maintain their status within the office, it often ends up reducing that status outside the office. Programmers, from their technically-astute vantage point, quickly realize when a manager's intervention is inadequate. Word spreads outside the users' office, and many people in the organization who once saw these managers as competent in their roles in a non-automated office now see them as inept in computerized contexts.

In situations characterized by highly visible managerial intervention and technical ignorance, manual writers must be political in getting their manuals treated as valued sources of information. Sometimes a manual writer's goals can be met by giving managers a separate supervisor's manual for the system so that managers can learn the system privately and painlessly. At other times, high level management must direct a top-down restructuring of responsibilities that will encourage greater dissemination of technical knowledge in the workplace. By conferring with administrators and drawing on insights gained from previous observations and negotiations, a writer can be instrumental in helping decision-makers develop policies that enhance the use of the manual, .

The Organizational Purposes of In-House Documentation

As we can see, the rhetorical situation governing the development of an in-house manual is far more complex than traditional documentation research allows. In-house writers must understand that rhetorical situations include far more than just users and their needs with new systems. Rhetorical situations encompass organizational dynamics associated with the implementation of those new systems. Thus, writers must re-define the purposes of their manuals. A narrowly focused, reader-writer-text perspective infuses a manual with merely an instructive purpose; on the other hand, a contextual view compounds that instructional function with the more subtle communication purposes of reducing uncertainty, diffusing conflict, and socializing readers into the knowledge and values of the new system.

This contextual view of an in-house manual assumes that formal organizational communications, such as in-house manuals, interact dynamically with their contexts. Written in response to new methods of operation, in-house manuals become suggestive of further organizational changes [26-27]. For example, the manual's standard procedures, originally intended to reduce uncertainty, become the basis for evaluating what approaches are appropriate for new problems. Similarly, through its tacit sanctions and censures of behaviors and alotted responsibilities, a manual provokes responses from workers that are assimilated into the social norms that direct future perceptions and choices. Therefore, when an organization stands at the crossroads of technological change, it is crucial to evaluate the effectiveness of an in-house manual in organizational terms.

As an organizational communication, an in-house manual helps an organization adapt smoothly to computerization. A manual has three organizational functions beyond instruction: reactive, proactive and policy-making. An in-house manual fulfills its reactive function by helping to resolve existing problems associated with conflict and uncertainty. It performs its proactive function by avoiding potential difficulties. The manual serves its policy-making function by enabling administrators to use its mere existence to represent an organization's commitment to a new system. Managers often cite that commitment to justify new policies for departmental responsibilities or training practices.

Reactive

The reactive function of an in-house manual results from the inevitable convergence of the documentation development process with the process of adopting a new technology. When users make errors in operating the system, members of an organization turn to a manual writer to document the correct on-line procedures. However, even after an error is resolved and an in-house writer has committed the accepted procedure to paper, the tensions between users and programmers that surfaced at the time of the error are apt to remain. Consensus about the correct procedure does not, in itself, resolve the discrepant expectations each group may hold about the other's responsibilities for operating the system and for sharing knowledge. Therefore, to help fully stabilize organizational operations the manual also has to deal with the complaints that each group levels against the other. The writer can help stabilize the organization in three ways:

(1) To identify who is accountable for what in various tasks, in-house writers can use techniques such as playscript procedures (charts that tie specific actions to particular job roles) [14].

(2) To establish a shared body of technical knowledge in the workplace, in-house writers can write sections explaining a system's inner workings, logic and built-in constraints, thereby reducing antagonisms that result when users and programmers withhold information from one another.

(3) To direct the attention of users to the areas of information that are missing in users' interpersonal exchanges yet essential for effective problem-

solving activities, in-house writers can put such sections first and use active headings to contextualize the information for users' purposes.

Proactive

The proactive function of an in-house manual can be more subtle and complicated. It is tied to insights that in-house writers develop as they act as liaisons in the organization. As they try to negotiate compromises among the priorites and needs of users, programmers, and managers, the writers gain a sense of the underlying tensions and ambiguities, which, if left to fester, could easily lead to future disruptions. For example, users might have negative attitudes toward computerization or believe that programmers are purposely refusing to build the programs that users want. Programmers, on the other hand, might claim such programs are impossible. Writers must explore and try to diffuse such conflicts by turning mutual suspicions into increased awareness of each group's motivations. In asking for improvements in the technology, users aren't rebelling aginst computers so much as they are requesting that programs correspond to the specialized approaches they take to their work. In refusing to make modifications, programmers aren't lording it over users; they're doing the best that they can with the structure that exists.

Proactively, writers might also perceive that users' negative responses to a new system result from their feeling alienated from the system that has changed their work lives. [19; 25] Often this alienation arises because users are given no part in planning for the system's implementation. Writers can use the processes of developing and maintaining the documentation to counter this alienation and evoke a greater receptivity to the technology. That is, the manual can make up for missed opportunities in user involvement. As writers and implementation teams devise strategies for implementing the manual, they can make sure that users become responsibe for composing and updating their manuals. Through this participation, users may increase their sense of control over computerization because they feel they have a part in determining how they are supposed to learn.

Some proactive approaches require textual solutions in addition to organizational ones. Complementing interpersonal negotiations, the text of the manual can help to arbitrate when users' demands for optimal programs are at odds with programmers' demands for feasible ones. Users' expertise in their task areas leads them to ask for programs that accord with the best means for performing their tasks. Programmers, however, speak from their area of expertise when they claim that some of these requested programs are beyond a system's capabilities. Whenever such disparities arise about documented tasks, the manual can ameliorate the situation by explicitly acknowledging the validity of each group's position. The manual can overtly admit that users' desires are warranted and true to the logic of their specialties and, at the same time, explain that programmers are locked into specific constraints in the system. This proactive approach for avoiding potentially damaging misunderstandings requires in-house writers to expand their scope beyond merely documenting operations to providing background and rationale for the choice of these specific operations.

Policy-Making

Finally, the policy-making function of a manual revolves around its role as a precedent for future actions. The manual stands as a testament to an organization's goal to train users to become independent operators of their system. The manual sets a precedent for pursuing that goal, and organizations operate on precedents [19]. Once administrators make a commitment to this precedent by investing time and money in the development of a manual, they are likely, in later policy decisions, to continue in the direction of training users . Even if, upon distribution, the manual does not effect users' independent operation, decision-makers will use the existence of the manual to justify their expectations that users become proficient on the system in the future. In short, they assign to the manual a political significance independent of the manual's demonstrated instrumentality. With the manual interpreted as an emblem of commitment to training, administrators will continue to pursue this goal, perhaps by restructuring managerial practices or instituting training sessions. By encouraging users to become more responsible for their system, these policy changes can indirectly provoke users to rely more on their manuals for instruction. Thus, the initial political interpretation of the manual leads back to its improved use. The policies that, in the end, can help to make the manual a more valued and functional source of information in the workplace are set in motion, in part, by its mere presence.

An Expanded Definition of Usability

All combined, the reactive, proactive, and policy-making functions of an in-house manual should tacitly negotiate stability in the midst of technological change. *Evaluating the usability of an in-house manual, therefore, entails more than testing whether the documentation is easy to understand, accurate, and comprehensive for users' needs.* Usability must also be judged by whether users actually turn to their manuals for information and whether the presence and use of the manual lead to more efficient operations, more tolerant interdepartmental relationships, more shared knowledge, and more positive attitudes toward computerization.

Usability, in these terms, is a slippery concept. The effect of an in-house manual merges with other dynamics of organizational behavior with no clear-cut distinctions as to cause and effect. Even so, to get a sense of a manual's organizational effectiveness, in-house writers can still do more than simply test its textual quality. They must study the extent to which users actually use a manual after it is distributed. Such studies can reveal whether the use of a manual, in fact, encourages the mastery of new knowledge, clarifies responsibilities, and dissipates frustrations and antagonisms toward the system. Findings from such studies have significance for the manual as well as for organizational practices. Writers can identify the sections of the manual that still need revision in order to achieve desirable organizational purposes, and they can also discover areas within the corporation that require administrative actions in order to promote a more successful adoption of the system. As with all other aspects of developing and implementing an in-house manual, a contextual perspective gives in-house writers the added responsibility of becoming political players in the process of testing a manual's effectiveness.

Usability Testing for An In-House Manual

Despite the difficulty in defining usability in dynamic, contextual terms, the usability of in-house manuals still must be tested. Measuring the usability of an in-house manual according to its success in achieving its organizational purposes does not preclude testing the textual qualities of a prototype before the manual is distributed. Quality testing is necessary for measuring comprehensibility [29-30]. Testing whether a manual is used and determining the effects of that use are separate aspects of usability. This "actual use" focus rests on the need to identify the function that an in-house manual plays as a formal communication in a newly computerized environment. Broadly speaking, "actual use" usability testing looks at the connection between the use of an in-house manual and larger organizational efforts to integrate a new system into the workplace. If users use their manuals, in what ways does that use facilitate a successful adaptation to the system? If users do not use their manuals, in what ways does that lack of use impair adaptation? Unfortunately, current literature on documentation neither addresses the need for such testing nor details a test design for it.

Testing Actual Use

Testing the actual use of an in-house manual can rely on a three-pronged approach that combines quantitative and qualitative methods. (For a discussion of qualitative research methods for technical writers, see Doheny-Farina and Gould in this volume.) For actual use testing, writers can collect data from three different sources: user logs; observations of users at work; and surveys and interviews with users.

User Logs. Writers could ask users to keep logs that record when they refer to their manuals and detail the specific sections of the manual that they refer to. The quickest and easiest way for users to keep such logs is to highlight and date pages in the manual as they use them. Users would welcome such an expedient approach to logging, especially when they feel pressed for time in their daily work . Writers could collect marked pages each month and replace pulled pages with clean copies.

Longitudinal Observations. Writers could conduct longitudinal observations in the users' office to discover how efficiently and productively the system is run. As users work on the system, writers should examine what system-related information users seek in their daily routines, where they access that information, what time and other constraints effect their preferences, and how effective the information they receive is in answering their questions and problems. From these observations, writers can qualitatively analyze how the manual fits into established patterns of retrieving information and, if necessary, project ways in which the manual might improve current methods for acquiring help.

Surveys and Interviews. Writers would follow up their observations with written surveys and interviews. Such surveys should gather demographic information on users and ask them to evaluate the system, their competence with the system, the usefulness of the manual, and their most valued sources of instruction, including the manual. Respondants would also cite the areas in which they feel the need to develop more competence and could give suggestions for future training and interdepartmental work sessions. Writers would analyze survey responses and pursue significant results in informal interviews with users . Through these interviews, users could elaborate on their evaluations and needs. The interviews could uncover a broad spectrum of users' previously unspoken concerns, such as calling for improved ergonomic conditions, finding ways to derive satisfaction from new modes of work, and suggesting improvements for particular on-line functions. (For a discussion of the relationship of product design to document design, see Baker in this volume.)

This three-pronged strategy is comprehensive enough to provide built-in checks on results. For example, if writers only relied on logs, they could draw erroneous conclusions. An absence of notations could just as easily be due to users having forgotten to mark their references as to their not having used the manual. Longitudinal observations enable writers to see whether, in fact, users actually do turn to their manuals in their daily routines. Also, writers could compare what they observe to be the most frequently sought information to what users mark in their logs. If there are discrepancies between these findings, writers could use interviews to ask users why they turn to a given source for particular problems. Finally, surveys and interviews offer a depth of interpretation that is not available from the surface results of logs and observations.

In analyzing results from this testing, writers should organize their findings so as to best lead to conclusions and recommendations for improving the potential use of the manual, in the redesign of the text and in the restructuring of organizational practices. Writers should follow four analyztical procedures. First, they should identify the recurrent as well as most important problems and issues that prompt users to acquire information. Second, they should enumerate the sections of the manual that users access. Third, they should analyze the information needs that are not adequately satisfied by users' current means of seeking help. Finally, they should establish the relationship between users' preferred sources of information (for example; co-workers) and various geographic, psychological, and bureaucratic factors in the work environment.

The Significance of Actual Use Testing

The conclusions and recommendations drawn from these analyses should focus on means for enhancing users' proficiency with the system in light of the ongoing interpersonal and structural dynamics of the workplace. The manual, as part of the organizational communication system, is one source for enhancing the performance of users. Writers should redesign their manuals to highlight the operational and responsibility-related information that seems most valuable to users on the basis of logs, obvservations, surveys, and interviews. When users feel pressed for time in their daily activities, they need ready access to the sections and visuals most crucial for their needs. The redesigned manual should also provide content that "fills out" the problem-solving discussions among co-workers so that users have adequate conceptual frameworks for making informed decisions. Similarly, the vocabulary, tone, and style of the manual should reflect the language of interpersonal consultations.

In addition to redesigning the manual, writers also need to recommend ways to make the surrounding organizational dynamics more conducive to reference to a manual. Possible organizational incentives for motivating users to use their manuals include: training sessions with the manual as the centerpiece of instruction; reward systems for using the manual; and increased user participation, either through regular updating sessions or through autonomous work groups responsible for particular procedures and their documentation.

Conclusion

Conducting "actual use" usability testing formalizes an in-house documentation writer's commitment to a manual as an organizational communication. Situated in an environment that is undergoing technological change, in-house writers face the challenge of tailoring the design, purpose, and content of their manuals to the evolving dynamics of the workplace . Because in-house manuals tacitly deal with large-scale organizational concerns in addition to immediate instructional concerns, an evaluation of the effectiveness of a manual hinges on its usefulness as a stabilizing document, not just its accuracy and comprehensibility as a guide to operations. To achieve this organization-based dimension of effectiveness, in-house writers need to pursue strategies during writing and testing that maximize their roles as liaisons and gatekeepers so that their texts adequately address organizational needs. Writers must reject the image of mere translators of technical information and become viable resources in the organization. Ironically, the "closed system" nature of an in-house context actually enlarges a writer's opportunities to create truly effective documentation.

This contextual analysis is intended as an exploratory study. What is now needed is further research grounded in a social theory of writing perspective. Contextual questions are very different from those posed in studies based on a reader-writer-text perspective, and we are only just beginning to raise those new questions. On the one hand, studies based on a reader-writer-text frameworks focus on targeted readers and ask what form and content best correspond to their levels of knowledge, prior experience, task-oriented needs, and cognitive strategies for processing verbal and visual information. From the perspective of a reader-writer-text orientation, usability -- that is, effectiveness -- is defined merely as optimal understanding in an individual, psychological sense, and this understanding is measured by a user's ability to correctly and expediently perform documented instructions. In contrast, a social theory of writing approach focuses on the functional rather than psychological success of a text and assumes that performance is tied to a range of interconnected contextual factors, not just to a relationship between a user and a text. For in-house manuals, contextually-based inquiries ask about the characteristics of the manual in relation to the context in which it is embedded and question how different arrangements within the manual and within the environment can evoke the desired organizational outcomes.

To conduct such inquiries, researchers have to venture into disciplines that have previously been considered outside the province of technical writing. They must examine the literature of sociology, anthropology, and organizational theory about the social processing and construction of information, about communication in organizational cultures, and about the adoption of technological innovations. The theoretical precepts as well as the ethnographic and statistical methodologies from such fields can help documentation researchers define their questions and design their analyses. For in-house documentation, we need several types of studies: more case studies so that we can distinguish the universal from the particular; comparative studies so that we can see how two sets of circumstances give rise to different results; and single, in-depth issue analyses so that we can see the impact that interconnected variables have on each other. Clearly, the frontier is wide-open.

References

1. For a comprehensive description of the documentation writing process coupled with theoretical explanations on why various approaches are effective, see R. John Brockmann, Writing Better Computer User Documentation: From Paper to Online (New York: John Wiley and Sons, 1986).

2. For a syntactic analysis of written instructions, see R. Charrow and V. Charrow, "Making Legal Language Understandable," Colombia Law Review 79 (1979) 1306-1379

3. For a discussion on manual designs, see Thomas Duffy, Thomas Curran and Del Sass, "Document Design for Technical Job Tasks: An Evaluation," Human Factors 25 (1983) 142-160

4. For issues related to audience analyses, see K. Eason and L. Damodaran, "The Needs of the Commercial User," in M. Coombs and J. Alty (eds.) Computing Skills and the User Interface (London: Academic Press, 1981)

5. For a synthesis of important, current research, see D. Felker, F. Pickering, V. Charrow, and J. Redish, Guidelines for Document Designers (Washington, D. C.: American Institutes for Research, 1981).

6. For audience-based rhetorical arrangement patterns, see Linda Flower, John Hayes and Heidi Swarts, "Revising Functional Documents: The Scenario Principle" in P. Anderson, R. J. Brockmann, and C. Miller (eds.) New Essays in Technical and Scientific Communication: Research, Theory and Practice Vol. 2 (Farmington: Baywood Press, 1983

7. For a discussion of the psycholinguistics of written instructions, see V. Holland and A. Rose, Understanding Instructions with Complex Conditions (Washington, D. C.: American Institutes for Research, 1980)

8. For a discussion on the effects of users' schema, see David Kieras, The Role of Prior Knowledge in Operating Equipment From Written Instruction, Technical Report No. 10 (Arlington: Office of Naval Research, 1985)

9. For an analysis of the theoretical principles useful for documentation design, see Judith Ramey, "Developing a Theoretical Base for On-Line Documentation," The Technical Writing Teacher 13 &14 (1986)

10. For issues related to audience analyses, see Stephanie Rosenbaum and R. Dennis Walters, "Audience Diversity: A Major Challenge in Computer Documentation," IEEE Transactions on Professional Communications PC-29 (December 1986) 48-55

11. Lester Faigley, "Nonacademic Writing: The Social Perspective" in Lee Odell and Dixie Goswami (eds.) Writing in Nonacademic Settings (New York: Guilford Press, 1985)

12. Barbara Mirel, "Designing Field Researvh in Technical Communication: Usability Testing for In-House User Documentation," Journal of Technical Writing and Communication 17 (1987) pp. 347-354

13. Barbara Mirel, "Actual-Use Testing for In-House Computer Manuals, Technical Communication 34 (November 1987), pp. 289-291

14. Sandra Pakin and Associates, Documentation Development Methodology: Techniques for Improved Communication (Englewood Cliffs: Prentic-Hall, Inc., 1982)

15. Jonathan Price, How to Write a Computer Manual (Melo Park: The Benjamin/Cummings Publishing Co., 1984)

16. Donald Cunningham and Gerald Cohen, Creating Technical Manuals: A Step-by-Step Approach to Writing User-Friendly Instruction (New York: McGraw-Hill, 1984)

17. Lawrence Mohr, "Organizational Technology and Organizational Structure," Administrative Science Quarterly 16 (1971) 444-459

18. Andrew Pettigrew, The Politics of Organizational Decision-Making (London: Tavistock Publications Ltd., 1973)

19. Charles Perrow, Complex Organizations (New York: Random House, 1986)

20. Susan Shimanoff, Communications Rules: Theory and Research (Beverly Hills: Sage Publications, 1980)

21. Linda Smircich, "Studying Organizations as Cultures," in Gareth Morgan (ed.) Beyond Method: Strategies for Social Research (Beverly Hills: Sage Publications, 1983)

22. Tom Burns and G. M. Stalker, The Management of Innovation (London: Tavistock, 1961)

23. Joan Woodward, Industrial Organization: Theory and Practice (Oxford University Press, 1980)

24. Larry Hirschhorn, Beyond Mechanization: Work and Technology in a Postindiustrial Age (Cambridge: Massachusetts Institute of Technology Press, 1980)

25. Lawrence Mohr, Explaining Organizational Behavior: The Limits and Possibilities of Theory and Research (San Fransisco: Jossey-Bass Publishers, 1982)

26. Gerald Salancik and Jeffrey Pfeffer, "A Social Information Processing Approach to Job Attitudes and Task Design," Administrative Science Quarterly 23 (1978) pp. 224-252

27. Karl Weick, The Social Psychology of Organizing (Reading,MA: Addison-Wesley, 1979)

28. James March and Herbert Simon, Organizations (New York: Wiley and Sons, 1958)

29. For a discussion of current approaches to usability testing see Gary Schumacher and Robert Waller, "Testing Design Alternatives: A Comparison of Procedures" in Thomas Duffy and Robert Waller (eds.) Designing Usable Texts (Orlando: Academic Press, 1985)

30. For a discussion on usability testing, see David Schell, "Testing Online and Print User Documentation," IEEE Transactions on Professional Communications PC-29 (1986)

14 Improving the Management of Technical Writers: Creating a Context for Usable Documentation

Richard M. Chisholm
Plymouth State College
Plymouth, NH

What Managers Should Know

Managers of writing in the computer industry are increasingly interested in improving the procedures for creating documentation. These managers may profit from thinking about computer user documentation from the point of view of the writer.

This chapter reports the results of research into the management of writing in the computer industry. Based on a survey of technical writers, this research shows that writers use a variety of processes for producing documentation, that they identify a wide range of problems, and that they have discovered numerous solutions. While recognizing their own shortcomings, these writers are helpful in pinpointing management problems and in suggesting concrete ways to improve management.

The purpose of the management of writing in the computer industry is the same as the purpose of management in any industry: to maximize profits by producing quality products that satisfy customers while keeping costs down. Effective and efficient management relies on the optimum use of resources -- time, money, personnel, and information. Keeping this principle in mind, I will explain practices that have proved effective in managing writing in the computer industry. In doing so, this chapter will explain:

1) three models of the documentation cycle,
2) practices that create problems for writers, and
3) practices that alleviate problems for writers.

Research Procedures

The comments and suggestions in this report are based on responses to a questionnaire in which writers were asked to describe the document cycle in their firm, to identify the problems they have experienced, and to suggest solutions to them. Here are the questions that writers responded to:

1) In your firm (or in the organization you know best), what procedures do documentation specialists follow when they design, write, re-write, revise, test, and edit documents? That is, what is the document cycle?

2) What are some typical problems and frustrations technical writers experience in their jobs? What management practices prevent writers from doing their best work?

3) What practical solutions to these problems have you discovered or experienced? How can writing be more effectively managed?

Of 310 questionnaires mailed to participants in the Conference on Writing for the Computer Industry at Plymouth State College, New Hampshire (1984, 1985, and 1986), 38 persons (12%) responded. In most cases, the writers asked to remain anonymous. The questionnaire gave these writers the chance to "sound off"; but they replied with the sober analysis and suggestions which follow. (1)

Let me make it clear from the outset that this presentation describes the process of writing computer user documentation. It is not concerned with the strategic aims of writing, with techniques for various kinds of writing (proposals, reports, archives, and so on), nor with how to write. The focus, then, is upon creating the context for usable documentation.

Part 1: Three Models of the Documentation Cycle

The respondents identified three models which represent the flow of information in the document cycle: a) the **end-loaded cycle**, b) the **middle-loaded cycle**, and c) the modern **team-based cycle**.

The first and second of these models have served for many years, but they are cumbersome and outmoded. The third one is favored more and more because it gets writers and product designers together from the beginning of the design process, facilitates communication throughout the process, and fosters orderly production of documentation. (For a further discussion of the relationship of product design and documentation, see Baker in this volume.)

Model 1: The End-Loaded Document Cycle

Managers who use Model 1 say to their writers, in effect, "The machine is almost complete. Come in and write the user manual. We need it in two weeks."

Diagram 1 describes this inadequate model for producing computer documentation. While it may seem to be a reasonably adequate model, it is inadequate because it leaves the task of documentation to the end of the product cycle. Writers are called in to document the system after it has already been designed and produced -- when it is ready to be shipped.

PROCEDURES

Line Procedures In the Direct Line of Product Development	**Staff Procedures** Support or Ancillary Tasks
Product created by: a Project Manager a Marketing Professional Project Engineers Project Programmers	**Documentation** created by: a Publications Manager Writers and editors Graphics designers Printers
Market Analysis Product Specification Product Design Product Development Product Programming Product Testing Product Manufacture	
	Installation Procedures User Documentation Maintenance Documentation
Out the Door Sales	

This flow chart represents a widespread concept of the procedures for producing computer documentation. While it represents the actual process used in hundreds of firms over the last several decades, it is an inadequate model for documenting modern computers for use by contemporary audiences. This line-and-staff model leads to many of the problems described in Part 2 of this chapter.

Model 1: The End-Loaded Document Cycle
DIAGRAM 1

Note that Diagram 1 ignores the larger context within which writing takes place. It ignores design teams and the ways that writers interact with managers, engineers, programmers, and other technical people. It ignores the ways that writers interact with other writers. It ignores, in fact, most of the ways that writers procure information and work it into usable form. The jog in the line flow in Diagram 1 suggests that writers have a lower status and less importance than managers, marketing personnel, engineers, and programmers; it suggests that managers can well ignore the contributions that writers can make to product design.

Finally, because the flow chart in Diagram 1 oversimplifies the process of writing, it is not adequate as a diagram of the process of writing documentation. It suggests that writers simply get information, write it up, have it checked, and produce it. That is, it implies that the procedure requires simple input-process-output. This concept is limited.

Model 2: The In-The-Middle Document Cycle

Managers who use the following model say to their writers, in effect, "The documentation for this project is in a muddle. Come in and straighten it out and make sense of it." Unfortunately, Diagram 2 represents the most common document cycle used in the computer industry.

PROCEDURES

Design Team	**Writers**
Market Analysis	
Product Requirements	
Product Specification	
Product Design	
Product Development	
	Writers Called In
Product Development Continues	Documentation Begins
Product Programming	(Documentation Continues)
Product Testing	(Documentation Continues)
Product Manufacture	(Documentation Continues)
Out the Door	
Sales	

This flow chart shows that writers are brought in only in the middle of the product-development cycle when things are in a muddle. There are stacks of documents everywhere, no plan for the documentation, and a crisis atmosphere. No one had thought to tell the writers anything (or to ask them anything) during the early phases.

Model 2: The In-The-Middle Document Cycle
DIAGRAM 2

Diagram 2 presents a variation on the end-loaded cycle. In this model, managers call in the writers only when a project is in crisis -- say halfway through the product-development cycle -- instead of waiting a few more months while that crisis ripens into panic. Model 2 is only a slight improvement on Model 1.

Model 3: A Collaborative Team-Based Document Cycle
Managers who use the following model (a growing number) say to their writers, "We are beginning to talk about a new product; we'd like you to be on the product development team from beginning to end." This form of the cycle is becoming standard in many well-run computer firms. There are some problems with it, but it seems to be proving the most satisfactory in the long run. Those managers who do not learn to use it, some writers have suggested, will probably not be around in the long run.

PROCEDURES

Team members:
Project Manager
Marketing Professional
Project Engineers
Project Programmers
Publications Manager

Team Procedures		**Participation by**
Market Analysis (documentation process begins)		All Team Members
Product Requirements	(doc. process cont.)	All Team Members
Product Specification	(doc. process cont.)	All Team Members
Product Design	(doc. process cont.)	All Team Members
Product Development	(doc. process cont.)	All Team Members
Product Programming	(doc. process cont.)	All Team Members
Product Testing	(doc. process cont.)	All Team Members
Product Manufacture	(doc. process cont.)	All Team Members
User Documentation Completed		All Team Members
Out the Door		
Sales		

This flow chart shows a full-fledged model of the document cycle in which all members of a design team participate. It suggests the writer's specific contributions at each point in the process. The publications manager (or documentation manager) meets with the project engineer and the project manager in early sessions; personnel from the publications department collaborate closely with the design team throughout the cycle of product design, development, and manufacture.

Model 3: A Collaborative Document Cycle
DIAGRAM 3

An adequate diagram of the writing process in the computer industry will show how writers interact with a web or network of information. Writers must have certain kinds of support if they are to perform their duties adequately. In return, they make significant contributions at each stage of product development. Model 3 is more adequate as a model of the writing process because it indicates more clearly that the processes are complex and that they depend on a writer's interaction with a network of information and a writer's dependence on certain kinds of support.

In the collaborative document cycle represented by Diagram 3, the product is created by a Design Team which includes writers as well as technical and professional persons from other departments.

Diagram 3 suggests that writers make specific contributions to the product at each point in the product cycle. In effect, the documentation cycle parallels the product cycle. Writers gather information on the market audience and write a preliminary market analysis. Writers describe the product from outside in. They describe, that is, both product functionality (what the product can do) and the user interface (the way the users interact with the product). Writers contribute design ideas. Writers advocate user needs. Likewise, programmers and engineers contribute to convert their information into user documentation. Revision goes on continually. Collaboration is the key.

It must be remembered that these diagrams are merely crude representations of complex procedures. But whatever the procedures are, they need to be appropriate to the task, company personnel, and company mores. Moreover, the procedures need to be generally understood and agreed to by everyone in the company. Finally, they need to be monitored, evaluated, and updated. As simplified as it is, the third diagram suggests procedures that produce computer documentation effectively and efficiently in an increasing number of computer firms.

Part 2: Practices that Create Problems for Writers

Writers in the computer industry have identified many policies and practices that impede their work. These are, in effect, obstacles that writers would like managers to remove from their path. They have identified three kinds of problems: a) managers fail to understand documentation and writers, b) managers fail to plan and schedule writing projects, and c) managers fail to support writers.

Managers Fail to Understand Documentation and Writers
One of the most common complaints among writers in the computer industry is, "My manager does not understand me." What does this complaint mean? Is it merely petty grousing that reflects job dissatisfaction? Is it a part of the inevitable slippage between practicioners and their supervisors? Does it stem from jealousy of more highly-paid managerial and technical employees?

Whatever the answers to these questions may be, there are two legitimate meanings in this complaint. First, management often does not understand the importance of documentation. For example, one respondent to my survey said, "Management pays lip service to documentation. They claim to recognize the importance to the customer of good documentation, but they are not really committed." Another said, "Documentation is considered low priority." Documentation typically has a low status and is relegated to a low priority. The fundamental problem is that documentation is seen as merely a support, not as part of the product.

Second, management often does not understand what the document cycle is or how it works. As a respondent said, "Management fails to understand how long it takes to write a good document." All of the other failures of management described in this chapter flow from these two.

Managers Fail to Plan and Schedule Writing Projects
Nobody in the computer industry needs to be told that time pressures are severe. But many of the time pressures that writers experience can be traced to poor planning of the time available. Poor timetables, with unrealistic deadlines, contribute to lowered morale and lowered quality. Under the old concept of the writing cycle (diagrams 1 and 2 above), writers are expected to create documentation on too short a schedule and after sources of information have evaporated. My respondents frequently commented that there is not enough time, but showed that their managers set unrealistic deadlines. Driven by market considerations, they fail to plan adequate time for good documentation. One respondent commented that "we do not seem to be able to convince the engineers that it pays off in the long run to do it right the first time." Too often, critical stages in the document cycle are omitted because of the pressure of last-minute changes.

Some managers create anxiety unnecessarily by sticking to deadlines and requiring heroic efforts. Some writers experience unnecessary pressure and anxiety because their managers demand that they keep original deadlines even when the hardware and software they are documenting fall behind schedule. They are expected to work as though original, but obviously untenable, deadlines be met. Then, at the last minute, the deadline date is miraculously extended. If writers -- and others -- are given "one month more," then "one month more" for upwards of a year, they soon feel baffled and frustrated by the changing demands. Such unrealistic estimates of time lead to poor performance.

The problem of time takes another familiar form. Simply stated, writers are caught in a double bind. Documentation cannot be completed until the equipment or software is completed. Once the product is completed, managers want it to hit the market immediately -- accompanied by the completed documentation. But some of the writing has to be completed after the hardware or software is completed, and publication takes a couple of weeks at the printers. Writers often face this dilemma. Even with the best of will and effort and timetables, writers find themselves in a difficult situation.

The most critical problem is failure to plan for updating the documentation at the same time that the hardware and software are updated. In many cases, by the time that the manual is drafted, it is no longer accurate. Few firms plan effectively to update documentation during the entire life cycle of computer equipment.

Managers Fail to Support Writers

Some managers fail to realize that writers depend on others in the firm for information, for review, and for products. What Helen Loeb wrote several years ago is still true: "When technical documentation managers and software technical writers are asked to identify the biggest problem area they have on the job, they respond unanimously: 'Getting information from developers.'" (2)

Time and again, writers comment that their sorest need is for information. Despite this fact, procedures for distributing information are too often tenuous or non-existent. My respondents report that technicians give them inadequate information; they keep 'secrets' from the writers, and they have little time for consultation. Even some firms that are otherwise efficient have not devised an effective way to get current information to the writers.

Management failure to support writers often takes the form of failure to promote collaboration. Failure to collaborate takes many forms. Lack of agreement on procedures, policies, and standards paves the way for capricious and arbitrary decisions and prevents a uniform corporate look. When various engineers use different ways to write documentation, editors must laboriously re-write their materials. Waste is inevitable. (For a discussion of collaboration among technical writers, programmers, and managers, see Mirel in this volume.)

Perhaps the most surprising result of my survey is the reported lack of consistent policies. Many respondents commented that procedures for editing and re-writing are entirely non-existent. Respondents reported lack of consistent markup language and lack of ways to settle disputes over content, length, and tone of manuals. The result is a series of re-writes of rather simple material. In some firms, writers and editors find it difficult to work together as a team because they are in different departments. As a result, minor problems that could be dealt with easily become major problems. Management at the highest level may not even realize that communication is difficult. The problem may thus be built into the organization.

Some firms that have established policies and routines fail to enforce them. Respondents report that editing is haphazard, terminology is inconsistent, and arbitrary editing by technical experts gets management approval while technical errors are allowed to remain. It is not sufficient merely to promulgate regulations and timetables. Management is responsible for monitoring and controlling them. When reviewers are not held responsible for the material they review, and when testing is omitted, or put into the hands of incompetent workers, or when personnel are allowed to exercise authority outside the area of their competence, the quality of writing declines.

In some large firms, on the other hand, the system sometimes works overtime, like a Sorcerer's Apprentice. The most common complaint from writers in large firms is that there are too many levels of approval. The procedures choke off the distribution of information to writers, and then clog their work with cumbersome approval prodedures.

Part 3: Practices that Alleviate Problems for Writers

Writers have identified solutions to the problems cited in Part 2. These writers urge managers to a) understand computer documentation and writers, b) plan and schedule writing projects, c) support writing with suitable procedures.

Understand Computer Documentation and Writers

The writing problems that managers in the computer industry deal with are not only organizational and procedural. Many of them are conceptual. To solve the problems outlined in Part 2, many successful managers of technical writers have developed new conceptions of the roles of documentation and writers in the computer industry. Managers can put these concepts into operation by the following five guidelines. These guidelines help managers better understand documentation and writers.

1. Understand the Changing Context of Computer Writing. Writers ask why managers often downplay writing. Part of the answer lies in their concept of documentation. They relegate it to inferior status. Nobody can argue with the traditional concept that hardware is primary and the software has to be right. There can be no doubt that these concepts are correct. But too often these correct perceptions are accompanied by inappropriate corollaries:

- Documentation is peripheral.
- Documentation is merely support for our products.
- The documentation can always be upgraded later.
- Writing is an afterthought.
- The users will figure it out somehow.
- Writers, after all, are merely writers.

The effects of these attitudes are overheated hotlines, customer dissatisfaction, personnel dissatisfaction, loss of reputation, and, eventually loss of customers. In fact, more and more managers recognize that writers are increasingly important to the firm's welfare because computing tasks are increasingly complex and being performed by more and more people who are not computer-trained.

Because computer user documentation is still a relatively new product, it is often puzzling to managers. It is puzzling for a very good reason. Not only are computers complex, they are by far the most complex machines ever produced for widespread use. But that is only half the picture. The users of these increasingly complex machines are more varied than ever; more and more non-technical persons are using them. This is the first time in history that such complex machinery, with such complex capabilities, has been put into the hands of such varied users. No wonder managers are puzzled. So is everyone else.

At the same time, writers and writing have begun to change:

- Writers are increasingly mobile, aware of their power, and free.
- Writers have access to new production technologies.
- Writers know new production techniques.
- The processes that produce documentation are increasingly complex.
- Writers can make significant contributions to computer design.
- The amount of information produced doubles every few years.

In response to these new perceptions, many computer firms have begun to place more emphasis on writing. They have put line officers in charge of publications. They have put writers on product-development teams. They have begun to see that writing costs are best thought of as development costs, not support or overhead costs. They have recognized that writing is not merely a cost but that it is a strategic asset. This shift of attitude in the computer industry is increasingly important for writers.

2. Understand the Nature and Importance of Documentation. The writing that people do in the computer industry is different form the kinds of writing they do elsewhere (say, writing in schools and colleges, writing for newspapers and magazines, and writing research reports). Computer-related writing has several characteristics that distinguish it from other kinds of writing.

The first distinctive characteristic of computer-related writing is that it is an essential product-related activity. Because it provides the link between computers and their users, it is not merely a peripheral or an add-on, but is central. Documentation is essential to a high level of computing. Not only can it relieve the fear of using computers, but it guides all users -- beginners through advanced -- in ways to use the machines. This point may seem obvious, but it is often overlooked.

Second, documentation helps to shape the system it describes. It enhances other products (hardware and software), and it is itself a product.

Third, good documentation is an important marketing tool. It can supplement or replace some advertising. In contrast, poor documentation can alienate customers.

The main point is that communication through written language is one of the most important activities of a computer firm. Obviously, the special kind of language used in computer documentation is a means of production; that is, it helps people use the machines. Customers use documentation to get things done.

This view of documentation may come as a surprise to those accustomed to thinking of the computer industry in other terms. The traditional view is that computers are products of mathematics and engineering, supplemented by programming. This view remains valid, of course, but it is incomplete. We can understand the computer industry only if we recognize that its chief components are not two in number (hardware and software), but three (hardware, software, and documentation). When we want to understand the industry, then, we need to look beyond hardware and software to the realm of communication in ordinary language -- that is, to documentation.

The trick is to get technical managers committed to the documentation as a part of the product. The advice from writers seems unanimous: give writing a higher priority.

3. Understand the Writing Process. One respondent boldly stated one of the main problems: "Management many times does not understand the writing process, and does not wish to learn." It is natural for managers to think of writing computer documentation as a simple process. After all, managers typically spend a good deal of their own time writing and reading. From the point of view of some managers, the writing of documentation seems as straightforward as writing memos and letters. But the writing of documentation is more complex. It requires similar kinds of resources, knowledge, and information as the most demanding kinds of technical writing. It demands the same skills and abilities as writing the most important documents in the firm. In fact, writing documentation is similar in scope and complexity to the writing of formal proposals and reports.

In a typical computer firm, formal proposals receive a good deal of attention. Proposals are its life-blood, and they map out the future of the corporation. For this reason, the best people from all parts of the corporation focus their attention to writing a proposal for a sustained period of time. All divisions contribute in a cooperative process. Everyone has a stake in the outcome, and everyone knows it. Their reputation, their very job depends on it.

But few of these same people appreciate the difficulty of producing documentation, even though it requires similar skills and knowledge. The following outline of some of the things a writer has to do will suggest the complexity of the task. A writer of documentation has to:

- Understand what the product can do.
- Understand how people will use the product.
- Gather information from a wide variety of sources:
  - * engineers, designers, programmers,
  - * marketing personnel,
  - * use of the machines themselves.
- Cull usable information from a mass of technical data.
- Analyze the audiences (management, peers, and users/customers).
- Plan interfaces for a variety of users.
- Select appropriate format and sequences.

- Select appropriate mechanics (punctuation, spelling, and usage).
- Select appropriate style.
- Test, revise, and edit materials.
- Rewrite material and prepare it for publication.
- Revise material as the machines are altered.

It must be emphasized that what I have called "the writing process" spans the entire product development cycle. That is not to say that writing merely parallels the product development cycle, but that it interacts with it. In addition, writing documentation requires most of the same creative abilities as other aspects of the product development cycle.

Managers who have not been writers themselves may fail to realize what writing entails. Writers not only write copy that describes machines and processes, but they produce human-relations documents. They are communicators who deal with audiences. What they do entails gathering information from a wide variety of sources, selecting and sequencing content, and selecting format and page design. It also entails analyzing audiences and their needs, selecting graphics, writing, revising, testing, and editing. These are all high-level cognitive skills that require training and experience.

What I am suggesting is that managers broaden and enrich their concept of writers and the way they work. In order for writers to create their best work, they must be able to rely on adequate processes. Other persons in the firm, such as technical personnel, cannot perform the tasks that professional writers perform. They often lack interest in writing as well as experience in writing documentation. Frequently they are isolated from users' needs; perhaps they are even indifferent to them. Writers, on the other hand, can bring the perspectives of users to a design team. Successful managers of writing in the computer industry increasingly appreciate these concepts.

4. Understand Information Networking. As noted above, it is apparent from numerous comments by writers that many managers fail to realize the degree that writers depend on an adequate flow of information. In order to write documentation, writers must have complete, timely, and accurate information about the hardware and software and how they work.

But the information that writers use comes from a wide variety of sources. It may not be too extreme to say that writers depend on a network of information more complex than that used by any other professionals in the computer industry. The network includes many different kinds of sources and many people at various levels within the organization.

One of the recurring themes in comments by respondents is that writers interact with many people. Writers get information from engineers, designers, marketing personnel, and programmers as well as from their managers. In most cases, this information is not handed to them; they have to go and get it. In the worst cases, information is dumped on them, in large undigested gobs and blobs. Or it has to be wheedled out, wiggled out bit by bit from persons who are no longer interested in the problem.

This means that writers often rely heavily on their inter-personal relations. They must develop cordial working relations with colleagues in other departments. For this reason, it is up to management to foster creative working relationships among professionals in various departments. It is also up to management to help writers develop and maintain the inter-personal skills that will help them procure information, so that when crises arise, writers can get the information they need. It is also management's responsibility, meanwhile, to reduce the degree to which writers must rely on these tenuous sources of information.

A recurring theme in the discussions by writers of their task is the fact that writers interact with many people in the course of their day-to-day work. Writers gather information from three principal sources: written documents, the equipment (the product itself), and co-workers.

Written documents may abound, but writers must often scan yards and yards of them to find the information they need. The people they rely on for information may not be available: they have moved to another project, moved to another division, or moved to California. Worst of all, the equipment they are documenting may not be available to the writers even when it is in production.

5. Understand the Document Cycle. Effective managers understand these aspect of the document cycle:

- *Document Flow:* They understand where each document goes, who sees it, who does what with it, who is responsible for it, who signs-off on it, and what its timetable is.
- *Information Flow:* They understand where information comes from, who generates it, where it flows, and in what form.
- *Information Processing:* They understand the differences between raw and cooked data.

Plan and Schedule Writing Projects

Writers increasingly insist on being included in the scheduling process because they recognize that the key to successful documentation is scheduling. Managers who involve writers in the scheduling process and define everyone's role in the project have a better chance of success. As one writer put it, "The main thing is to get technical managers invested in the outcome of the documentation."

An advance planning phase is essential to adequate documentation. Effective managers schedule adequate time for planning, gathering information, revising, reviewing, testing, and production. The time schedule must be realistic. A good contract will specify the requirements for documentation. Effective managers will follow these six guidelines:

1. Design the User Interface First. Some innovative firms begin product design by describing the user interface first, instead of the hardware or software. They ask not "What can this machine do?" but "How will someone use this machine?" Then they go about designing the software and hardware to meet those user needs.

This procedure runs in the opposite direction from the history of computing. During the early decades of computing, mathematicians and engineers designed general-purpose computing machines, then others tried to adapt them to serve practical purposes. But nowadays, computers are so powerful and so adaptable that it makes sense to ask first how people will use them.

2. Use Adequate Plan Sheets. Plan sheets spell out the details of cost, personnel, and time. They make explicit all of the assumptions about the product, the audience, the resources, the context of the work, and the document cycle. Wise managers will develop plan sheets for documentation just as they do for engineering and programming. They get a commitment for them from top management, from their peers, from people they supervise, and, ultimately, from the customer. Plan sheets provide a regular and systematic way to review progress. With a plan and a method for monitoring it, managers can profit from their mistakes and better prepare for the future.

3. Plan for Adequate Internal Communication. A frequent complaint by writers is well stated by one respondent: "Technical people are unavailable for help. Many times, if available, they are uncooperative. Too often the writer is perceived as a pain, a nuisance." The information needs of other groups in the firm are better understood and better provided for than the information needs of writers. Programmers get their information directly. It comes along with the assignment from the boss. It flows naturally to them in well-tended channels. When supervisors need information, they too get it directly, in the form of reports. The same is true for those who review, test, and produce marketing materials. The information needs of these persons are well understood. Consequently, their needs are met by procedures built into the organizational structure of the firm.

It is not so with writers. Writers, in contrast, get information second hand. It is often too little, too late, and of poor quality. First, they must wiggle it out from many sources. Then, since it is usually low-grade information, they must evaluate it, sift it, cull it. In addition, the tissue of information that writers deal with is more complex and more delicate. They get information from technical sources, then re-digest it for non-technical users. The main difficulty that writers encounter, in short, is that despite the complexity of the writers' tasks and the importance of information for them, less provision is made for them to get it -- and the larger the project, the more difficult it is to get information about it.

4. Plan for Updating. As noted above, wise managers plan to update the documentation. They realize that software programs are living, evolving organisms. As the software is updated, so must the documentation. As the system changes, the documentation must change with it. The firm must generate documentation throughout the life cycle of the system.

5. Develop a Concept of Teamwork. In many leading firms, it has become axiomatic that writers work as a team with product designers and developers. Writers participate in initial planning and scheduling as well as in software design. Each design team in these firms includes a documentation specialist. For large projects, it includes a publications manager and several writers. The team begins its work from phase zero with a writer as a full-fledged member. Writers, then, communicate closely with hardware and software engineers during every stage of product development. It is surprising to discover that in many firms, writers do not participate in product design. It is essential to involve writers in the day-to-day life of the technical aspects of the product.

Managers can develop common goals, as well as common standards and expectations, by fostering widespread participation in product design and development. Managers can develop commitment to projects and procedures, policies and standards if they make sure that everyone who has a stake in the project and everyone who contributes to the project is in on the planning.

Writers are often under-utilized in firms. Too frequently, their skills, abilities, and points of view are ignored and they are set to work at hack or menial tasks that neither challenge them nor benefit the corporation. Writers can contribute in several ways. Not only can they write proposals and specifications for new products, but they can contribute to an understanding of the user interface for new products. They can be the allies of marketing personnel because they understand the user's point of view, and their advocacy for users can make them invaluable in the firm. (For a discussion of the political role that writers play in the documentation process, see Mirel in this volume.)

6. Establish Priorities. Effective managers find ways to set priorities, implement them, monitor them, and control them. They help writers discover how important it is for the writing group to fulfill each specification. Managers rank the importance, for example, of the following goals:

- Publish documents with desirable aesthetic qualities.
- Publish look-alike documents.
- Respond quickly to new needs.
- Assure completeness of documentation.
- Assure accuracy of documentation.
- Assure appropriate style.

Support Writers with Suitable Procedures

Effective managers can motivate writers and engender trust by giving writers a challenge and then supporting them. Managers can provide writers with both physical and psychological support:

1. Provide Appropriate Publishing and Production Equipment. Effective managers let writers select their own word processors, text editing software, and printers. They provide dedicated terminals with adjustable 66-line screens and movable tables, paste-up areas, adjustable lighting, and software for document sorting, spelling, formatting, and editing.

It is important that writers themselves select hardware and software suitable for producing documentation. As every writer knows, a terminal designed for programming is a poor substitute for a dedicated word processor. When firms provide a desktop publishing system on each writer's desk, morale goes up immediately -- and along with it output and productivity. Installation of laser printers in one firm, which allows writers to produce their work in next-to-final form themselves, has cut production time 80%.

2. Be an Advocate for Technical Writing in the Firm. Part of the writing manager's job is to interpret writing to upper management -- that is, to educate upper management on the importance of writing in the firm. The task is to make others in the firm aware of the importance of documentation so that writing receives appropriate administrative support -- budget, personnel, status, recognition, timetables, and organizational relationships.

Conclusion

The comments on the questionnaires returned by 38 writers reflect a distinctive flavor that characterizes writers in the computer industry. First, the comments have been frank. Writers are serious professionals who are highly trained and who have thought long and hard about their strategies and their skills and techniques for producing computer documentation. They have all tried to be helpful and understanding. Even when they have found their jobs exasperating, they have been willing to examine their problems rationally, to share solutions, and to offer suggestions to help others overcome similar problems. Second, the comments by respondents reflect the excitement of writing for the computer industry -- its nervous bewilderment, its frantic, manic pace.

But most of all, the comments on questionnaires reflect the writers' feeling that writing is important and that writers in the computer industry are participating in an important enterprise. The responses reflect the zest that comes from working on the cutting edge of technology and communication and the realization that their efforts contribute significantly either to success or failure for themselves and for their companies.

Notes

1. This phase of the research, comprising a questionnaire-based survey of writers, was funded by Plymouth State College. The second phase commenced with a workshop on the same topic at the Fourth Conference on Writing for the Computer Industry, August 15, 1987 at the Massachusetts Institute of Technology. A third phase, including workshops, interviews, and on-site visits, is supported by a grant from the Society for Technical Communication.

2. Loeb, Helen. Writing for the Computer Industry. Unpublished textbook (author's advance xerographic copy.)

15 The Relationship of Product Design to Document Design

Lauren Davis Baker
Hewlett-Packard Company

The Quest For Usability

Increasingly, customers include documentation as an integral part of the products that they are buying. Customers are beginning to demand comprehensive, easy-to-use documentation. In the case of complex equipment, such as computer systems, documentation can influence product sales. The need for usable documentation is evident.

In response to this need, many writers are conducting usability tests to improve their documentation. However, they and the companies they work for should take heed: even excellent documentation cannot make up for flaws in the product itself. While poor documentation can make any product *less* usable, excellent documentation cannot make a poor product *more* usable. To create *both* a usable product and a usable document, usability must be a primary goal of members of the product team (documentation, marketing, research and development, and others) from the start of the project.

This chapter discusses how to move documentation testing from the end of the product development cycle, where most writers are forced to deal with it—to the beginning of the cycle, where it can best be used to improve product usability. This approach allows documentation and the product to be created concurrently, as a coherent system.

Shifting the Focus

In many corporations usability testing begins in the documentation department. One of the more interesting reasons for this is accountability. When a document is perceived as unusable (customers complain or there are a lot of support calls), the author will receive a lot of negative attention. This high degree of accountability motivates many writers to use testing as a means of ensuring that their documentation meets customers' needs.

Another reason for the focus on documentation testing is its high visibility. Consumer magazines are reviewing and rating documentation, along with product features such as ease of use, price/performance, and are asking to see documentation before buying computer systems and other expensive equipment. These trends are powerful incentives, encouraging corporations to produce usable documentation.

Documentation is relatively easy to test, and the benefits are becoming increasingly obvious and well publicized. Additionally, documentation is relatively easy and inexpensive to modify. Understandably, companies are more willing to rewrite chapters than software code, and are much more eager to rework manuals than hardware.

Many companies, therefore, begin usability testing in the documentation department, isolated from the rest of the organization. The result? Writers are trying to write easy-to-use manuals about difficult-to-use products. Focusing on documentation is a common, but ineffective approach to improving the usability of products; if a user's guide doesn't help the overall usability of a product, throw in a handy pocket guide or reference card. To quote Edmond H. Weiss, from *How to Write a Usable User Manual,* "In effect, we leave the hole in the road, but post warning signs; mistakenly, we then believe that the hole is no longer a danger."[1]

To accentuate the problem, evidence shows that customers don't like to read documentation, as discussed in the following section.

Following Instructions—When and Why

Product documentation is likely to be read in the following situations:

- the user is inexperienced
- the product is unique
- the user is concerned about damaging the product
- the user perceives the product as dangerous.

Unfortunately, in most situations people do not want to read documentation—they are eager to use the new product. Many people refer to documentation only after a trial and error approach doesn't work; hence the addage, "If all else fails, read the documentation." When people do read documentation, there is no guarantee that they will follow the instructions provided for them.

An interesting example of people failing to read instructions is recorded in a series of studies on the use of warning labels. Like manuals, labels provide product-use instructions. The results are especially dramatic because the labels warned of potential danger to users who might misuse the product. Because the stakes were relatively high, one might expect the subjects to be especially attentive to the instructions provided. Unfortunately, this was not the case.

A noteworthy finding in these studies was that 77% of the subjects could fully recall the label instructions, but failed to carry them out. Another 35% of the subjects read enough of the warning section to see what it was, and then stopped reading.[2] These subjects didn't feel that the warning was necessary!

If subjects are unwilling to read instructions when they are aware of personal risk, they are even less likely to read them when they feel they cannot be harmed by a product. Relying on documentation to make up for problems in a product's design is an unrealistic and unsafe practice.

Even when people consider information consciously, they still may not change their behavior.[3] This is especially likely when information is

- perceived as familiar or redundant
- perceived as inconsistent with the readers' beliefs or prior knowledge
- accepted as true, but the reader is not motivated enough to follow instructions or change his behavior.

Unless the customer is in an information-seeking frame of mind, the writer's message may not be received at all. To technical communicators, this means that the odds are against instructions being received and acted on unless the reader is motivated. And, even if the user wants to learn, he will overlook information if it appears redundant or too obvious—assuming nothing will be learned from reading the documentation. For example, how many of us read the instructions that come with a hairdryer? Most of us assume that the steps are simple and that the documentation won't teach us anything new.

Additionally, a document loses credibility if the information deviates too far from users' expectations. If the use of a product doesn't meet users' expectations, testing will invoke comments like "that doesn't make sense . . .," and subjects will attempt to use the product in ways they assume it should be used, based on preconceived ideas.

People approach products with assumptions based on their previous experiences. For example, they may assume they know how to use a product: how dangerous or safe it is to operate, how easy or difficult it will be to learn, how long it will take them to become a proficient user—all based on experiences with similar products.[4]

When users have related prior product experience they are less likely to use documentation before trying a new product. Most experienced users will not refer to documentation until they encounter a problem they cannot solve by trial and error.

Take the case of a new automobile. The average user assumes that familiarity with other automobiles will help him use the new model. The owner will probably open the documentation for reference only, when looking up the size of the gas tank, the type of air filter to use, or how to change the oil.

Unless there is something unique about the new auto, the user will act on assumptions about how cars work. He expects to be able to drive any automobile, based on his experience with some automobiles. Because it's true that past experience with some products (such as cars) will aid in using others, the user optimistically assumes this is true (to some degree) for all related products. If a new product is something users are likely to have had some experience with, such as appliances, computer equipment, or software, it cannot be assumed that the documentation will be read.

In some cases users will read the documentation and accept it as being true, but simply are not motivated enough to change their familiar behaviors. In such instances, the user responds to other motivating factors, such as deadlines, and adheres to the familiar patterns of behavior.

When designers acknowledge and work with users' preconceived ideas about how a product should work, users find the product easy to learn to use. As a result, the user feels successful using the product. Most importantly, the product must be foolproof enough to prevent users from hurting themselves should they fail to read the documentation. Unfortunately, this is where a surprising number of companies are at fault. Relying on user documentation to make up for such design requirements is not fair to the customer.

Changing Documentation Schedules

Most documentation testing occurs late in a product's development cycle. The writer waits to have a complete document to test and a "final" version of the product. This means that any problems in the product are found too late to correctly fix them: prototypes of the product have been developed, marketing plans are firmly in place, molds for parts have been created. At this point, product design changes are expensive and impractical. And, if major problems are found in the documentation, the writer has already invested a great deal of time and effort in the work.

As the following graphs illustrate, the number of possible solutions to problems decrease as product introduction nears; conversely, the cost of solutions increase with time.

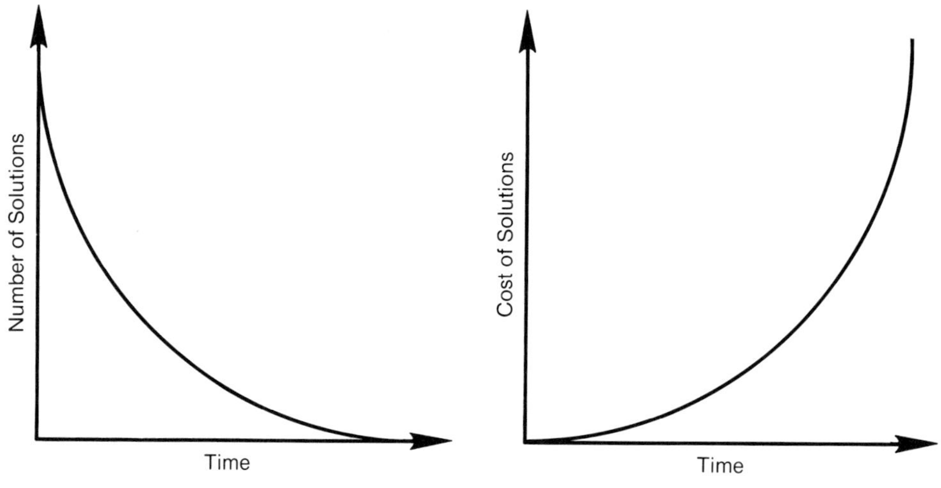

To effectively improve product usability, testing must begin early enough in the product's development to give product designers feedback when modifications are affordable and easily implemented. If testing is incorporated into the product development cycle rather than tacked onto the end, the benefits of testing (customer-motivated design improvements, improved ease of use and customer satisfaction, increased perception of company quality, ensuring product meets customer needs, identification of hidden problems/oversights) can be realized on a larger scale.

Working With Product Lifecycles

All products have their own lifecycles, or phases of development. The length of these phases and their names will vary from one company to the next, according to the nature of the product and development time required. The following illustrates a simplified product development cycle.

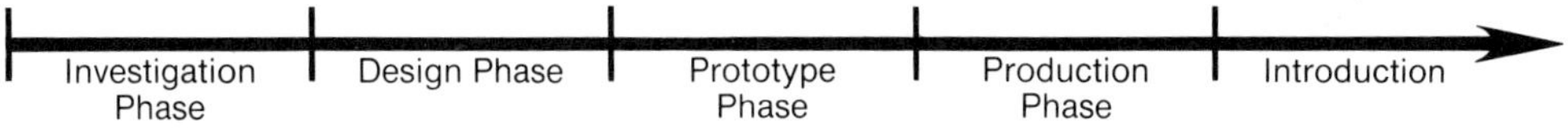

As shown, most documentation development occurs in the last quarter of the product development cycle, when the a prototype of the product is available.

By getting involved late in the product's lifecycle, writers can only help users use the product. If features are difficult to use, writers can try to make them appear more usable—if features are really bad, they must write a document full of warnings, cautions, and footnoted exceptions. Product fixes developed at this time are likely to be difficult to implement and provide only superficial improvements.

However, if writers get involved earlier in the design of the product, they'll be in a position to suggest improvements to product design problems. At this point, designers are more able to implement the writers' suggestions to create a more usable product.

The ideal time for the writer to get involved is in the initial "investigation phase". During this phase, the company determines which features the product will have. In a company with a strong marketing organization, market research techniques determine which features customers want. In a company with a strong research and development department, this department may suggest potential products to the rest of the company, based on technological advances they have made. In either case, the implementation of these features may or may not be usable to the customer.

The first time writers try to document features or procedures, it will be apparent whether or not these procedures are straightforward. If writers try to find the most natural way to describe the features or tasks, they will probably describe the most logical design solutions for the features. The technical communicators' approach as the first users of the products can be invaluable in spotting design problems.

The list of tasks and associated product features should be extremely detailed. Include every subtask and product feature involved in each major task. The next step is to prioritize the tasks, by identifying which are the most critical to making the customer feel successful. For example, if a customer can't find the ignition, he'll never be able to drive the car.

Next, take a more global look at the product. For example, consider compatibility with previous versions of hardware or software, whether or not the product can be connected to other peripheral products, which default settings will be most useful to the majority of customers, usability by disabled people, whether or not it provides feedback, whether or not it allows the user to make a major error (like erase a hard disc) without warning, product adaptability for future upgrades, and usability by international customers.

The task list will take more than one attempt to complete. As the product becomes more clearly defined, edit and update the list.

By creating a list of tasks during the "investigation phase," the product and the documentation begin developing as a system. The product team is working toward common usability goals, identifying issues early, and allowing the team the necessary time to consider multiple, cost-effective solutions.

Scheduling Testing

The product team should develop a product schedule, identifying when each aspect of the product will be designed and built, even if it is only an approximate schedule. The next step is to map the list of critical tasks onto the product schedule. This allows the team to determine the earliest possible date that product prototypes or prototypes of product features will be available. Use this preliminary schedule to determine when to test the documentation and tasks associated with each feature. A sample schedule is shown below.

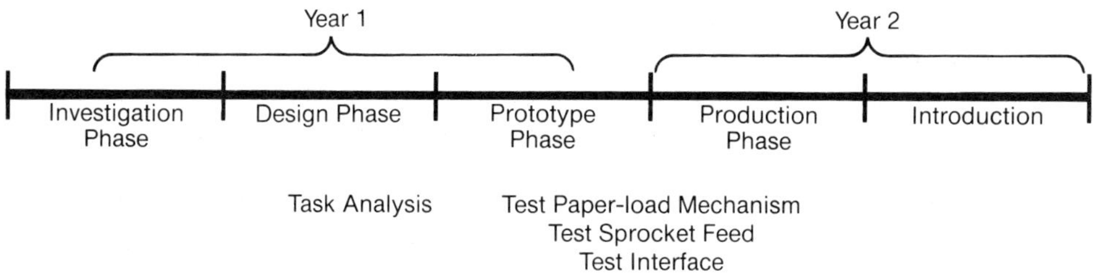

The list of tasks and features focuses on the most critical user interface issues. From it, writers can identify the tasks that must be documented. Additionally, product features will have been prioritized according to how strongly they influence customers' opinions of the product's usability.

Making the Most of Usability Testing

The following sections discuss ways to best use testing to improve both documentation and product design.

Identifying User Interface Issues
The initial "investigation phase" is the ideal time to identify the product's most critical user interface issues. If the company has a human factors department, they may lead this effort; without a human factors department, this list should be created with other members of the product development team. It is important to include a representative from each functional area (for example: marketing, documentation, customer assurance, manufacturing, and research/development)—each will bring unique viewpoints and concerns.

The product team should perform a task analysis. As the name implies, task analysis involves examining what the product's design requires of the user. Task analysis helps the team examine the feasibility of the product design from both a development and a usability perspective.

Start by identifying the *tasks* the customer will need to accomplish with the product. Next, list ways in which the customer will interact with the product to accomplish each task.

Two sample tasks are listed below. These examples illustrate the types of information that can be useful in performing a task analysis.

Example 1: Hardware Product, Printer

Task	Product Interaction
1. Loading paper	
a. Turn on printer	power cord, on/off switch
b. Open paper latch	paper latch
c. Feed paper into printer	paper bail
d. Adjust sprocket feed	sprocket feed

Example 2: Software Product, Word Processing Software

Task	Product Interaction
1. Underlining a word	
a. Load software	disc drive, keyboard
b. Select START	primary menu
c. Begin writing	keyboard
d. Highlight word to	cursor keys, f3 function key

Technical communicators must keep in mind that they are not waiting to test a finished product or document. They will use this method to test sections of documentation with product prototypes *as they develop.*

As each new version of the product or particular features are developed, conduct additional rounds of testing. If the new designs are improvements, subjects will have a higher success rate and will be able to complete tasks in less time. By the time a final product prototype is developed, the errors found should be relatively minor.

This is the best way to effectively influence product design. It will encourage the development of products that are easy to use, easy to document, and make the customer feel successful.

Developing Tests

The list of tasks is used to determine what needs to be tested. The schedule pinpoints when tests can be conducted. Using these tools, the product team can develop tests. The team should agree on test methods and procedures before implementing tests. David Meister's *Human Factor's Testing and Evaluation* gives a basic introduction to human factors testing, including test design. Wesley E. Woodson's *Human Factors Reference Guide for Electronics and Computer Professionals* may also be used as a reference during test design.

When testing one prototype after another, tests are developed more rapidly and are shorter in length than tests of finished products or entire systems. Tests are conducted iteratively, after each design change, with team members looking for very specific reactions from subjects. In many cases, feedback on product design can be obtained using ten subjects or less.

Tests should follow all the best practices of usability testing, such as using subjects that match characteristics of the product's targeted customers. For example, what age and level of education are customers expected to have? Is computer literacy a considera-tion? If the product is targeted for people with a wide range of experience, choose subjects with an equally wide range of experience—including both novices and experts. Each will teach you something about the usability of your product and your document.

To be fair, each test subject should be given the *exact* same information about the product and the task. Written test instructions are preferable to oral instructions because they ensure that subjects get the same information, in the *same wording,* for each test. When writing test instructions, avoid language that will bias the results or set expectations. Phrases such as "we think you'll like this design" or "this may be difficult" set an expectation for the subject.

Develop realistic test scenarios. This helps to take pressure off of the subject, by making the test situation seem less foreign. This is a commonly-used scenario: "It is Monday morning, and you find a new computer on your desk. Your boss has left you a memo, asking you to set up the computer and enter product forecast data (provided on the attached sheet). Set up the spreadsheet and get a print-out for your boss." The scenario provides the subject with a task that is typically accomplished with the product, without giving away the intent of the test designers.

Provide subjects with as "finished" a product or product prototype and documentation as possible. Draft documentation should include artwork and page numbers, in at least a rough form.

Product engineers and the technical communicators who developed the documentation should observe the test from a remote site or from videotape. By no means should they be allowed to interfere with tests in progress. Tests must be conducted by unbiased administrators to avoid biasing results.

Record how long it takes each subject to complete the assigned task(s), from start to finish. Additionally, record the success rate of subjects: how many succeeded, how many completed the task incorrectly, how many needed assistance to complete the task at all. This information will show whether or not one design is an improvement over another.

Record the types of problems subjects are having, and prioritize them. Concentrate on resolving the problems that are most likely to interfere with customers successfully using the product. Next, discuss solutions. Solutions can be as straightforward as changing the wording on a menu screen, using color more consistently in menus, adding color to highlight user-accessible hardware (such as levers or buttons), changing the sequence of menus, or providing audio or visual feedback. The technical communicator's experience in thinking like a user will help to reveal solutions that may be missed by product designers.

Recognizing the Difference Between Documentation and Product Errors

Technical communicators should learn to distinguish between documentation and product errors. With this knowledge, they can identify potential product flaws in the product design phase.

One of the most direct ways to focus on product design issues is to let subjects use product prototypes without documentation. If the use of the product is intuitive, subjects will be successful after some trial and error. If the design is extremely complex or illogical, subjects may never stumble on the correct use of the product.

An additional tool is benchmark testing. Look at alternate designs and compare the usability of the original product's design to those designs. If, for example, you are studying paper-loading methods for a printer, look at what the competition has developed. Are their methods intuitively obvious? How long does it take to complete the same task (in this case, paper-loading) using each product? This kind of information will provide invaluable feedback on the design of the product.

Here are some other indications that a product has usability problems:

- an expert can do the task in much less time than the neophyte
- documentation has been debugged, yet users still struggle with tasks
- subjects understand instructions but object to the procedure itself.

When usability problems are observed, the product team should discuss design options. If an improved design isn't possible, the information can be used to develop a product support plan, supplemental training, a second version of the product, or a retrofit of the current product. As a last resort, documentation developers may be asked to develop help cards, warning labels, or similar aids to supplement the product's design.

Developing Formal Guidelines

The work the product team accomplishes with its first product lifecycle can be carried over to future products, as a set of general guidelines. For example, product interface issues are identified in the early "investigation phase," usability tests begin in the "design phase," and so on. Additional tests, such as safety checks, should be worked into this schedule.

This approach requires the support of representatives of the departments involved in bringing a product to market. Each department helps to define when it is most efficient for them to do their jobs with respect to the product development cycle.

The guidelines developed will help to keep product teams focused on goals and issues through the product development cycle. Additionally, it will let all team members know the requirements of other departments to do their jobs most effectively.

The guidelines can be fine-tuned further, into product "checkpoints". For each checkpoint, the product team agrees on the criteria the product must meet before passing on to the next phase of development. The criteria and objectives must be tailored to fit the nature of the product, the company, and its customer.

A sample set of guidelines for an "investigation phase" follows. In this case the tasks have been divided among the departments responsible for bringing the product to market, in the absence of a Human Factors Department. Ideally, guidelines would be drawn up for each phase of the product's development.

Task	Responsible Department
Identify usability problems with similar or existing products.	Marketing Customer Assurance
Identify product features, considering technology, customer needs, and cost.	Marketing Research and Development

Conclusion

Traditionally, technical communicators have worked to develop the best possible documentation for their assigned product. Writers may have noticed product design problems, but felt helpless to do anything but try to "write around" them.

With the customers' increased focus on usability, corporations must look at the usability of the product and documentation as a system. Technical communicators can play an integral part in this effort, using their outlook as the first user of the product. By using information gained from documentation testing at an earlier stage in the product's development, technical communicators can help to create products that are both easier to document and to use.

References

[1] Edmond H. Weiss, How to Write a Usable User Manual. ISI Press, 1985. pp 26-29.

[2] Jill A. Strawbridge, "The Influence of Position, Highlighting, and Imbedding on Warning Effectiveness." Proceedings of the Human Factors Society—30th Annual, 1986. pp 716-720.

[3] D.P. Horst, G.E. McCarthy, J.N. Robinson, R.L. McCarthy, S. Krumm-Scott, "Safety Information Presentation: Factors Influencing the Potential for Changing Behavior." Proceedings of the Human Factors Society—30th Annual, 1986. pp 111-115.

[4] G.H. Robinson, Ph.D., P.E. Small, Robinson and Associates. "Toward a Methodology for the Design of Warnings." Proceedings of the Human Factors Society—30th Annual, 1986. pp 106-110.

[5] Wesley E. Woodson, Human Factors Reference Guide for Electronics and Computer Professionals. MacGraw-Hill, 1987. pp 159-161.

16 Studying Usability in the Field: Qualitative Research Techniques for Technical Communicators

Emilie Gould
IBM Corporation
Kingston, NY

Stephen Doheny-Farina
Clarkson University
Potsdam, NY

Nearly all the chapters in this book argue, either explicitly or implicitly, for more applied research into technical communication practices. The authors of several chapters (e.g. Baker; Bradford; Chisholm; Rubens and Rubens) urge technical writers and document designers to include usability testing in the documentation cycle. Others, like Charney, Reder, and Wells, argue that we should turn to basic, experimental research to discover the optimal ways to present technical information. Still others (Debs; Mirel; Ramey) discuss the benefits of going out into the field to study usability. In this chapter, we also urge writers and designers to go out into the field; that is, we urge writers and designers to study users operating in their natural work environments.

We make this argument by providing an overview of some field research techniques that can be useful for those of you whose job is to continually produce new technical documentation in industry. These techniques will enable you to a) learn more about the nature of your users, and b) explore the usefulness and accuracy of your documentation.

We must begin, however, with an important disclaimer: we do not expect anyone to read this chapter and then be able to go out and perform all of the techniques that we describe. Instead, we merely illustrate some of the possibilities, the constraints, and the complexities involved in field research. In many ways, the ability to conduct field research is *an art learned only by doing*. Obviously, no one can learn this art just by reading an article about it. Our ultimate purpose, then, is only to urge you to consider how field research may help you improve the ways that you evaluate your users and your documentation. We want to encourage you to expand your repertoire of usability research techniques.

What is qualitative field research?

Simply put, qualitative research involves investigating a few cases in great depth; field research involves investigations done in the natural environments of those under study. For the typical technical writer, the best qualitative field research relies on customer visits. By studying the uses of documentation in a customer's natural work environment, a researcher can learn much from only a few users.

Underlying qualitative field research is the belief that you only begin to understand usability by observing how people solve problems in their normal environment. How individuals act is based upon the ways those individuals interpret themselves, their actions, and the world around them. In order to understand users' actions, you must try to get close to their point of view; to understand **how** users act, you want to understand **why** they act as they do. Furthermore, you want to see how well or poorly your documentation is integrated into the users' work environments.

What are limitations to qualitative field research?

Qualitative field research is limited. While researchers using quantitative methods seek to learn from a sample group what an entire population thinks or does, researchers using qualitative techniques may not discover anything that applies to a larger population.

For example, by conducting "exit polls" across a state, television networks are able to predict the winners of statewide political elections. If those same networks studied, instead, only a few voters' perceptions of the issues, the candidates, and the campaigns, the networks would probably not be able to predict anything about the outcome of the entire election. However, network pollsters probably would have interviewed a limited number of voters before they constructed their exit polls.

In the same way, if technical writers and document designers wish to discover how *all* users will use mass marketed information, then qualitative studies of a few users will not give documentors the power to make sweeping predictions. Nonetheless, qualitative research enables documentors to gain insight into how *some* users act. Such limited knowledge can be useful both in itself and in relation to quantitative methods.

What can you learn in the field?

Even though you cannot predict how an entire population will behave, you can still learn something from how a few users act in a particular setting. In such situations you can learn:

1. Who your users are (company demographics and personal information): While abstract demographic information can be gained from surveys, a researcher who goes into the field to study actual users can begin to get to know a few users. That is, a researcher begins to learn how a few *unique* individuals perceive their jobs and the tools they must use to do those jobs.

2. What users' work environments are like: In the field, researchers can learn something about the physical environments within which information is used. This can include a range of information, from whether users work alone or in groups to whether they have room to read or store your library of manuals.

3. Which users have access to what information: In an ideal world, all users who need documentation would indeed have access to it. However, sources of authority in an organization may control the way information is accessed and used. In addition, corporate channels of communication may operate in ways that aid or hinder information use. By going out into the field, a researcher can learn whether the information that documentors provide actually reaches those who need that information. Such a discovery may lead documentors to new or enhanced ways to package and disseminate information.

4. How information is used in those environments: Field researchers can seek the answers to a variety of question about information use, questions such as: Do workers actually use the documentation that you provide them? Do workers rely on resident experts for answers? How do experts gain their expertise? Have users rewritten your documentation and made it more usable for their particlar situation? When following procedures, do users take shortcuts?

5. Why users behave the ways that they do (the meanings users attribute to their behavior): Not only can field researchers discover unexpected user behavior, they can learn *why* users behave in those unexpected ways. By implementing research techniques designed to elicit the meanings that users attribute to their own behavior, researchers can discover how documentation relates to the users' actions.

6. How accurate and useful the information is: When a researcher discovers that the documentation at a particular site has been rewritten, that may mean that the original was inappropriate in some way. It may also mean that the original was *in error* in some way. Researchers may be able to catch errors in the original analysis of the task by observing actual users, especially during preliminary use of new products during beta testing.

7. How satisfied users are with your information: While the typical survey questionnaires that accompany documentation ask users whether or not they are happy with the documentation, field researchers can explore those responses in detail. True, it may be scary to discover the depth of disatisfaction that users may feel about certain documentation; at the same time it is extremely important to understand why users feel the ways that they do. Researchers may discover that user attitudes can be altered with some simple, cost-effective changes. Or it may be that dissatisfaction is so deep that major changes must be undertaken or business may be lost.

How does qualitative field research fit with quantitative methods?

Usability is best explored in many ways. A complete usability program combines qualitative and quantitative research. Qualitative field research, quantitative surveys, and lab testing are interdependent and should reinforce one another. You should go into the field to:

1. Provide information about a task for which your company is designing a product: With this information, you can develop a prototype where the characteristics of user, not the function, mandate the design. As argued elsewhere in this book (Bradford; Baker; Chisholm), documentation specialists can bring a user's perspective to product design.

2. Help establish variables for later quantitative surveys or testing: When you observe people at work, you may discover features that affect how users perform tasks. You may eventually try to isolate those features and establish them as variables in a quantitative survey or usability test. Without observing users in action, you may never realize that a task involves those features.

3. Validate quantitative results and instruments after such testing: For example, in her chapter in this volume, Lauren Davis Baker discusses the uses of "scenarios" in usability testing. That is, a test subject is asked to read a scenario that describes a work situation and then use the product and documentation accordingly. The test administrator then records how well the test subject performs the task and can evaluate the effectiveness of the documentation and/or product. Through observation or by taking scenarios out into the field and asking real users to read them, researchers can learn how well testing matches experience.

Sometimes a complete usability program is impossible. You may lack the resources to distribute a quantitative survey or run quantitative or experimental usability tests. Statistical validity might be limited or unavailable because there is a small user population, the variables cannot be established, or you cannot find appropriate test subjects. In such situations, qualitative field research lets you explore usability in return for a limited effort.

You can use questionnaires, interviews, or on-site observations to learn how people use your documentation. However, before reviewing these techniques, you need to understand some of the problems you face as a field researcher and how to prepare yourself before going out in the field.

What are the constraints on you as a field researcher?

Field researchers have five primary constraints on their efforts to collect information on usability:

1. **Time constraints**. Unfortunately, customers can spare you only so much time. When you enter your users' workplace, you are unlikely to have more than a few hours, or a day, or at most a week to do your research. You must plan ahead to get the most out of your brief visit. At the same time, you must be very sensitive to the users' available time. You must try to study users without significantly delaying their work.

This can put you in a terrible bind. Ethnographers who study people as they live and work in their natural cultures can spend *years* in the field trying to gain insight into those cultures. In her study of the uses of in-house documentation (this volume), Barbara Mirel spent months observing and interviewing the users of the documentation. This is not to say that a brief visit to the field will yield little information. On the contrary, two days of well-prepared and active data collection can yield a surprising amount of information about a tightly defined topic. If you continue to make field visits to the same or similar users over a period of months, you can begin to develop a sophisticated analysis of documentation use.

2. **Political constraints**. You want to avoid straining company/customer relationships. The presence of a researcher in the midst of a workplace can be disruptive and intimidating. Whenever you are in the field, no matter how careful you may be to avoid disrupting users' work, you will be seen as an outsider -- and worse, an outsider who *"is watching us!!"* In addition, you will be seen as a representative of your company; if you are a poor representative, you can invite resentment and damage the relationship between your company and the customer.

You should also be concerned about relationships within your own company.

You may have to explain your research goals to other people who have their own relationships with the users. Since marketing relationships are particularly important, marketing personnel within your company may not want you "getting in the way." Thus, at some point in your research, you must show that learning more about customers -- what they need in documentation and how they use documentation -- is of primary importance to the mission of your company.

3. **Legal constraints**. You must observe the legal limits on handling all proprietary information. Ask your company for its policy on gathering information from the customer's organization as well as its policy on divulging information from your own organization.

4. **Ethical constraints.** Field researchers concentrate on the particularly personal way individuals use information. You are not collecting data from a large group of faceless, nameless, randomly chosen respondents to surveys. You are meeting, interviewing, and getting to know unique individuals. You are assuming that by learning how a few of these individuals do their jobs, you can gain some knowledge about how to do yours. You are asking them to allow you to probe what they think and how they act. In the process, you may learn some information that those users would not want their supervisors to know. Thus, you must be sensitive to the private nature of the information you collect.

You should not mislead users in any way. Be open about your agenda. If you are able to guarantee anonymity, tell them. If you are not, by all means tell them!

You must realize that you will bring a set of biases that will color what you see. You must continually attempt to let what you observe challenge your preconceived notions. The less that you do to manipulate those you study, the clearer your snapshot of the field will be. Some useful guidelines, such as the American Psychological Association's guidelines for research, can help you respect your user's rights.

5. **Budgetary constraints.** Obviously, it costs money for companies to send their writers out in the field to study usability. If your budget does not allow for such trips, you can modify several of the research devices described in this chapter and use them in less costly ways. For example, you may be able to set up data gathering sessions with users within your own company. You must always assume, however, that the information that you gather in these less expensive, but contrived studies, cannot necessarily be equated to studies of actual users. You may still gain insight into usability, but you may be gaining

insight into usability in an artificial setting because these users will share your own institutional bias.

How should you prepare yourself to go out into the field?

You must do preliminary research before setting up any research situations in the field. To be as well-informed as possible, you may wish to talk with fellow employees -- such as technical support representatives and marketing personnel -- who already have contacts in the field. These people may have some insights into user behaviors; but their interests are probably not the same as yours.

If your company has attempted to get information on documentation use in the past, you may be able to review the history of user feedback. This feedback may be in the form of user-surveys, trip reports, complaints, or personal accounts of users' responses to products and documentation. Most usefully, you may be able to either establish or consult "customer councils" -- user groups that are organized to discuss and develop requirements for new products or enhancements.

You can also gain some useful information by exploring some institutional channels, such as conferences, conventions, trade shows, the trade press, and the research journals and books. The trade press often prepares product reviews that discuss particular issues that you may want to explore in the field. Research publications may contain reports on the uses of products and documentation similar to yours. (For a review of some useful research publications, see Debs in this volume.)

Once you have done your preliminary research, put together a research plan. Establish the scope of your research: decide what types of documents, products, and users you want to study; make a list of questions that will guide your research; choose which data collections methods to use; get authorization for your program through proper internal channels; find customer sites that will allow investigations; and set up formal or informal meetings at the site. Of course, plans can change; therefore, you must remember that no matter what you **want** to investigate, you should only try to study what you are **allowed** to study when you enter the site.

Your own writing projects will probably determine the focus of your research. And, you must follow your company's own procedures to get your research program authorized, locate sites, and arrange your site visits. However, you do have some flexibility in choosing how to collect your data. Depending on your resources and your goals, you can use questionnaires, interviews, or on-site observations to learn how people use documentation.

What can you learn through questionnaires?

One useful way to gain qualitative information is to ask "open-ended" (as opposed to "closed") questions. One way to ask such questions is to employ open-ended survey questionnaires. The use of open-ended questions assumes that the researcher does not know the possible answers (while the use of closed questions assumes that the researcher does know all possible answers and can list them). With open-ended questions, the researcher lets users respond any way they see fit. There are no limitations on the length or content of user responses.

Even without a budget for travel, you can survey customers and gather feedback on your documentation through open-ended questionnaires. But, you may also want to send out a survey to help you decide which customers to visit for interviews or observations. Customers who put a lot of time into filling out a survey, or who bring up problems you hadn't thought of, are worth following up in the field. Conversely, once you have been out in the field you may be better prepared to ask the key, probing, revealing open-ended question -- stated in a way that ellicits a serious reply.

Open-ended questionnaires have several advantages. They can:

- enable the researcher to question users even when the researcher cannot imagine or list all possible answers;
- give control over the answer to the respondents;
- allow for lengthy in-depth responses;
- allow users to discuss underlying motivations, fears, or anxieties; responses may demonstrate uncertainty or intensity of feeling;
- reveal what users believe to be important; users will go in directions they feel are significant;
- reveal misconceptions or gaps in the users' knowledge;
- help discover answers to be used on future closed questionnaires.

On the other hand, open-ended questionnaires have some disadvantages. You must ask fewer questions than in closed questionnaires. (It is easier for respondents to mark a scale than to tell you what happens when they push Button B.) And, open-ended questions are more difficult to analyze than closed questions. Answers cannot easily be reduced to a simple category or number.

When writing open-ended questions, you should:

- provide clear instructions that explain how to fill the questions out;
- focus on a topic but leave questions largely unstructured; avoid leading questions;
- never ask double-barreled questions (one question that actually asks two different things);
- avoid jargon; use synonyms for potentially ambiguous terms;
- write questions in the affirmative; avoid negative words;
- stimulate responses by including sample passages from documentation.

Good questions are hard to create. This list, of course, represents only a sampling of suggestions for writing open-ended questionnaires.

What can you learn through interviews?

Interviews provide more information, in more depth, than do surveys. A user may scribble a brief comment in a survey that would lead to a half-hour discussion in an interview.

While there are several types of interviews that a researcher can employ, some guidelines apply to all interviews. Researchers must learn how to:

- establish a non-threatening persona as interviewer;
- choose settings and moments that are the most conducive for formal and informal interviews;
- form questions that prompt users to speak at length about the matters under investigation;
- get reticent users to open up;
- let talkative users speak naturally, yet keep them focused.

Some people are more effective interviewers than others. But anyone can learn to be a better interviewer. It is a matter of practice as well as personality. The more often you go into the field, the easier it becomes. With repetition, you can learn to control the unintentional messages you may send users through voice cues and body language.

While you may discover usability information through informal conversations, there are three types of formal interviews that are particularly useful:

1. Post-Hoc Interviews (Rose, 1984). This technique works best with a product that the user has not used before. Closely observe the user working with the product for brief sessions of five to twenty minutes. While observing, write very detailed notes -- identifying the points at which the user pauses, stumbles, rereads, makes errors, gets stuck, or engages in other noteworthy behavior.

Immediately after the session, you should interview the user by reviewing your notes. You want to focus on the noteworthy moments and ask the user to recall his or her thoughts about those moments. By pointing to those moments, you are trying to stimulate the user's memory. You must allow the user's responses to be open-ended and draw the user out.

2. Discourse-Based Interviews (Odell, Goswami, and Herrington, 1983). If you enter a site and discover documentation that has been rewritten by the customer, you can use those rewrites as the basis for a specific type of interview.

First, identify the parts of the original documentation that have been altered. Compare those passages to the user's version. In a tape-recorded interview, ask the user if the original could replace the new version for each of the changes. You want to encourage the user to discuss the differences between the two versions. Anytime you can ask users to discuss two **plausible** alternatives -- alternatives that could actually be implemented, you may be able to gain some useful information about the way users think and act.

3. Scenario-Based Interviews. You may go into the field to validate the task analysis developed for a product and its documentation. During your customer visit, propose various situations in which the user would operate the product, fix it, or recover from errors. Through these scenarios, you can discover the various preconceptions and strategies users bring to task -- and whether the tasks and user groups were correctly analyzed.

What can you learn from observing users at work?

A third way to learn more about the usability of information is to observe users working in their natural work environment. This is a difficult thing to do. You must be bold enough to go into an unfamiliar environment and try to watch "the natives" as they watch you watch them! At the same time it requires sensitivity and patience because you don't want to intimidate or alienate those who you wish to observe. Maintaining this balance puts more pressure on the researcher than sending out surveys or simply conducting interviews.

In order to observe users, you must enter the field site ready to:

1. Develop relationships with users who will serve as key informants. Whether particular users are "assigned" to you or whether you may choose users to observe, you must develop a relationship that will enable the user to work, while still allow you to record that activity. Some people may not want to be observed; others may want to do nothing but "shoot the breeze" with this stranger in the office. Obviously, you want to observe people who will go about their work but are willing to have you watch. Generally, if you are open about your agenda, *and if you make it clear that it is the documentation that you are really studying,* then you should be able to find some willing key informants.

2. Find effective vantage points from which to observe. Of course, you would like to minimize the effect that you will have on the activity under study, and for much of your observations, you would like to find unobtrusive vantage points within the workplace. But no matter how hard you try not to disturb the users you observe, your presence does make a difference. You need to anticipate this disturbance and deal with it. You must take your notes quietly, control your verbal messages and body language, and discourage the user from turning to you for reassurance.

3. Draw physical and social maps of the setting. That is, you must establish a clear sense of where users, products, and documentation are in relation to each other; you must also learn where users stand in the formal and informal hierarchies of the organization. Both "maps" will help you understand users' behavior, and, most importantly, will help you to more deftly maneuver through the physical and social territory.

Once established in the field site, you can record information through several means:

1. Writing Field Notes (Shatzman and Strauss, 1973). These are written observations and comments. You may write three types of field notes: observational, theoretical, and methodological notes. In *observational notes* you record activity as accurately and objectively as possible. Of course, you can never achieve true objectivity, but you will try to achieve a "disciplined subjectivity" in your observations. Write *theoretical notes* when you wish to express comments or analytical interpretations. These notes represent your ongoing analysis of what you observe. Finally, you can use *methodological notes* to remind you to do some further research-related activity. It is crucial for you to separate these three types of information that you record. You want to keep distinct your observations, analysis, and procedural comments.

2. Using recording technologies. Audio tape-recording is the most commonly used technology in field research. Tape recorders are small and relatively unthreatening, but some users are intimidated when they realize that they are being tape-recorded. Users have a right to know you are taping them. Explain that your tape-recorder saves you from having to take notes and saves them from having to repeat what they say. Tell the users how you plan to use the information so that they won't worry that their comments will be used against them. If people are still uncomfortable with the technology, put the tape-recorder away and write field notes.

While you might also want to make video-tapes or take photographs, both technologies can have even more negative effects. Both can be extremely intrusive. And, useful as these technologies seem, they still offer only limited perspectives on the behavior under investigation. Finally, many companies prohibit picture-taking as part of their procedures to protect proprietary information.

3. Conducting Read-Aloud Protocols (Flower, Hayes, and Swarts, 1983). With this procedure you attempt to intrude into the user's thought processes. (See chapters by Carroll, Mack et al, and by Ramey for discussions of the use of this method.) Similar to **post-hoc interviews**, this procedure is very effective with the user of a new product and its documentation. Instead of alternating note-taking and interviewing, ask the user to read the documentation aloud while performing the task. Urge the user to express his or her thoughts, expectations, and strategies for doing the task.

However, read-aloud protocols have a negative side. They can distract the user and actually worsen performance on a task. Some people spend so much time talking about what they are doing that they forget what they planned to do. And read-aloud protocols are very tiring. Users are being asked to carry on a monologue. As they get to the end of a task, they tend to run out of steam and stop talking. You have to pace the session and give the user breaks. You must be in control of the situation but not control the user's response.

How should you analyze data and report results?

Once information is collected through surveys, interviews, and observations, you face the difficult task of preparing that data for analysis and writing up a research report.

Analysis usually begins with a clerical task. You must review all your questionnaire responses. You must transcribe your information whether it is in the form of hastily scribbled field notes or audio tape recordings. This step is important and very time-consuming. Researchers often enjoy working in the field and then discover that the sheer volume of data is too much to review or transcribe quickly. Plan ahead and make sure you have the time and means to carry out this step.

At the very least, even if you cannot use some of the information immediately, make a thorough index of your field notes so that you can go back and transcribe them in more detail. Preview the tape and correlate general topics with the machine counter. Store the index with the notes or tape and attach a copy to your report. (Prepare an index even if you do transcribe your notes. Other people in your company can probably use your information. They will find it more easily in an index than in a long transcription. If you neither index nor transcribe your data, they will never find it.)

Number each line of data as you transcribe. You should make clear distinctions between observational, theoretical, and methodological notes. Others need to be able to read the data and interpret it without undue interference from the researcher's on-site interpretations.

Once the data is prepared, analysis is a complex process that is partly structured and partly intuitive. The book, **The Discovery of Grounded Theory,** by Glaser and Strauss offers a particularly detailed description of the ways to analyze qualitative data. The following is a simplistic summary of their advice: Begin by reading through the data chronologically, searching for patterns. These patterns may take the form of recurring actions and statements or similar actions and statements. While looking for these patterns, try to establish categories that link patterns together. Support the categories with examples from the data. Finally, develop themes that link categories and explain user behavior.

Analysis is completed by writing your trip report. Include in your report:

- User problems, including both documentation problems and product design problems.
- Examples of re-worked or annotated documentation.
- Particularly successful documentation, product design strategies, or features.
- The nature of the work environment (including maps of user and documentation locations).
- The strategic role that information plays within the company in terms of user tasks.
- Physical use of documents (how they are accessed, where they are

placed for reading).
- Users' views of their jobs.
- Your research methods (e.g. post-hoc interviews or read aloud protocols).
- Reports of problems that may have influenced the validity of the report (attitudes toward your company, limited access to certain user groups).
- Need for further research.

Conclusion

How a technical writer conducts research will be influenced by the unique demands of his or her company's business. Each company will develop unique research objectives. Technical writers can learn valuable information to meet these objectives by conducting qualitative field research.

Writers who go out into the field should not go unprepared. Unlike researchers in a laboratory setting, field researchers can control very little during an investigation. They must understand their research techniques and be flexible in implementing them. Most writers in the field will probably employ one of three research methods. They will use surveys, interviews, or observations to gather their data.

When they return from their fieldwork, the writers should prepare their data for analysis and write a trip report. Tapes must be transcribed; field notes must be reviewed and categorized to explain user behavior. These explanations will help writers understand why some users act the way they do, but this analysis will not necessarily help writers predict how their documentation will be received by others.

Note

1. This chapter grew out of a paper and workshop that the authors presented at the Technical Writers Institute, Rensselaer Polytechnic Institute, June 1987.

References

Flower, L., J.R. Hayes, and H. Swarts, "Revising Functional Documents: The Scenario Principle," *New Essays in Technical and Scientific Communication: Research, Theory, Practice,* P. Anderson, R. Brockmann, & C. Miller, eds., Farmingdale, NY: Baywood Publishing Co., 1983, pp. 41-58.

Glaser, B., and A. Strauss, *The Discovery of Grounded Theory: Strategies for Qualitative Research*. New York: Aldine Publishing Company, 1967.

Odell, L., D. Goswami, and A. Herrington, "The Discourse-Based Interview," *Research on Writing*. New York: Longman, 1983, pp. 220-236.

Rose, M., *Writer's Block: The Cognitive Dimension*. Carbondale: Southern Illinois University Press, 1984.

Shatzman, L., and A. Strauss, *Field Research*. Englewood Cliffs, NJ: Prentice Hall, 1973.

List of Contributors

Baker, Lauren Davis, Technical Writing Department, Hewlett-Packard Company, San Diego, CA

Bradford,Annette Norris, IBM Corporation, Kingston, NY

Carroll, John M., Thomas J. Watson Research Center, IBM Corporation, Yorktown Heights, NY

Charney, Davida H., Department of English, The Pennsylvania State University, State College, PA

Chisholm, Richard M., Department of English, Plymouth State College, Plymouth, NH

Debs, Mary Beth, Department of English Writing Program, University of Cincinnati, Cincinnati, OH

Doheny-Farina, Stephen, Technical Communication, Clarkson University, Potsdam, NY

Ford, Jim R., Federal Systems Division, IBM Corporation, Bethesda, MD

Gould, Emilie, IBM Corporation, Kingston, NY

Grischkowsky, Nancy L., Information Systems Group, Business Applications Systems, IBM Corporation, Norwalk, CT

Hunt, Peter, University of Wales, Cardiff, UK

Krull, Robert, Communication Research Laboratory, Rensselaer Polytechnic Institute, Troy, NY

Lewis, Clayton H., Computer Science Department, University of Colorado, Boulder, CO

Lewis, Elain, College of Communication, Boston University, Boston, MA

Mack, Robert L., Thomas J. Watson Research Center, IBM Corporation, Yorktown Heights, NY

Mazur-Rimetz, Sandra A., Micro Control Systems, Vernon, CT

Mirel, Barbara, Department of Humanities, Illinois Institute of Technology, Chicago, IL

Morgan, Meg, Department of English, University of North Carolina at Charlotte, Charlotte, NC

Ramey, Judith, Program in Scientific and Technical Communication, College of Engineering, University of Washington, Seattle, WA

Reder, Lynne M., Department of Psychology, Carnegie-Mellon Univeristy, Pittsburgh, PA

Robertson, Scott R., Department of Psychology, Rutgers University, New Brunswick, NJ

Rubens, Brenda Knowles, Myers Corners Laboratory, IBM Corporation, Poughkeepsie, NY

Rubens, Philip, Communication Research Laboratory, Rensselaer

Polytechnic Institute, Troy, NY
Smith-Kerker, Penny L ., Austin Laboratory, IBM Corporation, Austin, TX
Vassiliadis, Kalomira, University of Thessaloniki, Thessaloniki, Greece
Wells, Gail W., Department of Psychology, Carnegie-Mellon University, Pittsburgh, PA

INDEX

The MIT Press, with Peter Denning, general consulting editor, and Brian Randell, European consulting editor, publishes computer science books in the following series:

ACM Doctoral Dissertation Award and Distinguished Dissertation Series

Artificial Intelligence, Patrick Winston and Michael Brady, editors

Charles Babbage Institute Reprint Series for the History of Computing, Martin Campbell-Kelly, editor

Computer Systems, Herb Schwetman, editor

Exploring with Logo, E. Paul Goldenberg, editor

Foundations of Computing, Michael Garey and Albert Meyer, editors

History of Computing, I. Bernard Cohen and William Aspray, editors

Information Systems, Michael Lesk, editor

Logic Programming, Ehud Shapiro, editor; Fernando Pereira, Koichi Furukawa, and D. H. D. Warren, associate editors

The MIT Electrical Engineering and Computer Science Series

Scientific Computation, Dennis Gannon, editor